T0329259

AN ECONOMIC HISTORY OF AUSTRALIA

AN
ECONOMIC HISTORY
OF AUSTRALIA

by

THE LATE
EDWARD SHANN

Professor of History and Economics
University of Western Australia

CAMBRIDGE
AT THE UNIVERSITY PRESS
1948

CAMBRIDGE
UNIVERSITY PRESS

University Printing House, Cambridge CB2 8BS, United Kingdom

Cambridge University Press is part of the University of Cambridge.

It furthers the University's mission by disseminating knowledge in the pursuit of
education, learning and research at the highest international levels of excellence.

www.cambridge.org
Information on this title: www.cambridge.org/9781316601679

© Cambridge University Press 1948

First edition 1930
Reprinted 1938, 1948
First paperback edition 2015

A catalogue record for this publication is available from the British Library

ISBN 978-1-316-60167-9 Paperback

This book is dedicated to
the Memories of
FRANC CARSE
GRESLEY TATLOCK HARPER
GILBERT LAMBLE
GORDON CLUNES McKAY MATHIESON
and
ARTHUR JOHN PEARCE

"The love of liberty is the love of others:
the love of power is the love of ourselves."
W. HAZLITT

PREFACE

THE following account of Australian economic development attempts to keep in the forefront the private activities by which British settlers in Australia have transformed a prison-yard and hunting-ground of savages into a productive annexe to Europe and Asia, proud of using its labour-saving methods as means to general well-being. Little, therefore, is said of public finance. Studies of government expenditure on development are being made, notably in the work of the Hon. F. W. Eggleston, but it is fitting that they should be preceded by an outline of the private activity which they have been ostensibly designed to foster.

The scene of the new beginning here studied was a distant and at first despised part of the dowry of that fairest mistress "Trade", for whom Britain, Holland and France long fought. It was peopled first by outcasts, rebels and adventurers, stiffly governed for two generations by British officials, and to this day is largely financed by the British middle class. For a full century the little communities were outworks of the industrial revolution in Britain. In clearing the crowded gaols, in producing raw materials and food for the city-dwellers of the old land, they played a rôle of increasing importance in the grand speculation of industrialism—that experiment on which the British people have staked their capital, their mighty energy, their very life-blood. Australia emerged from the degradation of convictism by taking the place for which Spain had proved inadequate in the divided tasks of growing and manufacturing wool, both formerly discharged by Britain herself.

To-day the democracy that rules Australia is disposed to treat history as a record, as well forgotten, of the crimes, follies and misfortunes of others. And Britain's industrial responsibilities as centre of the world economy have again

been divided amongst pupils and partners. Three times
in the last fifty years, however, Australians of the rank and
file have had the chance to verify what "the papers" told
them of the changing world. On active service along
Australia's lines of communication with Britain, they have
felt the heave of big events. When W. B. Dalley sent the
New South Wales contingent to Suakim, colonials on
active service were scarcely taken seriously: John Bull
could thrash the dervishes easily enough. But fighting the
Boers on the veldt was another business; and Australians
came home from it to their federated Commonwealth
aware that strong nations were coveting the resources of
lands under the British flag. The sense of a permanent and
secure world was shaken.

During the campaigns of 1915 to 1918, in numbers as
great as the Commonwealth could muster and partly
equip—numbers whose going heavily checked the work
of farms, wharves and mines—Australians helped other
Britons and their Allies to meet the armed challenge. With
thinned ranks they came back, aware that the danger had
been repulsed at heavy cost. An era had ended. To them
too, as to Mr J. M. Keynes, "the most interesting question
in the world (of those, at least, to which time will bring
us an answer)" was "whether, after a short interval of
recovery, material progress would be resumed, or whether,
on the other hand, the magnificent episode of the nineteenth century was over."

At first it seemed that a prosperity greater than that of
pre-war times had come. Home and external markets
moved from strength to strength, with little faltering even
in 1920–21 when Britain plunged into the long depression
that grips her still. In this access of wealth, Australians
one and all talked of making their country more self-reliant.
Clever men stampeded the democracy into measures seemingly designed to make our economy a hermit one. The
coalition of parties in political power during the post-war
decade piled tariff upon tariff in favour of local secondary

industries, and sponsored crude plans to exploit the Australian market in favour of struggling export industries. Their talk ran high of making Australia another United States, drawing increased wealth from the interchange of products within the national boundaries. The realists in opposition applauded each tariff and marketing scheme, but, mistrusting American methods with labour, made haste, by control of state-administrations and by pleas before wage-fixing tribunals, to distribute income more favourably for their supporters.

Australia certainly has need of greater self-reliance, but she is not and cannot be another United States of America. In place of the Mississippi Valley and Middle West she has Lake Eyre and an arid, almost uninhabited, central region. On her fertile but limited coastal fringes live six or seven million people—about as many as inhabit Thibet. Their resources are too scanty to be the basis, as those of the United States are, of a Continental civilization, rivalling in economic power, by virtue of internal freedom of enterprise, all the rest of the world. The more the policy of a hermit Australia succeeded, the more surely would it bring slothful intellectual standards, and, as a consequence, material decay, until, with scorn, some sea power from the world where necessity had maintained knowledge and energy knocked in the closed door.

If she will but rouse her vigorous people to face facts, Australia's geographic position and relative immaturity offer her a rôle in the world economy of greater importance than that which she has already effectively filled. Incidentally her White Australia policy would then become internationally helpful. Seeking high efficiency and low costs by reverting to the tariff policy of the young Commonwealth (1902–1908), she can, for many generations to come, stimulate the production of a greater surplus of raw materials and foodstuffs. India, China and Japan are well started on the road to industrialism. In a review of "The Food Supply and Resources of China", read during a

recent Pacific Science Congress in Java, a Chinese economist, Shih Tsin Tung, concluded that industrialization
and rising standards of living in China would force an
increasing percentage of her 492 millions to rely on imported cereals. Rice-growing countries could not supply
them. His countrymen, already consumers of 235 million
"tan", or about 920 million bushels, of wheat, would
therefore find it imperative to change their food habits.
"The world's uncultivated areas are mainly wheat-pro-
ducing land." Geographically, with her wheat lands near
the coast, Australia is better situated to supply an in-
dustrialized Asia with foodstuffs than are the inland
prairies of America or the steppes of Russia. Her industrial
resources, well placed on the Eastern coast, would be
developed in due course as the internal economies of an
exchange kept technically alert by international competition.

Progress on these lines is the logical result of the broader
market for Australia's staple exports. She is now the
leading wool-grower for Continental Europe, Japan and
America, as well as for Britain. She is already finding
lucrative and growing markets for her wheat in Mediterranean, Indian and Asiatic ports.

Self-sufficiency in finance would be the reward of self-
respect. Without restraint upon external borrowing, no
economy can continue sound. But there is no inconsistency
between continued activity in international trade and
financial self-reliance. Britain's example demonstrates that.
Nor is there reason to doubt that all-round progress in the
arts would come unforced from a policy of fruitful trade
and international good feeling, and would make Australia
greater in the councils of the nations and a stronger member
of the British Commonwealth than she is to-day.

This book would not have been written but for the
encouragement given to the author by Professor Ernest
Scott, as Australian Adviser for the seventh volume of the
Cambridge History of the British Empire. The author's thanks

are also due to the Syndics of the Cambridge University Press for their permission to incorporate in this work the substance of his contributions to that volume.

The footnotes to the text make abundantly clear his obligations to others, and above all to Sir Timothy Coghlan, the first to labour in these fields. In the footnotes the writer has tried also to draw attention to the great need for further and more detailed studies. An attempt such as this at a wide synthesis is inevitably marked and marred by mistakes of emphasis and lack of knowledge. The author will be very grateful for help in correcting these, both from the new Australian schools of economics and from all students of this neglected subject. He already owes a deep personal obligation to the officials of the Mitchell Library, Sydney, and of the Melbourne and Perth Public Libraries, for their unfailing zeal in assisting him in his research among the books and papers in their custody. Professor W. K. Hancock of Adelaide University and Mr G. V. Portus, Director of Tutorial Classes in Sydney, helped him greatly with the earlier chapters, but must be held blameless for the substance and point of view. The conclusion emerges from the later chapters that since the war Australia has allowed her "national policies" to eat up the easy gains of a period of unusual plenty and to exceed the effort towards self-sufficiency which she can afford without over-capitalization. The writer hopes, however, that these pages may help to guide some of those engaged in the task of reconstruction.

EDWARD SHANN

SOUTH PERTH, W. A.

January 1930

CONTENTS

BOOK THREE

THE COMMONWEALTH

BOOK ONE

CONVICTS, WOOL, & GOLD
1788–1860

CHAPTER I

Governor Phillip and the Establishment

THE first British settlement in New Holland was planted on 26 January 1788 beside a little rivulet, known later as the Tank Stream, on Sydney Cove, Port Jackson. It was not scenic beauty that attracted the sailors, but the prime necessities of a seafaring people—sheltered anchorage and fresh water. Ages earlier, larger streams had carved out the deep valleys drowned under Port Jackson. The headwaters of those streams had been captured in some great earth change by the Nepean-Hawkesbury river-system. Thus the harbour formed by their submergence had escaped silt. Deep water slept in all its hundred bays and arms.

But the plain behind lacked a fit scene for immediate agriculture, the hard labour to which the convicts brought by the First Fleet had been condemned; and it was walled off from the rest of the Continent by the Blue Mountain cliffs. Till the mountains were crossed it was a port without a hinterland.[1] The great sandstone gorges thirty miles westward of the harbour beat back inland exploration for a quarter of a century. Possibly the officials of a colony that was primarily a prison cared no more than the aborigines to know what lay beyond the ranges. Like the aborigines, who obtained a sparse living from fish, game and roots, they clung to the harbour shores.

The only denizens of the virgin land were primitive

[1] See T. G. Taylor's article on "Economic Geography" in the *Australian Encyclopaedia*, vol. 1 (third edition), pp. 504 *et seq.* and the larger works it epitomizes, e.g. *Australia, Physiographic and Economic.*

hunting tribes who, by restriction of their numbers and by elaborate taboos, had adjusted their hunting to the supply of game. No competition with other races or cultures had narrowed their fields and enforced pasture or agriculture, the domestication of animals and plants in chosen spots. The intruders found a forest-clad country—unkempt, uncanny and unknown.

Prisoners, emancipists and officer-settlers tilled a few areas of alluvial soil which they found chiefly along the Hawkesbury valley. The best of these, however, were liable to sudden devastation by the flood-waters which the Nepean-Hawkesbury system hurled seaward along one narrow valley. As their harvests were swept away almost as often as not, the exiles found their main support in the stores and clothing brought from overseas and served out by the naval captains still in command. Unlucky delays in re-victualling the little white population made equal rations an established rule of early Sydney.

This was unfortunate. It confirmed in economic childishness that first company of marines and convicts. Neither criminals nor warders make a positive contribution to the social economy of production and exchange. In early Sydney this special department of British life was separated, isolated and given the appearance of a new community. But it proved difficult to introduce into it the main activities of a self-providing society. The First Fleet had been sent primarily to rid Britain of a troublesome accumulation of criminals. That good riddance was the dominant motive is plain enough. Several of the early batches of prisoners were sent without any record of individuals' terms of imprisonment. If any thought was given to their employment at the Antipodes, it was of the vaguest character. Perhaps the reports about Botany Bay made by Captain Cook and Sir Joseph Banks led the officials to expect an immediate and abundant return from cultivation of the soil.

Governor Phillip's instructions bade him treat "the

productions of all descriptions acquired by the labour of the convicts as a public stock".[1] Part of this he might use for the subsistence of the convicts and of his civil and military establishment. "The remainder of such productions you will reserve as a provision for a further number of convicts who will shortly follow you." But Cook's fertile meadows at Botany Bay proved to be sodden rush flats, and around Port Jackson Phillip found neither the land nor the men needed for instant and energetic tillage.

As far as eye could reach the country appeared "one continued wood". Trees "so large that the removing them off the ground after they are cut is the greater part of the labour" cumbered the whole country. Difficulties with his human material proved greater still. The convicts, numbering 717 at the landing, 529 being males, were the sweepings of the prison hulks. Artificers and useful hands had been retained in Britain. "The sending of the disordered and helpless", wrote Phillip, "clears the gaols and may ease the parishes from which they are sent, but if the practice is continued, this settlement will remain for years a burthen to the mother country."[2] His sinister charges were woefully unlike "farmers and emigrants who have been used to labour and who reap the fruits of their own industry....Amongst the convicts we have...many who are helpless and a deadweight on the settlement....Those who have not been brought up to hard work, which are by far the greatest part, bear it badly. They shrink from it the moment the eye of the overseer is turned from them".

The eye of the overseer was universally needed. The convicts were not led by the ordinary motives to honest industry—they had therefore to be driven. Phillip had counted on the loyal aid of the officers of the Royal Marines who had come as guard over the convicts. To his chagrin the officers, led by the lieutenant-governor Major

---

[1] *Historical Records of Australia*, series I, vol. I, pp. 11–12, Governor Phillip's Instructions.

[2] *H. R. of A.* series I, vol. I, p. 197, Phillip to Grenville, 17 July 1790.

Robert Ross, "declined any interference with the convicts, except when they are employed for their own particular service". The marines, they argued, had been sent as a garrison; their duty as guard over the convicts ceased at the landing. It was the first Australian strike, and one on the part of the directing class. They even objected to forming a court of criminal jurisdiction, an essential service in such a community. "Here", Phillip reported, "are only convicts to attend to convicts and who in general fear to exert any authority." Productive labour around Sydney broke down at once. In six months only eight or ten acres could be sown with wheat and barley. Even on these tiny patches the harvest failed: the seed had been over-heated on the voyage out. The sharing of the ship's stores continued, providing an effortless subsistence all too easily accepted by thieves and warders. The cult of energetic production had to make headway against this institution of paternalism.

In 1789 Phillip transferred the essay in public agriculture to Rose Hill or Parramatta, where, at the head of one branch of the harbour, he had found an open fertile area. But the change of soil did not mend matters. Under the only reliable supervisor, Henry Edward Dodd, a free man who had come as Phillip's personal servant, a hundred convicts raised 200 bushels of wheat, 60 of barley and small quantities of oats, flax and Indian corn. All of this was preserved for seed, and as Dodd would not contemplate remaining as a settler, the problems of food-supply and of supervising convict labour were not solved. In every despatch Phillip wrote of his need of continued supplies and of competent superintendents. "Men have been found"—this was in July 1790—"who answer the purpose of preventing their straggling from their work, but none of them are equal to the charge of directing the labour of a number of convicts with whom most of them are linked by crimes they would not wish to have brought forward." A time-expired convict, James Ruse, had been given in

1789 an acre of ground and a hut at Rose Hill "in order to know in what time a man might be able to cultivate a sufficient quantity of ground to support himself". His thorough tillage convinced Phillip that the colony would support itself on its own produce as soon as free settlers with convict servants worked for their own hand on their own land.

The attempt to grow food supplies by public agriculture brought the colony to the very brink of collapse by starvation. Phillip's careful plans for the expedition had made the voyage out a remarkably healthy one, but his foresight as a ship's captain could hardly be expected to extend to the needs and functions of a farming community at the Antipodes. No ploughs had been brought. Ground cleared by cutting down the big trees and "grubbing out" the smaller ones was hand-tilled between the stumps, with spade and hoe, a method the honesty of which could be ensured only by watching every stroke. Ruse said of his farm, "I dug in the ashes, and then hoed it, never doing more than eight or perhaps nine rods in a day, by which means it was not like the government farm, just scratched over, but properly done". Phillip's workmen were all too likely to quarrel with their tools, and those sent with the transports seem to have been of the poorest sort. "Bad tools", wrote Phillip in November 1791, "are of no kind of use. Two or three hundred iron frying pans will be a saving of spades. For cross-cut saws, axes, iron-pots and combs we are much distressed."

As herdsmen the convicts were of even less use. Phillip's instructions warned him to take the utmost care of the livestock, for breeding purposes. "The settlement will be amply supplied with vegetable productions and most likely with fish." But the convict herdsmen allowed the cattle to wander off into the bush and get lost. The forty-four sheep brought by the First Fleet also disappeared one by one, the losses being ascribed to dingoes and native spears.

With crops insufficient for seed at the next planting, with livestock disappearing into the bush, Governor Phillip, though he did not doubt "but that this country will prove the most valuable acquisition Great Britain ever made", had good cause to reflect that "no country offers less assistance to the first settlers, nor could be more disadvantageously placed with respect to support from the mother country, on which for a few years we must entirely depend".[1]

Phillip's early warnings prompted British officials to send him relief, but unluckily their first attempt to do so miscarried. The 'Guardian', a new fast-sailing 44-gun ship, sailed in June 1789 with two years' provisions for the settlement, clothing, sails and cordage, medicines, blankets, tools and agricultural implements. Having added plants and stock to her priceless cargo at the Cape, she should have arrived about the end of January or early in February 1790. "At that period the large quantity of livestock in the colony",[2] as it seemed to the Judge Advocate, "was daily increasing; the people required for labour were, comparatively with their present state,[3] strong and healthy,...the ration of provisions would have been increased to the full allowance; and the tillage of the ground consequently proceeded with in that spirit which must be exerted to the utmost before the settlement could render itself independent of the mother country for subsistence." Alas! On 23 December, after leaving Cape Town, the 'Guardian' collided with an iceberg. With great difficulty the gallant Riou worked her back to that port.

At Sydney her non-arrival and the rapidly approaching exhaustion of the 1787 salt pork and flour prompted

---

[1] H. R. of A. series 1, vol. 1, p. 51, Phillip to Sydney, 9 July 1788. The poor equipment may have been in part deliberate. W. Eden in a *History of New Holland*, 1787, wrote of the convict as "a forlorn hope", "a fair subject of hazardous experiments". "Offended justice in consigning him to the inhospitable shore of New Holland does not mean thereby to seat him for his life on a bed of roses."

[2] D. Collins' *Account of the English Colony in New South Wales*, p. 84.

[3] These reflections seem to have been written in June 1790.

Phillip to put his people on half rations.[1] He had somewhat earlier sent off the 'Sirius' to Cape Town for flour. Field labour had to be suspended through sheer weakness: The surviving sheep and cattle were eaten. It became a struggle to survive, hardly different, save in the hope of succour from overseas, from that of the aborigines around them.[2] Little flour was to be had at Cape Town. The 'Sirius' was sent on a second voyage to China, but *en route* she was wrecked off Norfolk Island whither she had taken a detachment of 300 convicts and 70 marines. The smaller store-ship 'Supply' was then despatched to Batavia. Some convicts sent into the bush to shoot kangaroos reported, after three weeks, that they had shot only three. In each fishing boat armed guards were set to prevent the complete plundering of the catch.

At last, on 3 June 1790, two months after the 'Supply's' departure, the long delay was explained by the arrival of a transport, the 'Lady Juliana'. She brought an "unnecessary and unprofitable cargo" of 222 female convicts mostly "loaded with the infirmities incident to old age" and "never likely to be other than a burthen to the settlement". But, as full counterpoise, came word of the 'Guardian's' stores salvaged at Cape Town and of other store-ships well on the way. A fortnight later, 20 June, the welcome signal of a ship in sight flew again at South Head, and in came the 'Justinian' heavily laden with stores. At the very end of the voyage each of these ships had passed through a critical moment. "The 'Lady Juliana', in standing into the harbour with a strong southerly wind, got so close to the North Head that nothing saved that ship but the set of the tide."[3] The 'Justinian',

---

[1] As to the scale of rations at various dates see *H.R. of A.* series I, vol. I, p. 44 *et passim*, vol. II, p. 358, and T. A. Coghlan, *Labour and Industry in Australia*, vol. I, pp. 55, 60, 62.

[2] What the early settlers thought of the aborigines may best be gathered from Phillip's despatch to Sydney of 15 May 1788, *H.R. of A.* series I, vol. I, pp. 24 *et seq.*; *Early Records of the Macarthurs*, pp. 33, 37; D. Collins, *op. cit. passim.*

[3] Phillip to Nepean, 29 March 1792, *H. R. of A.* series I, vol. I, p. 347.

on 2 June, in the same heavy rain and wind, "unexpectedly saw the land under her lee and was obliged to anchor on the coast, very fortunately so near the rocks that the return of the sea prevented her riding any great strain on her cable. Had those two ships been lost", wrote the stoical Governor, "the colony must have suffered very severely indeed". The relief was of brief duration. Hard on the heels of the 'Justinian' came the Second Fleet of convict transports—the 'Surprize', 'Scarborough' and 'Neptune' —and out of them landed a ghastly company of sick and dying. "Great numbers were slung over the ship's side in the same manner as they would sling a cask. Some died upon deck, and others in the boat before they reached the shore. There were landed not less than 486 sick."[1] The voyage, especially aboard the 'Neptune', had been badly found and abominably managed. By scurvy and "low fever" there died on board that ship 158 out of her 502 convicts. On the 'Surprize' 36 died out of 256, and on the 'Scarborough' 73 out of 259. Fifty more died within a month of landing. "It would be a want of duty", reported Phillip, "not to say that it was occasioned by the contractors having crowded too many on board those ships, and from their being too much confined during the passage." On 17 July 1790, three weeks later, he wrote of 450 sick "and many not reckoned as sick have barely strength to attend to themselves. When the last ships arrived we had not sixty sick in the colony".[2]

Finally, to dash all plans of making the colony self-supporting by agriculture, came drought of a duration and intensity unknown in English experience. The seed sown in 1790 was barely recovered at harvest. In November 1791 Phillip had to feed and clothe 2570 male and 608 female convicts and 161 children. What wonder that his

[1] Rev. R. Johnson to Mr Thornton, quoted in J. H. L. Cumpston and F. McCallum's *History of Intestinal Infections* (Commonwealth Department of Health), p. 34.
[2] The Rev. Johnson adds some reflections on the "astonishing villany

main thought was for a reserve stock of provisions to meet any future emergency due to a wrecked store-ship? "When the stores may permit the issuing of the established ration, the weekly expence according to our present numbers will be: Of flour 30,560 lb., of beef and pork 21,010 lb., of peas 179 bushels, of butter 1,432 lb., and our numbers will be increasing."

Was ever a member of the versatile race of ships' captains called upon to bear such a responsibility as his? In husbanding these stores he pitted his almost solitary will against thefts by convicts and marines alike. The former "were ever on the watch to commit depredations on the unwary, during the hours when they were at large, and never suffered an opportunity to escape them".[1] "Of the provisions issued on the Saturday the major part of the convicts had none left on the Tuesday night."[2] By issuing them on Wednesday and Saturday, and later daily, "the days which would otherwise pass in hunger, or in thieving from the few who were more provident", were "divided" and finally eliminated. Then the broken wards of a key found in the store-house padlock led to the detection of a conspiracy among the guard there. Seven of them had systematically looted it of liquor and provisions. The one on "sentry go" would admit two or more of the gang who could procure what they wanted even though the patrols visited the store while they were there. For the door was

---

of these wretched people....When any of them were near dying and had something given them as bread or 'lillipie' (flour and water boiled together), or any other necessaries, the person next to him or others would catch the bread out of his hand, and with an oath say that he was going to die and that therefore it would be of no service to him. No sooner would the breath be out of any of their bodies than others would watch them and strip them entirely naked. Instead of alleviating the distresses of each other, the weakest were sure to go to the wall. In the night, which at this time is very cold, and especially this would be felt in the tents, where they had nothing but grass to lay on (*sic*) and a blanket amongst four of them, he that was the strongest of the four would take the whole blanket to himself and leave the rest quite naked". *Loc. cit.* p. 36.

[1] D. Collins, *op. cit.* p. 81.
[2] D. Collins, *op. cit.* p. 65 and p. 30.

kept locked and the sentinel stood alert and vigilant at his post. But one night, after eight months of immunity, the key broke. All the culprits were executed, yet some of them had been held in high esteem by their officers. Such were Phillip's underlings. Against the depredations of rats he strove incessantly, but they defeated every attempt to clear the stores. The warping of timber, cut green and of necessity used before it was seasoned, made every building insecure.

Each of the benevolent despots, from Phillip to Macquarie, groaned under the load of responsibilities which the prison communism heaped upon his shoulders, but none with more reason than the first.[1] His command was a mere dump for human rubbish. Such was the misery of existence there that, out of sheer pity for the proposed victims, Phillip refused to correct the disproportion of the sexes by sending ships to take women from the Pacific Islands, as bidden by his instructions. Efforts to escape made by convicts were so determined that two men and a woman reached Timor in an open boat. Several parties set out to walk through the bush to China. Bass, when exploring, came upon a starving band of Irish escapees. He shared his dwindling rations with them and they parted, not without tears. But from the face of death they would not go back with him to Sydney.

Yet Governor Phillip, as even Macquarie was later to recognize, "with slender resources accomplished much". Not only did he house his charges and establish the beginnings of government with civil and criminal courts. His ration system, based on a central commissariat-store, was the economic last ditch, communism,[2] but it sufficed to hold off wholesale death by famine. Before the 'Justinian' brought relief the ration consisted of $2\frac{1}{2}$ lb. of flour, 2 lb.

[1] Cf. Philip Gidley King to Under-Secretary J. King, 3 May 1800, *H.R. of A.* series I, vol. II, p. 505.
[2] Cf. Gustav Cassel, *Theory of Social Economy*, vol. I, p. 72.

of rice and 2 lb. of salt pork per week, without trimmings.[1] The Governor refused to draw more for his own table, "wishing that if a convict complained, he might see that want was not unfelt, even at Government House".[2] By 1792, however, he had spent his strength, and in December, broken in health, he set out for England.

It was not a simple problem to convert this forlorn crew of exiles into a free community providing for itself. As instructed, Phillip made land grants to time-expired convicts, free even of quit-rent for the first ten years. Thirty acres were offered to each single man, 50 to the married men and 10 additional acres for each child. Fresh regulations, dated August 1789, allowed him to grant discharged soldiers 80 acres each, and free settlers 130 acres. But he soon found that to give a man land did not ensure his productive use of it. "Many inconveniences" attended the business. "With some the sole object in becoming settlers is that of being their own masters, and with others the object is to raise as much money as will pay their passage to England." At his instance, later governors were directed to make all grants non-transferable for five years.[3] Another "inconvenience" of small farming near Sydney was revealed in his request (17 July 1790) for permission to establish settlers in detached areas "where the stock will be less liable to suffer from the depredations which may be expected from the soldier and the convict and against which there is no security".

Governor Phillip granted only 3389 acres in all. Neither legal restrictions nor isolation made the "settlers from convicts" better able to read the riddle of agriculture in a climate fruitful at times but fatally capricious. General

---

[1] David Collins, *op. cit.* p. 46, tells of a herb called by the convicts "sweet tea" and held in great estimation amongst them: "The leaves of it being boiled they obtained a beverage not unlike liquorice in taste". Rapid consumption soon made it scarce.

[2] D. Collins, *op. cit.* p. 80.

[3] *H. R. of A.* series I, vol. I, p. 441, Dundas to Grose, 31 (*sic*) June 1793. Governor King improved on this by making grants to infant children which could not be transferred until they came of age.

Orders did not govern the weather nor direct the colonists' labours with foresight and imagination. These qualities came to the colony, however, in the person of an "ensign in the New South Wales Corps".

Among those who bore the torments of the Second Fleet's voyage were detachments of this force, which had been raised for the special purpose of relieving Major Ross and his Royal Marines from the task of superintendence to which they had objected. The New South Wales Corps were not a picked force, save perhaps in an evil sense. Governor Hunter described them as "soldiers from the Savoy (the military prison) and other characters who have been considered disgraceful in every other regiment in His Majesty's service".[1] In the Colony they stultified the efforts of every naval governor and kept the whole community in turmoil as long as they remained there.

The prime mover in these doings was invariably John McArthur. Though born in Devon, he was the son of a Jacobite of the '45. His father's brothers, it was said, had all been slain at Culloden, and the sole survivor had fled for a time to the West Indies. At John's birth, his father was an army agent at Plymouth, and in his service, no doubt, John learned about trade. Entering the army in 1782, he retired on half-pay at the peace of 1783, practised farming and read for the law. Then marriage and "every reasonable expectation of reaping the most material advantages"[2] led him to join the New South Wales Corps.

Even before Governor Phillip's departure, McArthur was eager to play the "spirited proprietor" and to develop, as was then the vogue in Britain, a capitalistic agriculture. He proposed to Phillip that he should retire from the Corps on half-pay and on the condition that he should be granted land and the labour of convicts to till it. Phillip had in

---

[1] *H. R. of A.* series I, vol. I, p. 574, Hunter to Portland, 10 Aug. 1796.
[2] *Early Records of the Macarthurs of Camden*, p. 2, Mrs John Macarthur to her mother, Mrs Veale.

1790 recommended the assignment of convicts to free settlers, but now he hesitated. "I am very far from wishing to throw the smallest obstacles in the way of officers obtaining grants of land" he told Dundas in October 1792,[1] "but in the present state of this colony the numbers employed on the public buildings, in procuring the materials and in other occupations equally necessary, does not leave more than four hundred and fifty for agriculture. From that number those convicts must be taken who are to be given to officers or settlers, which will increase the number of those who do not labour for the public, and lessen those who are to furnish the colony with the necessaries of life." The assumption that private settlers could contribute nothing to the Colony's supplies was born in Phillip's mind, perhaps, out of the feeble efforts of the expirees. But the alternative of relying on prisoners' tillage of Crown land continued to prove a delusive one. Dundas, in despatches dated 10 January and 14 July 1792,[2] gave Phillip a free hand to grant land, assign convicts and issue provisions to officers and others who became settlers "provided the allotments are made not with a view to a temporary but an established settlement thereon".

These instructions, and the relaxation of control which occurs in every despotism at a change of rulers, opened the way in December 1792 to a new economic policy.

[1] *H. R. of A.* series I, vol. I, p. 383.
[2] *H. R. of A.* series I, vol. I, pp. 328, 365.

CHAPTER II

The New South Wales Corps

IN the eighteenth century the power of the British ruling class was as yet untempered by constant responsibility to the opinion of the nation. In the army and navy, prize-money and the spoils of war had whetted the appetites of an island people never slow to seize their chances of enrichment by plunder or trade.

But a communistic system, such as they had to administer in early Sydney, demands, at least of its responsible chiefs, self-sacrifice and devotion to the common welfare. Its success depends upon the discovery of a successor to the patriarchs of old. He must apportion the pooled resources of the community in such fashion that each member of it may be moved, not by calculation, but by the primitive impulses of loyalty or fear, to do what in the sum of their efforts will suffice for the needs of all. Aboard ship, especially when tiny sailing ships ventured over wide oceans, a sense of common danger from tempest or lee shore might maintain this solidarity. Ashore, in a far land with a seemingly genial climate, the discipline of a little commune made up of the worst possible human materials went all to pieces. Such men as Grose and Paterson, and even Hunter and King, though they applied with a zeal that grew more ferocious with failure "the peculiar caste rules of the services", proved as unequal as Bligh at Tahiti to the changed demands on the sea-captain turned patriarch.

They and their fellow-officers were "for the most part simple, commonplace men, physically courageous and intellectually vapid, men guided by a strange jumble of uncomprehended motives—blind loyalty to the King, their regiment or ship—blind acceptance of the Church of England—mingled with love of liquor, greed of gain and indifference to the usual tenets of morality. Few were men of striking ability or forceful character, for the colonial garrisons, a backwater of the Services and the retired list, had little to show in those times of war in the way of brains or energy".[1] Probably not one of those called to fill Governor Phillip's place saw that the conversion of a prison camp into a free community was a sociological riddle of some complexity. Each was beset by his social equals for relaxations and concessions. Each was tormented by Whitehall's intermittent tugging on the financial reins. Each reached the breaking strain and returned home broken by failure. Yet for the most part their superiors remained as blind as they to the changed and changing realities in New South Wales.

To Phillip's civil officials, Surgeon Arndell and the Reverend R. Johnson, the changes which Lieutenant-Governor Grose made as soon as "the Governor's" back was turned seemed a deliberate plunge into anarchy. The civil court ceased to sit. Public agriculture was dropped. Phillip's admirable plans for the town of Sydney were ignored. The officers were granted land wherever they chose—land which soon included the former scenes of public agriculture. Public order collapsed and a general licentiousness raged unrebuked.

Grose and McArthur, on the other hand, reported a new energy and prosperity. In February 1793 the former, as Lieutenant-Governor, wrote of "the great spirit" with which the officers to whom he had granted land were clearing it "at their own expense. Whether their efforts result from the novelty of the business or the advantages they promise themselves I cannot say, but their exertions are really astonishing.... I shall be prepared and thankful

[1] Dr Marion Phillips, *A Colonial Autocracy*, p. 10.

B

to receive as many convicts as can conveniently be sent."
He thought the "settlers from convicts" an improvident
crew, but he encouraged them to bring maize to the
commissariat store by offering for it a fixed price of five
shillings a bushel, "it being at the same time a cheap
purchase for government and an accommodating market
for the settler".[1]

McArthur thought the changes since the departure of
Governor Phillip "so great and extraordinary that to recite
them all might create some suspicion of their truth". They
had in a short time lifted the settlement from "a state of
desponding poverty and threatened famine....As for myself I have a farm containing 250 acres, of which upwards
of a hundred are under cultivation. I have at this moment
20 acres of fine wheat growing, and 80 acres prepared
for Indian corn and potatoes. My stock consists of a horse,
two mares, two cows, 130 goats, upwards of a hundred
hogs. Poultry of all kinds I have in the greatest abundance.
I have received no stock from government but one cow".
That to the father of Australian pasture this petty goat
and poultry run should seem almost incredible progress
makes the "desponding poverty", against which it looked
well, dark indeed.

The surgeon and the parson in Sydney reported to
Governor Hunter other aspects of the military rule. "Crimes
of every sort increased to an alarming degree; thefts and
robberies became so numerous that they were spoken of
as mere matters of course."[2] "Assaults the most outrageous
were frequently committed....As no pains were taken to
inspire a reverence for religion, the Sabbath, instead of
being passed by the people in attendance at divine service,
was profaned as a day particularly appropriated to gaming,
intoxication, and uncontrolled indulgence of every vicious
excess." A drunken convict whom he met on the Parra-

[1] Grose to Dundas, 3 September 1793, *H. R. of A.* series I, vol. I, p. 448.
[2] Arndell to Hunter, *H. R. of A.* series I, vol. II, p. 183. Cf. Rev. R.
Johnson to Hunter, p. 178.

matta Road offered to break the good Surgeon Arndell's
head with a bottle of rum which he had refused to
share. When the clergyman failed to finish service in
the short half-hour allotted him by military orders, the
drum beat and, to his chagrin, out marched both guard
and congregation.

Agricultural activity and contempt for order, morals
and religion flowed, it would seem, from the same tap,
that is, from the rum used as a makeshift currency—a
strange instrument of progress but one congenial to that
strange company. Among the "articles to be sent to New
South Wales in consequence of Governor Phillip's representations" the store-ship 'Britannia' had carried in January
1792 "9,278 gallons of rum, being the allowance of half
a gallon per annum". Phillip was especially pleased at the
inclusion of the convicts "for it is a bounty which many of
those people well deserve and to the undeserving it will never
be given". He reckoned without his host. Not much longer
was his will alone to decide to whom it should be given.

By the same ship came word that recruits for the New
South Wales Corps in England had been promised, as a
condition of enlisting, "the usual ration except spirits,
without deduction from their pay". Dundas thought the
same offer made in New South Wales would be "a strong
inducement to some of the marines to enlist in the additional company".[1] He overlooked the fact that in the
communism of semi-starvation guard and convict alike had
been given, and had come to regard as their right, a share
of whatever was to be had and that the consignment of rum
was intended for both. Phillip saw that the soldiers would
think little of free rations.[2] Everyone drew them. But
the deprivation of spirits would put them on a lower plane
than the convicts. While he hesitated, and despite his
forebodings, Major Grose and his brother-officers chartered
the same store-ship, the 'Britannia', to bring a cargo from

[1] Dundas to Phillip, 10 January 1792, *H. R. of A.* series I, vol. I, p. 331.
[2] Phillip to Dundas, 2 October 1792, *H. R. of A.* series I, vol. I, p. 377.

the Cape which might "relieve the soldiers' necessities" and afford them "Comforts other than the reduced and unwholesome rations served out from the stores". Within a few days of Phillip's departure, moreover, an American ship, curiously named the 'Hope', arrived at Sydney, offering spirits and provisions, which the new Lieutenant-Governor bought, seemingly in fear of drought. He told Dundas that he had the less reluctantly bought spirits as well as provisions, "as it appeared from your letter of the 15th May[1] that it was intended to issue spirits to the non-commissioned officers and private soldiers". Dundas had foreseen that the coming of whalers would necessitate supervision over their usual rum-trading. In a later despatch, oddly dated the 31 June 1793, he warned Grose against allowing spirits to be secretly sold to convicts, and bade him subject the trade to "the view and inspection of proper persons directed by you to attend the same". But private exchange, however well watched, relaxes the commissary's grip upon a communistic economy. The 7597 gallons of rum obtained from the 'Hope' had long since been sold mainly to the only persons Grose was likely to direct as "proper to attend the same", that is to the officers of the Corps. They had quickly organised the bringing of more from Bengal, Batavia, and Rio de Janeiro as well as from Massachusetts, for they were finding it a most acceptable means of hiring labour and buying produce.

The home authorities, thinking an isolated prison would have no use for money, at first provided none. Convicts worked as punishment, and Whitehall paid in England for the freight of the store-ships. What use was there for money? If goods had to be bought from visiting ships or elsewhere, the Governor might draw bills on the Treasury. Things worked out much less simply at Port Jackson. Officers whose pay was due in London could draw bills

Grose to Dundas, 9 January 1793, *H. R. of A.* series I, vol. I, p. 414. The letter mentioned had arrived only a few days after Phillip wrote his comments on the exclusion of rum from the soldiers' ration.

as well as the Governor. Thus they too could buy goods from whalers and others. What they bought they bartered for labour with which to till or improve the 15,639 acres granted during the three short years of military ascendancy. Much of the labour they obtained at first for nothing from assigned servants victualled at the stores. Later it cost the price of its "keep" when under Hunter and King they were required to pay for such servants' rations. But thereafter they found it expedient to pay wages in "truck", either rum or provisions, to three grades of labour, (*a*) "government men" working in their own time, (*b*) assigned servants, and (*c*) expirees.

Phillip had at first set the convicts to work from sunrise to sunset, as part of their punishment. All did as little as the lax supervision of their fellows would exact. To encourage effort he therefore defined certain tasks as a day's work, and set the convict who had completed his task free to cultivate his garden or to do as he chose. In Phillip's time he seldom chose to work for others. The officers were forced to follow suit and define daily tasks for their assigned servants. Then, to keep control of their servants after the not exacting task was done, they too found it worth while to offer some reward as an inducement to extra work. Expirees were in a position to demand wages for the whole time worked. They had the alternative of applying to government for a settler's grant and for cattle from the public herd with which to make an independent home and start life afresh.

Rum, as Phillip foresaw, proved a much appreciated relief from the store rations. But it was more. So universally acceptable was it that it became a medium of exchange, a commodity for which convicts, whether in the government gangs or assigned, were ready to do extra work. Expirees would take payment in rum; and for rum, too often, settlers bartered their produce. Most who took it were content to consume it themselves. Provident habits were rare. The convicts drew rations from the stores, and expiree settlers did the same until their farms were producing. "Much work", wrote Hunter to Portland, in excusing his tolerance of rum, "will be done by labourers, artificers and others for a small reward in this article...which money could not purchase.... It is not by an extra allowance of the common slop clothing or the provision issued from the public store that this labour is to be obtained, for those men as well as women who have been some time here, and particularly those whose term is expired and who are disposed to work, aspire to a better kind of dress and are desirous of indulging with their tea and sugar, as well as the gratification of a little tobacco and spirits at times, which whilst thus applied with moderation is certainly not ill employed".[1]

Beyond a doubtful half-gallon per annum, however, the generality could get rum only by working for those who had it to give. So for the twenty years or more that it remained the customary means of paying wages, rum placed the key to wealth in the hands of those who could answer the convicts' insatiable call for it. Grose and his associates, with McArthur playing as ever a leading part, had supplemented Phillip's ship-board communism in necessaries by an exchange economy based on truck wages, with rum as the main item of consumption and motive for exertion. These officers may have known little and cared less about the implications and possible results of what they were doing. Perhaps such a change was inevitable to colonists of a trading race, and trade was in sight as soon as Ruse, the first expiree settler, grew more grain on his little farm than his family could consume. Its evil form, with rum as currency, expressed the neglect of Whitehall to provide a local money and the character of the ruling class who repaired the omission.

In their days of power they laid themselves out to make the best of both worlds—the wages system of England and the rations of her New Holland prison. Explaining to

[1] *H. R. of A.* series I, vol. I, p. 593, Hunter to Portland, August 1796.

Whitehall that it took time to make land fruitful, Grose allowed the officers, including himself, to draw rations and slops from the public stores for their assigned servants.[1] The expense soon roused the ire of the Treasury, which was paying for produce twice over—first in the rations used in growing it, and then in the fixed prices for the wheat, maize and meat delivered at the stores. Under pressure from home, and in spite of outcry from the subsidized infant industry, Governors Hunter and King charged the landowners for the rations drawn. Subsidized industries never willingly grow up. Whitehall then tried to set the clock back and to replace all purchase of settlers' produce by direct filling of the stores with grain and meat grown by the convicts on government farms.

The exchange economy, however, inevitably triumphed over communism. It called into play motives of self-interest and hope more continuous and powerful than fear of the government overseer. Using a common third as reward, it gave to all who would make the effort freedom to decide by what service they could gain more of that reward. Expirees and officers might grow grain and produce for the stores or for private sale. Even the convict, apart from the penal chain-gangs, might work for wages. These were paid in "truck" at computed prices,[2] and the officers, it is true, made their official privileges a screen for much that was villainy by our standards. Yet, even an exchange economy based upon tyranny and rum offered a freedom to experiment, a career open to talent, unknown in the lethargy of institutional communism.

Even the most selfish feature of the military regime, the assignment of convict servants to cultivators, was a step in advance of their serried degradation in the government gangs. When assigned to cultivators the convicts' services

[1] Dundas had given an implied permission to do this. See *H. R. of A.* series I, vol. I, p. 328.
[2] See the Rev. R. Johnson's statement of the cost of erecting the first church, reproduced in facsimile in vol. I, p. 263, of the *Australian Encyclopaedia.* Cf. *H. R. of A.* series I, vol. I, p. 451.

were in legal form lent, not sold. They remained "government men". Beyond question these assigned servants were harshly used.[1] In 1800 Governor Hunter made the presentation of delinquents before a magistrate the preliminary—for it very rarely proved an obstacle—to their punishment. Until then masters had assumed a right to horsewhip them. The effect of the system on the attitude of employers to labour must not be minimized, but there was a germ of economic freedom in the mere facts of trade and of payment of wages by "truck". All the degradation and extortion which accompanied the use of rum could not blot out the dawn, through that sinister method, of the freedom to produce and consume as he chooses which the use of money brings to the individual. A bad money may lead the individual to use that freedom ill, but it may later be replaced by a good money which does not.

From the first the new economy put power into the hands of those who rose superior to the evil of the money they used. Elizabeth McArthur's pen-picture of Elizabeth Farm at Parramatta, written shortly after Governor Hunter's arrival, is one of freedom confined to a dominant few.[2] "For such as have many in their employment it becomes necessary to keep on hand large supplies of such articles as are most needed, for shops there are none.... The officers in the colony, with a few others possessed of money or credit in England, unite together and purchase the cargoes of such vessels as repair to this country from various quarters. Two or more are chosen from the number to bargain for the cargo offered for sale, which is then divided amongst them in proportion to the amount of their subscriptions. This arrangement prevents monopoly, and

[1] See *Adventures of Ralph Rashleigh*, pp. 153 *et seq*. This book, though the epic quality of some of the adventures makes the element of fiction evident enough, has a value akin to that of the Homeric poems in its vivid portrayal of the customs and setting of old colonial days.

[2] *Macarthur Records*, p. 51. It is there dated 1 September 1795, but this is a slip. References in it to Macarthur's resignation of his superintendence of government agriculture and to the season of the year make it plain that it was written in 1796.

the impositions that would be otherwise practised by the masters of ships."

As to the market from which they obtained a return for this expenditure on truck, she says, "some thousands of persons are fed from the public stores, all of whom were formerly supplied with flour from England to meet the demand for bread. But since so many individuals have cleared farms they have thereby been enabled to raise a great quantity of grain in the country, which is purchased by the Commissary at 10s. a bushel, and issued for what are termed rations. In payment for which the Commissary issues a receipt, approved of by the Government. These receipts pass current here as coin. When any number have been accumulated in the hands of individuals they are returned to the Commissary, who gives a bill on the Treasury in England for them. These bills amount to thirty or forty thousand pounds annually. How long the Government may continue so expensive a plan it would be difficult to foresee. Pigs are bought upon the same system as would also be sheep and cattle if their numbers would admit of their being killed. Beef might be sold at 4s. if not 5s. the lb. A good horse is worth £140 to £150. Be it ever so bad it never sells for less than £100. From this statement you will perceive that those persons who took early precautions to raise live stock have at present singular advantages"

In Mrs McArthur's description one may detect a sense that the control of the market by the early birds was too good to last. Chafing at the officers' "singular advantages", such as their monopoly of imported goods, the settlers from convicts sought the intervention of Whitehall and of the Governor. A petition addressed in February 1800 by the settlers around Parramatta to the Secretary of State tells how that monopoly weighed upon them. It is the other side of the shield Elizabeth McArthur held up—a picture of "intolerable burdens which have not only cut off all hope of their independence, but reduced them and their families to a state of beggary and want, and incapacitated them from prosecuting the culture of their lands with vigour.... The tillage of land in this country", they explain, "is conducted in a different manner from what it is in Europe, the latter with the assistance of horses and oxen, the former wholly by men, who to keep pace with the growing extortion of monopolists and dealers, rise (*sic*) the price of their labour in proportion to the price of imported commodities. The price of grain being fixt, the poor settlers have no means of avoiding the impositions of the dealer and labourer, but are crushed under the heavy weight of expences attending agriculture, which frequently exceed the amount of their crops. In fact the whole of the very exorbitant profits of trade are extorted from them rather than the consumers of any other description, who in general are indifferent what prices they give for any article as the burden of expences falls on the land holders".[1]

The boon which the petitioners sought, as a remedy for all their ills, was a return towards government tutelage, the establishment by the government of "a public warehouse, from which the settlers might be supplied with every necessary article at such a rate as would not only enable them to meet the wishes of His Excellency Governor Hunter in his intended reduction of the price of grain, but also considerably diminish the expences of government by enabling the landholder to support his family, who from mere indigence are now dependent on the public store".

The settlers on the Hawkesbury, from whom were demanded prices even higher than those instanced by the Parramatta petitioners, solved the problem by direct action. They set up stills in the rough country behind Green Hills, and distilled "rum" from their own grain. So busy was the traffic in this "moonshine", sold at first at six shillings a gallon, that a grain shortage threatened.

---

[1] *H. R. of A.* series I, vol. II, p. 442. Cf. vol. II, p. 607, Governor King to Portland 28 September 1800.

More than the crooked ways of Sydney streets may thus be traced to the period of military rule. Wage earners under the wing of a benevolent government, traders meeting every increase of wages by exacting higher prices for their wares, a country population between the upper and nether millstones of regulated wages and prices seeking state assistance, but ready to pursue its own interests by the most direct means—all may be descried in the first dawn of exchange in New South Wales.

CHAPTER III

A Conflict of Evils

GOVERNORS Hunter, King and Bligh, who followed Phillip in the dynasty of ships' captains, were successively the focus of conflict between their masters at the Home and Colonial offices[1] and their servants in the New South Wales Corps. The period 1789–1810 also saw the stubborn maturing of the McArthurs' plans to grow fine wool for export, but the events in which the colonists were interested revolved in squalid turmoil about two bad businesses—public agriculture and the trade in rum.

General John Hunter's first impression of the colony he had last seen in the gloomy days of 1792 was one of admiration for a "state of agriculture and the breeding of livestock" far above his expectation. Under the spell of the "extremely well-qualified Inspector of Public works", Captain John McArthur, he concluded that this was the result of "the raising of grain and the breeding of live stock in the hands of private individuals. They are self-interested in what is their own property and it certainly succeeds better with them than in the hands of government". He assumed that the repetition in his instructions of the old direction to raise a "public fund" by the labour of convicts had been antiquated by colonial experience since its first issue. "If Government were to continue to cultivate land sufficient for the maintenance of whatever number of convicts may be hereafter sent out, there would

[1] As to the various offices and secretaries at Whitehall responsible at different dates for the Australian colonies see the article "Colonial Office" in the *Australian Encyclopaedia*, vol. 1, p. 282.

be an effectual stop to the exertions of industrious farmers, for want of a market for their crops. That we shall soon have abundance there is scarcely any reason to doubt." Rations, too, would provide an inelastic basis for a community bound to grow in numbers and wants and to escape out of the Governor's hand. Children of convicts were not born prisoners nor did expirees always sink again into bondage. The success of independent producers would incite and educate enterprise in others, and exchange would enable such folk to share their successes.

Hunter's superiors at home, however, refused to see that any conflict need arise between communism and freedom to produce and exchange. "Nothing", according to the Duke of Portland, "ought to be more reconcileable than the public interest of every State and that of the individuals who compose it, and as that union must be the consequence of proper management, I am persuaded it cannot be more likely to be effected than in a country the government of which is placed in your hands." This, from a Duke and a Cavendish-Bentinck to an old sailor[1] whose public duty had always been his conscience, was irresistible. Yet Whitehall's injunctions to keep down expenses and maintain prison agriculture made an uneasy and divided duty. Refusing McArthur a salary as inspector of public works, Hunter lost his services. To withdraw assigned servants and resume public agriculture on exhausted fields would, he clearly saw, jeopardize existing production and force him to draw more bills on the Treasury in payment for imported flour.

Even the herding of public stock by convicts was wasteful in the extreme. "The hog not being a grazing animal and there being nothing in the country yet discovered for their sustenance but grass, they cannot be allowed to run at large; they must be confined and fed upon corn; and very considerable is the quantity they require. Every little farmer can afford to feed a few upon the refuse or damaged

---

[1] Hunter was 58 when he returned to New South Wales as Governor.

corn, and sell to the government at less than half of what
it would cost the public if rearing large numbers. Numerous herds of such animals allowed to run loose would also
be dangerous to the farmer whose grounds are yet all
open." The only effective convict herdsman had been the
one who in 1788 lost in the bush a Cape bull and some
cows belonging to Governor Phillip and "Government".
Just after Hunter's arrival they and their progeny, numbering over forty, were found on the far side of the Nepean,
south-west of Sydney, in a fertile valley thenceforth known
as the Cowpastures. It was decided to leave the herd
unmolested, as a valuable reserve of beasts for future
emergencies.

The officers' estates continued to prosper despite Portland's insistence and Hunter's orders that the rations and
clothing issued to any assigned servants, other than two
batmen per officer, should be paid for in produce or
cash.[1] McArthur introduced a labour-saving device in
1796—the first plough seen in New South Wales—and so
kept up the profits of agriculture even under the new rule.

For the convicts remaining in or returned to government employ Hunter found work on public buildings
rather than in public agriculture. His efforts to enforce
attendance at divine service had been ill-received in that
cantankerous colony. Someone burnt down the church.
"Double-logged" gaols at Sydney and Parramatta were
equally or more unpopular and were "burnt by design".
Stone windmill towers, barns and storehouses and a few
roads and bridges lasted better. But McArthur undermined Hunter's credit with the Duke of Portland, already
endangered by his preference for private to public farming.
He reported the Governor's partiality in allowing some
cultivators the use of more than two assigned servants
victualled "on the stores".[2]

---

[1] General Order, May 1798, *H. R. of A.* series 1, vol. 11, p. 215. Cf. vol. 1,
p. 647.
[2] *H. R. of A.* series 1, vol. 11, pp. 89 to 93

Philip Gidley King, a man of smaller mind but greater energy than Hunter, bought the favour of Whitehall by undertaking to renew prison agriculture, and despite such crudities as hand tillage, harvesting with sickles and transport to the barns on convicts' backs, he did draw better returns from land at Toongabbie and a farm he rented on the Hawkesbury. But he, too, was soon lamenting the inferiority of public to private farming. In 1801, his first season of office, the "full rations victualled" numbered 2365 and required 29,640 bushels of wheat. The produce of government lands made up 8000 bushels, leaving a "deficiency to be supplied by individuals" of 21,640 bushels. "Individuals" that year won 60,000 bushels from some 4000 acres. "As the labour of prisoners working on public ground is exacted from them by the hand of authority, they are not actuated by the same motives as those who labour for their own profit. This, with their very bad characters and former pursuits,...requires a constant and unremitted attention to make their labour the least beneficial....The overseers are not much better. ...Notwithstanding the assistance given by the superintendents, every exertion necessarily falls on the Governor who alone is responsible and consequently interested in the advancement and prosperity of the colony." This is not a flattering picture. It exposes all too plainly the Achilles' heel of communism—its incapacity to organize production adequate to support its liberal consumption. Denying scope to ambition, it relies on the intermittent motive of fear.

The continued progress on officers' farms made it easy for King to enforce strictly the home authorities' ruling as to assigned servants. General Orders defined clearly the conditions on which such labour was lent, and required all who received assigned servants to sign these terms and to make regular returns of those they employed.[1] The Order

[1] See *H. R. of A.* series I, vol. II, pp. 622–4, for General Orders of 1 and 2 October 1800; vol. III, pp. 35–7 and 43 for later Orders.

of 31 October 1800 enacted quite a code of wages and
conditions of employment. From this it appears that
assigned servants and convicts working in their own time
expected, over and above their rations, about ten shillings
a week. By the end of King's term of office the assignment
of convicts' labour had become, in Coghlan's phrase,
"a legal covenant between the Government and the employer, that the latter should maintain a convict for a
certain period, receiving his labour in return". The
Government retained, as it had not done in the American
colonies, responsibility for the reasonable treatment of
convicts. Their labour was leased on terms which defined
the convict's living and relieved government of expense
but not of a certain care for the "servants of the crown".
In health their misdeeds could legally be punished by the
Governor alone. In sickness they were returned to official
keeping. By good conduct they might earn a conditional,
even an absolute, pardon. In any event the assigned
servant who satisfied his master escaped the degradation
of the government gangs.[1] He remained a protected
subject and escaped on sufferance from the heavy hand of
justice.

Prior to Governor Macquarie's time, little was done to
better the lot of the women convicts. The method of
selecting for transportation to New South Wales, as described by the Committee on Transportation in 1812, had
in view rather the riddance of Britain and Ireland of their
worst scum than the reform of those transported. "With
respect to female convicts it has been customary to send
without any exception all whose state of health will admit
of it, and whose age does not exceed 45 years.... Your
committee are aware that the women sent out are of the
most abandoned description, but yet with all their vices

---

[1] Cf. Hunter to Portland, 10 June 1797, *H. R. of A.* series I, vol. II, p. 20
"We frequently substitute for corporal punishment a certain time to labour
for the public...and this is more felt by the criminal than any other
punishment."

such women as these were the mothers of a great part of the inhabitants now existing in the Colony, and from this stock only can a reasonable hope be held out of rapid increase to the population".[1] Their early treatment had been a mixture of negligence and brutality. Some were taken as wives or servants by settlers, soldiers or convicts. Those left on the Government's hands were set to work at making up slop clothing, and, when a factory had been built for them at Parramatta, were employed in the weaving of a coarse cloth out of which blankets and rough jackets were made. Prior to the reforms instituted at Castlereagh's bidding after 1812, when the wretchedness of their lot had become known, the one gleam of humanity in this chapter of evil was Governor King's strong support of orphanages, primarily for girls, at both Sydney and Parramatta. "To save the youth of the colony from the destructive examples of their abandoned parents" he showed a continued zeal in appropriating minor sources of colonial revenue to the maintenance of the orphanages.

Governors Hunter, King and Bligh, each in his own manner, opposed the rum-traders' readiness to give such a public what it wanted, "a fiery poison" fatal to the consumer's sense of his own welfare. Here was free enterprize at its worst. The presumption on which the general case for free enterprize rests, of a harmony between individual wealth and general welfare, was in this instance obviously at fault. In three ways the naval governors restricted the supply of spirits; by licensing houses for its retail sale, by limiting imports and by suppressing illicit distillation from grain. More effective in the end were an alternative system of exchanging grain for stores, and the provision of a sound money with which anyone might safely trade for cash.

[1] *Report of Committee on Transportation*, 1812, pp. 9–12. The Committee was opposing Macquarie's representations against the sending of women convicts, e.g. 30 April 1810: "Female convicts are as great a drawback as the others are beneficial."

Hunter's attack on the officers' trading monopoly was easily bluffed off. As with the rationing of assigned servants, he hesitated and was lost. Though explicitly instructed to allow no spirits to be landed without his consent, he wondered whether such orders would be obeyed, and put it to Portland that there was much to be said for rum as a reward. By November 1796, however, he was alive to "the astonishing state of indolence and indifference about the affairs of the public which the private traffic of individuals have (*sic*) brought about". The general licentiousness arose, he thought, from the unseemly activity of the officers "in a most pernicious traffic with spirituous liquors". Considering the advantages given them, he felt the strongest astonishment "that they should have ever thought of condescending to enter into trade of any kind, except that of disposing to Government the produce of their agricultural labours".

Hunter's opposition proved, however, a mere wringing of hands. He forbade licensed dealers to pay for settlers' grain with spirits, but he could not bring himself to employ, against his social equals, a police recruited entirely from the convict class. Almost every official was in the ring, and the Governor was isolated and powerless. Field of Mars settlers asked him to give them an official credit on their grain, so that they might themselves buy part of a ship's cargo and escape the snares of "dealers, pedlars and extortioners". Hunter's only response was a fatuous General Order, 25 June 1798, desiring all settlers "to keep possession of their own money until they are apprised by public notice that a cargo has been brought, the officers having undertaken the trouble of officiating as agents for the general benefit of the whole colony".

This order led to his recall. It confirmed the impression of incompetence he had given by fumbling the project of selling imports at retail from the government store.[1] This

---

[1] *H. R. of A.* series I, vol. II, p. 19, 10 June 1797, and p. 114, 10 Jan. 1798.

he twice recommended, the second recommendation drawing the curt answer that he had already been told to do it. His General Order of June 1798 about the self-sacrificing officers meant, he was informed, "a sanction to the officers to engage in traffic" and therefore an apology for the disgraceful doings he had so hotly denounced. In January 1800, still unmindful of his fall, he frankly confessed his impotence to control McArthur's importation of spirits. "I am sufficiently experienced here to know that whilst the article sought after is in this harbour, or indeed any other on this coast, it is impossible to counteract the designs of those who wish to have it....To oppose its being landed, my lord, will be vain for want of proper officers to execute such orders as I might see occasion to give."

Philip Gidley King meant to be a Governor of tougher will. General Orders flowed from his pen like thunderbolts from high Olympus. Spirits might not be sold "from the beating of the taptoo[1] until the following noon, nor during Divine Service". Persistent unlicensed sellers should serve three months on the hulk 'Supply'. The clash was not long in coming. A creature of McArthur's was convicted of trading spirits with convicts for their rations of salt meat—a powerful incentive to theft by the hungry. He lost his licence and had his liquor staved.[2] Shortly after this declaration of war, McArthur found himself in temporary command of the New South Wales Corps, and, a disagreement having arisen over the court-martial of an officer accused of petty thieving, he contrived to isolate Governor King by a social boycott. He so far succeeded with the Junior Officers, that Colonel Paterson on his return could find no other means of answering the extension of the boycott to himself, for refusing to participate in it, than a

---

[1] This old form of the word "tattoo" is a reminder of its origin in the Dutch phrase "de taptoe slaan", to close the taps.

[2] *H. R. of A.* series I, vol. III, p. 323, P. G. King to John King. Also vol. III, pp. 45–6. The distinctive stripe on the convicts' dress was first used to prevent the sale of new clothing as soon as it was issued. Cf. vol. I, p. 308, Philip to Nepean, 18 November 1791.

challenge to McArthur. They met. Paterson was seriously wounded. King put McArthur under arrest. Then he ordered him to proceed to Norfolk Island in charge of a detachment. McArthur refused to go until his arrest was cleared by a court-martial. King, holding the only officers who could compose such a court to be "no impartial judges", sent him off to England.[1]

By a ship other than that bearing the official account of this turmoil, the Governor pictured to his namesake, the Under-Secretary, McArthur's ascendancy in the colony and his own predicament in "belling the cat". "He came here in 1790 more than £500 in debt, and is now worth at least £20,000....His employment during the eleven years he has been here has been that of making a large fortune, helping his brother-officers to make small ones, and sowing discord and strife." King counted on McArthur's resignation from the New South Wales Corps. "But come out here again he certainly must, as a very large part of his immense fortune is vested here in numerous herds, flocks and vast domains." Greater than these resources, however, King rated the "art, cunning, impudence and basilisk eyes" by which McArthur was able to achieve any object he pursued. "It is to these odds and the independence of his fortune I have to oppose my exertion for the tranquillity of this colony, the welfare of the public service, and my own reputation."

But Governor King's exertions against the rum traffic grew very spasmodic while McArthur was away. The Governor-General of India, at his request, checked the sending of Bengal rum. Warnings sent by the American minister in London to British consuls in the United States had less effect. The Yankees were old hands at smuggling, especially with rum. Much still came from Britain. King

---

[1] He made the voyage *via* India, and the ship, dismasted by a "willy-willy" off the N.W. of Australia, took refuge at Amboyna. For an incident which happened there, delightfully characteristic of the pugnacious McArthur, see *Macarthur Records*, p. 62.

sent away several cargoes, mostly of American or Indian origin, but his enforcement of the limit of 300 gallons which might be landed from any one vessel was never strict. "So great was the fame of the propensity of the inhabitants of this colony to the immoderate use of spirits and the certainty of getting any amount of payment in government bills", he complained to Portland, "that I believe all the nations of the earth agreed to inundate the colony with spirits."

Between September 1800 and October 1802, 37,891 gallons of spirits and 22,932 gallons of wine were sent away, but by his own account 69,980 gallons of spirits and 33,246 gallons of wine were landed, an annual consumption of five gallons three quarts of "rum" and two gallons three quarts of wine to every man, woman and child in the colony's average population of 5807 during that period. Though not an abstemious person, the average Australian of 1925–6 consumed less than two quarts of spirits (·44 of a gallon) and just two quarts of wine, including both imported and local liquors. He drank, it is true, 11·34 gallons of beer—quite another matter. By that alternative King was anxious to slake his subjects' thirst. Hop-plants were sent out in 1802 at Sir Joseph Banks' instance and brewing utensils followed. A brewery was duly started at Parramatta in May 1804. Simultaneously King laid a duty of £5 a hundred gallons on imported rum. Neither beer nor duty made any difference. The Governor himself still used rum as an official reward for the apprehension of criminals who had "gone bush".

Some odds and ends of metallic money scraped together during the period of the Napoleonic Wars were quite inadequate to displace rum from its general acceptance as a medium of trade. A thousand pounds of English silver had been sent to Phillip to pay marine artificers at work on ship-repairing. In 1801 this silver was supplemented by £2500 in "cart-wheel" pennies, clumsy ounce-weight things that went for twopence in the colony. They were good payment for debts up to £5, but the weight of them in such mass, and the Governor's refusal to take them at colonial value in payment for bills on London, marred their favour. Ships refitting in the harbour brought in all manner of strange coins—Johannas, ducats, gold mohurs, pagodas, Spanish dollars, rupees and guelders—but often both these and the British shillings were absorbed in paying vessels for imported stores when bills on London happened to be short. Rum, however, was always to be had. A little cozening would induce a settler to take it for his produce or as change when he "cashed" the commissary's receipt. Such receipts were then convertible into bills on London, the external currency that paid for imports, and more rum.

King continued Hunter's plan of retailing stores to the settlers, over and above the issue of free rations to convicts. This kept some out of the clutches of the rum-dealers and restrained the rate of profit at which private traders could sell imported goods. But the dishonesty of his underlings and the propensity of settlers to set up shop with the cheap government wares forced him to hedge with precautions the right to buy. First both Governor and Commissary scrutinized the list of the settler's wants. Then each customer was admitted singly to the warehouse in a loft, up a ladder at which a sentry mounted guard. For all that, the trade involved in retailing King's Sydney purchases of ships' cargoes and the consignments made by the Victualling Board encouraged independent merchants to take a hand in breaking the ring. First of these was one Robert Campbell. After acting as Sydney agent to a Calcutta firm that sold cattle, sugar and spirits, he started business on his own account in King's term of office.

The increase of goods due to the reduction of settlers' costs meant the production of more grain, and this augmented the settler's power to buy. Grain was thus occasionally in excess supply, but more often floods created dearth and the Governor found a great vacillation in the readiness of settlers to deliver their grain at the fixed price.[1] At first he ascribed this new trouble to McArthur's usual "art, cunning and impudence", and argued stiffly "that neither scarcity or plenty should influence the price" (8 November 1801).

Towards the end of his term King grew weary of the isolation in which every attempt at active rule involved him. Every move to regulate trade offended some interest and drew the fire of anonymous critics. Their "pipes" founded a species of lampooning journalism that still grows rank in Australia.[2] One represented King as anxious, on hearing that "Pitt and Portland were out", to feather his nest by every means while still in power.

> The convicts I'll starve and sell all their rations
> As well as their slops for my private occasions.
> From the orphan collection I take what I dare,
> Of whalers' investments I own I've a share.

He met such attacks sensibly by starting in 1803 the *Sydney Gazette*, but he was by then heartily sick of the too vast orb of his fate. In May he applied for leave to vacate the office he had once eagerly sought. Three years he waited impatiently for relief. The successor who arrived in August 1806 was a protégé of Banks, Captain William Bligh, who had seen service under both Cook and Nelson, and had won fame as "Breadfruit Bligh" of the 'Bounty'. To Banks he seemed a man of "integrity unimpeached, a mind capable of providing its own resources in difficulties, civil in deportment, and not subject to whimper and whine when severity of discipline is wanted to meet emergencies".

Bligh found at his coming a community sunk deep in depravity, whose most hopeful element, the farmers along the Hawkesbury, had just been impoverished by a recurrence of the floods. His task, as he saw it, was to revive

[1] For an account of the floods prior to 1806, see *H. R. of A.* series I, vol. v, p. 697, King to Camden, 7 April 1806.
[2] See *Australian Encyclopaedia*, vol. II, p. 301, article on "Pipes". Cf. *The Adventures of Ralph Rashleigh*, pp. 86–7.

agriculture, to build churches and schools and to amend by instruction the moral and spiritual shortcomings of his people. Most of the rising generation were entirely neglected, having no parents, "the mothers being dead, and their fathers having left the country as either sailors, soldiers or prisoners who became free".[1] Neither by word nor deed, however, did he exhibit a leader's power to transform his charges into a self-reliant society of families shaping their lives by a free exchange of services. His main instructions, repeating once more those given twenty years earlier to Phillip, still ordered him to create by prisoners' labour a public fund of foodstuffs, to be issued by authority. As a means of recovering from the recent disaster such communal subsistence-farming was hopeless. As a check on the speculative and fluctuating prices asked outside the stores by private cultivators it was no better. Since the institution of assigned service, public farming was perforce conducted at a high cost with convicts whom no private employer would take.

In his additional instructions to Bligh, however, Castlereagh had recommended the activity of free producers selling for an open market as the most hopeful chance of reducing dependence on England. Wheat and maize, except when floods swept away the harvest, were coming forward in ample supply. Castlereagh looked for live stock from the same source. In good set terms he propounded the new doctrine of freedom of enterprize. "Nothing, I conceive, will more essentially contribute to bring forward the supplies which the country is becoming able to furnish in most of the Articles of first necessity such as Corn, Poultry, Vegetables etc., than the abolition of all restrictions in the disposal of those supplies. In like manner it is not judged necessary for you to interfere in future in

---

[1] Bligh to Windham, 7 February 1807, *H. R. of A.* ser. I, vol. VI, p. 123. The weakness in early New South Wales family life may be judged from this short paragraph in the same despatch. "The inhabitants are healthy and Marriages increase; in my late Surveys I ascertained the Married Women were 395; Legitimate children 807; Natural children 1025."

respect to the demands of Adventurers bringing articles for trade to the Colony, further than to prevent improper communications between the ships and the convicts, excepting with regard to the Article of Spirits."

Bligh awaited the opportunity of an abundant harvest before abolishing the fixed official price of wheat.[1] He had hopes that the scarcity he found at his arrival would more effectively than any admonition "teach the settlers to be more provident and industrious". "Considerable importation", he reasoned, "would lead to great indifference, as it would reduce the price of grain and make it not worth their while to grow it." In this he was more considerate than his successor, whose importations were to produce precisely that depressing effect.[2] "When they begin to find a regular market for their grain", concluded Bligh, "agriculture will be the chief pursuit both here and at the out-settlements." But in taking the rôle of patron of agriculture, Bligh was moved by other motives than those of economic reason.

The exception to the rule of *laissez faire* which Castlereagh had noted—Bligh's duty to interfere "with regard to the Article of Spirits"—loomed larger to the new Governor than the rule itself. Here was a trade in which his charges wretchedly sacrificed their produce to the enrichment of an already wealthy few. He had been sent to repress it. His arch-antagonist in this duty had earned the displeasure of Sir Joseph Banks. Bligh's view of all John McArthur's energies in the colony was distorted by his determination to overthrow one who had baulked both Hunter and King. McArthur, we can now see, stood head and shoulders above his fellow-colonists in economic foresight as well as in money-making. When Governor Phillip

---

[1] This was 5s. per bushel in 1790, 10s. from 1791 to 1800, 8s. until 1804, 7s. at the Hawkesbury, 7s. 6d. at Sydney from 1804 to 1806, 15s. in 1806 and 10s. a bushel until 1822. See Coghlan, *Labour and Industry in Australia*, vol. I, pp. 142 and 277.

[2] See Marion Phillips, *A Colonial Autocracy*, p. 121, for the fluctuations of prices and their reactions on production in 1813 and 1814.

was hoping to find out how soon an expiree could be induced by the hope of independence to grow enough food for himself and his family, McArthur had proposed to use those "basilisk" eyes of his to keep a whole gang of convicts "hard at it", producing by their combined labour a surplus that would feed the colony and make him rich. When under Grose this plan was being tried, he foresaw that the home authorities would soon complain of the expense of feeding the assigned servants. He was therefore the first to offer to feed a hundred himself, and to press on Hunter a plan to render the colony self-supporting in animal food by distributing pigs among the better convicts. As soon as success in raising grain and animal food by private activity came in sight, his mind ranged in search of a way by which the colonists might pay for their needs from abroad. What could they export which, unlike the whale-oil and seal-skins already being won on the coast, would be permanent and expansive in supply, and secure against unthrifty exploitation by intruders? This forward-moving quality of his mind was of invaluable service to Australia in the end, but in his haste to reach each fresh objective, McArthur was ready to clutch every resource of his fellow-colonists which was legally within his reach, and with such weapons to fight relentlessly for more.

Neither opponent, indeed, was restrained by a conscience sensitive to the social consequences of his actions. Whatever Bligh's character may have been when in command of the ill-fated 'Bounty', his use of authority in New South Wales was often capricious and at times precipitate.[1] His main duty, as he saw it, was to restrain McArthur's traffic in spirits. Yet his first acts in the colony were hopelessly at variance with the rôle of stern rebuker of greed in high places. Before assuming office, he accepted from Governor King three grants of valuable land at Sydney, at Parra-

[1] See Macquarie to Castlereagh, 10 May 1810, *H. R. of A.* series I, vol. VII, p. 331.

matta and at Rouse Hill, amounting in all to 1345 acres; and the first grant he made was to his predecessor's wife, a grant of 790 acres in the district of Evan, to be known by the curious name of "Thanks". Local manners and customs, he wrote in November 1806, called for much correction. "The settlers in general, and particularly those from prisoners, are not honest, have no prudence and little industry; great chicanery is used in all their dealings, and much litigation. All this will require a great deal of attention on my part to remove."

He proceeded to question the validity of certain leases for fourteen years within the boundaries of Sydney. Phillip had set a limit of five years to such leases and King had confirmed this. At the end of his term, however, King had granted fourteen-year leases to McArthur, Johnston, Blaxcell and others. Farther afield, Bligh boggled at McArthur's grant in the Cowpastures beyond the Nepean, made by Lord Camden despite opposition from Sir Joseph Banks. Though McArthur's cult of fine wool had won many friends at home, Bligh threw cold water on it at every opportunity. On the farm he bought at Pitt Town on the Hawkesbury, he set an example of dairying and agriculture. His despatches made light of an export of wool. "In general, animal food is a greater object to the proprietors of sheep than the fleece, as there is an immediate demand for it." And again "Some wrong impressions were made in England by reports of the exportation (of wool) expected from this country. Some of the ships which arrived about the time I did had orders to purchase what was ready, but they found none for sale." When McArthur urged the superiority of his "peaceful productive sheep" over the herds of wild cattle—"fine animals" Bligh had called them—with whose title and possession of the Cowpastures the Governor was most sympathetic, Bligh burst into rage. "What have I to do with your sheep, Sir? Are you to have such flocks of sheep as no man ever heard of before? No, Sir!"

Yet the agriculture which Bligh favoured could at best only relieve the British Treasury of the cost of transporting provisions to New South Wales. The foodstuffs grown there must still be purchased before their issue as government rations. That demand, moreover, was limited and inelastic. In days of war, corn laws and slow transport, a big export trade in wheat, livestock or maize was inconceivable. The limit of Bligh's view in public economy was thus to save the cost and necessity of transporting saltmeat and flour from overseas. His express instructions and his naval training alike led him to rate higher than economic aims the disciplinary task—restraint on the use of spirits as barter. Was it not as a fearless disciplinarian that Banks had recommended him, at a doubled salary?

No evil, he thought, had resulted from the consumption of spirits. The trouble arose from the pull in hiring labour which their monopoly in importation had given to officers and big settlers, to the disadvantage of the small farmers. "To prohibit the barter being carried on in any way is absolutely necessary to bring labour to a due value and to support the farming interest." As examples of the effects of payment in rum, he cited: "A sawyer will cut one hundred feet of timber for a Bottle of Spirits—value two shillings and sixpence—which he drinks in a few hours. For the same labour he would charge two Bushels of Wheat, which would furnish Bread for him for two months. Hence those who have got no liquor to pay their Labourers with are ruined by paying more than they can possibly afford for any kind of labour which they are compelled to hire men to execute, while those who have liquor gain an immense advantage."

Bligh's conception of reform was a direct prohibition of the use of spirits as a means of purchase, coupled with police measures against private distillation.[1] Such measures, he knew, would provoke opposition from those who had

[1] Regarding the character and remuneration of these convict and ex-convict police, see M. Phillips, *op. cit.* pp. 77–8.

"so materially enriched themselves by" the trade. In social and official influence they were strongly entrenched, and he had the poorest opinion of the judge-advocate on whose legal decisions he must rely. "Mr Atkins the Judge-Advocate", he reported in October 1807, "has been accustomed to inebriety; has been the ridicule of the community; sentences of death have been pronounced in moments of intoxication; his determination is weak; his opinion floating and infirm; his knowledge of the Law insignificant and subservient to private inclination. Confidential cases of the Crown where due secrecy is required he is not to be trusted with." He advocated his removal in the strongest terms.

The stage was thus set and the chief characters cast for what the Sydney populace dubbed "The Rum Puncheon Rebellion"—Bligh's deposition by the New South Wales Corps on the twentieth anniversary of the colony's foundation, 26 January 1808. On one side a Governor blinded by prejudice to the ability of the little community's only first-class brain; on the other a group of officer-traders whom McArthur himself despised. "A more improper set of men", he told his wife, "could not be collected together".[1] As traders they drew their wealth mainly from a traffic which sapped the efforts of convict-settlers to make a new start by honest toil. Over their doings watched a court of law in which justice spoke by the whims of one despised as a drunkard even in that company.

On New Years' Day 1808 the small settlers and "emancipists", to the number of 833, petitioned Governor Bligh in the name of "the extensive rising greatness and enterprising spirit of the colonists" for "such privilege of trade to their Country vessels and themselves as other colonists have, and that the Law might be administered by Trial by Jury of the People as in England". Castlereagh's additional instructions clearly empowered Bligh to lend a favourable hearing to the former request. But the older

[1] 3 May 1810, *H. R. of N. S. Wales*, vol. VII, p. 370.

instructions which had been repeated to Bligh bade him
prevent by all possible means every sort of intercourse
between New South Wales and European settlements in
India, China and the Pacific. Only by licence from the
East India Company could English vessels trade in longi-
tudes east of the Cape of Good Hope. The officer-capitalists
of Sydney, long accustomed to pull the strings and to
exploit these special licences to their private advantage,
sniffed the tainted breeze when emancipist petitioners
asked for a general freedom of trade. Bligh, they knew
full well, meant to upset their system. It was high time
they captured, in defence of their privileges, the whole
machinery of government. The episodes of McArthur's
stills and of the seizure of the "Parramatta" were therefore
welcome opportunities to men already strongly tempted to
grasp for their own ends the Governor's powers to bind
and loose.[1]

The liberty for which they struck consisted in the privileges of a dominant few, but when they had grasped power
and imprisoned "the Tyrant" the usurpers fell out among
themselves.[2] McArthur, taking the official style of Secretary to the Colony, was soon involved in a furious contest
with the Blaxlands and Simeon Lord, a wealthy emancipist,
about the control of a sealing vessel, 'The Brothers'. This
culminated in further interference by the military in the
course of justice in the courts. So formidable was the
danger of chaos through these feuds, that in April, Major
Johnston, the rebel Lieutenant-Governor, addressed to his
fellow-conspirators a stern letter of rebuke, reminding
them of their pledged words to support him in assuming
the Government. He challenged any to aver that McArthur
had not fulfilled his share of that solemn engagement.
Such an appeal, backed by a challenge from two men who

---

[1] As to the operation of the restrictions arising out of the East India
Company's charter see M. Phillips, *op. cit.* pp. 16, 153; T. A. Coghlan,
op. cit. pp. 124, 138; and *H. R. of A.* series I, vol. x, p. 809 *et passim*.

[2] For an account of the mutiny, see Ernest Scott's *Short History of Australia*,
pp. 69-74.

meant what they said, went home. A revived sense of common responsibility curbed the feuds.

As time brought reflection on their position, however, financial apprehension made the rebel leaders cautious. How were the expenses of government to be met? If they drew bills on the Treasury and these were rejected, their signatures would put their private fortunes in jeopardy; and they had private fortunes. So they proceeded to meet current expenditure by selling the government herds and stores.[1] They did more. As under Grose and Paterson in 1793–5, so again under Johnston, Foveaux and Paterson the main activity of the military government was the granting of land and stock, the customary first capital for development.[2] Their proceedings, reported by Bligh's adherents, with no loss of unfavourable colour, did more to enlighten His Majesty's Ministers as to the folly of maintaining a standing garrison in such an environment than all the despatches of Governors fearful to confess their own impotence.

The "Rebellion", if the metaphor may be allowed, was a boil in an unhealthy body in which certain useless elements came into a conflict of mutual destruction which could be ended only by the surgeon's knife. It rid the colony of the New South Wales Corps and, for a time, of its ex-member but continued leader, John McArthur. It rid it, too, of naval governors and their habit of trying to order social and economic relations by the methods of the quarter-deck.

---

[1] Hence Major Abbott's laconic report to ex-Governor King, 4 September 1808: "The Colony is quiet. There is no money." Bills on London were then the only external currency for large amounts. *H. R. of N.S.W.* vol. vi, p. 835.

[2] Palmer to Bligh, 4 November 1808, *H. R. of A.* series I, vol. vi, p. 686: "Macarthur and Fitz has the chief management of Stock returns, as well as the Grain, and two such adepts in Villainy, they could not be in better hands." Also vol. vii, p. 108.

CHAPTER IV

"Governor Macquarie's Bank"

COLONEL Lachlan Macquarie, Governor-in-Chief of New South Wales and its Dependencies from 1 January 1810 to 1 December 1821, has been highly praised.[1] At a time when many were turning against him, his zeal and belief in the colony won this comment from his shrewdest contemporary: "Governor Macquarie is a man of unblemished honour and character, although it may not have been his lot to do that which I think no man ever will do—to give satisfaction to all".[2] His modern biographer, however, sums him up as "a man of very ordinary ability"[3] and an official historian half complains that he "left the development of the colony's primary industries and the pioneer experimental work to individuals undirected by the fostering care of government".[4] This he had been instructed to do. Yet, judging by his ideal of an emancipists' Utopia and his vendetta against free settlers, his forbearance sprang less from a thorough appreciation of his instructions than from "total incapacity"[5] to assess what the pastoral leaders could achieve. A splendid second-rater, he perceived things and hated opponents but could not judge the creative value of ideas.

Castlereagh's instructions plainly envisaged a colony

---

[1] As recent examples see (1) T. Dunbabin's *Making of Australasia*, p. 89, "Macquarie the Nation-Builder", "Second founder of Australia"; and (2) A. Jose's *Builders and Pioneers of Australia*, pp. 3–35.

[2] John McArthur. See *Macarthur Records*, p. 290. The opinion was expressed early in 1817.

[3] Marion Phillips, *A Colonial Autocracy*, Preface, p. vii.

[4] F. G. Watson, *H. R. of A.* series I, vol. VIII, Introduction, p. xvi.

[5] The phrase is J. T. Bigge's. *Macarthur Records*, p. 324.

developing its own economy.[1] There was to be an end
of naval paternalism over all residents in the prison
marooned on a distant shore. Fixed prices, government
trading and public agriculture were to go. Macquarie
furthered the new policy by providing a bank to keep the
currency sound and by building roads to the wider hinterland which the pastoralists had spied out beyond the
mountains. But much remained, notably in transportation
and the Navigation Acts, of an older system which had
treated all colonies as distant depots tied to British trade,
and the strong wine of despotic power let loose the Highland chieftain latent in Macquarie.

His first task was the unsolved riddle of rum. As his
public works pay-sheets bear witness, it was still in use to
pay wages. George Street between Brickfield Hill and
Bridge Street cost four hundred gallons. Prompted by
Castlereagh, Macquarie recommended the admission of all
rum sent to New South Wales on payment of "high" duties,
say three or four shillings a gallon. The home government, then contemplating a British duty of £1. 12s. 6d.
a gallon, at once chose the higher figure. It also informed
the East India Company, still in charge of licensing traders
and whalers in the South Seas, that any who traded to
"the colony of Botany Bay" might be allowed to carry
spirits thither "for the consumption of the inhabitants of
the said colony". Macquarie thought to take strict control
over this consumption by cutting down licensed houses in
Sydney from 85 to 20, and at the out-settlements in due
proportion.

Like King he was caught by a return wave which en-
gulfed every impediment. Official cancellation of licences
made little difference to the sale of rum in "The Rocks"
area, near the wharves. Macquarie granted fifty beer-
licences and took the administration of all licensing orders
out of the magistrates' hands, but the standards he required
of their holders proved to be such that one trader was

---

[1] *H. R. of A.* series I, vol. VII, pp. 80 and 83.

C

granted a licence who had been convicted of unlicensed vending four times in the two preceding years.

Nor were the wholesalers less adroit in finding the Governor's blind spot. Early in 1811 ministers at home were astonished to learn that Macquarie had granted a legal monopoly in the importation of spirits, other than on government account, to three men—Blaxcell, Riley and D'Arcy Wentworth! Blaxcell and Riley were typical speculative traders, but Wentworth, though by voluntary exile he had narrowly escaped transportation on a charge of highway robbery, was now Principal Surgeon and Superintendent of Police. He was taken into partnership by the other two during the negotiation of the contract. The three undertook to erect a large general hospital, including excellent surgeons' quarters, at no cost to the government other than (i) the grant to them of the sole right to import spirits for three years up to 45,000 gallons and (ii) the services of 20 assigned servants and 80 oxen. The Governor's enthusiasm for fine buildings (of which more anon) must have blinded him temporarily to the inconsistency of this monopoly with the policy of open imports subject to duty, and to the impropriety of making the Principal Surgeon and Superintendent of Police, with his repute as a retired highwayman, a partner in profits from the lavish sale of rum and the cheap erection of the hospital. Temporary blindness or no, when the Governor permitted breaches of this contract the partners exacted from him two extensions of the term of their monopoly. The "Rum Hospital" was duly built. Part of it still stands in the façade of Parliament House, hallowed to the legislators of to-day by the traditions of Wentworth junior, Robertson, Parkes, Dalley and Reid.

The four years of its building were an Indian summer to the rum-monopolists. Ruefully Hannibal McArthur reported to his Uncle John in England how they were making hay. Whereas he (Hannibal) had been forced under the terms of the monopoly to sell a consignment of spirits to government at 9s. a gallon, duty free, these contractors, after paying a duty of 3s. a gallon, were getting 36s. for theirs. Licensed houses increased more than threefold, and all complaints of disorder in them met with the cynical contention from Wentworth senior that the thriving trade meant good revenue for the police fund. Judging from the total of 144,000 gallons imported during the four years, a third of which may have been on government account, the monopoly imported more than was allowed in the original bond.

Earl Bathurst peremptorily ordered Macquarie to set importation free at the expiry of the contract, to raise the duty, and to put an end to the issue of rum at a fixed price to officials and military, "a practice which even under your Prudent Administration of it has the Appearance if not the actual Effect of encouraging the Barter of that Article". The contrite Governor raised the duty to seven shillings a gallon, and in 1818 to ten shillings.

Reduced consumption did not speedily follow the substitution of duties by no means severe for legal prohibition of import. Consumption during the Hospital Contract seems to have been about three gallons two quarts per head of population. From 1815 to 1820 it actually rose to over four gallons a head, apart from smuggling, illicit stills and beer. In England, though the consumption of spirits rose during the wars, the quantity drunk per head was in 1830 less than a gallon.

The provision of sound money and a central control of credit proved a more effective antidote. Governor King had dreamed of coin as an antidote to rum as early as November 1800. He proclaimed the approaching end of barter "when a sufficient quantity of copper coin is received in the colony". But the cart-wheel pennies were local tokens only. In December 1804 a British whaler, the 'Policy', captured near Amboyna a Dutch supply ship with fifteen chests of dollars aboard, worth £20,000. This was good silver money acceptable anywhere—a fact which disquieted the master of the 'Policy' who brought his prize into Port Jackson. He asked King to buy the silver and pay him in bills on London, a safer booty to carry on the open sea in time of war. King declined "so mighty a responsibility". He had apparent reason for his caution. Sealskins were, as he said, "the only staple yet discovered here", and, in the absence of exports, the more good money put into circulation the sooner was it drained out to pay for visiting traders' goods. So disappeared those of the 'Policy's' dollars that its master and crew spent in Sydney. Not even the cutting of the Spanish dollars into eight or ten parts kept them in circulation.[1]

Ministers at home were too much absorbed in war-finance, currency depreciation and "scarcity of specie" to pay heed to the monetary troubles of an obscure colony on the Pacific. Yet the principle of *laissez faire*, which Castlereagh enunciated for Macquarie's guidance, presupposed an honest and stable medium of exchange. In their search for a money less difficult to carry than rum or copper pence the colonists had already taken to issuing private "notes" or "cards", which circulated as "colonial currency".[2] A settler wishing to buy goods from a private trader tendered the receipt the Commissary had given him for his pigs and grain, and instead of taking out the change in rum, carried away an I.O.U. from the trader. Possibly the first issuers were the more reputable traders. To most ex-convict shopkeepers every settler was "fair game" and his store-receipt showed what he was worth to rob. Such a trader would count himself a failure if the whole amount were not promptly "melted down", i.e. taken in rum. Thus private notes may once have been *prima facie* evidence of a self-restraint akin to honesty.

[1] Spanish dollars were minted freely at Mexico City from 1535 and had become an excellent international cash in use from Maine to India. Little sterling silver was minted in Britain during the first half of George III's reign.
[2] Hence the mildly contemptuous terms "currency lad" and "currency lass" for children born in the colony.

Soon they varied as much in value as in style, or more. Some were in writing; others promised in impressive copper-plate future payment in sterling for value received. One group of leading firms tried printing in hot type as a precaution against old Sydney's expert penmen. With every precaution taken, however, such "petty banking", as Macquarie dubbed it, left open by its very nature "a door to grievous frauds and impositions". Traders who were still convicts on ticket-of-leave managed by free issue of currency notes to get hold of many commissariat receipts and to change these into substantial property, in goods or land. Then, declaring themselves insolvent, they would employ confederates to buy up their notes from their defrauded creditors, at a heavy discount. Apart altogether from such deliberate fraud, the general issue of colonial currency caused all its units to depreciate.[1] Governors strove in vain to limit to approved persons the right to issue "notes". Who was to draw the line and—a task still more difficult—to maintain it when it had been drawn? "Strong personal laws" ordering redemption in specie did no more under Bligh and Macquarie to stop fraudulent "currency" than they had done under King and Bligh to check the excess of rum. A spate of imports in 1812 made silver so scarce that in January 1813 it was at a premium of 75 per cent.[2]

At his first coming, Governor Macquarie advocated the institution of a bank for the provision of notes secured against land.[3] His advocacy of a plan avowedly derived "from the famous Bank of Pennsylvania" and promising a result "Eleven per cent. above what the Exchequer Bills

---

[1] For Macquarie's first impressions of colonial currency, see *H. R. of A.* series I, vol. VII, p. 264, Macquarie to Castlereagh, 30 April 1810.

[2] *Sydney Gazette*, 27 January 1813. "A difference of 15s. in the pound has been the present week demanded and no article laid in at the market price of the day can afford the difference."

[3] *H. R. of A.* series I, vol. VII, p. 265, Macquarie to Castlereagh, 30 April 1810. His Secretary, J. T. Campbell, had been in the service of the Bank of Ireland and had "had a principal part in the establishment and conduct of the Bank at the Cape of Good Hope".

yield in England" must have read like a lesson to the Old Lady of Threadneedle Street in sucking eggs. The Board of Trade, to which Lord Liverpool referred the proposal, would have none of it. New South Wales was a very different place from the Cape of Good Hope. The Board suggested that its Governor be sent £10,000 in dollars, through the East India Company. They arrived by the sloop 'Samarang' in November 1812, and Macquarie solved the problem of keeping them in circulation by punching a large hole in each, giving the ring or "holey dollar" an official value of five shillings, and the dump one of fifteen pence. As bullion the dollar was then worth five shillings for oversea trading. The government undertook to redeem "holey dollars" and dumps at the end of every two years by giving for them good bills on London. Thus they formed a local token currency, being in effect metallic promises to pay. But the supply was inelastic, and the way still remained open for creations of private "currency". Those who had no occasion to make payments to oversea traders passed on the depreciated notes.

By the *Sydney Gazette* the Governor warned issuers of currency that their safety and advantage lay in giving out no more. The main burden of a local money issued in excess fell upon dealers who had to pay importing merchants in sterling yet must sell their wares at retail for the depreciating currency. But, plain as the collective interest of the traders might be in calling a halt, the temptation upon each individual remained. So many tried to outrun the general disaster that the depreciation of "currency" was accelerated.

Only a Bank with exclusive right to issue could maintain the value of paper money at a par with specie and keep trade on credit sound. Unlimited credit means unlimited belief, an imprudent attitude in any community. In 1816 Macquarie succeeded in calling a halt to the unscrupulous. A fresh consignment of 40,000 silver dollars from India enabled him as a first step to re-enact Bligh's order that notes were to be redeemable at demand in sterling, then understood as including all specie. Prices and wages, too, were to be stated in sterling. But how was redemption to be made customary and easy? A general meeting of traders agreed early in 1817 that all contracts in existence were to be re-adjusted, two-thirds prices in sterling being substituted for those quoted in "currency". So much for past contracts. But who was to sustain for the future the collective interest in the equivalence of paper money and specie, of credit and international cash? Public meetings agree, resolve, dissolve and disagree. The responsibility for restraint in the issue of paper currency was placed and shouldered only when it was announced that a group of leading traders and officials had been granted a charter to form a bank.[1]

The capital of the contemplated Bank of New South Wales, gathered in the form of 200 shares of £100 each, was to be charged with the redemption on demand of all notes which the bank deemed it prudent to issue. Over-issue would thus endanger the bank's foundation, its stock of international cash. In issuing notes or otherwise granting the right to draw cash from its strong-box, the directors of the Bank were in this way made the colony's financial watchmen. They would hurt themselves first if they granted credit, *i.e.* the use of productive resources on condition of future repayment, to men unable or unready to put those resources to effective use. The bankers became in a sense the trustees of their clients' wealth and the guarantors of their honesty. They encouraged trade between the most dependable, and were bound by the special circumstances of the colony to pay good heed to its external trade.

In March 1817 the need for such a regulator of note issues had grown so clear that Macquarie, with the cautiously worded support of Judge-Advocate Wylde, granted a Colonial Subscription Bank a seven-years'

[1] *H. R. of A.* series I, vol. IX, pp. 217 *et seq.*

charter on his own initiative. He advised the Colonial Office not merely to confirm the charter but to become party to the subscription of capital, only £12,600 of which had been found in the colony. Government, he urged, "should at least make the Bank the Depository and Medium of all Government Monies and payments".

Though the Governor's secretary became its first President and deposits flowed in steadily[1], the paid-up capital at opening day was but £3625, and troubles soon came upon "my favourite Measure", as Macquarie termed it. The Colonial Office reported the opinion of the Crown's legal advisers "that you were not legally empowered either by your Commission or Instructions to grant such a Charter, and that it is consequently null and void".[2] Holding that no good purpose could be served by any "interference" in banking on the part of government, the Secretary of State ordered Macquarie to "intimate to the gentlemen composing that establishment that they can only consider themselves in the situation of persons associated for the purposes of trade, and as such not entitled to any of those special privileges which it was the object of the Charter to confer".

Foremost of these was the privilege of indemnity "against all risk or liability beyond the amount of the Shares respectively taken by each in the Capital Stock of the said Bank". Among banks of issue such limited liability was then the exclusive privilege of the Bank of England. In its absence the subscribers would become ordinary partners liable to an unlimited extent for the debts of the bank. Macquarie had hoped that the privilege of limited liability would induce the sound and cautious to subscribe adequate capital. A new currency chaos, he foresaw, would follow the denial of the charter's validity, and he

[1] The first depositor was Sergeant Jeremiah Murphey of the 46th Regiment, £50, the second John Harris of Ultimo, £138. 1s. 4d., and the third William Redfern, £51. 15s. 7d.

[2] Bathurst to Macquarie, 29 October 1818, H. R. of A. series I, vol. IX, p. 840.

fought with success, though in a somewhat disingenuous fashion, against the dissolution of his Bank. Possibly his reply to Bathurst was written promptly, but it was not sent until 1 September 1820. The Bank, it then announced, had succeeded beyond his most sanguine hopes. Its dissolution "would be attended with the most embarrassing circumstances to every member of the community". "So great a number of proprietors", he believed, "could not be legally united together otherwise than by a Charter of Incorporation".[1] In the dilemma of "venturing on the suspension of your Lordship's instructions" or producing "little short of a General Bankruptcy" by giving effect and publicity to them, he "ventured to take the weighty responsibility of embracing the former Alternative". Wherefore he asked for "direct sanction to his measures for the unexpired portion of the Original Charter of Seven Years". He did not get it; the question was referred to Commissioner J. T. Bigge, then conducting a general inquiry into the colony's affairs. In Bigge's report of 1823[2] a conflict is evident between accomplished facts in Sydney and Whitehall's new dogma of *laissez faire*, forbidding all legal privilege save to the Bank of England. Bigge bore testimony to the utility of the Bank in evolving order out of the commercial chaos of paper based on the honesty of individuals, and to the high credit it enjoyed. This had survived the loss of half the subscribed capital (£12,600) through defalcations by its chief cashier, discovered in January 1821. That credit, he thought, had grown in part from the belief in its possession of a royal charter, but as

[1] The right of "exclusive banking" granted to the Bank of England by the Act of 1697 and further defined by that of 1742 was interpreted as banking through the issue of notes "payable on demand or at any less time than six months from the borrowing thereof". No partnership of more than six persons could lawfully carry on such business "in that part of Great Britain called England". Macquarie seems to have been advised that he could do nothing repugnant to the laws of England, and was therefore bound by this second rule. See *H. R. of A.* series 1, vol. x, p. 351. Cf. A. Andreades, *History of the Bank of England*, p. 171, note 2, and A. F. Dunbar, *Chapters on Theory and History of Banking*, p. 195.

[2] J. T. Bigge's *Report on Agriculture and Trade*, January 1823, pp. 65–7

he could not be "insensible to the consequences of insufficient control that a chartered immunity from the ordinary risks of commercial partnership has a tendency to produce", he did not recommend the charter's renewal.[1] Yet in Brisbane's statement of action taken on Bigge's reports appears the bald entry: "Relative to renewing the Charter of Incorporation to the Sydney Bank after its expiring in the Year 1824: Charter renewed in 1824".

Whatever its standing in the eyes of the law, the Bank proved a vigorous custodian of the community's financial interests. It was an early example of the young society's power to create, independently of the state, organs for collective action. The coins that passed over its counter would have seemed to a modern teller fit only for a museum. In 1821 the Bank's clients were warned against such illegal and counterfeit money as "Dollars and Dumps which are not silver; Dollars having the usual holes in the centre but without the Colonial Stamp on them; Colonial Dollars from which a portion of Silver has been taken round the Centre; and Dollars that bear a counterfeit Stamp, intending to imitate the Colonial one surrounding the Hole in the centre, many of which may be detected by the figures for the date of the year being transposed from 1813 to 3181".[2]

It was not merely the opening given by imports of Spanish dollars for such private issues of mutilated coin which caused the Bank to take a strong line in advocating a purely British currency. Governor Brisbane displayed high enthusiasm for the Spanish dollar. To his scholarly mind it was "an invaluable coin which has for centuries been disseminating its benefits over every other portion of the earth—a coin which from the extension of its circulation over every part of the commercial globe may justly

---

[1] J. T. Bigge, *op. cit.* p. 67.

[2] These descriptions will be made more intelligible by reference to an engraving of the original issue of Holey Dollars and Dumps, e.g. in the *Australian Encyclopaedia*, vol. 1, p. 345, or in the *View of Premises of the Bank of New South Wales*, 1907.

be defined the money of the world". As Governor, he answered the Bank's dislike of the holey dollars by their recall and re-issue at 3s. 9d. But he admitted fresh dollars in great quantities, about 400,000 in number, making them legal tender at five shillings apiece. This official rate of exchange was more than the bullion value of the silver in them, and, as the colony's trading prospects improved, Spanish dollars were poured in to take advantage of the local over-valuation. In May 1825 the rate at the colonial treasury was lowered to 4s. 4d., and after Brisbane's departure in that year British silver was sent out in adequate quantity. Holey dollars were finally redeemed at 3s. 3d., and the unmutilated dollar was accepted only as so much bullion then worth 4s. 2d.

In these adjustments the Bank of New South Wales—"Macquarie's Bank", as it was called in lively reminder of his services in founding it—took a strong line in support of its first aim and reason, stable money. It denounced Brisbane's use of Spanish coins in government payments as a rejection of sterling cash payments in favour of a currency of fluctuating value. Now that the British had resumed specie payment on a gold monometallic basis, and war-expedients and depreciation (1798–1821) were no more, the Bank was right.[1] The colony's main trade being with Britain, a stable relation, even identity, in the standard money of the two countries was the first desideratum, whatever benefits may have been conferred "on the British and North American Colonies, on the French and Papal Canadas, on Mahomedan India and on the whole world" as scanned by the benevolent Brisbane.[2]

The same primary aim of sound currency was urged by W. C. Wentworth in support of a reduction of the discount rate in 1825 from 10 to 8 per cent., against a

---

[1] For the memorials and correspondence which passed between the Bank and Governor Brisbane in 1822, see *H. R. of A.* series I, vol. x, pp. 730–44.

[2] For two years, 1824 to 1826, the Bank issued notes in dollar denominations 1, 3, 5, 10, 20, 50 and 100. They were withdrawn in 1826 in favour of sterling notes for £1, £2, £5, £10 and £20.

minority of bank shareholders greedy for maximum gain. Out of this conflict arose the rival Bank of Australia to which many leading officials and squatters adhered, such as ex-President J. T. Campbell, John Oxley and John McArthur. Their knowledge of the inner counsels of the older bank and perhaps its record of independence explain but hardly excuse the partisan line taken by Governor Darling against the Bank of New South Wales. The success of the old Bank and the growth of the wool trade were attracting intending competitors from far and near. The promoters of a third bank in Sydney announced that their shareholding lists, in pointed reflection on the "pure merinos" who founded the Bank of Australia, were to be open to every free colonist. They were persuaded, however, to coalesce with the Bank of New South Wales by the offer of additional shares in it. While the terms were under discussion, Darling "discovered" a despatch (July 1823) forbidding his predecessor to renew the old Bank's charter. A run set in. Darling would agree to advance money from the Treasury to ward off panic only on conditions amounting to the compulsory liquidation of the Bank of New South Wales. Opinion rallied to its support. D'Arcy Wentworth and W. Redfern successively presided, and though the charter was declared invalid on the ground that Brisbane had had no right to grant it, the first president J. T. Campbell returned to pilot the Bank into re-organization as a joint-stock co-partnership, as from 1 January 1828. Even so the damage to its credit seemed likely to be mortal, and a government loan was accepted in the following year on the drastic condition that the Bank be wound up within twelve months.[1] But a new cashier and secretary, John Black, succeeded before the year was out in repaying both the Government loan and declaring a dividend. It is said that in doing so he depleted the cash in the Bank's chest to twenty-nine pounds! Under Black's management, however, Macquarie's Bank

[1] *Sydney Gazette*, quoted in *View of Premises*, 1907.

was to outlive the Bank of Australia and to outgrow in resources its competitors of British origin. The temporary superiority of the Bank of Australia by virtue of the favour and deposits of the Government did not save it from collapse in 1843.[1] The co-partnery form of the senior bank was strengthened in 1850. At the dawn of the gold boom it was incorporated afresh under a local act, with an augmented capital.

Macquarie's way of providing and regulating the colonial currency, as its determined survival shows, had taken early and deep root. The chief danger of Australian banks thenceforward may be traced to the multiplication of such regulators. The phase of competition was perhaps inevitable, but the rule of sound money like the rule of law calls for a single sovereignty.[2]

---

[1] See *The Hobler Papers* (Mitchell Library), 18 October 1848, vol. VI, p. 52, as to its liquidation. For the later history of the Bank of N.S.W. see the above cited *View of Premises*, 1907, *passim*.

[2] A. S. J. Baster, *The Imperial Banks*, a study of the development of colonial banks with headquarters in London, was published after this chapter was written. It is strongly recommended to students.

CHAPTER V

An Autocrat in a Hurry

BEING of a generation whose fathers had seen General Wade transform the Highlands after Mar's Rebellion and which was still learning from Thomas Telford the arts of civil engineering, Macquarie naturally set high store by the civilizing power of externals. And posterity has agreed in honouring him most for public buildings of a dignity which still charms the eye, and roads which first made land travel practicable. We are mainly perceptual beings. It is easy also to ascribe to these changes the growth of a pride in the colony as a permanent home. A generation was growing up in New South Wales which had known no other.

His General Order issued after a first tour of the settlements upbraided his subjects for their unsuitable houses, the absence of barns and their miserable clothing—a lack of standards bespeaking the despair of exiles. An early despatch asked for a well-qualified architect and warned the Secretary of State of heavy expenditure on the renovation of roads and bridges. But his free drawing upon the Treasury soon roused concern at home. In July 1811, Liverpool, in charge of the War and Colonial Office, trusted "that no public buildings whatsoever have been commenced, the construction of which was not indispensably required for the Public Service". Yet a Secretary of State at Westminster, beset by Treasury officials, and a Governor disposing in a virgin land of the labour of many bondmen could scarcely agree as to what was indispensable. "It is impossible", complained Liverpool, "to point out what expenses have been unnecessarily incurred or in the execution of what services retrenchments might have been made." The bills drawn mounted up. In 1808 they totalled £25,000, in 1809 £16,738—these were the years of inter-regnum—£59,378 in 1810, £71,085 in 1811, and £30,869 in less than four months of 1812. All this in time of war!

Long range fire from Downing Street was of course trained on the outstanding public buildings. No public architect was sent; that would have aided and abetted extravagance. By every mail there came instead pro-hibitions of unnecessary spending, comparisons, "not in your favour", with past governors.

Lachlan Macquarie was not the man to sing small. No governor "here or in any other of His Majesty's Colonies", he claimed, had been "more rigidly vigilant and watchful in the public expenditure of money, provisions and stores belonging to the Crown". "Conscious, therefore, of my own Integrity and Rectitude and of the Honourable Purity of my Motives"[1] he bade his superiors remember the pass Sydney was in when he assumed office. Less than a hundred bushels of grain were in store; two regiments were on his hands for four months; the settlers' crops were swept away by another Hawkesbury flood; new settlers on safer forest land had to be victualled while clearing their farms; Phillip's original barracks and quarters were collapsing because of green and unsuitable timber. "Without vanity and with great truth", he had already done in less than three years "more for the general amelioration of the colony, the improvement of the manners, morals, industry and re-ligion of its inhabitants" than Hunter, King and Bligh all together. By October 1814 he thought his annual ex-penditure, then £75,000, likely to fall by a third within two years, "if my plans of Reform and Economy shall be Approved and Meet my own expectations". Surely this man was the father of all Australian Treasurers!

[1] Macquarie to Liverpool, 9 November 1812, *H. R. of A.* series I, vol. VII, p. 526.

Many forces beyond his control combined to defeat his expectations. At his side was Mrs Macquarie, a lady of refined taste in buildings. As Whitehall sent no official architect, the Governor found one amongst those sent as prisoners. Francis Howard Greenway of London training had practised as an architect in Bristol and Bath. But times of war are hard for architects, and in 1812 he was "sent out" for fourteen years for concealing effects in bankruptcy. Reaching Sydney in February 1814, he submitted ambitious plans for a town hall and market house before the year was out. Though not accepted, they evidently won admiration, for in 1815 a more grandiose scheme included a bridge over the harbour at Dawes Point. His services in detecting faulty work in the foundations of the Rum Hospital led Macquarie to accept Greenway's offer to "erect more and better buildings in four years" than had been built since the colony's foundation. He was made civil architect in 1816 and assistant to the Inspector of Public Works, Captain John Gill, 46th Regiment. This partnership, employing convicts on day labour, set a new standard in colonial architecture which influenced private as well as public building throughout Van Diemen's Land and New South Wales.

Greenway's late Georgian work may still be admired in Hyde Park Barracks and St James's Church, Sydney, in St Matthew's at Windsor, perhaps in Burdekin House in Macquarie Street, in "Subiaco" at Rydalmere and "Newington" on the Parramatta.[1] He worked in a style "simple and stately, although of humble execution". The secrets of his strength are scale and proportion. He brought into the convict colonies a quality which dignified the pleasant homesteads of the "Old Colonial" days, in their shady gardens of great trees, both native and exotic, and preserved for a time the tradition of an earlier elegance.

[1] See Hardy Wilson's incomparable treasury of drawings, *Old Colonial Architecture in New South Wales and Tasmania.*

But the flame of his genius flickered and was gone, for his days of public employment were sadly few. Macquarie emancipated him in December 1817, and induced the Secretary of State to confirm, temporarily at least, his appointment as civil architect. But expenditure was rising again, to the scandal of Whitehall. Scapegoats were being sought, especially among the emancipists Macquarie had befriended. Plans and work for a new church of cathedral proportions, where Sydney Town Hall now stands, were vetoed in 1819 by Commissioner Bigge. He thought Greenway slack and "indulgent", given to a love of ornamentation. So his plans for a water supply to town and port, and for the City which was to be, passed into limbo. In 1821 the most talented and far-sighted of Macquarie's servants went back to private practice and obscurity.[1]

The renewed activity in public works rose, however, out of more than personal influences. A way had been found over the Blue Mountains. Great fertile plains and teeming rivers were there. And a big influx of convicts came out after the peace with France and the onset of post-war depression at home.

Before 1813 explorers looked for a way inland up the river-valleys such as the Grose and the Warragamba. With possibly one exception they had been baffled by gorges "of the most barren and forbidding aspect", where even the crows seemed to have lost their way. Perhaps the taciturn George Caley had caught a glimpse "of better country farther out"—the lure ever since to squatters gambling with drought. But Caley was stopped in 1804 by mutiny when within "cooee" of success.[2] It was left to Gregory Blaxland to hit upon the plan of working along the crests of the confused ridges. He was a substantial grazier whose pastures drought had scorched. In May 1813, with Lawson, a surveyor, and D'Arcy Wentworth's

[1] See article on F. H. Greenway in *Australian Encyclopaedia*, vol. 1, p. 581.
[2] See article on George Caley in *Australian Encyclopaedia*, vol. 1, p. 228.

son, William Charles, aged 22,[1] he hacked and tore a way through undergrowth and over rises to Mount Blaxland, 53¾ miles west of the Nepean. They turned there, battered and sick, but triumphant. They had looked West over open grass lands boundless in extent. Winter broke; when it was over, Macquarie sent G. W. Evans, his assistant-surveyor, with four convict servants and a guide from Blaxland's party, to test the hopes aroused. Early in the new year (1814) they returned, having traversed a hundred miles of rolling grassy plains, abounding in game, with rivers full of strange but excellent fish, "vast areas of grazing country not divided by barren spaces as on the east side of the mountains", "soil exceeding rich" growing the finest grass and herbs, "hills green to the tops and country like a park and grounds laid out".[2] A cart-road thither, said Evans, could be made in three months by fifty labourers.

Could a Governor hesitate at such a prospect? In July Captain Cox began making the road. "The Expence of constructing it", Macquarie explained to Bathurst, "will be very trifling to Government, the Men Employed in it being Convicts who Volunteered their Services on Condition of receiving Emancipation for their Extra labour. This is the only Remuneration they receive except their Rations".[3] In sanctioning a road even to these attractive Bathurst Plains there was need of explanatory caution. He had already found the Colonial Office very stiff in its criticisms of roads and bridges. "Making Permanent Roads and Bridges is one of the first steps towards Improving a New Country", wrote the sententious Governor in justifying a turnpike road to the Hawkesbury. Liverpool

---

[1] See A. W. Jose, *Builders and Pioneers of Australia*, p. 38.
[2] These phrases are from Evans' Journal, *H. R. of A.* series I, vol. VIII, pp. 165–77.
[3] Macquarie to Bathurst, 7 October 1814, *H. R. of A.* series I, vol. VIII, p. 315. This emancipation as reward for extra labour would take the place of the wages they could earn about Sydney "in their own time". Cf. Macquarie to Bathurst, 28 June 1813, *op. cit.* vol. VII, p. 781.

agreed, but questioned whether the British taxpayer should be the paymaster. "Permanent roads and bridges", it seemed to him, "will be the off-spring rather than the cause of internal prosperity"—a doctrine logical enough in an old country. But Macquarie was facing the needs of a country still to be occupied and notably lacking natural means of access such as navigable rivers. "Permanent roads through this Wide Extended Colony", he persisted even in 1812, "cannot be Constructed at the entire Expence of the Inhabitants for many Years to Come, and they imagine they have a right to expect that at least a part of the Colonial Revenue, particularly that part of it Collected on the Very Spirits of which they drink such Quantities, ought to be laid out and Appropriated to the Construction of Permanent Roads and Bridges, Streets and Wharves, Wherever these are essentially necessary."[1]

He had already constructed turnpike roads over the coastal plain to the Nepean River and to Liverpool. The tactful name of the latter destination did not, indeed, persuade its eponym that there was a difference between colonial and other revenues of the Crown. If the spirit-duties were spent on roads, they could not be used to lessen the burden of sending and maintaining the convicts. He begged the question by arguing that if the free settlers could not pay for the roads, this proved that the colony was not advanced enough to need them.[2]

When, however, news of Bathurst Plains confirmed Macquarie's every hope for the colony's future, he put aside the plea that Britain could not afford roads into this wonderland. A new Secretary of State had sanctioned the other turnpike roads on the ground that tolls would recoup the expense, but had boggled at transmontane

[1] Macquarie to Liverpool, 17 November 1812, *H. R. of A.* series I, vol. VII, pp. 604–5.
[2] Liverpool to Macquarie, 5 May 1812, *H. R. of A.* series I, vol. VII, p. 480. The same despatch calls for a quarterly or at least an annual statement of colonial revenues under nine heads.

roads "while His Majesty's Treasury at home is subjected to an Expence of from Seventy Thousand to One Hundred Thousand Pounds per Annum for the Support of the Colony".[1] The demurrer came too late; it crossed a despatch in which Macquarie announced his new programme of buildings and roads, asked leave to build a new church, large-scale convict barracks and a better court-house. After that he would reduce the gangs of artificers and labourers.

The works already begun Bathurst allowed, "as they are to be defrayed from the Colonial Funds". The court-house he vetoed; the church and barracks were to be built if the colonial revenue would stand the charge. But this, with a general promise to second improvements that took the form of schools and glebe-houses, threw the leash from the straining ambitions of Greenway and his vice-regal patrons. "Availing myself of the discretionary power Your Lordship has been kindly pleased to grant Me of erecting such Public Buildings as Can Conveniently be paid for from the Colonial Revenue",[2] Macquarie let contracts for churches at Sydney, Windsor and Liverpool, set about building by convict gangs a new Factory for female convicts at Parramatta, glebe houses at Liverpool, Parramatta and Castlereagh, and planned a new Civil Court House.

How could ministers at Whitehall control such a man? Could such ambitious plans possibly be sound? The colony was certainly growing: 16,493 male convicts were sent out between 1810 and 1820, 11,250 of whom embarked in the last four years. Colonial revenues from import and port duties had increased from £10,000 in 1811 to £25,884 in 1820. But this obstinate builder's calls on them, amounting to £3,005 in 1811, £6,920 in 1815, £16,486 in 1819, had increased also. More floods along the Hawkesbury in 1816, 1817 and 1819 had thrown

---

[1] Bathurst to Macquarie, 3 February 1814, *H. R. of A.* series 1, vol. VIII, p. 132. This despatch must have been written before the news reached England of Evans' exploration of the interior.

[2] Macquarie to Bathurst, 4 April 1817, *H. R. of A.* series 1, vol. IX, p. 353.

back many assigned servants upon government rations. Macquarie's bills drawn on the Treasury for rations and stores and its own expenses in fitting out convict transports had mounted to a total of £227,000 in 1814, and almost £240,000 in 1817. Rebukes had been met by protestations of future amendment, regularly falsified by the event. A grudging approval had been twisted into a programme of extravagance.

Most disquieting was another aspect of Macquarie's rule, his preference for emancipists, and the bad relations with the respectable settlers and officials to which that preference had given rise. Was the man a despot basing his power on mob-favour? His lineage and career bespoke an aristocrat of high and dependable character. Yet every vessel out of Port Jackson brought rumours and, after 1815, official word of discord in high places. Could public order in New South Wales survive recrimination between the Governor and the judges? By what idea of the colony's future could Colonel Macquarie be inspired or possessed?

In January 1819, to set such doubts at rest, the Secretary of State commissioned John Thomas Bigge, chief justice of Trinidad, to ascertain "how far in its present improved and increasing State" the colony was "susceptible of being made adequate to the Objects of its original institution". In Whitehall's view New South Wales was still a prison, and transportation thither a punishment to deter men and women in Britain from crime. "The Settlements in New Holland must clearly be considered as Receptacles for Offenders....So long as they continue destined to these purposes by the Legislature of the Country" (i.e. of Great Britain and Ireland), "their growth as Colonies must be a Secondary Consideration, and the leading Duty of those to whom their Administration is entrusted will be to keep up in them such a system of just discipline as may render transportation an Object of serious Apprehension".[1] It seems to have been all this

[1] Bathurst to J. T. Bigge, 6 January 1819, *H. R. of A.* series I, vol. x, p. 4.

in the days of the naval governors. As evidence that transportation to New South Wales under that iron discipline had answered "every end of punishment", Bathurst quoted "instances on record in which convicts have expressed their desire that the sentence of transportation might be commuted even for the utmost Rigour of the Law". Such action was intelligible in any who had heard of the horrors of the Second and Third Fleets, the voyage out being thought the worse half of the punishment. But speculation by contractors in the lives of the convicts in transit had been checked by the appointment to each transport of at least one naval surgeon, with powers which even the captain overrode at his peril.[1] In New Holland also the scene was changed, and transportation had lost its terrors. "Numerous applications are made by those who are sentenced to imprisonment for minor transgressions that they may be allowed to participate in the Punishment to which the greatest offenders are condemned." This was outrageous, thought Whitehall.

"The great End of Punishment is the Prevention of Crime", wrote Bathurst. "If, by ill-considered Compassion for Convicts, or from what might under other circumstances be considered a laudable desire to lessen their sufferings, their Situation in New South Wales be divested of all Salutary Terror, Transportation cannot operate as an effectual example on the Community at large, as a proper punishment for those Crimes against the commission of which His Majesty's Subjects have a right to claim protection". Thus Bigge's commission virtually dictated the condemnation of Macquarie's active employment of convicts on public works for an emancipists' Utopia where, when they had expiated their crimes, they should enjoy a new Britain under blue skies.

Macquarie's emancipist leanings, it may be argued,

[1] An account of the conditions aboard convict transports under these more humane conditions may be read in *The Frew Papers* (Mitchell Library), the vessel on which the Frews reached South Australia having encountered an outward-bound transport near the Cape.

were a result of the party leadership which came to him from Bligh. When on his twelfth day of office he raised to the magistracy one Andrew Thompson, leading settler on the Hawkesbury, he was rewarding the man and the district for loyalty to Bligh and rebuking the usurpers the more pointedly by disregarding Thompson's ex-convict status. Colonel Foveaux had warned Macquarie against the Revd. Samuel Marsden, and when the chaplain attacked Thompson's appointment his criticisms served only to arouse the despot in Macquarie. He adopted as a deliberate policy the very elevation of emancipists at which Marsden cavilled. Possibly the Scots laird enjoyed out-Christianing the Anglican parson.[1] In August 1810, Simeon Lord, a wealthy Sydney trader, but an ignorant and low-lived ex-convict, was also raised to the bench, and Macquarie tried to associate both Thompson and Lord with Marsden, the senior colonial chaplain, as trustees of the public roads. Marsden would not act with them, giving as his reason their notoriously bad characters.

Fate was not kind to Macquarie and his friends. Thompson died within nine months of his elevation, leaving to his patron a large share of a fortune based on trade in spirits. The legacy was accepted by Macquarie as proof of the giver's good will, but it became a target for gibes. Lord, subjected to insults in open court,[2] was persuaded by Bigge and Macquarie, at Governor Brisbane's coming, to retire from a position he had neither strengthened nor adorned. Redfern, a naval surgeon transported for being an accessory to the mutiny at the Nore, was promoted by Macquarie in the teeth of Bigge's advice and Bathurst's disapproval. At the accession of George IV Macquarie was flatly ordered to omit his name from the new commission of the peace.

---

[1] Cf. *H. R. of A.* series I, vol. IX, p. 499, where Macquarie in submitting a list of secret opponents places Marsden at the head of "this List of Malcontents".

[2] "You are a great man now, Mr Lord", cried a woman expiree, "but you came into the colony in the same situation as myself."

Frowns from high places and social boycotts of his "pets" in Sydney[1] merely provoked in the Governor a fierce antagonism to colonists who had not been prisoners. From thinking ex-convicts the most useful members of the community, he passed in November 1812 to asking that "the Free Settlers sent out from England may be limited to as small a number as possible.... These Free Settlers are the most discontented Persons in the Colony".[2] This may have been true, and may also have been to the discredit of a majority of them, sent out as ne'er-do-wells on family sentences of "conditional remittance" and always clamouring for government grants and donations. But discontent may have been justified in those who were pioneer stockraisers despite Macquarie's disfavour.[3] They acquired no merit in his eyes by success. Blind like his predecessor to the importance of any rural pursuit but tilling the soil, he sneered at graziers who gained "a very large Fortune without any trouble to themselves, the laborious parts of Husbandry being entirely left to the poor Emancipated Convicts or free persons of Inferior Origin". He repeatedly accused of laziness John and Gregory Blaxland, pioneers of the cattle industry.[4] In the colony the Governor acknowledged Gregory Blaxland's merit as the conqueror of the mountain barrier. In his reports to England he suppressed that merit.

In advocating the concession of trial by jury of the people, another plank from the pro-Bligh party's platform,

---

[1] See Ernest Scott, *Short History of Australia*, pp. 101-4.

[2] Macquarie to Liverpool, 17 November 1812, in *H. R. of A.* series I, vol. VII, p. 597.

[3] As to the method of distributing convict servants between government and private employers, see M. Phillips, *op. cit.* p. 130, and note to p. 13. "From 1814 to 1820 2418 mechanics arrived, and of these 1587 were assigned to government".

[4] See for examples, Macquarie to Liverpool, 17 November 1812, and Macquarie to Bathurst, 1 March 1815, *H. R. of A.* series I, vol. VIII, pp. 427-8. More than a year after Gregory Blaxland had, with Macquarie's full knowledge, planned and carried to the point of success the crossing of the mountains, Macquarie wrote of them as "having never benefitted the Colony since their arrival in it now nearly nine years ago".

Macquarie gave his emancipist principles free rein.
Bathurst had doubts whether the rule of trying men by
their peers could be applied to a society of such "peculiar
constitution". "Would that principle be fairly acted upon,
if free settlers were to sit in judgment on convicts?...
Would it be prudent to allow convicts to act as jury-
men?...Would not their exclusion be considered an
invidious mark...at variance with the Great Principle
upon which the institution is founded?" The Governor
agreed that only the free should be eligible but laboured
to put aside all distinction between free and freed. "Once
a Convict had become a Free Man, either by Servitude,
Free Pardon or Emancipation, he should in All Respects
be Considered on a footing with every other Man in the
Colony, according to his Rank in Life and Character."
The rub was in this last clause. The emancipists by whose
advancement Macquarie chose to prove the vigour of his
faith only demonstrated that punishment as then practised
had certainly not exalted the characters of the most
eminent ex-convicts. This was fatal to the success of his
generous policy. As Bigge complained, Macquarie was
trying not to restore to such emancipists their rank in life
but greatly to raise it. Like many despots he thought to
press folk into the designs he premeditated. Public
buildings are things on which, as on the Perth Town Hall
(W.A.), the broad arrow may be a pleasant historical
decoration. But human beings are otherwise constituted.

Macquarie, his biographer thinks, "had neither the
education nor the natural good taste to distinguish one
man from another in the ranks below him". Too impatient to await the slow process by which each free
generation appraises its leaders and culls its recruits for
this and that calling, he thought he could build a community like a barracks or a church with convicts and
emancipists only. But it was a destructive party spleen
which inspired such notions and they took a fatal hold
on the inferior mentality of many around him. Should

his policy be dictated, Macquarie asked ministers at home, by the wishes of those who came free to the colony, or should he "so construct it as to hold out the greatest possible rewards to the Convicts for Reformation of Manners by Considering Them, when this is the Case, in every way entitled to the Rights and Privileges of a Citizen who has never come under the Sentence of Transportation"?[1] He did not stay for an answer, but took it as a foregone conclusion and, though the fame of the wool pastures was already growing, his measures reduced free immigration to a mere trickle during the later years of his term of office. "In Coming to New South Wales (Free Settlers) should consider that they are coming to a Convict Country, and if they are too proud or too delicate in their feelings to associate with the Population of the Country, they should consider it in time and bend their Course to some other Country in which their Prejudices in this Respect would meet with no Opposition".[2] Seven-eighths of the men-convicts available were employed on public works, leaving few to be assigned to the settlers. When in 1817 "a low Rabble", in the vice-regal phrase, signed a memorial to the Commons against his arbitrary acts, they found themselves shut out from land grants and the customary indulgences of stock and labour, for daring "to asperse my personal honour and Government".[3]

Ministers sought by light hints to turn this hard-mouthed steed, but their touches were taken by him for a shaking of the reins in encouragement. Macquarie read Bathurst's warnings against the effects of a forcing policy

[1] Macquarie to Bathurst, 28 June 1813. For anticipations of restrictions on immigration see Macquarie to Liverpool, 17 November 1812, *H. R. of A.* series I, vol. VII, p. 594, and Bathurst's reply, 8 February 1814, vol. VIII, p. 128. Macquarie again, vol. VIII, p. 303.

[2] Macquarie to Bathurst, 28 June 1813, in *H. R. of A.* series I, vol. VII, p. 775.

[3] See *H. R. of A.* series I, vol. IX, note 77, on p. 866. Cf. p. 736. The acts of which the memorial complained included influencing the decision of a jury of inquest, ordering corporal punishment without inquiry, and seizing lands and houses. On the disputes between Macquarie and the judges, see Marion Phillips, *op. cit.* ch. VII.

in favour of emancipists as a full endorsement of his doings. "Some illiberal Men in this Country Would destine a fellow Creature who has once deflected from the Path of Virtue, to an Eternal Badge of Infamy....I am happy in feeling a Spirit of Charity in Me which shall ever make Me despise Such Unjust and illiberal Sentiments".[1]

Doubts grew. What would be the effect of such Charity on the convicts? It indited bitter despatches against judges, clergy and free-settlers. It built "good and comfortable accommodation" to house 1200 male prisoners. It made the saying proverbial that the surest way to vice-regal favour was having worn the badge of conviction for felony. Was it practicable to "hold out the greatest possible rewards for Reformation of Manners" without inviting clever rogues to seek them?

Jeffery Hart Bent, when Judge-Advocate, had cut Macquarie to the quick by contending that the Governor's doings were against the wishes of His Majesty's Government; but Downing Street managed its puppet despot on very slack strings. A mild reproof of extravagance drew from him in December 1817 a letter of resignation. Bathurst's reassurances, inviting its withdrawal, although the despatch containing them reached Sydney, were somehow kept from the Governor. He fretted under what he thought the unacknowledged suspension of his resignation.[2] Bigge's arrival in September 1819 limited his policies by a sort of consular veto. Chafing under the Commissioner's constant criticisms, he asked again to be relieved. Yet at the end he quitted his realm with reluctance. After his successor, Sir Thomas Brisbane, had come in November 1821, Macquarie went on progress through the scattered settlements.

Like James I he had "felt himself as an immense brood-fowl set over this land, and would so fain gather it all

---

[1] M. to Bathurst, 7 October 1814, *H. R. of A.* series I, vol. VIII, p. 316.
[2] For the resignation see Macquarie to Bathurst, 1 December 1817, *H. R. of A.* series I, vol. IX, pp. 495 *et seq.* Bathurst's reply is in vol. IX, p. 838.

under his wings". "Under the Divine protection", he told the Hawkesbury farmers, "we have been advancing towards a degree of civilization and comfort which can only render life one of enjoyment to those who have been accustomed from early habits to the manifold blessings extending to the whole population in the Mother Country". The oft-quoted passage in the apologia for his work which he wrote after his return to Britain still stirs Australians to sympathy with a great-hearted lover of the infant colony.[1] "I found the Colony barely emerging from infantile imbecility, and suffering from various privations and disabilities; the Country impenetrable beyond 40 miles from Sydney; Agriculture in a yet languishing state; commerce in its early dawn; Revenue unknown;[2] threatened by famine; distracted by faction; the public buildings in a state of dilapidation and mouldering to decay; the few Roads and Bridges, formerly constructed, rendered almost impassable; the population in general depressed by poverty; no public credit nor private confidence; the morals of the great mass of the population in the lowest state of debasement, and religious worship almost totally neglected....I left it, in February last, reaping incalculable advantages from my extensive and important discoveries in all directions, including the supposed insurmountable barrier called the Blue Mountains, to the westward of which are situated the fertile plains of Bathurst, and in all respects enjoying a state of private comfort and public prosperity, which I trust will at least equal the expectation of His Majesty's Government. This change may indeed be ascribed in part to the natural operation of time and events on individual enterprize. How far it may be attributed to measures originating with myself and my zeal and judgment in giving effect to my

[1] Macquarie to Bathurst, London, 27 July 1822, *H. R. of A.* series I, vol. x, pp. 671–3.
[2] On p. 675, in the same letter, he mentions Port duties of £8000 per annum which by 1821 had reached £28,000 to £30,000.

instructions, I humbly submit to His Majesty and his Ministers."

These claims reveal more than the egotism of the despot, swallowing up all credit for the activities of his subjects. By their emphasis on the comforts of civilization and by the slightness of the references to colonial flocks and herds, they suggest that Macquarie's mind stuck in the bark of externals, and missed the inner meaning of efforts to make New South Wales a colony of self-providing and permanent homes.

The social and economic weaknesses of the convicts were not to be exorcised by a spirit of charity which gave them comfortable employment on public works. These measures concentrated more than half the population of the colony in Sydney and subsidised unemployment there as early as 1817.[1] Convicts and emancipists were necessarily a wasting as well as a weak foundation. In October 1821 they numbered 19,126 adults out of a total of 29,783 inhabitants, but the disproportion of the sexes meant that most could know no family life. There were 15,939 convict men and only 3187 women. Of their children, who numbered 7224, many turned away from Macquarie's design of copying the comforts of Britain.[2] They with the free settlers—1489 adults and 1884 children—were the active elements in the advance over the inland plains which followed the collapse of his building boom. When Brisbane discontinued public works, the "old hands" passed into the service of the squatters, as hut-keepers and shepherds.[3] The white-trash of Virginia and the Carolinas perished as Lee's incomparable infantry. In a nobler cause the ex-convicts died as sentries beside

[1] See Marion Phillips, *op. cit.* pp. 134, 149.

[2] "Nationalism", thinks Dr Phillips, "the strongest characteristic of the Australian of today, is a legacy from these sons of exiles, for whom Australia was a land of hope and promise." *Op. cit.* pp. 260–1. It certainly has at times a psychologically suspicious stridency.

[3] As to the overwhelming of the convict blood by the free immigration of the gold-discovery decade, see T. A. Coghlan, *Labour and Industry*, pp. 562 *et seq.*

the peaceful productive sheep who won Australia for the white men.

Macquarie had shown good sense and resolution in his reform of the currency, but his vacillation about public agriculture suggests that a laird's paternalism prevented his seeing the economic futility of convict labour in public employ.[1] His public buildings, for all their innocent charm to-day, were laxly supervised and so continued the enervating precedent of reliance on government. He was, maybe, the second founder of Sydney, but not of Australia. By his vendetta against free settlers he roused the first whisperings of a hostility towards immigrants which still comes ill in a spacious land from the beneficiaries of John McArthur, Caroline Chisholm and William Farrer. And how could his or any other Bank discharge to the best advantage its function of entrusting the material resources of the community to those most capable of directing their increase if the Governor set his face against the free activity of the free? The days of paternalism were over.

[1] In his first despatch, still mindful of Castlereagh's instructions, he condemned the government farming which was shortly afterwards discontinued. See 30 April 1810, *H. R. of A.* series I, vol. VII, pp. 250–1. When, however, Bigge suggested that convicts could be productively employed thus, he tried again at Emu Plains in 1820. See vol. X, p. 680, and *Adventures of Ralph Rashleigh*, chapters VIII and IX.

CHAPTER VI

John Bull's Greater Woolsack

IN the eighteen-twenties, the figures in the foreground of the Australian scene suddenly shrink into insignificance. Governors still rule with little ease the turbulent Sydney populace. Officials still push their friends' interests, or plan the better training of the unspoilt generation. Traders still serve their own turn. But a curtain has been raised. These petty folk and their coastal land grants, totalling, since the colony's foundation, less than 325,000 acres, are dwarfed by the mighty drama of free settlement inland. More than Blaxland's cattle have escaped from vice-regal restriction. John McArthur, who had traded, ruled, intrigued and made money for a quarter of a century at Parramatta, at Sydney and at Westminster, had all along insisted on wasting his substance in pursuit of a dream that the colony would some day export fine wool. Suddenly men realize that he is right—that fine wool is no dream but the masterstroke of a pragmatical genius.

His wool-gathering originated in a deduction he made in 1794 from the results of putting a young Irish ram with some Bengal ewes. "By crossing the two breeds I had the satisfaction", he told Bigge in 1820, "to see the lambs of the Indian ewes bear a mingled fleece of hair and wool. This circumstance originated the idea of producing fine wool in New South Wales".[1] The Bengal sheep produced a covering which when shorn in early summer for the animal's comfort went as a matter of

---

[1] See generally S. Macarthur-Onslow, *Ear Records of the Macarthurs of Camden*, chapters III, IV, IX, and T. A. Coghlan, *Labour and Industry in Australia*, part I, chapter VII.

course to the rubbish tip. The Irish sheep's wool was little better. At a time of high values it was worth only 9d. a pound at home. But the mingled hair and wool on the lambs of this cross suggested to McArthur that if he used the right sheep he might breed wool worth shillings a pound. This, if grown on free or cheap land, would bear the light expense of convict labour, and would cost little freight as back-loading on returning transports, which, at that time, went empty to China to load cargoes of tea.

The fate of 44 sheep brought by the First Fleet was not encouraging. They had been worried by dingoes and stolen by convicts till but one remained. But "Elizabeth Farm" at Parramatta was twelve miles from Sydney and partly guarded by water. Through Captain Waterhouse of the 'Reliance', McArthur obtained in 1797 the sheep he wanted—four or five Merino ewes and three Merino rams from the flock of one Colonel Gordon, a Scot in the Dutch service at the Cape. This nucleus of the first Australian Merino stud was supplemented in 1805 by five rams and one ewe from the Royal Stud at Kew.

In buying these, McArthur, sent home under arrest by Governor King, had become involved in a feud with Sir Joseph Banks which almost wrecked his plans. The two men were seeking independently some export which would give the colony a means of self-support. Banks, when urging in 1798 that Mungo Park, the African explorer, should be sent to solve the riddle of the interior, held it to be inconceivable "that such a country, situate in a most fruitful climate, should not produce some native raw material of importance to a manufacturing country as England is". If found, such a material might repay the cost of establishing and maintaining the colony.[1] McArthur, in search of influential patrons for his project, took much trouble with a collection of African natural history specimens for Sir Joseph which was carried on from St Helena by the East Indiaman on which he reached England. His pains over

[1] Sir Joseph Banks to Under-Secretary King, 15 May 1798.

the safe delivery of the cases earned only a dry acknow-
ledgement from Banks, the colony's chief advocate and
friend at court.

McArthur found other aid. In July 1803 the clothing
interest was promoting a bill in Parliament to relieve
their industry from the restrictions imposed by the Eliza-
bethan Statute of Artificers. In the name of the fashionable
doctrine of *laissez faire*, they sought the same freedom as
obtained in the cotton manufacture. They had been met,
however, by the formidable argument that expansion of
employment in their craft was impossible because of a
notorious dearth of the raw material.[1] Out of the blue
came Captain McArthur with his samples of wool grown
on Spanish sheep at the Antipodes, telling of wide empty
pastures from which they might expect the coming of
quantities beside which Spain's nine million pounds would
seem a mere bagful. He wrote, in October 1805, of "tracts
of land adapted for pastures so boundless that no assignable
limits can be set to the number of fine-woolled sheep
which can be raised...with little other expense than the
wages and food of the shepherds".

Sir Joseph Banks, whom the Office of Trade consulted
as President of the Royal Society and an explorer of the
scene, disparaged McArthur's project. "I have seen
fleeces imported from New South Wales the quality of
which was equal to Spanish wools of the second or third
rate piles, but I have not seen any equal to the best piles
of old Spain....I have never heard of any luxuriant
pastures of sheep till I read of them in Captain Macarthur's
statement, nor did I ever see such when in that country."
What could be more authoritative? "I have my fears",
he continued, "that it will be found on enquiry that sheep
do not prosper well there, unless in lands that have been
cleared and manured with some labour and expense....
The freight of wool from Spain to England costs from

---

[1] See Memorial to Treasury from Woollen Manufacturers, quoted in
Macarthur Records, p. 67. Also Coghlan, *op. cit.* p. 101.

D

1*d*. to 1½*d*. a pound....What the freight of a ton of wool from New South Wales will be I am not able to ascertain, but it will certainly add very materially to its actual price when brought to market." Sir Joseph advised against encouraging McArthur in "a mere theoretical speculation".

Such advice from one whose first-hand knowledge of the land in question had been gained nearly thirty years before in the swamps around Botany Bay would have aroused a less pugnacious man than John McArthur. He met it first by a letter from Captain Waterhouse who had also run sheep in the colony. "The Universal mode of feeding Sheep in that Country", Waterhouse reported,[1] "has been by driving them into the Woods, on the Natural Pasturage. When I left the Colony there was not artificial grass sufficient to feed a Lamb a week....My Flock were driven into the Woods after the Dew was off the Grass, driven back for the Man to get his dinner, and then taken out again until the close of the Evening, when they remained in the Yard for the Night....When brought home earlier than usual, and finding fault with the Shepherd for it, he said that they were so soon full that they had lain down for hours." As to freight, McArthur called before the Committee one John Princep, a London merchant, who quoted a freight of £16 per ton on wool as backloading in time of war, and £8 per ton in time of peace. So fortified against Banks, the Committee recommended a grant of lands to McArthur, subject to resumption with compensation if the land were wanted for cultivation. It supported, too, McArthur's idea that the Governor should be instructed to feed the convicts on mutton rather than salt meat, and to pay a premium on mutton from finewoolled sheep.

McArthur sought a grant of ten thousand acres around Mount Taurus in the Cowpastures, well beyond the lands under tillage. Lord Camden, then in charge of colonial

---

[1] The letter and McArthur's covering memorial to the Committee of Trade and Plantations are reprinted in the *Macarthur Records*, pp. 78 *seq.*

affairs, was ready to make it, and McArthur sold his commission in the New South Wales Corps in order to devote fuller attention to his Merino flocks. For a time Banks himself joined in talk of a company which should be granted a million acres and be managed by McArthur.[1] In August, however, there was a sale of Spanish Merinos from the Royal Stud at Kew, where the antagonism between McArthur and Banks flared afresh. The sheep were the progeny of Merinos presented to the King in 1791 by a Spanish Marchioness. They afforded McArthur the chance of adding to his Cape Merinos another strain. Gordon's Merinos were of the Escurial type[2], while those of the Royal flock were Negretti. Which was superior is largely a question of fashion. The prestige of the Royal flock no doubt favoured the Negretti, but in 1830 James McArthur, John's son, reported after a visit to Saxony that "with their ample folds of skin and large dewlaps" they were completely out of favour there.[3]

The sheep offered at Kew were culls and in poor condition, but McArthur bid with determination and secured more than his share. The highest price he paid was twenty-seven guineas for a four-tooth ram, with fleece of 7 lb. 2 oz. At the sale he met Banks who "at last when his aid was needless evincèd a strong desire to promote and patronize the introduction of the merino sheep into Australia".[4] McArthur, resenting a patronage ill-distinguished from tuft-hunting, forgot the rule "Agree with thine enemy quickly" and offered the coldest front to the older man's advances. The sheep and their proud owner were

[1] It was to have a capital of £10,000 and to pay for the manager's services by allowing him all the mutton. The plan might well have tempted the manager to be unfaithful to the plan of breeding first of all for wool. It remained a mere theoretical speculation.

[2] See J. D. Stewart, Presidential Address to the Royal Society of New South Wales, August 1928.

[3] See *Macarthur Records*, p. 439.

[4] From James Macarthur's notes written in 1859 for Sir Roger Therry's use in writing his *Reminiscences of N.S.W. and Victoria*, and quoted in *Macarthur Records*, p. 99.

ready for embarkation on the 'Argo'[1] when a paragraph in the *Morning Chronicle* reminded the purchaser of an old statute forbidding the export of English sheep on pain of forfeiture, fine and branding. Repairing hot-foot to Downing Street, McArthur met Banks leaving Lord Camden's office. The legal obstacle was evaded by a special Treasury permit, but McArthur had to content himself with a grant of five thousand acres at the chosen spot, to be supplemented by a similar area when his hopes of increase should have been realized.

He returned triumphant on the main issue, bringing back five rams and a ewe from the Kew purchase, expert wool-sorters, two new settlers, vines and olive trees. After a little demur at disturbing the sacred grove of the wild cattle, Governor King did Lord Camden's bidding, and for three troubled years McArthur watched his flocks increase at Parramatta and at Camden Park, his new estate in the Cowpastures.

That increase failed, however, to fulfil the hopes he had held out to the clothing interest. Among other sheep-breeders in the colony it excited scorn for the puny Merinos. Bengal sheep always bred twice a year. Cape ordinaries often did so. McArthur had based his reckoning of increase on the growth of the colony's total flock from 1531 in 1796 to 6737 in 1801. Assuming that on protected pasture his flock would double in two and a half years, he had predicted a production comparable within twenty-five years with that of Spain. But he had reckoned without his sheep. At his return he found that the crossing of Merino rams with crossbred and comeback ewes gave sheep of weaker constitution.[2] The coastal lands, we know now, are not favourable to Merinos. They are more at

---

[1] The ship which McArthur had purchased and adorned with the figure-head of a golden fleece.

[2] See Memo. by John McArthur, in *Macarthur Records*, p. 72. "As the cross with the Merino blood advanced the young sheep became delicate and sickly and the Ewes seldom lived to rear more than three Lambs—often not more than one, and the Lambs were as tender as their Mothers."

home on the drier Western slopes.[1] But the fading out of the hybrid vigour set colonial opinion against the whole project of breeding for wool alone. McArthur did not budge from his conviction that the colony must find a staple: the British taxpayer would not always foot the bills for rations, roads and public buildings. The Revd. Samuel Marsden and others bred sheep for immediate returns of mutton as well as wool. They found the type hard to fix. But as McArthur's sheep became more deeply imbued with Merino blood they regained constitution. With Cox of Windsor and a chosen few he made the future of fine wool safe by sticking to pure Merino, and by standing ready to supply Merino rams for all who would breed first for wool, and for fine wool.

Nothing daunted him. He remained in exile from 1809 to 1817 rather than purchase immunity from arrest by an apology for the part he had taken in deposing Bligh. His wife Elizabeth trained his sons and watched the flocks during his absence. When he returned in 1817 to the colony he had roughly served, even the judges protested against a move by Macquarie to raise him to the magistracy. He retorted with energy upon their petty souls but his later letters grew low-spirited under the torments of gout. They still witness, none the less, to his old tenacity on the main issue. "My feeble attempt to introduce Merino sheep", he told an absentee neighbour in 1818, "still creeps on almost unheeded and altogether unassisted. Few settlers can be induced to take the trouble requisite to improve their flocks, or to subtract a few guineas from their usual expenditure—tea and rum—to purchase Spanish rams."[2] "By storing the Country with Fine-Woolled Sheep"—he is here coaching in colonial economy his son John, then at the Inns of Court—"a most valuable export would be

---

[1] This is strikingly shown on the "Sheep Map of Australia", *Commonwealth Year Book*, No. 20, p. 627.

[2] J. McArthur to W. Davidson, 3 September 1818, *Macarthur Records*, p. 317.

obtained, the returns of which would increase the demand for labour and gradually prepare the colonists to depend on their own exertions and in time enable them altogether to provide for their own expenditure."[1]

The routine work was within the competence even of convicts. The main thing was that stockowners should grasp the need of purity in the breed. It was a sure sign that the old man's fad was at last being understood when about 1820 Sydney speculators began to sell as "Pure Merinos" coarse-woolled sheep showing a trace of that blood. Finding Bigge receptive to his ideas, McArthur offered to make the true breed accessible to all by selling to government all the rams they would take for a price in land valued at 7s. 6d. an acre. He wanted elbow room, some 50,000 acres. Only strict supervision in enclosed ground had kept his stud pure. When he shifted it out to Camden Park he would need a bigger scene for his main flock. He offered to pay in fine-woolled rams for "a certain proportion of such lands a Government now bestows gratis and with no other object than the production of corn and cattle, for which they are obliged to pay by Bills on the English Treasury".

While only the coastal plain was known, horned cattle had multiplied almost as fast as McArthur had expected of his sheep, 12,442 head of cattle in 1810 becoming 102,939 in 1820. After 1813, however, the sheep began to countenance the First Flockmaster's hopes. From 50,000 in that year they multiplied to 290,000 in 1821. Between 1814 and 1820, from 60,000 to 90,000 pounds of wool were exported annually, forming as yet but a tiny fraction of the imports from all sources into Britain. In 1821 New South Wales and Van Diemen's Land exported between them 175,433 pounds of fine wool. In 1822 a gold medal was awarded to John McArthur "for importing into Great Britain wool the produce of his flocks equal to the finest Saxony". This meant that Australian wool could

[1] *Macarthur Records*, pp. 328 *et seq.*

reach a standard well above that of "the best piles of Old Spain". In 1827 he obtained 196d. a pound for a bale bearing the famous "I.McA." brand, a record price that is still unbeaten.[1] In 1831 New South Wales sent 1,134,134 pounds and Van Diemen's Land 1,359,203 pounds. The 1,100,000 sheep in New South Wales in 1832 had by 1838 become 2,750,000. By 1849 there were 13,159,000 sheep in the mother colony, 6,000,000 of them being in the Port Phillip District. Within less than three decades a mighty expansion in the despised convict settlements of New Holland "had changed the balance of forces in the wool-world and had made Australia's greatest contribution to the strength of the Empire".[2]

John McArthur, well-loved and devotedly followed by his own family until his death in 1834, was indeed the happy warrior who had "wrought upon the plan that pleased his boyish thought". But age, gout and the fierce scorn of a superior mind for time-servers made him a poor apostle of an idea which had by this time won some trial in many another temperate country.[3] His contemporaries obstinately refused to retract their mockery of his "pure Merinos". "Many do not like to apply to me because they have always scoffed at the project from its commencement.... Many will not move unless in a string.... At present (1820) there are not ten sheep-breeders pursuing any measure for the improvement of Wool and not more than six of them that pursue judicious ones."[4] He even sought to push upon government, through its grants of stock to new settlers, the work for which his powers of persuasion fell short. "I wish to God", he communed with young John, "Government could be induced to

---

[1] See *Commonwealth Year Book*, No. 20, p. 635 for recent price records.

[2] Stephen Roberts, *Cambridge History of the British Empire*, vol. vii (to appear), ch. vii, "The Wool Trade and the Squatters"—the best short account of the period.

[3] For the attempts to introduce Spanish sheep into the U.S.A. see L. G. Connor, *Report of American Hist. Association*, 1918, vol. i, p. 101. As to Britain, Germany, France and Bohemia, see below, pp. 89–91.

[4] *Macarthur Records*, p. 332.

adopt some plan of supplying settlers with Merino Rams of undoubted purity of blood at a moderate price.... I care not what price Government take them at: let them fix it themselves and let me have the honour and satisfaction of seeing the universal spread of what I have so long and so anxiously laboured to establish, and I shall be satisfied." Suddenly, in the early 'twenties the tide of opinion turned in Britain. There was a rush for Australian land and Saxon Merinos with which to furnish unlimited and superior raw materials for the woollen and worsted industries. Army officers, tenant-farmers, younger sons of the middle class came out to compete in taking up "runs" with "currency lads", surveyors and shepherds-turned-graziers.

The way to the unlimited expansion of colonial wool supplies had been opened at home only after a sharp clash of protectionist and free-trade opinion. British flock-masters had long been dismayed by "the awful fact that this country which once boasted of its native wool as the staple commodity...has now become wholly dependent on a supply of foreign wool for its clothing manufacture".[1] This had come about as an indirect result of the rising demand for mutton and the success of Bakewell and his pupils in breeding sheep to supply it. From home flocks whose masters were indifferent to their needs the woollen manufacturers had turned for fine wool to Spain and the Continent. Under Pitt's liberal policy, wool had come in free of duty from 1784 to 1802. Thereafter a revenue duty had been slowly raised from 5s. 3d. a hundredweight to 6s. 8d. in 1818. Post-war protectionism, listening to the cry of the woolgrower for higher prices, imposed in 1819 a heavy duty of 6d. a pound on foreign wool. Colonial wool was admitted at a duty of 1d. a pound. The duty on foreign wool caused a contraction in imports of raw material and in exports of woollens. In 1825, when

[1] J. K. Trimmer, *Improvement of British Fine Wool* (1828) (Mitchell Library). Cf. p. 78.

Huskisson codified the Customs, high protection gave way to a revenue duty of 1*d*., subsequently ½*d*., a pound, and the banked out supplies of foreign wool came in with a rush. No doubt, as Earl Stanhope complained,[1] the price of English wools fell in sympathy with those of the fine wools imported. But a wider public than the beneficiaries of an artificial dearth of wool, to whose interests the noble lord appealed, stood to gain by the freeing of trade. The high cost of raw materials during the five years of restriction had cramped the woollen industry and raised cloth-prices to the loss of both consumers and exporters.[2] British flock-masters had long known the manufacturers' needs of "quality wool" but had followed other ambitions. In the eighteen-twenties they well knew of the waning of Peninsular supplies and of the attempts to acclimatize Spanish wool abroad.

One of them had watched Saxon and French attempts to divert from Spain the fine wool industry without being much impressed thereby. He urged that Southdowns improved by Merino rams would make a safer, and a British, base for its continuance. The chance, if it ever existed, of acclimatizing fine wool in Britain was not taken. A joint production of mutton and coarser wool paid better. But Australian pastoralists, though without experience of their own, were quick to seize the lessons of failures and changes, and to exploit a more favourable climate elsewhere.

Spanish wool had been grown by unchanging and traditional methods. Flocks ten thousand strong had been guarded by head shepherds, each aided by fifty assistants and as many dogs. According to the season, they were conducted north or south, from mountain to plain, travelling about 2 leagues a day. The dogs of mastiff type more than matched in size and strength the

---

[1] In his *Letter to the Owners and Occupiers of Sheep-Farms* (1828) (Mitchell Library).
[2] See James Bischoff, *The Wool Question Considered* (1828), p. 84.

wolves against which they defended the flocks; the sheep were trained to gather to them at any alarm. As a rule the sheep were folded till the dews were gone. Lambs' tails were cut and their noses branded. The sheep-owners shore their flocks unwashed and sold the wool in the grease. Dealers washed and sorted it at river-side establishments, and packed it for export in bags holding about two hundredweight. After shearing, the ewes were housed from the night cold in narrow "sudatories", and crowded so closely that they perspired freely, the aim being, it was said, to make the new wool softer.[1]

In Germany and France several flocks of Merinos had been established during the age of the Enlightened Despots, notably in Saxony and Bohemia, and also at Rambouillet in France, by Louis XVI. The Saxons had coddled and housed their flocks to safeguard them from lung troubles in a rigorous winter climate. The delicacy of un-acclimatized constitutions may have increased with the in-breeding of small and isolated studs.[2] The wool produced, however, had scored heavily with British manufacturers owing to its fine texture and "kindness" to the touch. This "kindness", which gave a "small face" on the finished cloth, was produced by washing the wool on the sheeps' backs and allowing the "yolk" to rise again. Fine as was the Saxon wool, Trimmer thought the Saxon Merinos a puny race, growing but half the weight of wool yielded by the stock from which they sprang. Yet at the close of the wars (1814), Britain imported 3,595,146 pounds

[1] See J. K. Trimmer, *Improvement of British Fine Wool* (1828) and Thomas Southey, *Observations addressed to the Wool-growers of Australia and Tasmania*, 2nd edition (1831) (Mitchell Library).

[2] Thomas Southey, *op. cit.*, quotes an account of the introduction of Spanish sheep from Moravia to Graf Hunyadi's Hungarian estates, which emphasizes the minute care taken of them. "Out of 17,000 sheep there is not one whose whole family he cannot trace by reference to his books. The sheep are driven under sheds when it rains or the heat is oppressive. They always lamb in the house, the ewe being placed in a little pen by herself. One shepherd looks after every hundred sheep."

"A little barley-meal should be placed in the water-trough to increase the ewe's milk. Ewes failing in milk should be given meal and salt in water."

from Germany, while the Spanish supply was stagnant at 9¼ million pounds. By 1827 the German supply had grown six-fold to over 22,000,000 pounds, while the Spanish quota was down to 4,349,643 pounds.

According to Trimmer, French armies had seized 200,000 Merinos during the wars, and had spread the blood far and wide through France. But on inspection, the Rambouillet stud-flock pleased the English flock-master no more than the Saxons did. The French Merinos, albeit large in frame for that breed, seemed "the most unsightly flock of the kind he had ever met with", their fleeces deformed with the most exaggerated wrinkles. "If such be the victory" over his smaller but neat Southdown-Merino flock, close in body as in fleece, "I am well satisfied with my share in the defeat."

His plea for breeding fine wool in Britain came too late. The war-time demand had been for mutton and coarse clothing wools. War had been more usual than peace in the previous half-century, and Bakewell, with his improved Leicesters, had shown British graziers how to meet its calls. The great breeder had even talked of preferring a breed without wool, his great aim being mutton and fat, which in his day was produced six inches thick on the sheep's ribs.

Woollen manufacturers, watching the decline and progress of Spanish and Saxon supplies, noted with joy the improving colonial wools. Here was a supply where mutton could not long be a distracting factor. The colonial market for it must soon be glutted. The loss of the preference of 5d. a pound in 1825–6 coincided with a drought in Australia and accentuated the financial troubles consequent on a stock boom in the year following. But by this date admiration for colonial wools had become vocal before Parliamentary committees. A Blackwell Hall factor reported them "more sought after than any other description",[1] and a London merchant spoke of the cloth they made as beyond equal "for fineness of texture

[1] H. Hughes in evidence before a House of Lords Committee, 1826.

and softness of quality. Equal to the wool of any country and of any time, it has the strength of wool with the softness of silk". Two million pounds of it were said to have arrived that year, and sea transport was no longer held a handicap. Some claimed they could bring wool home from Sydney or Hobart Town at less cost for carriage than from Vienna or Leipzig.

Van Diemen's Land graziers made most rapid progress at first. The lands in the eastern half of the island were open and accessible through the Derwent and Tamar estuaries. The climate was that of South Devon and Cornwall in the river valleys, of a sunnier Scotland on the mountains, snow-clad during the boisterous Southern winter. While Governor Macquarie was short-sightedly spoiling his emancipists, Lieutenant-Governor Sorell grasped the magnitude of McArthur's idea. Early in 1820 he bought 300 of the Camden Ram Lambs at five guineas a head and induced the island settlers to use them by an offer of prizes for the finest wool.[1] In the late 'twenties, the Van Diemen's Land Company obtained 350,000 acres in the north-west of the island, and spent £40,000 on introducing the finest Saxon Merinos and over £100,000 on the development of its properties. A smaller company, the Van Diemen's Land Establishment, spent £40,000 on its lands around Cressy near Launceston. Its stock maintained a high repute for many years, although the Establishment collapsed. The Van Diemen's Land flocks increased from a doubtful 182,000 very ordinary Teeswaters in 1820 to 663,000, virtually all Merinos, in 1830. Backed by Sorell's guarantee to buy all wool at 4d. a pound, the export from Van Diemen's Land exceeded in the late 'twenties that of all the mainland runs.

"Vandemonian" stations, however, were all too accessible. "Bolters", as escaped convicts or bushrangers

---

[1] Sorell to McArthur, 4 February 1820, *Macarthur Records*, pp. 343-4. Only half of the rams were successfully landed in Hobart Town.

were first called in the island, became an intolerable plague.[1] Sheep-stealing was all too easy where flocks numbering hundreds might be driven off in daylight into secluded glens of the Eastern or Western Tiers, the brands blotted at leisure, and the sheep sold at the other end of the island with small chance of detection and less of punishment. The nearest criminal court was in Sydney.

When in 1824 the colony was separated from New South Wales, it received a court of its own. Its first Governor, Colonel George Arthur, ruled in despotic style for twelve years. By sheer assiduity he hunted down the bushrangers and maintained a semblance of discipline. The capture of Matthew Brady in 1826 ended the days when a "Governor of the Ranges" affected to correspond on equal terms with the "Governor of the Town". Arthur prohibited the payment of wages to assigned servants and relied on watchfulness to maintain control of the prisoners. Though these measures might prevent the worst excesses, they had in them no germ of improvement; the mountain glens were still fatally accessible. Such advantages as the river valleys had possessed for English agriculture[2] were discounted by the lack of appropriate town markets for its mixed products, as well as by the presence of such evils as thieving natives and bushrangers. When the Hunter Valley in New South Wales was settled, and good seasons came to that colony again, Van Diemen's Land slumped. Similar

---

[1] See Calder MSS. (Melbourne Public Library), vol. 1, pp. 83, 132; *H. R. of A.* series III, vol. III, pp. 252 *et passim*, Hobler MSS. (Mitchell Library), vols. 1 and II, and article on "Michael Howe", *Australian Encyclopaedia*, 1, p. 630.

[2] See Hobler MSS. (Mitchell Library), vol. II, pp. 133 *et seq.* for George Hobler's account of his little farm at Killy-faddy outside Launceston, in 1826. He congratulates himself on his 150 acres of fine meadows, into 10 acres of which he has dibbled roots of sweet scented vernal grass. This he thinks will give the hay a scent that will puzzle "the natives and cockney farmers". Apple trees, quinces, peaches, almonds, apricots, plums, cherries, gooseberries, raspberries and strawberries are planted in his orchard, and "several thousand forest trees in the seed bed and nursery" are ready. Of 50 acres cleared for cultivation, 30 are ploughed and part sown. He is preparing to plant sweet-briar hedges under the "dead fences" and has "three bushels of haws of colonial growth".

episodes of quick prosperity were to recur in the 'fifties and 'eighties, in reflection of mainland booms. But her neighbours so surpass Tasmania in climate and fertility of soil that the island has never been able to hold back its energetic sons from crossing the straits. Hobart newspapers were complaining in 1826 of artisans and mechanics who went off to Rio or Valparaiso. Since Port Phillip and New Zealand were settled, these nearer centres have attracted Tasmanians still more strongly.

The concentration of convict-transports into Tasmanian ports after the cessation of "the system" in New South Wales (1840) only made matters worse. Four thousand convicts a year poured into the colony between that year and 1853, when the system was finally abandoned in Eastern Australia. Over 67,000 in all had been sent thither. An official who had entered the service in 1829 shuddered after half a century at his first memories of Hobart Town—rough streets of squalid houses, drunkenness, robbery and frequent murder. "But the immense chain-gangs or files, two or three hundred yards long, of men undergoing secondary punishment, all in heavy irons, dressed in yellow clothing and closely guarded by armed soldiers and police, passing along the streets with chains rattling most dismally all the way, were the most striking sight that caught my eye after landing. My first impression of the place was that there was nothing beautiful about it except Mount Wellington and the clear blue sky overhead."[1] The "better class" convicts manned the Customs Department as "writers", receiving sixpence a day and "board wages". "Men of this stamp were, of course, not much to be relied on. They required a very Argus to keep watch over them in a revenue office."[2]

A few entries in a settler's diary of October and November 1829 indicate how the better convicts fared when

[1] J. Eskine Calder, in the *Hobart Mercury*, 4 June 1879. From their clothing the convicts were known as 'canaries'.
[2] *Calder Papers*, vol. II, p. 98.

assigned to private employment. When a convict servant's zeal at "burning off" displeases the master, he is taken to the Police Officer and ordered 50 lashes forthwith. Within a fortnight comes this eloquent entry: "3 November: I have now fifteen prisoners who do the whole of the work of the farm without my paying a shilling in wages, but how much looking after they require! C——l, the fellow who was flogged well for his idleness, is now learning to thrash and after this week he shall thrash or be thrashed, without putting me to the trouble of looking after him".[1] Within ten days he was again flogged 50 lashes "and the chief constable directed to make a new cat for him". Within a month the same servant was in trouble for letting the oxen feed on the wheat-field and was sentenced to six months in the government gang. Then "18 December: Surprised by a letter from C——l, from the chain gang, promising better behaviour if I would intercede for him and take him back. That I certainly shall not do". Criminals driven by such means to uncongenial tasks not unnaturally chose, whenever the faintest chance offered, to "go bush" in the hope of at least a spell of liberty, though in so doing they "put their necks into a halter".[2]

As the great age of squatting dawned in New South Wales, and as free farmers spread over the Adelaide Plains, all that could do so fled the ill-omened island whose very name had become a byword for discord and criminality. There fell upon it the palsy of inferiority.

On the mainland, where the climate offered a more difficult problem to those sons of foggy Britain, the pastoralists' craft was slowly articulated under the stress of necessity with many blunders and small successes. "Considering", wrote one of the pioneers at the end of a long life of learning, "that they had nobody else's experience to

---

[1] Hobler MSS. (Mitchell Library), vol. II, pp. 157 *et seq.*
[2] Hobler records being "stuck up" by such a bushranger, Bevan, in June 1829, vol. II, p. 120. His wife's quickness saved his life.

work on, and that hardly any of them had had anything to do with sheep or cattle or horses in their lives before, they managed to flounder along and do wonderfully well."[1] John McArthur's account of how they kept the native pastures sweet in his day suggests blackfellows driving game. "The natural grasses are in all seasons rich and abundant," he said. (He was always heroic and at the moment he was persuading the Privy Council who knew nothing of Australian droughts.) "When they become too rank they are burnt off, and are almost immediately succeeded by a younger and sweeter herbage which the sheep eat greedily and keep bare." On alluvial flats, where periodic floods top-dressed the soil and the constant small tillage of a myriad hoofs compacted the turf, the spread of European plants "electrified the country". On the drier uplands with a lighter covering, deterioration followed the loss of humus by such burning. Flocks increased in the favourable seasons up to the limit of carrying capacity. Then came the sudden droughts of a warm temperate zone as the whip and spur of expansion in search of grass.

In the 'twenties and 'thirties, however, all seemed easy to the young pioneers. With an established repute for the quality of their product, and an unlimited market as a result of the release of English manufacturers from fiscal burdens, the boom in Colonial "wool establishments" was no mystery. Flock-masters and wool-brokers proffered advice· to the new graziers how to tend their sheep and to prepare their clips for market. Companies were formed in London to seize on a large scale the great chance that had so long gone begging at the Antipodes. Sailing ships, and even an occasional steamer, went rolling down wind in the roaring forties, their gunwales no longer lined by the tristful, hopeless faces of convicts, but by free settlers fired with ambition to make their fortunes by filling John Bull's greater woolsack.

[1] R. D. Barton, *Reminiscences of an Australian Squatter* (1883), p. 35.

CHAPTER VII

Pioneering in the Pastoral Industry

IN 1815 a party of convicts escaped from the settlement at Bathurst established by Governor Macquarie for small expiree farmers, and sought a way to New Guinea down the Macquarie River. They soon came back, nearly starved, but telling of endless grassy plains. In 1817 and 1818, Surveyor-General Oxley traced both Lachlan and Macquarie Rivers into flooded marshes. Was there an inland sea beyond? Working back to the coast northward of Sydney, he crossed rich grasslands on the New England plateau and Liverpool Plains. In 1820, Wild reached Lake George, and in the next year Throsby found the Murrumbidgee not far from the site of Canberra. Bigge, noting the attractive climate and foreseeing the accessibility of a colony on Bass's Straits, urged a careful survey of the inland pastures by an expedition from the head of Port Phillip to Lake George, to be followed by the introduction of free settlers. Brisbane thought of landing a party of convicts at Wilson's Promontory and rewarding with free pardons all who reached Sydney.

On the saner advice of Alexander Berry, a Sydney merchant, he finally selected Hamilton Hume, a colonial-born bushman who had shown exploring talent beyond Bathurst, to lead an expedition south-west from Lake George. With six assigned servants and Hovell, a ship's captain who had opened up the Illawarra country, Hume crossed the Murrumbidgee in October 1824, half-climbed the snow-clad Monaro tableland, worked round it inland, rafted the party over a deep westward-flowing river on a dray covered with tarpaulin, forded more rivers flowing north-west, worked west again round rough snow-clad country, found Kilmore Gap and emerged on an inlet which both he and Hovell took to be Western Port, but which was actually Corio Bay where now stands Geelong. When Western Port was occupied in 1826 by a party of soldiers and convicts, they found sealers there and some acres of land under wheat and vegetables.

In 1827 and 1828, Allan Cunningham, botanizing north of Oxley's New England, reached another attractive table-land, the Darling Downs, and saw a gap through which, on a second coastwise expedition, he climbed to the Downs from Moreton Bay.

These successive thrusts over the range had shown that well-watered grasslands extended north and south for at least a thousand miles and were approachable through three or four gaps in addition to the difficult Blue Mountains road to Bathurst. But how far west did they stretch? Did their slope in that direction reach the shores of an inland sea? In winter, rain-clouds banked up from the west and north-west, yet in September and October, the southern spring, parching winds regularly blew over the mountains from the west.

A severe drought between Cunningham's two journeys dried up the marshes that had baulked Oxley's way westward, and Captain Charles Sturt pushed out with Hume to find the sea to which the westward rivers flowed. Leaving the reed-beds, they rode over dry plains till they came upon a stream between high banks trending southwest, with water too brackish to drink. They named it the Darling. Sturt saw it again in 1829 when he tracked the Murrumbidgee by dray, and when more marshes stopped him, by a whaleboat, brought overland in sections and put together by his convict servants on the river bank. Making their way into the Murray and naming it, the party rowed with the current for 26 days, passed what they guessed to be the Darling Junction, saw Mount Lofty Ranges in the dim west, and turning south, emerged in Lake Alexandrina.

Finding no relief ship in Encounter Bay beyond the mighty surf of the Murray Mouth, they rowed upstream for 56 days on a ration of less than half-a-pound of flour a day, against a river swollen by flood-waters. Uncomplaining, the men fell asleep over their oars. Then they camped and sent on the two strongest to Wantabadgery depot for relief which came just as the last ounce of flour had been eaten. Sturt, a "verray perfigt gentil knight" among the explorers, went blind for many months.

Oxley's successor, Major Thomas Mitchell, was one of Wellington's Torres Vedras men, and had envied Sturt the honour of being chosen to explore the inland rivers. In 1831 he struck north-west to find a great "Kindur" river of which a runaway convict told native tales. He crossed the Peel and the Namoi and found the Macintyre. The blacks called it the Karaula, but there was no sea, nor light-coloured men seeking scented wood. And the aborigines stole his stores. In 1835, working west-north-west, he reached the Darling and built a stockade at Fort Bourke. Thence he followed the flowing river through well-grassed land, but not to the Murray. When he knew that Sturt had guessed right, he turned back. In 1836, however, he went from Orange down the Lachlan and Murrumbidgee to the Murray-Darling junction, reascended the Murray to the Loddon, traced it south, crossed to the Grampians and the Pyrenees and followed the Glenelg to the Southern Ocean. Peninsular names—Nivelle, Arapiles, Trafalgar—still mark his route across "Australia Felix" as he named the fertile Wimmera and western districts. He marched back from the Glenelg in military order, and his cart-tracks, "the Major's line", became the route by which Sydney-side stockmen made their way overland to Port Phillip district. But "in this Eden" he was not, as he supposed, "the only Adam". His little column was drawn to the coast again by a glimpse of Edward Henty's farm and whaling station on Portland Bay. And on 30 September 1836 from the summit of Mount Macedon he made out, at the northern corner of Port Phillip, "a mass of white objects which might have been either tents or vessels". It was the beginning of Melbourne. Batman and Fawkner, both young colonials, the one a blacksmith-settler and the other a journalist of rebellious habit, had been there for six weeks, founding from Launceston an unauthorized base for the settlement of Port Phillip district. They had discovered the scene to which David Collins had shut his eyes when in 1803 he lost heart at Sorrento and fled to Van Diemen's Land.

Sturt's heroic boat journey and Major Mitchell's reconnaissances proved that wide inland horizons lay before the quiet battalions already being deployed through the gaps in the ranges. Their occupation of "runs" and "stations", spreading out fanwise to north, west and south-west, was the first detailed exploration of the land.

No General Orders directed their advance. On the contrary, in October 1829, Governor Darling had marked out nineteen counties in a rough semicircle around Sydney and had forbidden settlement beyond their boundaries. His gesture only demonstrated the waning power of the Sydney government in economic matters. Ten years later, there were 694 holdings between the Gwydir and the South Australian border, and the rush to take up runs in Port Phillip and its wonderful Western District was fast gaining momentum.[1]

The adventure of taking up a run has been incomparably described by Professor Stephen Roberts.[2] "A man of small capital acquired a flock and simply set out.... Each was a land-freebooter scanning the horizon for unoccupied or unclaimed land. He was an 'overlander', nursing his sore-footed flock, watching every pinch of flour in his bullock-dray of rations, and looking for his plains of promise or his long-dreamt of mountain-pastures. Over

---

[1] See S. Roberts, *History of Australian Land Settlement*, ch. XIII, on "The Tracks of the Squatters".
[2] Appearing in *Cambridge History of the British Empire*, vol. VII, ch. VII.

the desert and the mountains, over the sun-baked plains and the flooded marsh-lands he went, either seeking some vague landmark dimly hinted at by a previous explorer or one of his rivals or, more often, trusting to his destiny, and his bushman's sense to find virgin country in the general direction in which he was moving.... He kept on despite distance and drought, starvation and disease, attacks by the blacks and desertions by his men. He was staking everything, often his life, on finding a suitable 'run' for his sheep, and until he reached this haven, nothing else counted."

When Darling set his limits on the official maps he meant to take control of this pastoral expansion. An un-licensed occupation of Crown land within and beyond "the limits of location" was stultifying the issue of his new annual grazing licences over defined runs. Yet within a few years, a greatly swollen majority of the graziers in the colony were "squatters" who had placed their "stations" wherever they could find room, regardless of a government which hardly existed beyond Bathurst.[1]

The new economy did not establish itself without two bad stumbles on the part of the new directing class, the booms of 1826 and 1838–9 and the financial crises which followed them. Yet each of these episodes served to emphasize the importance of the pastoral industry, for each arose through the failure of the leaders of the free community to justify their leadership by a single-minded activity in developing

[1] When first used in Van Diemen's Land the term "squatter" had the same contemptuous ring in Australia as in America, and it long retained a suggestion of criminal origins, at least in the ears of the "pure merinos" or free settlers. "Station" originally meant a folding place where the sheep were shut up at night as a defence against dingoes or "warrigals". The transition to the later use may be seen in a letter dated 12 May 1830 in the Hogan MS. (Mitchell Library). The owner of Cuttawally writes of "going up the country in about three weeks and then we will settle where the different stations are to be". But the whole run is already known as "Cuttawally Station" as well as "Cuttawally Establishment". This older name "Establishment" and the ranks of superintendent and overseer which still survive on the stations may be traced at Emu Plains Agricultural Establishment in *The Adventures of Ralph Rashleigh*, pp. 88, 93, 94.

that industry. In each instance the crash of speculation drove men back to hard work on the main task which they had thought to leave to others.

The first boom may best be described as it appeared to the critical eyes of John Dunmore Lang, the fiery Scots parson whose zeal for Australia, though marred by a bitter sectarianism, burned with a flame that consumed many a sham during his long life in New South Wales (1823–1878).[1] "The Australian Agricultural Company commenced operations in 1826.[2] As cattle and horses had to be purchased for the company wherever they could be got the price of agricultural stock rose rapidly throughout the colony, insomuch that cattle of colonial breed were actually sold to the company's agent for twelve guineas and sheep for four or five guineas a head....No sooner had the existence of the A. A. Company been announced and its operations commenced in right earnest than the sheep and cattle mania instantly seized on all ranks and classes of the inhabitants. The mania impelled whomsoever it seized to the cattle market....Barristers, attorneys, military officers of every rank, civilians of every department, clergymen, medical men, merchants, dealers, settlers were there seen promiscuously mingled together every Thursday outbidding each other in the most determined manner for the purchase of every scabbed sheep, scarecrow horse or buffalo cow in the colony that was offered for sale. It was universally allowed that the calculations of the projectors of the A. A. Company could not be inaccurate. It was made as clear as daylight to the comprehension of stupidity itself that the owner of a certain number of sheep and cattle in New South Wales must in a certain number of years infallibly make a fortune. It was determined on all hands that the A. A. Company should not be the only reaper of this golden harvest....

"In all cases where the purchaser had money to pay

---

[1] A short biography in the *Australian Encyclopaedia*, vol. I, p. 719, gives a fair outline of his career.

[2] See S. Roberts, *History of Australian Land Settlement*, ch. VI, and Appendix I.

for his sheep and cattle money was paid. Where money was not forthcoming, as was generally the case, credit was allowed....It was not at all to be wondered at that persons who were to be so speedily enriched beyond their highest previous expectations should begin to speculate prematurely. Articles were accordingly ordered and bills given for their payment and so favourable was the prospect of demand for the future that colonial merchants or importers were induced to order large quantities of British and other foreign goods till their warehouses were filled and almost every article of British manufacture could be obtained in Sydney at a cheaper rate than in London.

"It pleased Divine Providence to visit the colony in the midst of these speculations with an afflictive drought of nearly three years continuance, the effect of which, combined with the natural result of the sheep and cattle mania, was to open the eyes of the colonists to their own folly and madness, to blast the golden hopes of thousands and to bring many families to poverty and ruin....Month after month herds of cattle and flocks of sheep were seized and sold for the payment of debts incurred by their original purchase....The ruin thus experienced in all directions was just a little less extensive than the mania which had originally caused it. Those who had commenced with capital found that they had lost it in great measure. Those who had salaries found that these must in future be appropriated for the payment of debts which their own cupidity and infatuation had led them to contract. Those who had neither capital nor salaries at the first had their property brought to the hammer and themselves to poverty or prison."

During 1830, although the rate of interest allowed by law was only eight per cent., twelve, fifteen, twenty and even twenty-five and thirty per cent. interest was obtained to meet the urgent necessities of individual settlers.[1]

[1] Dr Lang's description is quoted by Edward Pulsford in his *Rise, Progress and Present Position of Trade and Commerce in New South Wales*, written in 1893 for the N.S.W. Commission to the World's Fair at Chicago.

In 1838 there was for a second time speculation, such as marks the adoption of any new and promising expedient of economic advance, on the increase in stock and land values. The population of the colony had grown from 30,267 in 1827 to 68,795 in 1838. Old and new colonies were expanding rapidly in Van Diemen's Land and South Australia. "New chums" were again buying up flocks and herds without the experience necessary to calculate the income they could be made to yield. The proceeds of government land-sales at Port Phillip and at Sydney were being used to bring out numbers of assisted immigrants. Graziers were tempted to believe that high prices and abundant labour made big profits certain. Again there was a fevered zeal to buy stock and equip stations. Speculators "put it about" that land values must rise still more. On the wings of hope the reckless soared into the inane.

In 1839 the Government announced that the price of land would be raised to 12s. an acre as soon as the 300,000 acres of land already offered at 5s. had been sold. The authorities thought to check the speculative buying of what was deemed cheap land. Their action had just the opposite effect; men rushed to buy at five shillings what would soon be worth twelve. Auction sales of Melbourne town allotments realized £131,000 in 1838, £152,000 in 1839 and £313,000 in the first ten months of 1840. Some allotments that had been sold in 1837 brought within three years eighty times what had been paid for them. Even in the proposed suburbs of Melbourne, a twenty-five-fold increase was not unknown. Private re-sales were made on credit, the amounts outstanding to bear interest at ten per cent. To finance this gambling in title-deeds there was general borrowing on the collateral security of land at the inflated prices. Payments of town wages and for government land were the only occasions for the use of cash.

New banks were competing for a footing in this land of the golden fleece. At the beginning of 1834 there were only two colonial banks—the Banks of New South Wales and of Australia, the latter having been founded in 1826 on an unlimited liability basis with a capital of £400,000. In 1834 the Commercial Banking Company of Sydney opened its doors and the Bathurst Bank was founded in 1835. These were followed by the Bank of Australasia and the Chartered Bank of Australasia in 1836, the former of which boasted a capital of £400,000, and by the Union Bank of Australia and the Sydney Bank in 1839. By that year the total capital of the banks serving the colony's trade in Sydney or in London was over £2,300,955. In 1841 out of their total assets of £3,050,000 the banks held £2,610,000 in discounted bills. London merchants in haste to make money out of such a well-provided community poured in on consignment masses of goods, largely luxuries. Governor Gipps marked the profusion in which all classes were living by declaring that around Melbourne the country was "strewn for miles, almost for hundreds of miles, with champagne bottles".[1]

As the pressure increased, rates of interest as high as 15 per cent. were promised, but, unless the prices at which title-deeds changed hands continued to soar steeply, such rates would soon ruin speculators using borrowed funds. In 1839 financial stringency in London checked the flow of capital to Australia. In the new province of South Australia land sales and credit collapsed, and "scourging drought" in New South Wales from 1838 to 1840 accentuated the mistrust felt in England about the future of all the colonies. Within the colonies, the drought undermined credit by forcing heavy exports of coin to India, Java and Chili to pay for rice, maize and wheat. Governor Gipps relieved the banks' need for a time by placing on deposit with them the cash it had been customary to hold in the Treasury, but the cessation of land sales soon forced him to call up his deposits. A quarter of a million was withdrawn between July 1840 and November 1841 to pay

[1] T. A. Coghlan, *Labour and Industry in Australia*, vol. 1, pp. 473 *et seq.*

the public service. Heavy payments by government of bonuses to assisted immigrants came due as the delayed result of activity in sending them out during the boom period. The banks called• in advances and stopped all "cash credits"; spending ceased, save on bare necessaries. The regular merchants found their business paralysed by the sale of speculators' consignments at auction without reserve. Banks which nursed trader-clients whose stocks were unsaleable only added to their losses. Farmers and pastoralists who offered bullocks or wool in payment for stores had to sacrifice them on a glutted market into which all were forced by drought. Sheep had brought 35s. a head in 1839: in 1843 they were sold at "sixpence a head and the station given in". Horses worth "£50 to £70 for the commonest hack" in 1839 went for £7 in 1843. Fat cattle went at 50s. as compared with £10 to £12.

Settlers, merchants, storekeepers and working house-holders were alike glad of the shelter of a new Bankruptcy Act passed by Council in 1842 at the instance of Judge Burton. It left debtors their freedom on condition that they surrendered their estates to their creditors. The estates as a rule fetched little. When in 1843 the Banks of Australia, Port Phillip and Sydney failed, the assets of the first, in which many leading colonists had already lost their share-capital, were liquidated by a lottery—the only way that would attract a little cash.

Financial oracles, including the majority in the Legislative Council, were insistent that the Governor should "stem the tide of disaster" by issuing new cash, notes backed by mortgages on land. The distant Colonial Office, however, put a veto on such heterodox money. But out of "the Bad Times", as these years of despair were long called, came two expedients that helped the insolvents set free by Burton's *Seisachtheia* to find their feet again.

To start wool-growing the first requisite was a waggon-load of stores and some sheep with which to make the westward march. How could pastoralists give security for payment? They had no land, and in any event it was almost unsaleable. In September 1843 an Act of Council was passed permitting banks to lend against liens on live-stock and wool. Again the Colonial Office demurred. It relied on London ideas of sound banking, the first rule of which was that the banker must draw a firm line between commercial bills and mortgages on property. Bills, to London financiers, had behind them goods on their way to consumers. Before the bill was due, the sale of the goods would put the drawee in funds to meet his obligation. Land might be drought-stricken: movable property might prove sterile or perishable. In a crude new country, however, such bills were not to be found. Behind the best of the bills which the banks had discounted during the boom the assets were often land, stock and wool; and if banks could not or would not lend on such security they would not lend at all—their capital would lie idle. The Council stood its ground and the Act was maintained against every threat of disallowance. As it had already given the relief intended, the Colonial Office let well alone. In finance accomplished facts must be respected.

The other saving expedient was boiling down sheep for their tallow. This was first tried by Henry O'Brien of Yass as an escape from scab[1] and from the ruinous prices which sheep were fetching. When the tallow from a sheep was worth four or five shillings and the English market for it was firm, the boiling down vat, however wasteful of good mutton, was an effective retort to bids of 6d. a head. In 1844, forty-four boiling-down plants rendered 350,000 sheep into 48,758 cwt. of tallow. The maximum output was 233,757 cwt. from 1,700,000 sheep in 1850. As the demand for stock revived, the need of this gruesome last resort quickly passed. "The value of the discovery", thought Sir Timothy Coghlan, "lay more in its effects

---

[1] On this highly contagious disease and the obstacles which long hindered its suppression, see E. M. Curr, *Scab in Sheep*, Melbourne 1865. The annual loss caused in Victoria alone for many years was £500,000.

upon men's minds than in the actual use to which it was put."

The ruin brought on many by their boom-time projects forced them to work again as active producers. The result was a spurt in exports almost as prompt as the decline of imports. The latter fell away from £3,014,189 in 1840 to £931,260 in 1844, in which year exports surpassed imports for the first time in the colony's history, being worth £1,128,115. New production was attempted along many lines. George Hobler contrived to make champagne on his Hunter River property, but rain spoiled his vintage, and the boom thirst did not revive. Then he tried fresh fruit, but the Sydney market was too soon glutted, and the vigneron "determined to make raisins for our own use". "It is a most uncertain country for agricultural pursuits" he reflected. "The day before the rain commenced the corn seemed to be scorched up past all help. Now there is every appearance of a good crop which may have the effect of making it all but unsaleable. Prices now are about 3s. 6d. for wheat, 2s. to 2s. 6d. barley, 1s. 6d. maize, 45s. hay, butter 9d. and meat 1½d."[1] The only way, he found, was to persist with wool and tallow. Stores were cheap and there was still plenty of labour competent to run sheep after the fashion which suited a semi-nomadic economy.

Many descendants of the pioneers hold firmly to "Banjo" Paterson's faith

> That nothing in the ages old
> In song or story written yet,
> On Grecian urn or Roman arch,
> Though it should ring with clash of steel,
> Could braver histories unfold
> Than this bush story yet untold.
> The story of their westward march.

Others in Australia would reduce the merit of the pioneers to the sheer luck of having been the first favoured few

[1] Hobler MS. 1844 (Mitchell Library).

with flocks and herds to drive into rich empty pastures. There they had but to watch wool grow and numbers multiply while the excluded many, equally capable, did all the hard work. Either view is imaginative and false. The true "story of their westward march", as revealed in the diaries and memoirs of its participants, is no epic of disinterested bravery. They waged no public war, but each devoted his slender resources to a more thorough and truceless conquest—the occupation of land by a new economy. What drew them to Australia was not quest of glory, but the main chance of making good a family's foothold in a new and, as they held, unused land. It was neither child's play nor high romance. And the measure of their deserts and their success in comparison with those of the workers they employed was the measure of their courage and endurance.

Anthropologists still protest at their and our "neglect" of the aborigines—and even active extermination of them.[1] They ask for the native a few crumbs from the proceeds of a more provident use of his country, and for authentic reserves in which the "outback" survivors of its primitive huntsmen may maintain themselves as of old. This is both just and, for the high purpose of knowing the taciturn mind of an archaic race, also wise. But there was and there can be no consistency between a hunting and a pastoral use of land and beasts. The blacks' morale and their elaborate code of honour crumbled as the squatters and their servants drove multitudes of strange beasts across the tribal boundaries, shot down warriors and the native game, even those tabooed to the tribe, ensnared the gins and children into dishonour and drudgery by gifts of rum, tobacco and flour. In numbers the older race was too weak, in organization too divided, to resist a folk who, despite their still feebler numbers, had food in plenty,

---

[1] See F. Wood Jones, *Australian Association for the Advancement of Science*, Perth 1926, vol. xviii, pp. 497 *et seq.*, a restrained and powerful statement of the claims of the Australian Aborigines.

weapons of incomparable power, and a ruthless mutual loyalty.

A tribe could for a time be formidable to a solitary pastoral household or an isolated hut, with stores half-watched and flock unyarded and astray. But their half-instinctive "duffing" from the newcomers' abundance would soon or late be answered by a "rounding up" and "dispersal" of the blacks in the vicinity of the "theft". Of the survivors, a few proud old men might stand aloof still living on game and grubs, their only belongings a few skins, spears and firestick. Outwardly scornful, their hearts were benumbed with broken memories and despair. The youngsters, laughing at the defeated spirit and traditions of their elders, accepted the white man's food and excitements, rode his horses, even wore his uniform, and as native police tracked down their fellows. The old hunting skill of the blacks was thus fatally domesticated and turned against the "myalls" or untamed blacks on the edge of pastoral occupation. But disease thinned off with hideous rapidity the domesticated blacks, and no disagreement between the whites regarding their mutual rights to the land prevented their joining to treat the myalls as vermin whose destruction was to be achieved by any means, from shot-guns to poisoned damper.[1]

The squatters and their servants came by degrees. They used the land in a pastoral economy, demanding, above all, security from the hunters' spears for their beasts and from

[1] For an account of the massacre by blacks of a benevolent squatter named Wills, and his household, at Cullin-la-ringo in the Comet country, Queensland, 1861, see Nisbet MS. Mitchell Library. Another pathetic murder was that of a small squatter, Maclaren, stalked all day and slain close to his hut near Gurumbah, after he had put down his gun and gone back for some sick sheep, while his family sat waiting for "tea". In *Christison of Lammermoor*, chs. VIII, IX, X, and on pp. 226–8, may be read the methods and difficulties of an exceptional squatter who "worked in with" the blacks. "Kurry used to be as shy as a frightened fawn with white people.... A few years later in Hughenden town nobody would have recognized the shy pretty girl in the drunken woman screaming larrikin filth at a half-caste urchin."

his firestick for the grass. They obtained it, occasionally by bribing and befriending the blacks, usually by brutal intimidation. Then disease and the depression of manifest impotence wasted the survivors all too rapidly for the squatters' liking—for they had found in the young blacks, who were handy with stock, a supply of docile and cheap labour. In undisputed possession, as far as the spearmen were concerned, the squatters pursued their plans, watching over, cajoling and shepherding the white shepherds whom they set to watch their "faint flocks and herds".

Their care was made fruitful, their isolation tolerable, by a regular exchange of goods at the coastal ports between "bullock waggons toiling down to fetch the wool away" and sailing-ships bringing cargoes of clothing and hardware over the tumbled Southern Ocean. Individuals, "undirected by the fostering care of government", developed the pastoral industry which still remains the principal activity and support of the white man's Australian economy.

CHAPTER VIII

Shepherding and Marketing

"WOOL-FARMING"—the term is John McArthur's—called neither for skill nor assiduous labour. It adjusted itself to the quality and quantity of the human material available.[1] Shepherds and hut-keepers were placed at the various "stations" on a run, in deliberate isolation from the temptations to which they had formerly succumbed. In the days of open boundaries, a run was simply a string of such stations stretched out over perhaps forty miles of country. The overseer was expected to visit each in its turn, taking the men their rations, tobacco, newspapers and any other odds and ends they had bespoken from the "headquarters" store. He would count each flock and, of course, discuss the state of feed and water. This incessant round with rations was "a dingo's life" for the overseer, but the existence of the shepherds and hut-keepers at the stations was a soul-destroying monotony. Seldom or never had they the resources of mind from which to build an inner life to compensate for the loss of Sydney's gregarious pleasures.

A slab-hut with a stringy-bark roof, rough-hinged flaps in lieu of windows, a mud floor, a packing-case table, seats made from split logs, and beds, if any, of bush saplings and hessian, was their home. Often a blanket on the floor and a saddle for pillow served as "shake-down". Pasted on the walls might be a few fly-specked cartoons from the

---

[1] The convict, according to Dr Lang, "is better clothed, better fed, and better lodged than three-fourths of the labouring agricultural population of Great Britain and Ireland. While at the same time his labour is beyond all comparison much less oppressive".

satirical press, or coloured prints from the Christmas numbers of the "weeklies", usually representing famous race-horses. No enclosure surrounded the hut, save when an exceptional hut-keeper had put in a few pumpkins or cabbages. "In dry weather dust, in wet weather mud up to the uncertain line at which bush ended and house began" made "a home little better than an animal's lair" and equally attractive to flies and vermin. For heaps of sheep's dung stood feet high at older "stations", and the dam or river near-by made admirable breeding-places. To light a candle indoors in summer was to fill the place with mosquitos. The only way to escape them was to sit or sleep in a smoke from smouldering cow-dung so dense that it weakened the eyes' resistance to "sandy blight". Just before daybreak the mosquitos would stop, but at dawn the flies were up for the day. "You can seldom lift a piece of food to your mouth without one hand driving away flies to make room for it. Anything like gravy in your plate is a sort of fly-trap and most successful in its operations. Fleas are as abundant as may be expected from floors of dust and so many dogs about, cats and parrots, and the thermometer indoors usually from 90° to 100°".[1] Any abrasion of the skin tended to fester. The flies helped to spread an infectious condition known as "Barcoo rot".

At "headquarters" the squatter or his superintendent might enjoy the co-operation of wife and family in fighting such discomforts and maintaining some amenities of life. But in the first pioneering the menfolk were often, from choice, "roughing it" alone.[2]

Station labour came from four sources—"old hands", "wild colonials", "new chums", and, a little later, ex-

---

[1] *Hobler Papers* (Mitchell Library), vol. v, p. 4, 21 January 1847, on the Lower Murrumbidgee.

[2] See M. M. Bennett's *Christison of Lammermoor*, p. 116: "They ate portulacca to keep off scurvy and made tea with wild marjoram. 'It's a hungry place, Lammermoor', a traveller told a neighbour. 'Nothing to eat but pigweed and mutton. No flour. No stores of any description'".

diggers. They had small chance of family life. A disparity in numbers between the sexes persisted in extreme degree until the 'fifties, especially up country where the squatters for pastoral reasons looked askance upon "encumbrances".

"Old hands" formed the vast majority of the shepherds and hut-keepers. Such callings suited the mentality of many sent out for trying to live without working. They were "found" with rations adequate for fairly valiant trenchermen, the customary scale being 8 or 10 lb. of flour, 10 to 12 lb. of meat, 2 lb. of sugar and a quarter of a pound of tea per man per week. In addition, wages were "allowed" at rates varying from year to year, but seldom in pre-gold days above £25 per annum for shepherds and £20 for hut-keepers. Against these amounts were charged all clothing and extras drawn from the headquarters store. When, at long intervals, the victims of monotony announced themselves "dead sick of it" and "wanting a spell", the balance to their credit would be paid in the form of a cheque on some distant bank, probably in Sydney. Most of them were expirees too weak in initiative to take up land grants or, when grants ceased, to work at city or farm wages till they could buy "blocks". The rations-and-cheque system offered such men no escape from degradation, no real chance of self-respect.

Rations had been issued continuously from the days of assigned service. The issue of them set up in the minds of the old hands an implicit belief that so long as they "kept out of trouble" their animal wants would be supplied without forethought or exertion on their part. Rations to the "sundowner" seeking a place seemed to them one of the rights of man. To the squatter they were a kind of insurance-premium; for a disgruntled swag-man could so easily be careless with matches when the grass was dry.

An indirect result of this "right to tucker" was that the paid-off station-hand fell a willing prey to another class whose prototypes had inhabited "The Rocks", and who waited for custom in the bush "public houses". For the Nirvana of intoxication, and to escape for a few weeks from consciousness of a life thrown away, the old hand would surrender a cheque representing the reward of a year or two's work with no more compunction than "a child surrendering a sovereign for a coveted handful of sweets".[1] What escape was there when they were paid by cheque? Seamen at the end of a voyage are at least paid off in coin, and may stand by one another. The pastoral hand, coming in alone, was unable to pay for anything until he had cashed his cheque at the "pub" or store. The moment he showed it, he ticketed himself as worth so much if he could be induced to "melt it down".

Long accustomed to rations, the old hands had no knack of cash payment, no sense of relative values. The warm welcome at the "house of accommodation", however pleasant to their lonely souls, often covered the treachery of "doped" liquor. At a certain shanty in Central Queensland, known as "Billy ——'s Private Cemetery", the publican was asked if there were any chance of getting a couple of "handy men" to take out to a station. "Looking round to the 'bar' end of the 'pub' he pointed to one fellow lying in a drunken sleep. 'You might get that cove in another three days. His cheque is nearly done. He only brought £40 with him. Those other two are good rough carpenters, but they won't be ready for a fortnight yet. They had over two hundred pounds between them when they came in'."[2] The last scene in such a bout would be the publican's refusal to supply more liquor. The cheque, by his reckoning, was duly "melted". And then the victim would depart, thanking "mine host" with tears of maudlin gratitude for his final "gift" of a bottle of rum to see him on the way.

[1] See generally "Bushmen, Publicans and Politics", in *The Pastoral Times*, Deniliquin, 1869 (Mitchell Library).
[2] Nisbet MS. (Mitchell Library), pp. 78 *et seq.* Cf. *Hobler Papers*, vol. v, pp. 29, 34 *et passim.*

Licenses were granted by the Colonial Treasury at £30 per annum, often over the heads of the local bench of magistrates, who were nominally in charge thereof. The calculation whether it would pay to buy one turned, as of course, on the number of work-people in the vicinity. Any station hand who left the neighbourhood without "melting down" his cheque was spoken of by the publican as having done him an unwarranted injury.[1]

To the squatters, the lapses of their men were at the least a constant vexation and impediment; at the worst a source of tragedy. An overseer on Ghinghinda (Queensland), by name Salter, was murdered by a shepherd recovering from a spree for no cause but a few words of rebuke. At Christmas 1848 the manager of Nap Nap (Lower Murrumbidgee) was "shot dead on the shearing floor by one of the shepherds who, upon some slight quarrel in which McKinlay had been only too forbearing, had gone to his hut, loaded a double-barrelled gun, returned and discharged both balls through his heart, at a few feet distance". Nobody interfered with the murderer's escape. All too commonly, attacks by blacks on isolated homesteads were provoked by ill-usage from the station hands. Bosses and men were alike at fault in this, but the criminal element among the "hands" made them a source of added risk.

Station employment was thus in early days primarily a backwater of the tragic stream of transportation. The squatters preferred men "without encumbrances" for the semi-nomadic life when wool-growing was half exploration and all experiment. They cost less in rations. They did not hanker after allotments which might prove the land fit for agriculture and which always led to disputes about "clearskins". They bred no "wild colonials" to be "bush telegraphs" or worse.

[1] "They notice nowadays", wrote C. E. W. Bean, *On the Wool Track* (1910), pp. 205–16, "even in the Far West (of New South Wales) that the new generation of Australians manages to keep its cheque in the country towns, reach Sydney or Melbourne and lose it there." More centralization!

From small settlers' farms along the Hawkesbury or the Hunter, and from the few married couples that found employment on stations came the "currency lads", "natives" or "wild colonials"—"the results of the results of the system". Or were they a new type fashioned by life in a wild, wide land? As early as Macquarie's reign they were spoken of as a new type, tall, loose-limbed, fair, small-featured and, though strong, less athletic-looking than Englishmen of the upper classes. None denied their versatility with horses or on ship-board. In truth these children of the First-Eleeters were reverting in a healthier environment to "the type of which their parents were debased examples". John McArthur's shrewd eye sized up their active, intelligent ways. "They will be enterprising whenever a proper field is opened to their industry. At present many of them have but little instruction and their future prospects are very confined."

For twenty years after his death (1834) their prospects remained confined. Born in the worst period of New South Wales or in Van Diemen's Land, they laboured, a contemporary noted, "under the disadvantage of having seen a larger proportion of questionable morality than do the children of our peasantry at home". Yet many a record stands of touching devotion to their education by expiree parents. There was need of it. In the late 'sixties, the Riverina, one of the first occupied squatting areas, had 20,000 people scattered over 150,000 square miles with "scarce a dozen schools and certainly not a dozen clergymen".

The lithe horsemanship of the young "natives", thoroughly at home in the bush, fitted them for more active tasks than shepherding. They were the drovers, bullock-drivers and horse-breakers. As shearers they were hard, fast workers when they liked, but quarrelsome. Not specially addicted to liquor, they were fond of horse-racing, card-games and dancing. After roving awhile, they would marry and settle in their native districts, but their "innate Bedouinism" came out in a sympathy for bush-rangers and skill in "sweating" a horse. They resented the police as enforcers of a code never their own. The more worthy their parents, the less likely were they to remain in districts where their children's chances were so small. But though settled on a coastal farm, the married "native" would still turn up on the runs at shearing time, and shearers were early noted as a class intent on a good cheque which they knew how to carry past the publican. Having homes, they knew the value of money.

The puzzles among station hands were the "new chums", "limejuicers" or "Johnny Newcomes"—awkward immigrants from specialized England, serving a hard apprenticeship to the rough parts of the work as contractors' mates or as sheep-washers. They liked jobs at weekly wages, and though as a class they were neither loafers nor dissipated, every lapse at a bush shanty made self-respect harder to retain. Many sought the towns in disgust; others "escaped to New Zealand and a kindlier folk".

When transportation had ceased, but before Caroline Chisholm had humanized country life by promoting the immigration of families and by mothering the single girls, pastoralists were growing restive at the "dangerous demoralization" of station labour. A magistrate in the Bacchus Marsh area notes in his diary, 17 September 1849, "Mr Labilliere called to ask for warrants for the apprehension of two of his servants who have absconded without cause or notice. The rascals only hired just to get through their time until shearing came on. I issued warrants, and if I have the handling of the scamps they shall spend the shearing season in the body of Her Majesty's Gaol....It will take a great many more immigrants to force upon these scoundrels the practice of propriety or common honesty.. .To pay such fellows high wages the whole of the proprietary of the country has been sorely pinched for years past".[1]

[1] *Hobler Papers* (Mitchell Library), vol. v, p. 125. Cf. L. Thomas, *Development of the Labour Movement*, 1788–1848, ch. v.

Far more hands were employed on a run in shepherding days than now. A shepherd was expected to look after flocks gradually increased from 300 at Camden Park to 1500 or more on Queensland stations; his annual wage was £25 or less in bad times. Rations in pre-gold days cost a squatter at most another £12 10s. A hut-keeper's wage was from £18 to £20; sometimes, where flocks were small on hilly country, one hut-keeper served for two shepherds. Thus the prime cost of running sheep might be as low as 1s. per annum.[1] Then there were sheep-washing and shearing costs. Men were paid a pound a week and a full ration for washing 700 sheep a day.[2] The work was thought to be done at reasonable cost when over 5000 sheep and 300 lambs were washed in October 1849 at a total expenditure on wages and rations of £14 10s.; that is about two-thirds of a penny per sheep. The customary wage for shearing was 3s. a score, but a total shearing cost of 4d. a sheep wrung from its recorder a wail that "we are working and scheming, employing capital and time just to fill the pockets of insolent scoundrels who thereby enrich blackguard publicans, often of their own class. The state of the country is hopeless, unless wages are much reduced".

Any money wages, whether well or ill spent, seemed high to pastoralists who had run their stations with assigned servants paid by "truck" through the station store.[3] In 1835, when such labour was still plentiful, Captain Sturt estimated that a sum of £2814 invested in wool-growing would amount after five years to £9845, after paying 7½ per cent. all through. The price of wool was high at the time. New South Wales wool brought

---

[1] This allows no profit on the extras issued from the store to the men.

[2] For a description of the method of "creek-washing" see *Macarthur Records*, pp. 442–7. On most stations extra labour was needed at lambing, concerning which see Nisbet MS. (Mitchell Library), p. 18, and E. Shann, *Cattle Chosen*, p. 179.

[3] As to the prevalence and effects of the "truck system" see T. A. Coghlan, *op. cit.* pp. 207–8, and pp. 430–1. Cf. article on "Industrial Law", by F. A. A. Russell, *Australian Encyclopaedia*, vol. i, p. 662.

from 2s. to 3s. 6d. per pound in London in the early 'twenties, and the island fleeces, which were better sorted, somewhat more. The abolition of the preferential duty caused a temporary decline after 1825, but best fleeces were bringing between 2s. and 3s. a pound in 1829, and inferior greasy fleeces as low as 6d. Prices rose in the 'thirties, but fell heavily in the bad times after 1840, recovering to an all-round average of 11½d. in 1844, 14d. in 1845 and 15d. in 1846, and weakening to 13d. in 1848 and 10½d. in 1849. To meet the fall in values, wages were cut and flocks increased in size, but what helped most was a rising yield per sheep. Averages are not full evidence of this, for they include the flocks of the unsuccessful with those of the profit-makers. Though John McArthur cut 2 lb. 7 oz. per sheep in 1820, the average then was only 1¼ lb. By 1828 it was 1½ lb., in 1835 it was 1¾ lb., and in 1839 2¼ lb. and almost 3½ lb. in Van Diemen's Land.[1] In the 'twenties, high freights and port charges made the export of any but best fleece wool unprofitable, but by 1836 freight to London or Liverpool might be had for 1½d. or even a penny a pound.[2] At such charges it paid to send the skirtings as well as the fleece.

Nevertheless, the labour problem of the late 'forties perturbed squatters who had been used to the old system. By 1848 there were no convicts in private employ on the mainland, and, although immigrants filled the places deserted by expirees, they all asked for and obtained wages, though few could long endure the isolation of the bush. The squatters of Port Phillip, the most prosperous employers at this time, formed associations to bring over time-expired convicts from Van Diemen's Land; even these stood out for £20 a year. In 1845 and the following three years, several shiploads of "exiles" who had been

[1] See T. A. Coghlan, *Labour and Industry in Australia*, vol. 1, pp. 254-5. These are apparently creek-washed weights not comparable with the scoured weights of to-day, being somewhat higher.
[2] Cf. C. R. Fay, *Great Britain from Adam Smith to the present day*, pp. 152, 157, as to falling port dues after 1825.

taught trades in English prisons were sent out and set free on condition that they did not return to England during their sentences. They were employed, usually as shepherds, until it was found that the squatters had no means of preventing their drifting into the towns. Thereafter, all classes united to stop the transportation of such "Pentonvillains". Chinese were tried, but those brought were from Southern China and could not stand the shepherd's lot in the Victorian winter.

It was the gold discoveries, however, which caused such a labour shortage that entirely new methods of running sheep became imperative. When towns swelled into cities calling urgently for wages-men at high rates of pay under sociable conditions of work, the abundance of cheap station labour was gone for ever. At the first news of gold, before the occurrence and size of the deposits could be gauged, Governor Fitzroy expected a glutting of the labour market by the rush of voluntary immigrants, most of whom he thought doomed to disappointment. The assistance of migration by grants from the land revenue was dropped. But as finds of fabulous riches succeeded one another in Victoria, the difficulty of manning the stations and shearing the sheep grew acute. The cessation of assistance to immigrants was countermanded. New South Wales, shorn of its rich Port Phillip District and bereft of its most vigorous sons by the rush to its own and the Victorian diggings, was hard put to it to maintain the staple industry. Wages rose to unheard-of levels, especially in districts near the Victorian border. In 1854 shepherds were asking £40 a year with rations, and farm labourers £50; while in Sydney carpenters were getting as much as a pound a day, and masons and plasterers 30s., when employed on the urgent tasks of building houses and business premises for the swelling population.

These, and the even higher rates paid in Melbourne, were not to last; only skilled tradesmen could command the high day-wages. And the advance in station wages was largely covered by the increased value of wool, which rose to 13·3*d*. in 1853 and 17·7*d*. in 1854, and by the keen demand for butcher's meat at high prices. Yet the sheep-men felt the threat of a new restlessness; their men had become unwilling to engage for long terms. Why, indeed, should a shepherd tie himself to the dullest servitude with El Dorado a few score miles away, and nuggets as big as eggs or footballs awaiting a lucky blow by the first-comer's pick? The contrast between the monotony of station employment and the roaring life of the diggers' camps makes intelligible the renewal of restlessness among the "hands" at every word of a new find. One need hardly go beyond that contrast to see how gold accentuated the harsh relations between squatters and labour, and the Australian antipathy to regular pastoral employment. A general exodus from the stations released from its baleful associations all who by hook or crook could gain a living in the mining camps and port towns. The number of "shepherds and persons engaged in the management of sheep" fell, it is estimated,[1] from 27,000 in 1851 to about 20,000 in 1856, in spite of considerable recruiting of assisted immigrants.

For several years the pastoral industry barely held to its pre-gold size. With the aid of immigrants, of aborigines, and of the dulled and unenterprising remnant who would not or could not break away from old ways, sheep were somehow shorn; they could not be washed, so the wool was sent home in the grease. Great numbers of stock were sold as butcher's meat to the new populations on the "fields"; this occasioned a steady shifting of sheep and cattle into Victoria. Yet the total of flocks there declined during the period 1851 to 1861. There was no great increase in the total number of sheep in Australia, though seasons were not unfavourable. In 1851 there had been 17,450,000 in all the colonies. By 1861, when the stations were again employing as many men as "before the gold",

---

[1] By T. A. Coghlan, in *Labour and Industry in Australia*, p. 680.

and flocks were again increasing fast, the total was less than 21,000,000.

The limiting factor throughout the decade had been labour. In 1856 one person was employed per 950 sheep: the quota in 1851 had been one per 650. In South Australia, from which the exodus had been almost general, each shepherd was tending in 1856 an average of 2500 sheep. Such tending was so near to a formality that the question pressed whether the shepherd might not be eliminated altogether. John McArthur, in his experimental way, had tried leaving sheep out in the open, but the wet climate of the coast gave them foot-rot, catarrh and other ills. The dingo, too, was very prevalent there in his day, and given to worrying and killing sheep for sheer love of hunting or mischief. In the drier interior, now the main and almost the only scene of Australian sheep runs, many an anxious squatter had noted that little harm befell sheep left out at night by careless shepherds, so long as the wild dogs were absent. In the late 'fifties, Victorian squatters, especially those who had attained the security of freehold, began under the pressure of the labour shortage to fence their holdings. Increasing population made the extermination of the dingoes practicable, and there were manifold gains to be made and only one danger to be feared in fencing the runs into paddocks. They had found out Australia's greatest advantage in the raising of sheep and wool. It is the one wide area where sheep can safely be left to run wild for months on end.

The gains by fencing were such that it quickly repaid those who could face the heavy initial cost. Primarily it did away with the crabbed old shepherds. Fewer men[1] of a more dependable type, the mounted boundary-riders, took their place. Often they found their own horses and

---

[1] Earl of Belmore to Duke of Buckingham, 12 August 1868. "The reduction caused by fencing in the number of persons employed permanently upon a run may be estimated at 80 per cent." In an Appendix to the Nisbet MSS. Gregson estimates the reduction at 10 per cent. only.

saddlery. Married men, in Victoria and the central division of New South Wales at least, would keep a cow and cultivate a garden. The effects of the change upon the sheep were even more important and proved to be cumulative. Not being daily driven back and forth over the dusty and bare area extending hundreds of yards around each folding-place, they were less parched and worried. Hence they produced better grown fleeces, and there was no imperative need to wash them before shearing. Merinos are by no means as gregarious as most breeds, and when left to camp or roam, they did not destroy the herbage nor waste their energies needlessly.

The one danger was that of increased losses by fire. "When the flocks were shepherded the area grazed was kept tolerably short and within considerable radius of the stations there was but little grass to burn. In any case the stock were under safe and handy control. In the wide and spacious paddocks, however, the sheep were anywhere and everywhere. In good seasons there was an abundant coat of grass over all the run, not fed bare in any place particularly, so that there was little protection against fire for either run or sheep."[1] The danger was greatest in the grassy plains of the Victorian River valleys, in the Riverina District between the Murray and Murrumbidgee, on the Western Slopes and the Queensland Downs. The mountain pastures were moister and in the mulga country out west the bushes and dwarf trees which provide the "top feed" are usually too wide apart to let a fire travel. The menace of fire in the best sheep country, however, taught every good bushman to smother the embers of his camp-fire before breaking camp, and made safety matches which "strike only on the box" preferable to the older wax vestas. That one danger among the many economies due to fencing led the squatters to view without regrets the thinner spreading of the country population when shepherding declined.

[1] Nisbet MSS. (Mitchell Library), "Notes on Fencing" by J. Gregson.

Different kinds of fence were used according to the materials to hand. Log fences helped to pack away much dead timber in the ring-barked country. In open forest many a hundred miles of post-and-rail fences were put up by the ex-diggers who, when alluvial gold became scarce, took fencing contracts rather than don the blue overalls of miners on wages. All through the plains wire-fencing was the rule. The ex-diggers won the admiration of the squatters by their energy, the pride that would not accept sundowners' meals without payment, and their relative success in refusing to be "lambed down" at bush shanties. They fenced paddocks which grew larger and larger as the carrying capacity grew lighter "out-back"— where paddocks of 20 or 40 thousand acres are not rare. Then they went on their way. While they fenced, little out-back towns were busy handling fencing materials and stores. Sleep deeper than ever came upon Dandaloo and Nevertire when the fencers went farther north.

Developed in Victoria during the late 'fifties, the new method became at once the vogue where wages were highest, spread through New South Wales in the 'sixties and to Queensland in the 'seventies. The isolated and poverty-bound Western Australians began log-fencing in their timber-covered land during the late 'eighties, and are still busy wire-netting against dogs in the mulga country where miners' curs have mated with and strengthened the native dingoes.

The pastoral industry owes much, however, to that same Australian dingo. It is proverbial among the boundary riders that a good dog is equal to three men; and you may see under the verandah of the "store" in any out-back Australian town a type of dog, lean, smooth-haired, prick-eared, ill at ease because of the folk about, watching eagerly for its master. That is the kelpie, a breed which dates back at most to the eighteen-sixties, but one so fashioned to the conditions of "the wool track" that it saves the squatter as much labour as his most expensive

fences, and provides the boundary-rider with his favourite
subject of conversation, when he has any. With small flocks
constantly "worked" the collie served, but out on the great
plains he has neither the stamina nor the habits required.
"No day is too hot, or cold, or long for the kelpie. Endowed with muscles of steel and a coat that defies all
weathers, he finds it all the same whether the heat be
110° in the shade or the biting winds and sleeting rains
are sweeping across the plains and chilling the larger stock
to the bone. Away on either wing, far enough out for the
wild merino sheep not to take fright and so split in all
directions, he gallops with his long tireless stride; or when
his wisdom tells him that they need it, stops and stands
like a statue facing them, then drops to the ground for a
space and creeps towards them like a dingo stalking game
till they turn and go the way he wishes.... The one thing
that can upset the kelpie's working is the bindi-eye, a
wretched little three-cornered thorn which grows on the
plains and sticks in his feet; but when this happens the
owner shoes him with little boots of basil, and he goes on
working as usual."[1] Of the four types of kelpie—black-
and-tan, blue, red, and "barb" or black—all owe much
to a Victorian black-and-tan sheep bitch named "Kelpie",
whose appearance and quiet working plainly told of dingo
blood. Among true kelpies, only barbs bark when working
sheep, and they are fitted for cross-breds rather than for
the wilder Merinos. The original barb was so called after
the black horse called "The Barb" that won the Melbourne
Cup the year he was born (1866) near Forbes, out of
Sally, one of Kelpie II's pups. But the sheep men are not
as proud nowadays of their dogs' pedigrees as they might
be with advantage.

Prices of New South Wales wool ruled high in the 'sixties,
twice averaging over 19*d.* a pound in the grease, and only

---

[1] R. L. Kaleski, *Australian Encyclopaedia*, vol. II, p. 452, whose charming
article the reader should consult for the steps by which the kelpie breed
was evolved, and also the Australian cattle dog.

twice below 16*d*. prior to 1869 when they fell to 12·9*d*. and to 9·9*d*. during the Franco-Prussian War. After a sharp recovery in 1872–3 they steadied at about 12*d*. a pound during the decade from 1876 to 1885. Victorian greasy wool brought a few pence more in most seasons. The lower level after 1873 may be attributed in part to a higher demand for gold by Europe which was turning monometallic. Men gave more goods for a unit of gold and thus all prices stated in gold trended downwards, especially as gold production decreased. A special cause of lower wool values was the continued increase in the production of wool on fenced stations and on the backs of better-bred sheep.

An indirect benefit of "paddocking" was that run-owners had more time and money to apply to the improvement of their flocks. The average weight of the fleeces cut in New South Wales rose to 5 lb. 7 oz. in the grease or 2 lb. 9½ oz. scoured in 1880, and to 5 lb. 11¾ oz. in grease or 3 lb. 4½ oz. scoured in 1890. As the number of sheep in the colony also rose from 6,119,163 in 1860 to over 35,000,000 in 1880 and nearly 56,000,000 in 1890, the amount of wool coming on the market was large enough to test its powers of absorption even though new countries were sending their buyers to London and, as communications improved, to the showrooms of Melbourne and Sydney too. So squatters turned on their "account sales" the same critical scepticism which had served them well when they reshaped Spanish and German methods of running sheep, and cut their own costs to the minimum by fencing. They began to scrutinise the charges made for brokerage, tare and draft, entry and warrants, commission et cetera.

At first the "pure merinos" had followed John McArthur's example in sending their wool to be auctioned by London selling brokers. At Garroway's in Change Alley, Cornhill—the very coffee-house from which Mr Pickwick sent Mrs Bardell that compromising letter about chops and tomato sauce—Australian, Saxon and Spanish wools were sold a lot at a time, "at per lb., bids to advance one penny". The daily session lasted while an inch of candle burned.[1] After 1835, however, the increased scale of the consignments from New South Wales and Van Diemen's Land led to regular auctions at the Royal Exchange to which Germans came to buy rather than to sell. The London selling brokers, by pamphlet, by word of mouth to home-visiting squatters, and by letter, did much to teach their clients nicety in the arts of washing, pressing and sorting the clip.[2] Washing, if overdone, gave the wool a harsh and staring appearance—it was better to have too much yolk than too little. Too tight a pressing with the screw matted together all parts of the fleece so that it required a man's force to separate one from another in the bale and produced a noise like the tearing of coarse linen. "With the chance of having this market to yourselves you Australians should be doubly careful in getting up wool....Some of the fine marks have acquired a preference with buyers principally from the various qualities and descriptions being kept by themselves."[3]

The brokers were certainly capable schoolmasters on the "get-up" of the clip, but were they as effective in securing for the grower its full market value? When the novelty of Australian wool had worn off and the quantity had increased, there were signs that it was not bringing the best price by public auction. Bales bought in at Garroway's and sold privately made an advance on several occasions, once of no less than 20 per cent. Squatters asked indignantly whether the opinion prevailed among buyers that Botany Bay wool-growers wanted money and must

---

[1] See *Macarthur Records*, p. 440, for a facsimile of an 1821 Catalogue.
[2] See letters from James and John Macarthur junior in chapter XII of the *Macarthur Records*: J. W. McLaren to Frew Bros. Adelaide, 19 September 1843, Frew Papers (Mitchell Library), and T. Southey's *Observations addressed to the Wool-growers of Australia and Tasmania*, 1831.
[3] J. W. McLaren to Frew Bros. 19 September 1843.

sell at once? Those in that unhappy position might be bound to sell their wool through local merchants as a condition of obtaining stores on credit.[1] As early as 1823, Sydney commercial houses were purchasing and consigning wool to London. But the "pure merinos" knew too much of the tradition of the New South Wales Corps to sell through such intermediaries. For a generation they bore with the London brokers, despite their qualms. In the 'fifties the time involved in a journey to London grew less. The clippers attracted by the gold rushes took only half the hundred and forty days reckoned usual with the old frigate-built Indiamen.[2] Squatters, visiting "home" more easily, began to look more closely into the customs of the London brokers.

The more prominent of the brokers were joined in an association styled "The New South Wales and Van Diemen's Land Commercial Association". Its members, so a band of inquiring pastoralists reported, had made it their study, by deliberations and conferences, to acquire an intimate knowledge of every matter of importance affecting wool, and to continue to act in protection of the permanent interests of the entire trade. The inquiring squatters were evidently dubious of the brokers' qualifications for their high calling. "It may not be out of place", they commented drily, "to observe that the association's unremitting and valuable services to the flockowner might

---

[1] *Hobler Papers*, vol. vi, pp. 147–9, 27 April 1849. "Watson and Wight to my great relief were disposed to give me the assistance I required upon the pledge of my shipping my wool through their house and melting my stock at their establishment; I to pay 2½ per cent. for their endorsement to bills and 5 per cent. (per four months) for cash they might be called upon to advance." Cf. Nisbet MS. (Mitchell Library): "The biggest handicap to the pioneer settlers was the rate of interest that they had to pay on the money they had to borrow in order to carry on....I found a friend of mine, who was a capital manager and judge of stock but no book-keeper, was paying 17½ per cent. in addition to the obligation of getting all his stores from the same firm at their own prices".

[2] The 'Thermopylae', of George Thompson's Aberdeen White Star Line, ran from Start Point to Melbourne in 63 days 17 hours. In 1852 came the P. & O. steamer 'Chusan'.

acquire a readier recognition if its proceedings were better known, and a larger body of importers enrolled among its members ".[1] Shortly afterwards the association changed its name to "The Colonial Wool Merchants' Association", but it remained an alliance of selling brokers. Manufacturers and growers were excluded. Its customs forbade bids of less than a half-penny, and the disclosure of the successful bidder's name. Much wool, it was suspected, was knocked down to the selling broker's own employees, and manufacturers might obtain wool only through buying brokers or wool-staplers.

Warehousing methods, too, came in for criticism. A Riverina pastoralist who insisted on seeing his Booligal clip weighed into the warehouse in London found an increase on its colonial weight of no less than 5298 lb. for the 938 bales, worth 2s. 4d. a pound in London. Hitherto this increase in weight had been masked by wasteful sampling and unchecked weighing, so that London firms, it was said, picked up their office expenses off the warehouse floors. When the associated brokers stiffly refused, however, to modify their customs at the instance of the colonial pastoralists, many of these turned to the local wool sales in Sydney and Melbourne.

Local sales had sprung from small beginnings. Yorkshire buyers had early scented the big profits that were being made by buying small lots of wool direct from the growers. P. B. Whitfield, an expert wool-buyer, was sent out to Sydney to sell a station and remit the proceeds in the form of wool; finding the operation lucrative, he remained in the land. Another, James Johnson, landed in Sydney in 1838 and at his death in 1906 was worth £216,000.

Wool might reach the coastal ports at any time throughout the year. A bullock team seldom averaged more than twelve miles a day, and rains might make the black-soil

[1] *Report of Committee on Sales of Australian Wools in London*, February 1870.

plains impassable for weeks at a time. There were no telegraphs till the 'sixties nor railways beyond the coastal areas until later. As soon as word came of bullock-waggons toiling in with wool, the cash-buyers rode out to "Jack Ireland's Corner", at the junction of the Parramatta and Liverpool roads, or to "Bark Huts" on the way to Liverpool. Having satisfied the owner-driver that his accoster was not a bushranger—though the distinction seems to have been a conventional one—the buyer would clamber on the waggon and slash the bales to inspect them, the owner pretending utter indifference and refusing the first offer as of course. An atmosphere more favourable to business might be reached in the bar-parlour of the "Farmer's Home", "The Woolpack", "The Emu Inn", or the "Square and Compass", while the working bullocks were being watered at the Haymarket waterhole. What margins the buyers could allow themselves in this unequal contest may be gathered from Johnson's avowal that in one fortunate run of prices he obtained at least double in London what he had paid in Sydney for each and all of 8000 bales, with the solitary exception of one lot for which he paid 6d. and received only 10d. in return.

After 1843, however, this wayside selling was superseded by local auction of small graziers' clips. An auctioneer named Thomas Sutcliffe Mort began to include bales of wool in his weekly general sales. His first wool-store, erected by the Tank Stream in 1844, was a primitive affair without walls or gates—just an iron roof, a single-bale weighing scales, and a dump. But small growers found they secured better prices there than at the Belmore inn-tables. Yet Sydney remained "a delightful antediluvian hollow" during the dècades when the colony's best men were going north to the Darling Downs and beyond, or south to the Riverina and Port Phillip. Richard Goldsbrough, a wool-classer from Shipley in the West Riding, bettered Mort's example by erecting at Melbourne stores on a scale undreamt of before in Australia. His were the first properly lighted floors, and in the thirty years after 1848 he spent over £100,000 on show-rooms and warehouses. In this, as in much else, Sydney was for a time eclipsed by her wealthy southern rival.

When in the 'seventies the big squatters began to favour local sales, Mort was still holding his weekly auctions in a low two-storied building by Circular Quay. At the door a small boy would jangle a bell for half an hour before the sale began. The bidding went on in relative silence, save for the auctioneer's eloquent exposition on the virtues of each lot. By nods, winks and raisings of their pencils, the buyers sought to bid without disclosing any keenness. An old-timer from their ranks, returning after many years of retirement to witness a modern sale, shook his head at the babel of tongues. "They make more noise, but we made more money!" As wool came to market at all seasons, buyers lived on the spot, and their ways were leisurely. Perhaps a buyer would ask the auctioneer to stop a moment, while he went down to have another look at the bales, set out on the ground-floor. The request would always be granted; it put spirit into the subsequent bidding. Or the auctioneer would appeal to the owner as to the acceptability of the price offered, a practice which once drew from a purple-faced grazier the stammering outburst, "Don't you dare sell my...wool for sevenpence. Don't you dare!"

Another oft-quoted *contretemps* was the occasion when the wool-buyers' chairman demanded in market overt the withdrawal of a lot of wool which had been found to contain rubbish in the middle of the bales, and called for the name of its owner. The auctioneer's finger pointing out a prominent Legislative Councillor "did much to forward the cause of honest packing".[1]

Thus by an incessant elimination of waste and wasters

[1] Many of these details are from a series of articles on "The Romance of Wool-Selling" by R. J. W. in the Sydney *Daily Telegraph*, Sept.–Nov. 1914.

the Australian pastoral industry kept up its competitive efficiency. The full adjustment of the scene and method of marketing to the world-wide demand for Australian wool came later. As Britain's manufacturing leadership passed, wool-buyers of all nations sought the local wool-sales.

CHAPTER IX

Free Colonies and Assisted Migration

UNTIL the eighteen-twenties the Governors had been the "prime-movers" in the economic as well as the political affairs of New South Wales and Van Diemen's Land. The price which Britain paid for the clearing of her gaols was largely left to their discretion. Macquarie, for instance, pursued for a decade policies of which his superiors increasingly disapproved. Yet even Macquarie could only postpone, he could not set aside the veto of a distant oligarchy upon extensions of vice-regal expenditure. If it were burked for a time, the call from Whitehall for greater economy became all the more emphatic when unmuffled. Under Governor Brisbane there was such retrenchment in the public employment of convicts that soon not a road in New South Wales remained in repair, even by the rough standards then prevailing.

Britain no longer needed to pay for convicts' keep while constructing public works. The squatters had become eager for their assigned service on the inland "runs", and until assignment ceased in 1839 the supply of convicts seldom exceeded even momentarily the call for station hands. Wool had made the squatters freer paymasters, in the sense that their doings were subject to no ministerial veto. In the mass they were also paymasters of more labour than Governor Macquarie had ever employed.[1]

Though the assigned servants were bondsmen, the way was plainly opening by which the prison settlements would become colonies of free men. The changed status of the leading free colonists was politically recognized by

[1] See generally on the convict population at this time Samuel Butler's *Handbook for Australian Emigrants* (1839), ch. III.

the institution in 1823 of a Legislative Council to which seven and, after 1825, fifteen of them were summoned to advise the Governor. The first step in the political education of substantial householders followed in 1824, when trial by jury was at last substituted for the semi-military procedure of earlier days.

Restriction and free enterprize are always hard to mix. The essentials of prison life as then understood were confinement and close supervision; these were maintained with difficulty when New South Wales and Van Diemen's Land were no more than open, isolated prisons. But the comings and goings of busy wool-ports were quite incompatible with such discipline. Brisbane sent Surveyor-General John Oxley to spy out new sites for the main prison. In 1823 Oxley picked upon Moreton Bay, named the fine river there after the Governor and supervised the founding of a new penal settlement under Captain Logan, the perfect martinet.[1] In England, however, other counsels prevailed. After a period of limited continuance in Van Diemen's Land and Norfolk Island to 1853, and then in Western Australia from 1851 to 1867, transportation was abandoned as inconsistent with the healthy growth of free communities. Between Bigge's Reports of 1823 and that of the Commons Committee in 1839 Australia passed from the eighteenth century into the nineteenth.

Many currents mingled and eddied at the turn of the tide. At Westminster the ruling aristocracy's ambition to hold imperial sway, though chastened by the loss of the American colonies, was swelled afresh by the aggressive philanthropy of the middle class. Industrial triumphs were giving a new dimension to British trade and the middle class felt itself called to spread civilization—some according to the evangelical gospel, some according to the principles of political economy—through all lands and climates. This new social and political partnership at Westminster made

---

[1] Concerning his labours and tragic death compare the accounts given by T. A. Coghlan, *op. cit.* p. 156 and the *Australian Encyclopaedia*, vol. 1, p. 762.

practicable experiments in free colonization with land grants at the Swan River and in systematic free colonization around Adelaide. It also made possible the rapid success of the anti-transportation movement, the clumsy essays in state-aided migration, the maternal crusading of Caroline Chisholm and, finally, whether as a gesture of despair or as a daring venture of faith, the grant of colonial self-government.

The new prosperity based on wool put a speedy stop to free land grants. Both bases of that system—the grant of areas proportioned to social standing and the payment of quit-rents to the Crown after a few years of development—had long been crumbling. The plan had fitted the phase of experiment, when the climate was a riddle and the land had no ascertained value, no proved utility in production. But once free settlers came out in force, eager to take up sheep runs, the grant and withdrawal of land at the will of the Governor had become an anachronism. In a colony sure of its future, investors of capital asked for security of possession as the *sine qua non*. The change was registered by the waiving in 1825 of the Governor's "permission to settle", previously essential to free settlers as well as expirees. With it went the Governor's power to "huff" a man's land, which Macquarie had freely used against grantees guilty of insobriety and even at the expense of some who petitioned the House of Commons against him.[1] Oxley suggested the sale of any area in excess of 2000 acres which a settler might require. Combinations of free grant and sale were tried, but naturally led to very few sales. Land grants were finally abolished in 1831.

The years of transition witnessed the coming not only of scores of individual capitalists but of more than one great joint-stock company. These ventures, recalling seventeenth and eighteenth century methods of colonization, aimed at exploiting John McArthur's discoveries on bold

[1] See Macquarie MSS. (Mitchell Library), "List of Grants cancelled through Seditious Conduct".

lines. They did notable work in exploring difficult country, both in New South Wales and in N.W. Tasmania. They opened up a coal trade; they introduced Saxon and Spanish sheep of the highest quality. According to a French contemporary, Pilorgerie, the "gigantic enterprise of the Australian Agricultural Company", which expended £300,000 in the northern area of New South Wales, "awakened public attention and directed it towards Australia". But privileged companies, exonerated from quit-rents on their huge estates because they relieved the public of the expense of maintaining thousands of convicts, sorted ill with the doctrines of natural liberty and equal opportunity—at least for those with property—which Adam Smith had popularized. Nor did their resemblance to the East India Company help them with British middle-class or Australian opinion.[1]

Philanthropists were critical of the assignment of convicts and of transportation generally. Wilberforce's long crusade against negro slavery was soon to be followed by a sharp and decisive attack on the export of criminals. Thus it fell out that the last company projects, those of the Swan River Colony and South Australia, ended in an odd mixture of private adventure and public responsibility. As fields for investment they suffered by this confusion of ideals, yet the delayed success of the latter province showed the way to free colonization and sowed the seed of self-government, though not in the drilled and systematic lines its projectors first planned.

In April 1827 Governor Darling appealed for a permanent settlement on the Swan River. Glowing accounts of the fertile soil there had come from Captain Stirling,

---

[1] For accounts of the two principal companies, the Australian Agricultural Company and the Van Diemen's Land Company, see Stephen Roberts, *History of Australian Land Settlement*, ch. vi and Appendices i and ii. Professor Roberts' acceptance of Jorgensen's claims to have forestalled Hellyer, the V.D.L. Co.'s surveyor, in discovering the Surrey Hills in N.W. Tasmania, is adversely criticized by Mr A. L. Meston in his paper before the A.A.A.S. 1928, on "The Work of the V.D.L. Co. in Land Settlement".

R.N., who visited it after revictualling a military post under Major Lockyer sent in 1826 to guard King George's Sound against French occupation. The Colonial Office, at first favourable, drew back in fear of the expense of founding a free colony. In November 1828 a syndicate, including Thomas Peel, Sir Francis Vincent, Colonel Potter McQueen and E. W. H. Schenley, offered to settle 10,000 persons there and to provision them for four years if granted land at 1s. 6d. an acre in return for their expenditure. This they estimated at £300,000 and they asked for four million acres. They had in mind a proprietary colony like Pennsylvania. To set the ball of production rolling they planned to give each male settler 200 acres out of their grant. The balance they would sell as production gathered momentum and the demand for more land grew.

The Colonial Office virtually destroyed their project, first by limiting the grant to a maximum of one million acres, and then by issuing regulations (December 1828) which threw open to everyone the whole area of the colony. Not only the projectors, but any who brought out property for the occupation and development of the land, were to receive 40 acres for every £3 thus invested. Grants proportioned to property had long been the rule at Sydney, but the application of such a rule where there was as yet no centre was fatal to the syndicate's plan. It had thought to create such a centre and to draw profit from a monopoly of the land around it. How else could it recoup initial expense? All but Peel saw that this scheme would fail, and withdrew.

The colonists who went out in 1829 included, according to Governor Stirling, "more than the usual number of men of property and family". Both rich and poor expected, from Stirling's account of the soil and vegetation, to find rich loams and succulent native grasses. They looked about for open plains and park-like downs on which to repeat the rapid progress as pastoralists which had so lately fallen to the lot of many in New South Wales. If some "expected the moment their feet touched the shore to find inns, turnpike roads, smiling orchards and cornfields in a country untrod by civilized man", this only showed how few can picture the complex, unending drudgery involved in beginning at the beginning—in clearing the virgin forest and building up by faith and toil and sheer fatigue the setting of a good life for others. The officials of Whitehall had not made much progress between 1786 and 1828 in imagining the task.

The first-comers took up the best land they could find along the coastal rivers—the Swan and the Canning, the Serpentine, the Murray and the Harvey. Little of it was good land, and they went far afield in search of better. Their homesteads were scattered over a coastal plain with few areas of loam, where through the long hot summer land-transport over deep sand tracks is exceptionally arduous. Two defects beat down their high hopes: lack of grassy plains on which to depasture flocks and herds, and lack of labourers. Grasses are markedly absent from the forest floor of the great belt of "mahogany" or jarrah along the escarpment behind the sandy coastal plain. Even where they found grass under the open tuart trees on the limestone hills nearer the Western Coast, the amazing contrast between the dry desolation of summer and the verdure of the wet, mild winter caught them unprepared. The lack of labour was paralysing to middle-class folk accustomed to over-populated England.

Edward Gibbon Wakefield—fixing his attention on the failure of Thomas Peel, who landed 300 settlers, spent £50,000 and quickly reduced himself to beggary and isolation—attributed all these evils to the 1828 regulations, as he, from Newgate Prison, imagined their working. But the picture he painted to a Commons Committee on Waste Lands, though admirable as propaganda for his own system of colonization, slurred over other reasons for Peel's misfortunes. Peel, though a cousin of the great Sir Robert, was no leader. The land was unsuited to sheep and hardly less so to cattle. Poison plants killed scores of stock. Both stock and settlers were speared by blacks. The more experienced farmers, such as the Hentys, after a hurried search for better land, re-emigrated to Van Diemen's Land. The die-hards, facing terrible natural obstacles to pioneering, put up a grim and for long a doubtful struggle. Pastoral production grew very slowly out of explorations that revealed an almost waterless interior.

Wakefield told how the 1828 regulations gave priority to the grantees of immense estates, separated the settlers by "great deserts", condemned some to die of hunger because they did not know where to find the governor's house and food, and the governor to impotence because he did not know where to find his poor subjects. Too long his fancies passed current as an historical account of this "scarecrow of colonization".[1] Wakefield was bred to the trade of a land-agent. In writing about the Swan River Colony he was concerned far less with truth than with a background against which he might depict the harmonies of "systematic colonization", his own panacea.

Success in starting a free colony, he held, depended on selling land at a "sufficient price". Out of the land-sales-fund the immigration of labourers should be subsidized. These, unlike Peel's men, would be impelled to remain in service by their inability to pay for land a price deliberately raised high enough to baulk their land-hunger. Till they had served an apprenticeship in colonial conditions and saved the "sufficient price" of a little farm, these free labourers were to be the "combinable labour" for lack of which the respectable Swan settlers had endured such woes. A colony adopting Wakefield's plan would escape all tribulation. The "sufficient price" would adapt the supply of labour to the supply of land. Land sales—assisted immigration—more sales—more labour, and the

[1] See R. C. Mills's admirable book, *The Colonization of Australia*, 1829-42, pp. 64-72.

thing was done. In truth, it was to be a land-agent's Utopia.

The experiment of a Wakefield colony at Australind, on Koombana Bay, a hundred miles south of the Swan River, should have been decisive in showing the virtues of the "sufficient price". Land there was sold at a pound an acre, surely a "sufficient price". Otherwise the conditions were remarkably similar to those on the Swan. There were labourers in plenty at Australind in 1842, effectually prevented by the "sufficient price" from buying the land—combinable labour or landless proletariat after the best English model.[1] Yet the cycle of land sales and subsidized migration would not revolve. Once the character of the soil and the problem of marketing its produce had been tested, the Australind Company could not dispose of its blocks at 2s. an acre. The land market was glutted in Western Australia; earlier buyers were willing to cut their losses and sell at a farthing an acre.

Such stumbling was perhaps inevitable in a territory of "mottled" soils, like Western Australia. After all the puffing and booming, land values must be based on the net production, a singularly individual fact which varies widely from block to block. The control or fixing of a uniform and sufficient price for all the land in a colony, by a group of gentlemen around a table on the other side of the globe, necessarily imported into its sale the atmosphere of a lottery. And when all the previous numbers had proved to be blanks, the interest of the public in the lottery naturally grew cold. But Australind was an afterthought, a trial of the Wakefield plan in a scene damned in advance by his own propaganda of earlier years.

Wakefield's system for the planting of free colonies dated back to a dismal picture he had sketched in Newgate during 1829 of the plight of well-to-do settlers in New South Wales. On his release in 1830, he set himself

[1] For the story of the Australind Settlement, see Miss E. L. Burgess's paper in the *Report of the 1926 Meeting (Perth) of the A.A.A.S.* pp. 478–96.

to use the growing interest in Australia and the long-standing concern over British unemployment as the bases of an experiment in systematic colonization in an unspoilt field. Free grants of land were not only wasteful now that wool was booming; they were also offensive to the political opponents of privilege. In January 1831 the new Whig Government went half-way towards adopting Wakefield's plan when they abolished grants and substituted sale as the sole means of disposing of colonial land. But by that time 3,344,030 acres had been granted in New South Wales, and 1,200,000 acres at the Swan River. Ricardian principles were in the air and it was presumed that the first-comers had picked the best land there. Wakefield, therefore, behind the screen of propagandists, sought a virgin field where his system of selection, concentration and sale of land for the support of emigration might work unthwarted. The area around St Vincent's Gulf and Encounter Bay—praised by both Flinders and Baudin, remote alike from the iniquities of Sydney and Hobart Town and from the miseries of Swan River—had already attracted him when at the end of 1830 word came that Captain Sturt had traced the great inland rivers to an outlet in that very region. To the enthusiasm Sturt aroused, there ensued, as in the Swan River project, a conflict between plans for a proprietary colony and precautions for public control. Again the Colonial Office stumbled into an incoherent compromise.

In June 1831 Anthony Bacon, a Peninsular and Waterloo veteran, proposed a colony in South Australia that would cost Government nothing. He was to be its Governor. Under-Secretary Hay, with the Swan River on his mind, replied that such schemes were "always liable to end in becoming in some way or other a source of expense to the revenue of this country". Then the Wakefield group put forward proposals for a proprietary company which should quickly transform itself into a self-supporting free colony. The Company was to raise half a million of capital, to spend a quarter of this on buying land in the colony, and another £125,000 on advances to settlers. The other half of its capital it was to employ directly on its own land. A Governor recommended by the Company, but appointed by the Crown, was to have despotic authority until the population reached 5000. When they numbered 5000 and could meet the expenses of their government, they should be allowed annually elected Assemblies, liberty of the press, freedom of trade, no interference with religion, and a militia of all adult males for purposes of defence.

Such ideas seemed to the Colonial Office "wild and impracticable". Prompted by its Counsel, Mr James Stephen, it objected to "transfer to this Company and ultimately to a popular assembly the sovereignty of a vast unexplored territory, and erect within the British Monarchy a government purely republican". Wakefield, blaming the Whig chiefs for the opposition, commented drily: "If the Company should revive their project they would do well to put a House of Lords into it, with a Baron Blackswan, a Viscount Kangaroo, a Marquis of Morrumbidgee, and a Bishop of Ornithorhyncus".

At the end of 1833 Captain Sturt came in person to the aid of the projectors, impressing the value of South Australia and urging that the Murray River navigation must be "the grand attraction of the Scheme". Suspicions of the promoters' money-making designs were smothered by the adoption of a form of government by officials. Thereafter events moved quickly. In 1834 a South Australian Association successfully lobbied through Parliament an Act (4 & 5 W. IV, c. 95) to establish the British Province of South Australia. The crux of the compromise was to be a Board of Commissioners appointed by the Crown to manage land sales and migration on Wakefield's lines.[1] Initial expenses of foundation were to be met out of a loan of £200,000 to be raised on the future revenues of the Province, with the land fund as collateral security.

[1] For a summary of the provisions of the Act see R. C. Mills, *op. cit.* p. 233.

Colonization was to begin after £35,000 worth of land had been sold and £20,000 lodged with the British Government as a guarantee fund. The scheme was weak in that it divided responsibility. Though the Commissioners raised the money for government as well as for migration, the governing officials were not directly responsible to them. It is true that the Commissioners could enforce their views by their control of the purse, but only with a maximum of friction and mutual antagonism.

The ablest of the Commissioners, George Fife Angas, resigned in 1835 to form a South Australian Company. This was a purely private venture, not to be confused with the 1831 project of a proprietary company to found and rule the colony. Angas's Company, with a capital of £320,000, made extensive purchases of land which gave the movement a decisive fillip. He was a man of capacity and imagination, witnessed by his share in founding more than one Australian Bank.[1] At the very start his care included the education of settlers' children, and in 1838 he succeeded in attracting to the new colony over 600 Lutheran zealots. By the end of 1850, 6000 more had followed them. Their descendants have played a very honourable part, especially in the active agriculture of the Province. Few of the colonial leaders, however, equalled Angas in foresight. The officials and resident Commissioner, by wrangling over every step preliminary to the settlers' private exertions, almost brought the settlement to a standstill.

Some officials were energetic and competent, notably Colonel William Light, the Surveyor-General. Others were not, and were distracted from their duties by the leave to trade, which in a spirit of false economy had been granted to eke out small salaries. Arriving in August 1836, only a few weeks in advance of the first fleet of colonists, Light had to choose the site of the first town, to survey it and also

[1] The Union Bank of Australia and the Bank of South Australia, as well as the National Provincial of England.

the country blocks so that the first subscribers might exercise their right of "first choice of land throughout the Colony". Foremost in importance was the decision to be made between (i) the coast of Gulf St Vincent, praised by Flinders, (ii) Port Lincoln, considered by one of Baudin's officers a harbour worthy to rival Port Jackson, and (iii) the Murray Mouth, *prima facie* the key to a great riverine hinterland. To Governor Hindmarsh's surprise he found when he arrived (28 December 1836) that Light had chosen the present site of Adelaide, attracted by a fair harbour and an abundance of fertile open land. Contention raged, but Light's choice was upheld against the Governor and the Company's local representative by a big majority of the settlers, now numbering 600 (Feb. 1837). But his progress in surveying was beset by demands from investors that he should mark out the lots in the first town, Adelaide, before measuring land for farms, and hindered by the preference of the unacclimatized farmers for pockets of good land in the cool Mount Lofty ranges, rather than on the Adelaide plains.

Rapid arrivals of colonists caused the demands for land to accumulate. Light's request for more surveyors, voiced by his deputy G. S. Kingston, drew from the Commissioners nothing but criticisms and absurd instructions to expedite the work.[1] Light resigned, and few of his staff would take service under Kingston. The survey broke down. The would-be-farmers missed the favourable seasons of 1838–9 and 1839–40, when they might well have been able to export wheat to drought-stricken New South Wales. Much capital, badly needed for development, was spent on the import of foodstuffs at high prices. Denied practical use of an evidently fertile territory, the colonists turned to wild speculation in town lots. Governor and Commissioner, still quarrelling, were recalled, and in

---

[1] For some detail of the part played by the incompetent Kingston see A. Grenfell Price, *Foundation and Settlement of South Australia*, pp. 75–8, 85–8. This work supersedes all earlier accounts.

F

October 1838 Colonel George Gawler took charge as both Governor and Resident Commissioner. The population of 3680 had been concentrated all too successfully; they were almost all in Adelaide.

Gawler saved the situation. In place of Kingston, who "left the service to perform duties of equally dubious value as City Engineer",[1] Captain Sturt, who had sold his station at Mittagong in New South Wales and brought cattle overland from the Murray, was set to survey the country lands. A staff was gathered from Light's men, from the eastern colonies, and a belated detachment of sappers. Then the work was retarded and disorganized by some thirty "special surveys", giving big purchasers their pick of 450,000 acres from the unappropriated land. But even this meant progress in the pastoral use of the Province. Overlanders, beginning with Joseph Hawdon (3 April 1838), were rapidly stocking the excellent open pasture lands. By December 1840 there were 4400 people in the country districts, 8000 acres under cultivation, 67,000 cattle and a quarter of a million sheep. More came overland than sheep and cattle. Runaway convicts were of good service as sawyers at a time when building and fencing materials were very scarce, but their turbulent doings in the Mount Lofty Ranges made an inopportune call on the colony's slender funds for extra police.[2]

Perhaps because he knew that Stephen of the Colonial Office expected the collapse of the Commissioners, Gawler went on with free energy to repair the colony's lack of police, roads, harbour and public buildings—"the necessary permanent outfit". In 2½ years he drew on the Commissioners for £270,000 not covered by the colony's revenue. Torrens, their leader, had been inspired by Wakefield to object to the use of the land fund for govern-

---

[1] A. G. Price, *op. cit.* p. 133. Cf. p. 178, for his supervision of the construction of a Government Wharf at Port Adelaide.

[2] See A. G. Price, *op. cit.* p. 130.

mental expenses. It was reserved, somewhat pedantically, for the sending of immigrants. The coming of these in spate constantly forced Gawler into more urgent building. Yet the Commissioners failed to borrow the balance (£120,000) of the loan that had been authorized for first expenses of government such as this. The antinomy between private adventure and public authority inherent in the Foundation Act of 1834 was still unresolved. In December 1839 Lord John Russell replaced the South Australian Commissioners, who had asked him for salaries, by a Colonial Land and Emigration Board which was to manage migration to all British colonies. The change might promise an extension of systematic colonization to all, but what was to be done to relieve the congestion in Adelaide and to meet Governor Gawler's bills?

While this problem was being fumbled at home, there came adverse reports of the South Australian hinterland. It was but a fertile island ringed by salt lakes. The colony's credit slumped. When the new Board tried to raise the balance of the authorized loan not a single subscriber offered. They refused (Sept. 1840) to accept any more of Gawler's bills, ordered him to dismiss the police, and asked the Colonial Office to take up the financial burden. It refused. The colony was bankrupt and remained so until after months of deliberation a Commons Committee recommended government assistance. Gawler was recalled and superseded in May 1841 by Captain George Grey. With much gusto Grey exposed the laxity of Gawler's control of expenditure. He put an end to its demoralizing effects on the labourers who preferred Adelaide to the bush and on the contractors who gaily swindled the distant taxpayers of Britain. Yet Grey insisted on the payment of the bills that had given the colony an effective start, and if his policy of keeping public expense within the colonial revenue was due and salutary, it must be recognised that Gawler had retrieved the land situation, pushed on the surveys and settlement, and left the Province "with all its problems solved save those of unemployment and finance".[1]

In the last resort the Province was saved by the quality of its land and climate, which now enabled the settlers to produce their earliest abundant harvests. Wakefield's system was well adapted to finding funds and launching a colony by well-planned puffing. Such puffing, however, provoked speculation. Raising the sufficient price of land after a specified time only aggravated that phase. Whether the colonists could make good their investment or even survive it depended, of course, upon the quality of the soil chosen. "The calibre of the early settlers", wrote George Grey long after, "gave me trust in the new Anglo-Saxondom of the Southern Hemisphere. There was a worth, a sincerity, a true ring about them which could not fail of great things." Anglo-Saxons in either hemisphere, and possibly others too, are given to emphasizing the human merit behind success. But the same human factor was present at the Swan River and its outposts where success was slower to come.[2] South Australia had the other essential, an endowment of agricultural land needing small initial expense for clearing. Adelaide is within what remains to this day the most uniform and continuous stretch of first-class wheat land in Australia. At the end of 1842 a harvest worth £98,000 was gathered, more than half of which was exported. Such progress made the colonists sure of triumph over temporary straits.

Wheat exports oversea were not very profitable, however, and New South Wales had now escaped from drought. Duties continued to be levied in Britain on Australian wheat, while that of Canada was being admitted free. The price in Adelaide during 1844 fell as low as half-a-crown a bushel.

[1] A. G. Price, *op. cit.* p. 209. See, too, his rehabilitation of Gawler's land policy, pp. 145–6, and works expenditure, pp. 188, 194. Grey's success was built upon what Professor Scott (*Short History of Australia*, p. 151) too strongly terms "Gawler's failure".

[2] For an instance consider the persistence of the Bussells, Turners and others in the face of defeat by the big timber at the Leeuwin, *Cattle Chosen*, *passim*.

Yet wages were maintained and increased by the proving in that year of big deposits of copper ore a little north of the capital town. Copper-mining at once set up a new era of speculation and prosperity. No system of migration nor minimum price for land could keep agricultural labourers from turning miners at high wages on the Burra and Kapunda lodes. But an ingenious young Northumbrian saved the farmers. He greatly reduced the cost of producing grain by inventing, out of a hint from Livy and ancient Gaul, a horse-driven machine that stripped the ears only. Ridley's "stripper" made feasible a profitable export trade in wheat and was a masterstroke in reconciling high wages with low costs. In this it antedated fencing in the pastoral industry by several years.[1]

In South Australia, as subsequently in every colony, mining played a most useful part in attracting colonists. Looking back into the past, a South Australian attempted in 1892 to state a norm of Australian settlement, departure from which had always brought difficulty. "The proper order of events is first pastoral occupation of large areas—practically detailed exploration of new territory: then mining in the all too few localities where minerals exist: then the gradual subdivision and development of the land for higher utilization".[2] Every historical formula carries an insidious suggestion that its phases occur inevitably and automatically. This is not so. Western Australia, for instance, with its minerals in arid country, had to wait long for the miners and for adequate people and wealth to develop her refractory though rich resources. To South Australia the miners early brought their unsystematic but strengthening impetus. As soon as the copper and silver

[1] A. S. Ridley, *A Backward Glance* (1904), collects the evidence as to the origin of Ridley's stripper and its claim to priority over other South Australian attempts at a solution. According to David Gordon, *The Central State*, Ridley's stripper reduced the cost of harvesting from 2s. per bushel to 3½d. or from £2 an acre to 5s. 10d. for a 20 bushel crop.

[2] Quoted by Stephen Roberts, *Land Settlement*, p. 289, from Holder, a South Australian squatter.

ores found in 1843 had been proved, capital and labour flowed again into the Province. Where minerals were known to exist, Governor Grey delayed for the maximum of three months the sale of the "waste lands" containing them in order to ensure active bidding. "A few weeks ago", reported an astonished merchant in May 1845, "a hundred acres of land adjoining a copper mine at work, distant fifty miles from this, was sold at the Government sale for £2201...Adelaide is now obtaining a good name amongst our hitherto jealous neighbours." But private knowledge often ran ahead of government precautions, and two areas of 20,000 acres of metalliferous land were bought at the minimum price of £1 an acre.

Governor Robe, Grey's successor, was baulked in an attempt to secure by royalties a public share in the profits of mining. A legal decision ruled that his insertion of a clause in land-titles, reserving to the Crown a fifteenth of the value of metals won, was inconsistent with the statute governing such titles. And the Legislative Council would not amend the Act. A Land League was formed among leading buyers which kept down competitive bidding and divided by lot what was bought.

The Province steadily gained in population and prosperity. By August 1848 it had 38,666 inhabitants, and an ordinary revenue of £82,411. Land sales since its foundation had totalled £530,877. Western Australia at the same date had about 4600 colonists. The stagnation of trade and production there led this handful of people to petition the Home authorities for convicts, whose employment on roads and public buildings might galvanize trade and improve the means of transport. The grant of their petition and the arrival of the first prisoners at Fremantle in June 1850, though worth a hundred thousand pounds a year of Imperial expenditure, accentuated the contrast between Eastern and Western Australia. For by that date the movement against transportation had in the eastern colonies reached the eve of complete success.

CHAPTER X

From Transportation to Family Life

DURING the eighteen-thirties, Archbishop Whately of Dublin led an effective attack on "the system of transportation".[1] The sending of convicted men and women oversea, he reasoned, neither deterred others from crime nor reformed the criminals, and it hideously contaminated the new communities in Australia. The British public and Parliament, roused by his logic, were left unsatisfied by the apologies of Governor Arthur (V.D.L.) and of Archdeacon Broughton (N.S.W.). A Select Committee of the Commons reported in 1839 "that transportation to New South Wales and to the settled districts of Van Diemen's Land should be discontinued as soon as practicable". They found "inefficacy in deterring from crime and remarkable efficiency in still further corrupting those who undergo the punishment" to be inherent in the system, and inveighed against the "monstrous evil of calling into existence and continually extending societies or the germs of nations most thoroughly depraved".

In Sydney the prospect of abolition at first provoked opposition rather than support. The Legislative Council, representing the squatters and large employers, urged "that the sudden discontinuance of transportation and assignment must necessarily curtail the means of purchasing Crown Lands and consequently the supply of funds for the purposes of immigration". The Secretary of State paid small regard to this special pleading, though he approved Governor Gipps' suggestion to restrict assignment to the

---

[1] The subject-matter of this part of the chapter is more adequately treated in Ernest Scott's *Short History of Australia*, ch. xvii.

country districts, "as a step towards the entire discontinuance of assignment throughout the colony, at as early a period as practicable". More complex must have been the motives of a Sydney public meeting (9 February 1839) which promoted a petition for continuance signed by 4000 people. Sir Timothy Coghlan attributes the petition to an idiosyncrasy of the emancipists which led them to identify their self-respect with the retention of convictism. Vulgarity in a king is said to flatter the majority of his subjects, and a steady supply of criminals may have assured to the emancipists in Sydney a social status often based on ill-gotten wealth. Colonial opinion, however, whether bond or free, played at first a minor part. The initiative came from British humanitarians.

The Order in Council which on 22 May 1840 abolished transportation to New South Wales left Norfolk Island and Van Diemen's Land as "penitentiaries" to which for the future only long-sentence criminals were to be sent. At Norfolk Island, Alexander Maconochie[1] made trial of reformatory methods as opposed to those of exemplary punishment. At Port Arthur and Macquarie Harbour in Van Diemen's Land severity passed the limits of human endurance, often driving warders and victims alike into stark insanity.

Before Peel's reform of the criminal code had had time to bear fruit, 4000 felons were still transported annually from British prisons. "Mr Mother Country" still held it "indispensable that within the Australian colonies receptacles should be found for all the convicts and exiles who may be sent from this country in execution of judicial sentences." This he considered "so momentous an object of national policy that we can acknowledge no conflicting motive as of sufficient importance to supersede it". The fate which the momentous object of national policy implied for the "receptacles" had by 1846 become all too

---

[1] See *Australian Encyclopaedia*, articles on "Convicts", vol. I, pp. 301-2, and on "Maconochie", vol. II, p. 14.

plain in Van Diemen's Land. Apart from emancipists and expirees freed by servitude, there were in the island 29,949 prisoners out of a total population of 66,105. The plan by which, according to their conduct, prisoners were drafted through probation gangs into private employment had broken down. Squatters and farmers, in spite of the working of a sort of Gresham's law that bond labour drives out free, could not find places for the "good-conduct men". Of 10,480 in the probation gangs, 3852 were due for good-conduct passes into private service during the year, but 3509 of the 12,240 already holding such passes were still waiting for masters.

On the mainland the threatened cessation of bond labour led landowners to give ear to the suggestions of the Colonial Office that some of the surplus convicts should be smuggled into New South Wales under a modified "system". W. E. Gladstone, observing the glut of labourers in the island and knowing that the squatters north of Bass Straits were in need of labour, made certain qualified and involved proposals to Governor Gipps.[1] "It will be acceptable to Her Majesty's Government if the members of the Legislative Council of the colony will show a disposition to concur in the opinion that a modified and carefully regulated introduction of convict labourers into New South Wales, or into some part of it, may under the present circumstances be advisable. It seems probable that we may again be approaching a period—if indeed such period has not already arrived—when the supply of free labour in the Australian colonies is on the whole below the demand." A Committee of the Legislative Council, under the chairmanship of William Charles Wentworth, duly reported in favour of the revival of transportation under Gladstonian safeguards (Oct. 1846). There were to be no government gangs and no assignment in the towns. This would placate

[1] The text of the despatch may be read in the *H.R. of A.* series I, vol. xxv, pp. 34–7, or in Coghlan, *op. cit.* pp. 336–40. According to Ernest Scott, *Short History of Australia*, p. 193, Mr Gladstone was a partner in a Port Phillip sheep station.

immigrant labourers and artisans. Both convicts and ticket-of-leave men were to be confined to the country districts. For each male convict a female, free or convict, was to be sent, and as many free migrants as prisoners. Though quietly forwarded to England, the committee's report, when published in Sydney, provoked a strong public outcry against any form of transportation. Colonial opinion had by this time hardened into virtually unanimous opposition to any renewal of the system, and in September 1847 the Council repudiated the work of its committee.

While this was yet unknown in England, Earl Grey, Gladstone's successor, had prescribed a way of diluting the bitter draught. He suggested sending "ticket-of-leave" men as exiles to New South Wales, after they had served the main part of their "times" in British penitentiaries and on public works. Their wives and families would be helped to join them, and free migrants sent in equal numbers. But Earl Grey's plan involved the re-proclamation of New South Wales as a "receptacle" for convicts. The step gave rise to such an explosion of wrath in Sydney and Melbourne that Governor Fitzroy sent the next transports laden with "Pentonvillains" to Moreton Bay (August 1849). Their landing at either of the southern towns would have provoked riots. In all, less than 2000 of these "exiles" had been sent, but in 1850 and 1851 men of all shades of opinion joined the branches of an inter-colonial Anti-Transportation League. In the newly constituted colony of Victoria, where free migrants were dominant, their zeal against convictism was intensified by an ugly inrush of "Vandemonian" expirees and probationers to the gold-diggings. The Victorian Legislative Council passed a bill restricting immigration from Van Diemen's Land to those who could prove their freedom from the taint of penal servitude. It was vetoed by the Crown, but the Colonial Office had already yielded on the main issue. After 1852 no more convict transports were despatched to Tasmania. The squatters of Moreton Bay petitioned more than once for assigned convict servants, but in vain. When in 1859 the new colony of Queensland was created, only a few survivors remained of the penal settlement there.

Within a decade of 1853, when transportation to Eastern Australia ceased, Britain was unable to deliver from her gaols the thousand convicts a year that Western Australia was anxious to see employed on her roads and public works. In part the change was the outcome of Peel's mitigation of the criminal code. With the aid of his new Police he made certainty of detection a better deterrent from crime than savage sentences against the small proportion of criminals who were caught. The wholesale depopulation of Ireland after the potato famine and the new prosperity in Britain that had come with rising gold prices alike relieved the pressure of poverty in the United Kingdom.

Since transportation ceased, Australian governments have often busied themselves with the problems of attracting free migration, but the "ill odour in which government emigration was and is held among the superior class of hard-working men"[1] has been intensified by every successive attempt. Reacting strongly against the "evident selfishness" of the systems propounded by Wakefield and Ben Boyd, the writer just quoted—though conceding that poverty, real or comparative, was, and ought to be, the great recruiter for emigrant ships—stickled at the favourite deception of the emigrant with the notion "that some other country is more pleasant to live in than his own". "All schemes based on a mere desire to get rid of troublesome paupers or to supply rich colonists with cheap servants will fail and always have failed. To be continuous and not spasmodic emigration must be for the benefit of the emigrant." When Sidney wrote, the easy gains to be made on the alluvial diggings offered to many, for a time at least, abundant benefit. Before and since that decade, however,

---

[1] S. Sidney, *The Three Colonies of Australia*, 1852, p. ix.

the man who sought to persuade migrants to venture from Britain to a far land, whence return was difficult, laboured against real difficulties. The dull servitude of agricultural and pastoral labour before gold was discovered was not unknown in Britain. The hardship, the distance and cost of the voyage were great. In the days of transportation the voyage out was counted the worse half of the sentence. During the decade when transportation had ceased and the gold was yet unknown, low passage-money was a necessity for those making the journey in pursuit of the wage-earner's humble standard of life. As soon as the policy of land-sales came into vogue, some of the revenue thus derived had been set aside to pay the passages of free labourers; and so great was the disparity of numbers between the sexes that this category was interpreted as including unmarried women. The excess of men in the colonies certainly suggested that at the Antipodes emigrant women might pursue with some confidence the ambition of matrimony. In 1832 a ship went out with women and children from the charitable institutions of Dublin and Cork. Plans for repayment of passage money worked badly, and after 1835 unmarried women were granted official as well as virtually free passages. Labouring families were assisted by liberal grants. In 1836, however, the poor quality of the migrants gathered by shipping agents anxious only for full government cargoes led New South Wales to send three naval surgeons to select the best applicants. "No females were to be accepted unless they belonged to or accompanied a family group. The men, preferably under thirty years of age and married, were to be one-third agricultural labourers and overseers, two-thirds mechanics." Thus, even before self-government, colonial authorities sought to improve by selection the evil quality of the human material which Britain had first thrust on them.

To some colonists, it is true, selection did not seem necessary. On grounds of expense New South Wales dropped her appointment of special selectors in 1840, and made the new Land and Emigration Commissioners her agents in the matter. "The real objection", thinks Sir Timothy Coghlan, "was that the immigrants, being of a superior type, were disposed to look for higher wages than the settlers were willing to pay, and the married man with a family was apt to seek to 'better himself', whereas the settlers sought to have men who would remain with them permanently." Now that transportation was coming to an end, they wanted shepherds and hut-keepers in addition to the agricultural labourers, overseers and mechanics sought by government. A bounty system was started by which, apart altogether from government selection, private persons might bring out approved numbers of migrants so long as these complied with certain age limits and occupational rules. The first intention (1839) was that by this means colonial employers might bespeak in the United Kingdom the labour which they needed. Such a close correspondence between demand and supply soon vanished, if in fact it ever obtained. The increase of the bounties to cover the full cost of the passage made the recruiting of bounty immigrants an easy speculation for ship-owners. In 1839, 2814 were brought out, in 1840, 6675 and in 1841, 20,103. Having no claim on the government that had selected him, the bounty migrant was forced by his necessity to accept the first job that offered. In 1840 the local government found that it had given permits for the bringing of 71,315 migrants of this kind and had pledged itself to find £979,600. Luckily, when "the Bad Times" came, the Land and Emigration Commissioners took alarm at the number of bounty emigrants setting forth, suspended their own well-managed selection of emigrants for whom the land fund provided, and did their best to supervise the vessels and emigrants sent out under the bounty scheme.

But the damage had been done. Bounty migrants, largely from Ireland, where they were more easily recruited, crowded on Sydney wharves and foreshores, homeless and unprovided for after the ten days grace allowed on board the immigrant ship. The second colonial boom had burst, and employment was paralysed by waning credit and low prices. Sixty-four girls who had just landed possessed between them 14s. 1½d., twenty-two being literally penniless.

Into this hopeless scene came Caroline Chisholm, "a second Moses in bonnet and in shawl".[1] She was a yeoman's daughter, from Northamptonshire. At 22 she had changed the name of Jones for that of Chisholm, marrying a Captain in the East India Company's Army. They and their family came in 1838 to spend a period of sick leave in New South Wales. One of their first experiences in Sydney was an encounter with some Highlanders, wandering disconsolate and workless through inability to speak English. Chisholm, having Highland blood in him, turned interpreter and set them on the way to success as wood-cutters.

His wife's interest in emigrants needed little kindling. In early childhood an old soldier visiting her father had excited her curiosity by his tales of other lands, and his talk of them as colonies where emigrants might reap fortunes. The idea at once spurred her to childish action, and her first attempts at colonization were carried on in a wash-hand basin, before she was seven years old, with boats of broad beans, and touchwood dolls. With these she contrived a busy family migration and sent the boats, filled with wheat, back to their homeland on the other side of the basin.

In Sydney she found herself face to face with the realities

[1] London *Punch*:
> "Who led their expeditions and under whose command
>   Through dangers and through hardships
>   sought they the Promised Land?
> A second Moses, surely, it was who did it all?
> It was. A second Moses in bonnet and in shawl."

For her life and work see Mackenzie's *Memoirs of Mrs Chisholm*, 1852, and Margaret Swann's *Caroline Chisholm*.

of emigration—hundreds of homeless girls with neither friends nor protection. For three years, there and at Windsor, she did what she could to find places for them, sheltering many in her own home. It was in 1841, however, when her husband was recalled for service in China, and the financial collapse increased unemployment, that her efforts became public in scale. At Easter of that year she decided to devote herself wholly to this urgent task, and in it "to know neither country nor creed".[1] Newspapers and public men admired her projects but privately assured her that she was attempting the impossible. Sir George Gipps told her she much overrated her powers of mind and declined to help, but finally gave her the use of an old building for her Immigrants' Home.[2] For four nights she fought for possession against rats, and finally won with the aid of arsenic.

There she began a systematic campaign. Her free registry office substituted proper agreements in triplicate (one being filed at her office) for the verbal "contracts of service" which had till then left servants helpless before the masters and magistrates. A day school kept children from the streets. Her first report of the work of the Home showed that within a year 735 young women had been provided with situations; 291 going to the country districts. The Governor, as soon as he realized her genius for detail, franked her letters so that she might place country labour more easily. This was a valuable help when to send a half-ounce letter to Parramatta cost 4d., to Windsor or Campbelltown 7d., to Bathurst 10d., and the postage for 300 miles was a shilling. Her inquiries about

---

[1] See Margaret Swann, *op. cit.* p. 10. In her wash-basin experiment she "had a Wesleyan minister and a Catholic priest in the same boat".

[2] Sir George's account of her first interview with him gives a glimpse of Mrs Chisholm in the flesh and the spirit: "I expected to have seen an old lady in white cap and spectacles, who would have talked to me about my soul. I was amazed when my *aide* introduced a handsome stately young woman, who proceeded to reason the question, as if she thought her reason, and experience too, worth as much as mine". See, for other contemporary descriptions of her, Margaret Swann, *op. cit.* p. 5.

the places offering were thorough. Sir George Gipps was at first a little perturbed at their range. "When I gave you the privilege of franking", he told her, "I presumed you would address yourself to the magistrates, the clergy and the principal settlers, but who, pray, are these John Varleys and Dick Hogans of whom I have never heard since I have been in the colony?" She replied that if she had inquired of prominent settlers they must have gone to their overseers and would have then answered her vaguely. "I want to know what number of labourers each district can absorb and of what class and what wages. I have applied to men humble but intelligent, able to afford exactly the information I require."

Success in finding country places for the girls was baulked by their fear, probably justified, of making bush journeys by dray. They hesitated to set out alone. Mrs Chisholm went with them. Quickly the journeys grew into expeditions under her command, not of girls only, but of immigrant families. These became the invaluable nuclei of a social development in fostering which she was doubly faithful to her girlish vision of family migration.

Beginning with journeys to Parramatta, Liverpool, Campbelltown and Maitland, she was soon venturing as far as Goulburn, Bathurst, Yass, Gundagai and the Murrumbidgee. At times she was on the road for as long as five weeks. One party numbered 147 men, women and children on setting out, and grew *en route* to a maximum of 240. She would ride ahead on her favourite horse "Captain" while the migrants followed by dray. From farm to farm, from homestead to homestead, she sought places for them, judged the mutual fitness of place and servant, drew up agreements and meantime supplied her charges with their daily needs.

Her general plan was first to place a female servant, relying on the rivalry of housewives to make the coming of one the stimulus to a demand for many. The girls married best among the farms, but even the stations, with their prejudice against "encumbrances", did not baffle her strategic cult of the family. She would never set about match-making direct. There was little difference to a squatter or farmer, she reasoned, between a single man's wage and rations and those of a married couple.[1] She would persuade an employer to engage a married couple and, if need offered, use them as employers of the eligible girls.[2]

She was not, however, a mere match-maker by instinct, led on by a sympathy with the joys of matrimony. When an admirer praised her masculine mind, he meant to note her finest quality—insight into the main defect of transportation and subsidized migration. Great alike in brain and heart, she knew that the unit cell of society is a family. She settled 11,000 souls in new homes during the decade before the gold discoveries, and deliberately evolved a new art of family colonization. To her mind it was not good husbandry to uproot individuals from a crowded land, to cull the worst and cast them out on a rubbish heap, and then, when some throve in the rotting mass, to call it a new garden. She saw that, as certain plants can only thrive together, the sexes must be balanced to make a sane community. Between 1840 and 1850, the period of her greatest prestige and activity, the ratio of males to females in the Australian colonies dropped from 2 : 1 to 1·43 : 1. The number of females in all colonies was 63,102 in 1840 and 166,673 in 1850: of males 127,306 in 1840 and 238,683 in 1850. Confining attention to New South Wales, and taking the dates 1836 to 1851 in order to exclude the

[1] The rate of wages for a single man then averaged £20 per annum with weekly rations of flour 9 lb., meat 10 lb., tea 2 oz., sugar 1½ lb. A man and his wife with one child £25 per annum and a double ration.

[2] E. Mackenzie, *op. cit.* p. 67, reports "On one of her first journeys she was met by a discontented party of emancipists, shepherds and shearers of the district who said: 'We believe you are a very good sort of a person, Mrs Chisholm, and have great respect for you, but we cannot allow emigrants here to lower our wages'. Her answer was, 'I hear you want wives. Is that true?' The reply was a universal 'Yes'. 'Then, don't you see, I can't send single girls to a district where there are only bachelors. Let me fix a few married families down on the different stations, and I will send to them decent single lasses that you can marry'."

free settlement at Port Phillip, one obtains more striking figures:

New South Wales Population

Year	Males	Females	Ratio
1836	56,677	22,252	2·55 : 1
1851	113,155	84,110	1·34 : 1

The credit due to Mrs Chisholm is not that she achieved these results but that she altered the attitude of the community towards female immigration and by spreading family life raised the self-respect of all grades and set new standards in the development of social life.

The worst feature of transportation, she held, had been that it denied its victims the normal motives of human ambition, ability to hand on to one's children the lore of family life, a very present immortality and a renewal of youth. To her the convicts were victims of a "close and galling bondage", "incarcerated together by hundreds like a menagerie of wild beasts"—"victims of a principle promulgated but too successfully by a modern popular author".[1] At its worst the system produced the horrors of Port Arthur, and filled the gaols and asylums for long after 1840 with the demented wrecks of prison discipline. But none escaped unbranded, and the solitary hopeless life in the bush into which the old hands drifted only confirmed "the frightful and deteriorating effects of this more than savage life".

Her deliberate aim was to bring to all in Australia the opportunity of family life. Accustomed in her journeys to find shelter at the nearest hut, and to share the hospitality of all classes, she had learned to know the kinder side of the emancipist settlers, "their extreme, nay, nervous anxiety regarding the welfare of their children—the efforts they

---

[1] The phrases are quoted from a letter on "Emigration and Transportation Relatively Considered" which she addressed to Earl Grey in 1847. The "modern author" would seem to be Jeremy Bentham, and his *Panopticon v. New South Wales, Constant Inspection the only security against Escape* (1812).

make to educate them—the miles they travel to attend a place of worship—their deep sympathy for the unfortunate—their Christian liberality and charity—their open-hearted hospitality". She denounced and sought to remedy the effects of a system "that has doomed tens of thousands to the demoralising state of bachelorism". She appealed to the "paternal government" to entitle itself to that honoured name by promoting family and female migration. "For all the clergy you can dispatch, all the schoolmasters you can appoint, all the churches you can build, and all the books you can export will never do much good without 'God's police'—wives and little children."

In such a cause she obtained unstinted support from almost all in the colony. A prominent member of the Legislative Council asked her to draw on him for any money she required on her journeys. But in the country districts none would accept payment for the needs of her charges; she at no time found need of his help. By 1843 her plans were taking wider scope. She did not relax her efforts to find places for migrants. A contemporary describes her[1] "making forced marches at the head of armies of emigrants, as far as 300 miles into the far interior, sometimes sleeping at the stations of wealthy settlers, sometimes in the huts of poor immigrants or prisoners; sometimes camping out in the bush, teaching the timid, awkward peasantry of England, Ireland and Scotland how to 'bush' it; comforting the women, nursing the children, and putting down any discontented or froward spirits among the men; now taking a few weary children into her covered tandem-cart, now mounting upon horseback and galloping over a short cut through the hills to meet her weary caravan, with supper foraged from the hospitable settlers."

She realized very soon that in ninety-nine cases out of a hundred the emigrants had come in hopes of obtaining land and independence. The best way of national coloniza-

[1] Samuel Sidney, *The Three Colonies of Australia* (1852), pp. 155–6.

tion would be to settle families on small farms. The Governor and his Council, however, were left under the new constitution of 1842 without power to "interfere in any manner with the sale or the appropriation of the lands belonging to the Crown in the colony or with the revenue thence arising". And the minimum price, raised from 12s. to a pound an acre, at which the Land and Emigration Commissioners sold land on strict Wakefield lines, debarred small settlers, both because of their poverty and the less lucrative use they could make of the land, from competing at land sales against the shepherd-kings.

Baulked of the aid in family land-settlement which Governor Gipps would gladly have given, Mrs Chisholm found a wealthy landowner, Captain R. Towns of Shellharbour, willing to give her 4000 acres on which to make an experiment, together with five months' rations for her party. There in December 1843 she settled a group of 30 families, including over 240 persons. She watched over their early troubles and nursed to humble success a little colony of 30-acre farms.[1] In 1846, having built up a stable organization for placing migrants in New South Wales, she returned to England to found a national scheme of colonization.

In London she quickly created "The Family Colonization Loan Society" which encouraged the migration of undivided families by supplementing their savings with loans. After a winter of pleading backed by full proofs of actual instances, she extorted from the Land and Emigration Commissioners a remedy for the evil of families divided by partial emigration. Two shiploads of children were sent from British workhouses to rejoin their parents oversea. Free passages for convicts' wives and families were more sparingly given. With the active aid of leaders of opinion like Lord Shaftesbury and Sidney Herbert, the Family Colonization Loan Society conducted a vigorous educational campaign in favour of New South Wales. "Tell the

[1] See S. Sidney, *op. cit.* pp. 153–4.

truth. The country can stand it" was Mrs Chisholm's watchword, and she was able not only to arouse great interest and energy in emigration, but also to charter ships and institute sweeping changes in the accommodation and food on board. For this she was attacked by shipowners, who did not scruple to suggest that all her philanthropy cloaked plans to enrich herself. The 'Slains Castle', the first ship to fly her blue flag with the monograms F.C.L.S. and C.C., sailed with 250 passengers in September of 1850, and was followed at six-monthly intervals by others. Where the Emigration Commissioners had allowed from 600 to 800 to be carried, these vessels chartered by the Loan Society carried less than 300. By 1852, however, news of the gold discoveries had reached Britain and the need of Mrs Chisholm's labours to find colonists was over. After her return to Australia in 1854, she remained there for twelve years. One of her first activities was to persuade the new Victorian Government to erect rough shelters along the tracks to the diggings. But her health was broken, and her constant insistence on the need of unlocking the land dimmed her popularity with some. Between 1862 and 1866 she kept a girls' school in Newtown, Sydney. She was given a pension of £100 a year by the Crown and died in 1877.

Work such as hers could not be undone. The Land and Emigration Commissioners renewed in 1844 their sending of selected migrants—agricultural labourers, shepherds and domestic servants—4500 of whom went out under their auspices in 1844-5. Thereupon a committee of the Legislative Council asked in 1845 for £12,500 per annum for three years, with which to renew "bounty immigration". They adduced in support elaborate calculations of the new land and increased flocks that would absorb the newcomers' services. The assumption of unchecked and abundant prosperity was perhaps not as naïve as it sounded. Governor Gipps put aside their pleading, thinking the effect of such a renewal would be to flood the labour market again and to force down wages. The land revenue was not as buoyant as these pastoral hopes, and he put the annual need of fresh labour at 4000 only. No funds, however, were available in 1846 and 1847. There was talk of Indian coolies, and of a limited trial of Chinese and South Sea Islanders. In 1848 loans on the security of future land sales were raised to promote selected immigration again, £50,000 being allotted to Sydney district and a like sum to Port Phillip. The more humane and business-like handling of migration was shown in the reservation of half the passage money until the selected migrants had been landed in Australia and their treatment *en route* had become known to the authorities there. The new spirit prompted, too, the provision of depots for the reception of new arrivals at country centres such as Goulburn, Bathurst, Maitland and Moreton Bay, where they were lodged at government expense until offered work at rates deemed fair by the superintendent.

Other societies formed to promote emigration, such as Sidney Herbert's Female Emigration Society and the Highland and Island Emigration Society, were not as successful in their choice of migrants as Mrs Chisholm's Family Loan Colonization Society. Like her organization they failed to collect the sums advanced to eke out small savings and pay passage money, but the migrants they selected being less worthy of support, they received no such grants from the legislature as maintained her Society's work.

Mrs Chisholm's crusade for family life was a personal task, the realization of an enthusiast's dream. In the decade of confused trekking to and fro by excited diggers from the first gold discoveries to the final rush to Otago in 1861, family desertion was painfully frequent all through Australia. Mrs Chisholm's effort may then have seemed vain and soon forgotten. Her plea for access to the land, even when freely granted in form, for long seemed equally barren of the consequences hoped for. Yet both are very real achievements in Australia to-day.

CHAPTER XI

The Gold Rushes of 1851–1860

THE grant by Britain of colonial self-government, to the Eastern Colonies in 1851, to Western Australia in 1890, was immediately followed in each instance by energetic discoveries of gold. The causal relation is not plain but the economic and political results were revolutionary. Gold drew in new populations which swamped the old colonists, and which, as their easy gains from gold declined, used the new political freedom for ends of their own, not approved by the pastoral communities they had disturbed and reinforced in numbers.

The Crown Colonial officials in New South Wales did not welcome the finding of gold. They may fairly be said to have delayed it in the interests of prison discipline and a quiet life. In 1823 a convict produced a small nugget which the officer in charge promptly took to be stolen gold melted down; the discoverer was duly flogged. Rumours of other finds floated around shepherds' huts and Sydney bars. Officialdom frowned. A Polish explorer, Count Strzelecki, told Governor Gipps in 1839 of gold-bearing pyrites near Lithgow. Gipps bade him be silent and similarly advised the Revd. W. B. Clarke, a schoolmaster and amateur geologist, when he too found gold in 1841. A British geologist, Sir Roderick Murchison, came to the conclusion, from a study of published papers on Australia, that gold would be found there. He based his argument on the similarity of the mountains with the Urals, and urged that unemployed tin-miners from Cornwall should be sent to look for it. Earl Grey at the Colonial Office snubbed him for his enthusiasm, and such "cousin Jacks" as were

assisted to migrate turned their steps to the South
Australian copper-mines. Even a mild rush to California
only half thawed the chill with which officials thought of
similar doings in New South Wales. A certain W. J. Smith,
who in 1849 showed the Colonial Secretary a nugget em-
bedded in quartz, was offered a reward in proportion to
the value of the find. He declined terms that would have
thrown him upon the generosity of an evidently hostile
and sceptical Government.

In 1851 the atmosphere suddenly changed. In February,
E. H. Hargraves, a squatter who had returned from
California, tested his theory that the rocks and flats near
Bathurst closely resembled the gold-bearing country over
the Pacific, and found it true. Taking the gold to Sydney,
he persuaded the Colonial Secretary that an announcement would stop emigration to California and end all
possibility of renewed transportation. He accepted the
offer which Smith had declined, and within a few weeks
his "Ophir" field had infected the whole colony with the
gold-fever. By mid-May, 400 miners were "puddling" for
nuggets and gold dust. From stations, farms and city
streets came "new-made miners, some armed with picks,
others shouldering crowbars and shovels, and not a few
strung round with wash-hand basins, tin-pots and cul-
lenders".[1]

It was now the pastoralists' turn to take fright at the
consequences. Some asked for martial law and a down-
right prohibition of gold-digging. The latter was actually
proclaimed by Governor Denison in Van Diemen's Land
in 1852, avowedly in the interests of "the ordinary pursuits" of the colony. Governor Fitzroy proclaimed the
gold to be legally the property of the Crown, and required
all miners to take out monthly licences to dig for it. These
were to be issued at 30s. a month by resident Commis-

---

[1] Quoted from the *Bathurst Free Press*, 17 May 1851, by G. V. Portus,
"The Gold Discoveries and their First Effects", appearing in vol. VII, ch.
IX, of the *Cambridge History of the British Empire*, the most spirited and
thoughtful account of the period.

sioners. The *Sydney Morning Herald* doubted the efficacy of such restraints. It clung to the hope "that the treasure does not exist in large quantities". Should it do so, "let the inhabitants of New South Wales and the neighbouring colonies stand prepared for calamities far more terrible than earthquakes or pestilence!" (19 May). Standing, however, was the last thing the inhabitants were prepared to do when in July a certain Dr Kerr produced a mass of gold and quartz containing 1272 ounces of gold which an aboriginal shepherd had knocked off the outcrop of a reef. A new field called the Turon became the scene of a rush of men more excited than ever.

The colony of Victoria, separated from New South Wales on July 1 of that year, made a prompt bid for a share in the "calamities". It was intolerable that separation should be, even in appearance, the occasion for the loss of the most active spirits in its population of 77,000. In Port Phillip District, too, there had been tales current of shepherds' finds, and the inevitable "man named Smyth" had been told by Superintendent Latrobe in 1844 to hush up a discovery of gold on the Ovens River. A Gold Discovery Committee (9 June 1851) now offered a reward for the finding of gold within 200 miles of Melbourne. It was immediately claimed by W. Campbell of Strath Lodden near Clunes. Louis John Michel brought in samples of gold-bearing quartz from Anderson's Creek. Thomas Hiscock of Buninyong found gold a few weeks later on the south side of the Dividing Range, and the Ballarat diggings nearby soon eclipsed all previous finds by their amazing richness. Early in September, Melbourne papers received word of very rich diggings that had been quietly developed since mid-July at Mount Alexander. In December, Henry Frenchman found at Golden Gully the first of Bendigo's big deposits. During 1851, gold worth over a million pounds was won in Victoria, which became the centre of attraction before the gold discoveries were known overseas. The Victorian fields were from 70

to 100 miles out of Melbourne. The Dividing Range was
an easily crossed watershed quite unlike the formidable
Blue Mountains behind Sydney. In the size and abundance
of their nuggets and surface enrichment the diggings were
unique.[1] Governor Latrobe reported having seen eight
pounds weight of gold washed from two tin dishes of
dirt. Three years later a nugget weighing 98½ pounds,
found on Dalton's Flat during a visit by Governor and
Lady Hotham, was called the "Lady Hotham" in her
honour.

Ordinary mortals could not be expected to regard such
wonders as calamities. The diggings seemed rather the
first real chance of independence that Australia had
offered the poor man. Childhood's dreams were coming
true. Wealth in big lumps might be picked up from the
ground. All that was necessary was hard work with pick
and shovel, turning over the soil in gullies where long
ages had washed down and lightly covered the unheeded
metal. Food was rough, and water often scarce. Colonial
fever, as typhoid was then called, was soon prevalent
about the makeshift camps. But to men inured to a bush
life these were trifles when weighed against the virtual
certainty of high holiday from sheep and loneliness, and
perhaps the means of returning to the old land rich and
respectable ever after. Until September 1852 most of the
diggers were pre-gold colonists concentrated into Victoria
from station, farm and township. Nearly a quarter of the
population of pastoral days, it is said, tried their luck
along the gullies in the Great Divide. Expirees, emancipists,
free-immigrants, escaped convicts from Van Diemen's
Land, policemen and civil servants, sailors and clerks,
shepherds and shopkeepers went digging and puddling
where, with persistence and energy, fortunes were to be
won by the simplest method.

But not all were diggers. The idea of selling goods
to the fortunate at fancy prices occurred to so many that

[1] For a list of famous nuggets see the *Australian Encyclopaedia*, vol. 1, p. 561.

at Bathurst, the first diggings, prices in June 1851 were below those ruling in Sydney. In Victoria, however, the proffer of new gold was so sudden and so strong that the level of all Australian prices (taking those of 1896–1900 as base, 1000) rose from 1036 in 1846–50 to 1607 for 1851–5. The main source of quick trading profits from the diggers was the sale of spirits. Up to the end of 1853 the Victorian Government refused to issue publicans' licences on the diggings. Opinion on the goldfields attributed this to the influence of the Melbourne public-house keepers. The lucky digger with his bag of gold-dust was expected to come to town and there replace the station-hand or shearer with his cheque. Whether that charge was well or ill-founded, the sly-grog shanty became a regular feature of the mining camp. As beer was too bulky to be easily smuggled, the grog sold was usually spirits. Teamsters could always be found who would risk the loss of horses, dray, harness and cargo plus a fine of fifty pounds. Brewers' casks were much in demand on the fields for "puddling" the gold-bearing dirt, and very handy to stow goods in during wet journeys by bullock team. Detection was not easy, and if the worst happened bribery was not unknown. What charges the traffic would bear may be deduced from the average of £1500 a week for cartage which a Ballarat publican is said to have paid during part of 1853. The sly-grog shop bore no sign and carried small stock. Its front curtain was always down, but the way in was well known, the storekeeper being usually a "tout" and sleeping partner. When the evening gun, fired near the Commissioner's tent, put an end to the day's strenuous digging, the lull of the meal-time was soon followed by a roaring business to which the police were ordinarily deaf and blind.

In general, however, the mining camps surprised observers by the order they maintained. Their capacity for spontaneous organization in religious congregations and in the usual Anglo-Saxon multiplicity of sporting, social

and friendly societies enabled Governor Latrobe to re-
constitute his police and civil service, and to convert, with
no more disorder than his own and his advisers' blunders
provoked, a fortuitous collection of newcomers into a self-
governing community.

The Victorian Government in 1851 was a mere scaf-
folding. The Imperial "Act for the better government of
Her Majesty's Australian Colonies", 1850 (13 & 14
Victoria, cap. 59) set up a Legislative Council, two-thirds
of whose members were elected on a ten-pound rental
franchise. This meant a present supremacy of the old
squatter leaders. But the Act endowed the new Council
with power to draw up a new bi-cameral constitution.
Thus its moral authority was overshadowed; its status being
that of a house of caretakers under notice to quit. It represented a landed interest at loggerheads with the Governor
as to its legal title to the land and by no means willing to
welcome an upstart industry spreading everywhere and
threatening to paralyse pastoral pursuits. In November
1851 the Council declined to find from general revenue
the cost of governing the mining camps. Latrobe, in the
habit of following Governor Fitzroy as his official superior,
continued to levy the licence fee imposed in accordance
with Californian precedents before Victoria's separation
from New South Wales. He considered the licence plan
unsound. It penalized heavily the unsuccessful diggers.
He would have preferred an export duty by which diggers
would have contributed to the cost of government in
proportion to their success. But that would have placed
the revenue, as part of Customs and Excise, within the
power of his factious and inexperienced Council. He
certainly needed more revenue. Diggers could average,
men said, an ounce of dust a day. It was little enough,
in the circumstances, to offer a constable 6s. a day. To
pay this he sought in December 1851 to impose a doubled
licence fee of £3 a month. The gold-miners, knowing that the
Council was pressing the Governor to grant pastoral leases

for long terms, raised a great clamour against this doubling of the "poll-tax" on their own energies. With few police and only 80 soldiers to enforce his commands, Latrobe withdrew. The Legislative Council, whose hostility had tied his hands, then passed a resolution favouring the levy of an export duty on gold in place of the unpopular licence fee.

The knot should have been cut when in June 1852 word came from Britain giving the local legislatures control of the licence fees from gold-digging, and suggesting that whatever additional revenue was needed might be raised "either by an export duty on gold or by a royalty". But an Export Duty Bill, proposed as an added impost, not as a substitute for licence fees, was howled down on the diggings. The outcry against it, very probably, was inspired by the gold-buyers, who represented that it would necessarily reduce the price they could pay for gold dust. Doubtless this was so, but they had been giving as little as 55s. an ounce, at least a pound less than the mint value of gold, and were discussing the relative qualities of the "colonial gold" won on the different fields.

Thus antagonism between the diggers and the Government was already marked when in September 1852 the first wave of a new type of free immigration broke on the shore of Hobson's Bay. The newcomers came mainly from Britain. Nineteen thousand landed in Melbourne in September, and 94,664 during 1852, seven times as many as the arrivals during 1851. Only 1648 of these were foreigners. Possibly the exceptional qualities of the foreigners, many of them exiles of the 1848 disturbances, impressed their contemporaries. More probably the insular prejudices of a population that had hitherto been selected from those under British jurisdiction made it gape at every foreign type. There were sources enough, without looking beyond the United Kingdom, for the indignant radicalism which soon leavened the mining camps. The hungry 'forties and the Chartist movement, the Irish

potato famine and Smith O'Brien's "rising" had repressed
in the old country popular ambitions to make a new social
order by political or revolutionary action. In Victoria the
emigrants, whose very coming showed them to be men of
confident initiative, faced no such repressive powers. At
first they were too intent upon trying their luck inland
to care for politics. Dumped pell-mell with a medley
of goods on Liardet's Beach (later Sandridge and Port
Melbourne), they sorted themselves out in Canvas Town,
trudged or rode through the scorching dust-laden north
wind, or, in the bitter winter of 1853, picked a way over
the muddy tracks to Ballarat or Bendigo. They felt no
respect for a ruling oligarchy without traditional dignity
and but lately seized of power. Whatever the Legislative
Councillors and Governor Latrobe might seem to the
old hands, to these newcomers, soon a growing and
self-conscious majority, they were men using temporary
political power to fasten on a new country a land monopoly like that whose claws the Anti-Corn Law League had
lately clipped by popular agitation. Throughout the colony
the diggers won wealth where these men had missed it.
Yet when the easy gold gave out they found themselves
debarred by new land laws from acquiring the stake in
the country which, they were told, was the proper condition of a share in its government.

The diggers proved ready critics. Now it was Tasmanian ex-convicts who excited their scorn, now Chinese
intruders. Those who returned to Britain shocked their
home-keeping friends with tales of the rough life and
rougher people on the stations and the diggings, of the
snares that lurked in Canvas Town south of the Yarra and
beyond the ken of the police, of the quagmire three-parts
of a mile wide across the Keilor Plains which served as
the road to Bendigo and Mount Alexander.[1]

[1] See *The Diggings, the Bush and Melbourne*, by James Armour, Glasgow,
1864; "The Gold Diggers", by C. B. Newling, *Journal of the Royal Australian
Historical Society*, vol. XI, pp. 262–80; and "Gold Seekers of the Fifties" in
The Argus, May 1899.

They had reason for much of their criticism. Neither officials nor legislators showed imagination or foresight in shaping channels for the broadening current of Victorian life. The population reached 236,798 in 1854, of whom 68,790 were able-bodied miners on the gold-fields. In the following year it passed that of the mother colony: in 1857 the population of Victoria was 410,766 and that of New South Wales 305,487. But though rich alluvial finds continued and the total yield remained amazing, that total fell from £16,776,250 in 1852, the *annus mirabilis*, to £8,661,161 in 1854. By then, three times as many were digging as in 1852.[1] To men led into an uncouth life by the motive of monetary gain through free and intense effort, this waning of their chances made the monthly licence fee an offence and an irritation. It was clumsily collected by a police force recruited from old Tasmanian military warders, London Metropolitan Police—culls, no doubt—and inexperienced youngsters locally pitchforked into a rank of "cadets", between commissioned and non-commissioned officers. Periodic "digger-hunts" were made by parties of police armed with fixed bayonets. Diggers caught working without the licence were marched to the "lock up" or even chained to a log outside the Commissioner's tent, to be heavily fined when they came under his summary jurisdiction. These digger-hunts were insultingly reminiscent of searches for bushrangers or runaway "government men".

Only a lead was needed to stir mass resentment into action. It was given unwittingly in June 1853 by a proposal in the New South Wales Legislative Council for the abolition of licences. The revenue from the fees was not important there. In August, after a short and orderly campaign known from the badge they used as the Red Ribbon Agitation, the Bendigo (V.) diggers sent a deputation to ask Governor Latrobe to reduce the licensing fee

[1] T. A. Coghlan, *Labour and Industry in Australia*, p. 587, bases these figures on the estimates made by dealers in bullion.

to 10s. a month, and to explain to him their subjection to armed force, their lack of access to the land, and their desire for a voice in making the laws. Latrobe answered that at 30s. a month the revenue from licences did not meet the cost of governing the fields. The miners' delegates talked to popular audiences in the capital of 100,000 diggers ringing Melbourne with fire, and were applauded. Reinforcements from "The Fighting Fortieth" were sent to Bendigo Camp and their coming was met by a general refusal to take out licences. A hasty measure was passed by the Council reducing the fee to £2 for three months. The formal refusal to reduce it to 10s. a month was intended to save the face of a legislature nervous of being "dictated to" by the mining population, but the concession emboldened the element that talked of using force. Stump-orators grew fonder of comparing the military resources and prowess of the diggers with those of the government.

When Latrobe left the colony early in 1854, order had been maintained at the diggings, but only by a big sacrifice of revenue and authority. The new Governor was Sir Charles Hotham, a naval officer as sure of the value of discipline as Latrobe had been conscious of the injustice of the licence system. A severe commercial crisis had followed speculative over-trading, and the diminution of revenue from imports and licences had left a public deficit of a million sterling. Hotham called on the Commissioners to mend matters by a stricter collection of the fees due. In 1854 a new rush had gathered the worst elements from the various diggings to Eureka Valley in the usually orderly Ballarat field. In October a digger was stabbed at the door of a rough "hotel" in an altercation "after hours". A venal magistrate acquitted the owner, an ex-convict from Tasmania, and a mob of some thousands thereupon swept the police aside and burnt the hotel. Hotham, after inquiry, dismissed the magistrate and ordered a new trial. The hotel-keeper was convicted of manslaughter, but three of the incendiaries were also sentenced to prison. A force of 450 soldiers and police was sent to keep order. Thereupon the "Ballarat Reform League" demanded of the Governor the release of their comrades and talked of revolt against "tyranny" and of a Victorian Republic. Hotham firmly refused the "demand" for release, inviting the spokesmen to temper it to a petition. He explained, in answer to talk of political rights, that a constitutional amendment giving votes to all licence-holders had been sent for the Queen's approval, as such amendments had always to be sent, but that if they would elect a representative he would at once nominate him to the Council. With clumsy obstinacy they repelled his conciliation and reiterated their "demands".

At Ballarat, on their return, a tall German called Vern began a provocative public burning of licences. At the next "digger-hunt" the Commissioner and his men were pelted with stones. The diggers bought up and seized arms; drilling began. On a rise in Eureka Camp they built a crude stockade of stakes, ropes and broken carts. The miners obtained some ammunition by rushing a military convoy; shots were fired into the government camp. Captain Thomas decided not to wait for General Nickle, known to be on the road with reinforcements. By a surprise attack early on Sunday morning, 3 December 1854, the stockade was carried, the rebel flag, a white Southern Cross on a blue ground, was hauled down and 120 insurgents were marched off to prison. An officer and four soldiers lost their lives, and so did 30 of the garrison. Thomas had admirably timed his rush when the family-men among the rebels were spending the week-end at home.[1]

Governor Hotham insisted upon the trial of the leaders for high treason, but juries refused to convict. One at least, Peter Lalor, made lifelong political capital out of

[1] For more detail see H. Gyles Turner, *Our Own Little Rebellion*, pp. 64-75, and W. B. Withers, *History of Ballarat*.

G

his escapade. He became a Minister of the Crown and Speaker of the Legislative Assembly. But neither "the last picturesque pose of an order that was passing", as Mr Portus aptly sums up the Eureka episode, nor the measures passed at the instance of the Royal Commission which was sitting when it occurred, could save alluvial digging. The Commission recommended an annual licence or "Miner's Right" (qualifying for the suffrage as well), at a fee of one pound. It favoured also an export duty of half-a-crown per ounce of gold, a poll-tax on Chinese immigrants, and the sale of land in small blocks near the gold-fields. These changes were made mostly in 1855, but the land reform came much later. No laws, however, could prevent the exhaustion, by the diggers' own restless energy, of the gold available at shallow depths.

The Victorian gold yield rose again in 1855 to a value of £11,708,088, and in the following year to almost £14,000,000; but gold mining, as Governor Fitzroy had predicted in August 1851, had become an industry of companies and capitalists. The number of alluvial miners continued to increase. It rose from 68,790 in 1854 to 82,428 in 1857 and 83,116 in 1861, but the Victorian yield fell off again to less than £11,000,000 in 1857 and less than £8,000,000 in 1861. An ever-increasing proportion of the gold became the property of the companies' shareholders, who installed machinery to work the ground systematically and at depths the diggers could not reach. Steam was first used in crushing quartz during 1855. By November 1861, 711 steam engines were generating 10,782 horse power on the fields.

Two influences buoyed up the diggers' hopes of keeping open the free man's chance. On some fields the partly elective local courts, which the 1855 Act substituted for rule by Commissioners, set their faces against amalgamation of claims. On the Mount Alexander and McIvor diggings their preference for individual mining prevented the more economical but socially less attractive company system from gaining ground. At the Ovens, at Bendigo and at Ballarat, consolidation proceeded steadily. In place of individuals with their methods of shallow sinking and tub-and-cradle work came larger parties who, with a little capital, made good profits by turning over systematically the partly exhausted shallow ground. This was known as "paddocking". Claims were combined or an area taken conjointly and the whole body of ground cut away systematically on a face. "Headings" which would not pay the handwashing digger were put through a circular trough, or horse puddling-machine. Harrows attached to cross-bars were dragged by horses travelling round the circumference of the trough while a stream of water flowed through it. Even so the "paddocks" were but alluvial deposits, and this systematic work completed the exhaustion begun by the individual diggers. When deeper ground had to be worked, and reefs or lodes followed down, well-timbered shafts called for more capital. Steam-batteries became a pre-requisite to puddling or more complex processes of treatment. Whatever the courts might wish to see, such methods meant wages-men and "bosses" rather than prospectors "on their own" or even as working partners.

More substantial was the aid given the diggers by the establishment in 1855 of the Sydney Mint. As a result the miners did not feel the new export duty, for they then obtained for the first time approximately the mint value of their gold. Hitherto gold-buyers on the fields, partly by taking advantage of their clients' ignorance and partly to offset the banks' charges or the risks of transport to the coast and to Britain, had given less than 70s. an ounce. The presence of the Sydney Mint, freely coining gold into sovereigns at the rate of £3. 17s. 10½d. per standard ounce, forced the dealers to give the local equivalent of that rate.[1]

[1] The pastoralists benefited substantially also by the presence of the Mint, for the greater ease in making specie remittances put an end to the wide fluctuations in exchange rates which, in the early days of the gold rush, had operated as a burden on all trade.

Nevertheless, such a price-change, being necessarily limited and possible only once, could not long stay the inevitable catastrophe. By the end of the 'fifties, the Victorian diggings were too thickly peopled to keep up the standards of extravagant living to which miners had grown accustomed. The scenes of the later rushes proved all too limited in resources to reward the numbers that swarmed off from old hives. In 1858 there was a rush to far-away Canoona near Rockhampton, in what became Queensland during the year following, but this venture ended in such misery that the governments of Victoria and New South Wales were constrained to bring back many of the 10,000 who had gone, in order to save them from starvation. Many of them tramped past the scene of the great Mount Morgan mine of later years. Men of New South Wales, returning disappointed from Victorian diggings, increased the yield of the older colony's gold-fields from £674,477 in 1857 to £1,806,171 in 1861.

In Victoria the struggle for a living was embittered by the presence at the diggings of large numbers of Chinese. A few had appeared in 1853; by March 1854 they numbered 2000. There were 25,370 Chinese in Victoria by the end of 1857 and 20,000 of them were digging for gold. They would not work for wages under white "bosses", many of them being bound financially to their own countrymen.[1] If better chances did not offer, they could make a living by re-washing "tailings". Wherever they appeared there was bad blood between them and the white diggers, charges of the most varied character being made against the Celestials. They were "picking the eyes of the fields". But had not all come to do that? They were insanitary in their habits, and immoral. They took money out of the country. Popular outcry dictated a Chinese Restriction Act in June 1855 by which every Chinese coming into Victoria was subjected to an entry tax of £10. Ships were forbidden to carry more than one Chinese to every ten tons registered measurement. All

[1] See P. C. Campbell, *Chinese Coolie Migration in the Empire*, *passim*.

Chinese resident in the colony were subjected to an annual poll-tax of £1, which was raised in 1858 to £6. "Protectors of Chinese" were appointed to enforce these taxes and to control Chinese camps.

The raising of the poll-tax in 1858 marked a realization that other obstacles did not prevent the Chinese from coming. In formidable numbers they made their way to the diggings across country from Guichen Bay in South Australia and from the south coast of New South Wales. After 1858, the heavy poll-tax and the waning alluvial yields sent many across the Murray from Victoria to the New South Wales diggings; yet there were still 25,000 in Victoria at the 1861 census. New South Wales had then 12,988, mostly engaged in gold-mining. Popular dislike was shown there in a Restriction Bill passed in 1858 by the Legislative Assembly but rejected by the Council. The Council's hands were forced, however, by outbreaks of violence in December 1860 and January 1861 at a new field called Lambing Flat or Burrangong.[1] A Miners' League virtually superseded the Commissioner and police as local authority, and twice drove the Chinese off the field. Foot, horse and artillery were sent from Sydney to restore order. The Premier, Charles Cowper, followed with counsels of moderation and promises of legislation. His first proposal was to segregate the alien miners on certain fields to be proclaimed as open. Fresh riots at Lambing Flat and the acquittal of those accused of participation punctuated the passage of this Act and of another drafted on the lines of the Victorian measure (passed November 1861).

The Colonial Office was embarrassed by the inconsistency of the New South Wales Act with the Convention of Peking, signed with China in 1860 by Great Britain and France. In this Convention, Chinese emigrants had been conceded, at the instance of the European powers, "perfect liberty" to take service in British colonies and to ship

---

[1] There had been a similar *émeute* at Buckland River diggings in Victoria on 4th July 1857. For details of the Lambing Flat riots see T. A. Coghlan, *Labour and Industry in Australia*, p. 777.

themselves and their families on British vessels. The new Act was allowed because of the "exceptional character of Chinese immigration" to Australia. In form it was certainly unlike the indentured labour which the framers of the Convention had intended to promote, in opposition to the traditional Chinese prohibition of emigration. When, however, the Chinese diggers had been deterred from coming or had been driven home again by poll-taxes, by popular violence and by waning alluvial yields—they seldom ventured below as wage-earners in deep mining—the Chinese Restriction Acts were repealed in all the colonies —by South Australia in 1861, by Victoria in 1865 and by New South Wales in 1867. But the deep-seated animosity of the Australian working class against Chinese competitors was not extinguished. It blazed again in 1875 on the Palmer diggings in far northern Queensland, and was so notorious in the 'nineties that no Chinese ever ventured to dig for gold on the Western Australian fields. It was not their vices that provoked animosity; they were orderly and content to be left alone. The prejudice against them was fundamentally economic, the resentment of a free-spending folk against men whose racial standards of effort and endurance bore the marks of stern competition to survive. Every habit of theirs was a threat to impose such standards on Australia.

As events shaped themselves, the gold rushes did not materially alter the preponderance of British blood in the colonies. The census returns of 1861 showed the following percentages of population classified according to birth-place:[1]

Birthplace	Victoria	New South Wales
Australia	29·2	47·0
British Empire (outside Australia)	61·4	46·2
Foreign countries	8·6	6·6
Unspecified	0·8	0·2
All countries	100·0	100·0

[1] Tables quoted, G. V. Portus, *op. cit.*

The best informed of Australian historians holds that "the strong current of vigorous manhood attracted to the country on the discovery of gold" overwhelmed the ex-convicts and "recipients of assisted passages obtained by charitable agencies" who had formed the ordinary population of pre-gold days.[1] But he is not blind to "the indifferent material of a large minority of the people who came to Australia during the gold rushes.... During the quarter century following the gold-rush, thousands of persons whom no inducement to better their condition could incite to steady work lived almost from hand to mouth, without care or thought for the future".

In their days of good fortune, the newcomers clamoured for democracy, and it was given them. The constitutions shaped by Legislative Councils during that decade of excited progress were quickly revised in response to the cry of the easily enriched for a right to mend all ills by new laws. Chartism was orthodoxy among them. Its dominance is plain both in the methods and in the programme of the Bendigo Red Ribbon Association (1853). Manhood suffrage became law in South Australia in 1855, in Victoria in 1857 and in New South Wales in 1858. Vote by ballot came at about the same time, and triennial parliaments have made the laws of South Australia since 1856 and of Victoria since 1859.

If democratic laws could reshape for the better the means by which folk get their living, the way was open and the will was there. At the end of the decade the pressure on legislators became urgent. The Australian population had risen from 405,000 in 1851 to 1,168,000 in 1861. Under the stress of diminishing returns in mining, the diggers clamoured for economic reform. The independent took up Mrs Chisholm's cry for homes on the land. Others joined the unemployed of Sydney and

[1] T. A. Coghlan, *Labour and Industry in Australia*, pp. 874–6. Cf. his discussion of the permanent traces of convict blood in Australia, pp. 561–2.

Melbourne and demanded government works.[1] The latter palliative, however well it agreed with older colonial practice in road-making and public building and with the poor-law relief of which many had been recipients in Britain, in no way solved the problem. It did not necessarily broaden the basis of colonial production or make room for the permanent settlement of the restless prospectors. Whether it could do so depended on the expansion of economically sound industries. Both land settlement and public works programmes were enacted in every state, as will be shown later.

Yet the gold which so greatly reinforced Australian life went mainly to confirm the strength of the pastoral industry. Of the wonderful legacy unearthed by alluvial digging— £125,000,000 in gold—the Victorian population had the first use of some £110,000,000. It was spent mainly on meat, drink and clothing in the first instance, and thus more than made amends for the dislocation which the first rushes had brought to the farms and stations.

The demand for more meat at higher prices quickly caused the closing of the few boiling-down establishments which remained. Meat prices in Melbourne rose from 1½d. in 1851 to 4d. and 6d. in December 1852 and 1s. in May 1854. Later in that year they fell forty per cent., but in 1857 good joints of beef cost 9d. a pound and mutton 7d., and these prices rose to 11d. and 9d. respectively in 1858.[2]

In comparison with other commodities, meat seemed cheap to the newcomers, and their consequent adoption of Australian meat-eating habits made them very profitable customers to butchers and stock-raisers. The good market for meat and the less demand for labour on cattle

---

[1] Three planks in the economic programme of the Labour Movement of later generations may be traced in the demands of the Sydney unemployed in 1858–60, viz.: (i) opposition to piecework, (ii) preference for government employment, and (iii) belief in reduced hours of work rather than maximum earnings. See T. A. Coghlan, *Labour and Industry in Australia*, pp. 700, 711, 726.

[2] As to prices at this period see generally T. A. Coghlan, *Labour and Industry in Australia*, part IV, chapter VIII, pp. 783–829.

runs caused an increase in the proportion of cattle, and this helped to promote the occupation of new country, mainly in northern South Australia and Queensland.

Everywhere fencing, as already described, enabled the squatter to lessen his total labour-costs. Ex-digger contractors also brought a new energy and economy into the transport of wool and stores, previously carried out by unreliable station hands. Most striking of the transport changes due to the new volume of Australian trade was the fall in freights on wool. Faster and bigger ships came out in greater numbers, bringing full cargoes of eager immigrants and eagerly bought goods. Wool went as back-loading for freights as low as a half-penny a pound, and the abundance of shipboard space removed the necessity for "dumping" or compressing the bales, a practice which had always troubled the London brokers because of its effect on the appearance and "handling" of the wool. To the squatter the best consequence of the gold discoveries was the rise in prices in which his wool shared to the full. Both Victorian and New South Wales wool doubled in market value during the 1851–61 decade.

The pastoral industry, having successfully solved its labour problem by fencing the runs, and having added to its oversea market a growing local demand for meat, came out of the period of stress stronger both in possessions and in prospects. Agriculture was at first harder hit, but benefited equally by the bigger demand for its wheat and dairy produce, and recovered by paying similar attention to labour-saving. Less than half a million acres were under crop in 1850 and over a million in 1858. But the farmers were not yet able to feed the colonial populations and could win no such profits as those which enabled the pastoralists to buy out the free selectors of the next period. History and geography still joined in raising high the squatter's throne.

BOOK TWO

COLONIAL PARTICULARISM
1860—1900

CHAPTER XII

"Unlocking the Land" in New South Wales

THE names of Cumberland, Argyll, Cornwall, Buckingham, Gloucester and Glamorgan—which were given to the counties into which the coastal area near Sydney was divided in 1829, and to those of Van Diemen's Land—spoke of a purpose to make a southern Britain there. And, doubtless, the Colonial Office felt in 1831 that at five shillings an acre purchasers of colonial land were being endowed with the means to found new county families, gentle and simple, squires and yeomanry. The systematic colonizers thought of smiling farms, with ploughland, hedgerow and meadow pushing back the primaeval forest. By 1839, however, the Secretary of State, Lord Glenelg, realized that in some untidy way flocks and herds were occupying the back country before the named counties had been properly cleaned up by "combinable labour". The Wakefieldians explained that the price set in 1831 had been too low. "The check which it was intended to impose upon the undue dispersion of the inhabitants of the Colony had not been sufficient." Governments have been fighting that "undue dispersion" ever since, sometimes by free selection for agriculture, sometimes by subsidies and protection to "industries".

By new regulations Glenelg raised the price of land to twelve shillings an acre, and brought on a land boom. Here was an asset whose value had been raised 140 per cent. in a day. Collapse followed in 1841, as it must follow every mania for buying land regardless of the net income it can yield. The good Wakefieldians sitting as Land Commissioners in Westminster diagnosed the malady as the outcome of Glenelg's timidity in working the magic wheel of land-sales, emigration and settlement. They persuaded Lord John Russell to raise the upset price to a pound an acre, and hoped to stimulate sales and revenue, while curbing speculation, by selling the land at a flat rate rather than by auction. All thrifty folk might then share in the unlimited bargain, and with the proceeds ample labour could be sent out to construct roads and buildings worthy of a new and freer community.

This dream of neat farms and combinable labour ignored the pastoralists with their flocks and herds, making their slow way over the dusty inland plains, now passing the precious flour, tea and sugar over a flooded stream on a tarpaulin raft, now checking the bullock-waggon down a "breakaway" by hitching on a fallen gum-tree—those skirmishing explorers whose wild doings seemed flatly contrary to the dogma of concentrated settlement.[1]

Governor Bourke, in October 1835, confessed that he could not "avoid perceiving the peculiarities which in this Colony render it impolitic and even impossible to restrain dispersion within limits that would be expedient elsewhere". The Colonial Office, not living in a warm temperate land and fearing that he was unsound on the fundamentals, lectured him for his lack of faith. There was unlawful squatting in old Wales, he was told, and of course in every new country. But "under a good and responsibly administered law of colonization colonial squatting would be as rare as the invasion of private estates in this country". Bourke was not abashed. These squatters, he replied in effect, are not gipsies but the very leaders of colonial prosperity. "Not all the armies of England, not a hundred thousand soldiers scattered throughout the bush, could drive back our herds within the limits of our

[1] The ideal of concentrated settlements was not the Wakefieldians' invention. Cf. *Report of Committee on Transportation*, 1812, p. 4.

Nineteen Counties." He wholeheartedly supported his advisory Council in an Act that granted annual licences to the occupiers of "runs" of indefinite extent "outside the bounds of settlement", charging them ten pounds apiece for licence and run. To settle boundary disputes by local ideas of equity and good conscience, he named district Commissioners of Crown Lands. These steps gave official recognition to the occupation of the "unsettled areas".

This was worth much. The squatter was becoming a Crown tenant; he had a right to his run, which, once it was noted by a friendly Commissioner of Lands, was good against everyone but the Crown. Fights over boundaries and water-rights, formerly settled arms in hand, gave place to legal enforcement of possession. The tract of country occupied by the squatter and his establishment was legally in his possession. He could bring an action against any intruder; so ruled Chief Justice Stephen.[1] "He was not bound to show his title. He simply said 'the Crown does not interfere with me and I had possession before you came in'." To provide a border police, an assessment on each squatter according to the number of his stock was imposed by the Legislative Council in 1839. The power of government was to be made effective in the back country.

Neither Bourke nor his successor Sir George Gipps had the least inclination to treat the squatters as "systematic violators of the law". "As well might it be attempted to confine the Arabs of the desert within a circle drawn on the sands", Gipps informed Lord John Russell (19 December 1840), "as to confine the graziers or wool-growers of New South Wales within any bounds that can possibly be assigned to them: and as certainly as the Arabs would be starved so also would the flocks and herds of New South Wales, if they were so confined, and the prosperity of the colony would be at an end."

[1] Quoted by Stephen Roberts, *Camb. Hist. of Brit. Empire*, vol. VII, ch. VII.

But while impressing the graziers' importance on the authorities in England, Gipps opposed the programme of further privileges for which they contended in his Council. Under William Charles Wentworth they sought security of tenure, compensation for improvements and first right to buy their runs. Without the first and second they could hardly be expected to build substantial homesteads, and to make expensive improvements. Purchase, however, if left to the squatters' option, might mean such a picking out of the oases that control settlement as had marked the sale of "special surveys" in South Australia. The net of a land monopoly would early enclose the land to the prejudice of future comers.

Australian land was then regarded, both in Britain and the colonies, as a trust vested in the Colonial Office for the benefit of generations to come.[1] Gipps' superiors at home held that the free access of graziers to the land conflicted with that trust. The Australian pastoralist, they reasoned, had no more right to occupy the waste lands of New South Wales, without Her Majesty's express sanction, than a Berkshire farmer had to feed his oxen on the Queen's demesne of Richmond or Hampton Court.

Gipps, under such pressure, resisted the squatters' demands for security, and they, caught in "the Bad Times", made him the scapegoat of their sudden penury. Yet in reality he was contending for the admission of their freedom to use the land, while maintaining his trust by refusing them virtual ownership and monopoly. When in 1844 he judged the worst of the financial collapse and drought to be past, he tried to expedite recovery by increasing the number of pastoral runs—a first essay in "bursting up the big estates". He persuaded the Council to constitute each twenty square miles one run, subject to

[1] As late as 1882, a Newcastle surveyor, W. Christie, in *Our Land Laws*, wrote: "The land belongs to the people. We have no more right to the appropriation of the whole of it or any part to the prejudice of posterity than the First Fleet of colonists had to our prejudice, or than Captain Cook had to claim the ownership to the prejudice of them".

the annual charge of ten pounds per run. While he hoped thus to find room for many more runs with a carrying capacity of about 4000 sheep, he did not debar any squatter from holding as many runs as he could use and rent at a profit. Twelve out of the fifteen district land commissioners had recommended this step.

In new Land Purchase Regulations (3 April 1844) Gipps sought, further, to define each squatter's "right to purchase part of his run", granting security while avoiding exclusion. Each run-holder, he proposed, should be required to purchase his homestead block of 320 acres at the end of five years' occupation, and a similar area in addition after every eight years. If the run-holder would not buy, any other purchaser might obtain the run by paying the retiring holder the value of his improvements. The plan offered the pastoralist a regulated pre-emptive right which meant either security or compensation. Its aim was to use the Crown's ownership of the land to enforce the admission of the most vigorous users of it. Yet it provoked such an outcry that within three years a Pastoral Association, formed to resist it, bore down almost every safeguard against monopoly.

Emotion rather than logic inspired the Association's cry of "Ruin or Rebellion". Any suggestion of a new obligation was torment to nerves overstrung by speculation, by drought and the despair of "boiling down". The pastoral leaders, with relatives in every British shire and clients in every port or manufacturing town, brought heavy pressure to bear on the Colonial Office. At first Lord Stanley stood by Gipps and his regulations. Deputations, pamphlets and petitions poured in on his successors, W. E. Gladstone and Earl Grey; and in 1847 Orders in Council under a new Imperial Waste Lands Occupation Act (1846) conceded in effect all that the squatters had asked—security of tenure, "independent" valuation of holdings and pre-emptive rights. The obsolete limits of location between the coastal counties and the more productive area "beyond the bounds of settlement" were dropped, and the land was classified into "settled", "intermediate" and "unsettled" districts. In the settled districts pastoral tenants might have annual leases only; in intermediate districts they might have leases up to eight years' duration, subject to resumption with compensation at the end of any one year; in the unsettled districts they could obtain leases of not more than fourteen years. The pre-emptive right given during these leases, though it did not prevent the Governor from reserving land for public uses, excluded all other purchasers during the term of the lease.[1]

Too late, the popular party, which had rallied under Robert Lowe to vilify Gipps and support Wentworth, saw that they had helped the squatters to gain a firm grip of the land. Whether the pre-emptive right applied to any part of the run and shut out all other buyers, as the squatters argued, or covered only the homestead and the sites of improvements, as the Duke of Newcastle read it in 1854, it certainly gave effective power to buy the "eyes of the land"—to "peacock" the country as this was called. "Sir George Gipps needs no defender now", wrote a Sydney weekly as soon as the purport of the 1847 Orders in Council was understood.

When Port Phillip District became Victoria, the pastoralists dominant there managed by hard-driving in the Legislative Council and in the law courts to obtain an interpretation of the Order that obstructed all sales cf Crown lands under lease, save to the lessees. Latrobe thereupon refused to issue leases, and the pastoralists had to be content with yearly licences carrying the other privileges intended by the Orders in Council but not this exclusive possession. Under such licences or leases, however, nearly the whole of Victoria outside the mountain mass in North Gippsland was in the possession of less than a thousand pastoralists. As it was held that cultivation

[1] See *V. and P. of N.S.W. Leg. Council*, 1847, vol. I, no. 120, cap. II, sect. 6–9.

would create a presumption of permanence in their tenure, the Orders in Council prohibited the pastoralists from cultivating more land than was needed to grow grain, hay, vegetables or fruit for their establishments. This prohibition was relaxed somewhat during the years of dislocation, but in 1854 the squatters were officially reminded that they held their land on pastoral licences, not as cultivators.[1] Before the gold rush, one of them had noted in his diary a private opinion that the lands between Geelong and Bacchus Marsh were the finest wheat fields in New South Wales. Hobler wrote this when New South Wales was undivided. In the new circumstances, pastoralist spokesmen were ready to contend that Nature had "passed an eternal sentence of sterility" upon Victorian land.

The implication that the pastoral runs were to be locked up on this indeterminate sentence was anathema to men who knew what had been done in similar climates elsewhere.[2] Before the diggings began, Victoria had been producing nine-tenths of the wheat she consumed. The area under cultivation fell while country labour could find far higher rewards at the diggings and on the roads thither. In 1855 only a tenth of Victoria's breadstuffs was locally grown. The contention that this was due to sterility was specially galling because California, by dint of granting "homesteads" on easy terms to her surplus diggers, was already exporting potatoes and flour to Australian colonies of similar climate.[3]

[1] *Victorian Government Gazette*, 24 April 1854. "His Excellency the Lieutenant Governor directs it to be notified that as it cannot be considered necessary for the welfare of the residents at the various gold-fields or other populous districts that the cultivation of Crown Lands should still be permitted in order to facilitate the better supply of the necessaries of life to them, the provisions of Her Majesty's Order in Council of 9 March 1847 (ch. 2, p. 1) subject to which the occupants of Crown Lands are licensed must be respected and will be enforced."

[2] Cf. W. Howitt, *Land, Labour and Gold* (1855), *passim*.

[3] Addressing a committee of the Melbourne Chamber of Commerce (1855) on the Waste Lands of Victoria, a merchant named Train cited "the all-sufficient fact of their paying £21 per ton for Californian potatoes and £40 to £50 per ton for American flour". California, he said, "had been four years in becoming an exporting country".

By 1860 the progress of cultivation was again very marked in all the colonies. Victoria had 387,000 acres under crop, South Australia 359,000 acres, Tasmania 152,000 and New South Wales 246,000. Yet the last-named colony was importing in that year grain to the value of £580,176, as compared with £16,939 a decade earlier, and two-fifths of Victoria's bread still came from imports of flour and wheat.

The transitional governments did find ways to retain or regain land from the pastoral net. In New South Wales a million-and-a-half acres were reserved for public purposes, which prevented the complete tying up of the land under pastoral licence which troubled Latrobe in Victoria.[1] In both colonies a power was re-asserted in 1854 which had been overlooked in the heat of controversy—power to resume lands in the intermediate districts at the end of any year. But more radical solutions were in the air. The imperial Act granting self-government vested in the new colonial legislatures "the entire management and control of the waste lands belonging to the Crown" in each colony, and also "the appropriation of the gross proceeds of the sales of any such lands". In the new legislatures the pastoralists soon surrendered control to the democracy of gold-diggers and other immigrants. But they handed on with it no torch of enthusiasm for the interests of posterity.

When manhood suffrage was granted in 1858, alluvial gold-mining was palpably profitless. Thousands of diggers had rushed to Burrangong (N.S.W.) in 1859, but by the year's end most of them were stranded in Sydney. Many tried and missed again at Kiandra in the Australian Alps. But why should this unprofitable scouting for gold continue over land of evident fertility and abundant rainfall? Why did not the mother colony follow South Australia's lead and unlock the land for wheat and dairy farming? A reform recently passed in Adelaide had greatly simplified

[1] See S. H. Roberts, *History of Australian Land Settlement*, ch. xvii.

the sale and transfer of land.[1] "Forty-niners" from California told of free selection on the prairies and the Pacific coast. Recent British history showed that even a landed aristocracy strongly entrenched could not stand against a determined popular movement. So it became the law in Sydney that every man, woman and child should have the same chance to select a farm as John McArthur had enjoyed at Camden in the Cowpastures. Surely there was still enough for all in the 196 million acres that remained of New South Wales after Victoria and Queensland had been carved out of it.

The leader of this popular movement for "free selection before survey" came from the ranks of the squatters themselves. John Robertson had been a youthful pioneer "beyond the bounds of settlement", but had no liking for Wentworth's campaign for security of tenure.[2] He was a Londoner by birth and, though afflicted with a cleft palate, his good looks and rough candour endeared him to a devoted political following for a full generation.[3] In 1861, after a sharp constitutional conflict in the Legislative Council, he pushed through both houses measures which were designed to begin an agricultural revolution and to give every family that desired it a stake in the country. The first, a Crown Lands Alienation Act, permitted anyone to select 40 to 320 acres anywhere from the Crown lands, the limit being raised to 640 acres in 1875. Each selector was to pay five shillings an acre, a fourth of the price, when his "selection" was duly surveyed, and was to

[1] See S. H. Roberts, *History of Australian Land Settlement*, pp. 218 *et seq.* for the origins of the Torrens system of registering titles and transfers of land, and its rapid extension.

[2] For another contemporary squatter's critical analysis of the claims of pasture and agriculture, see Colin Campbell's *The Land Question: A Lecture at Ararat*, 1861 (Mitchell Library).

[3] B. R. Wise, *The Making of the Australian Commonwealth*, speaks of his "natural gift of profanity" and tells how in his old age, when still the admired oracle of the anti-Federal or Geebung Party, a spirited young lady told Sir John of a portrait of his which had appeared in the papers. It was so like him that she had kissed it. "And did it kiss you back?" "Oh! No, Sir John!" "Then it can't have been much like me."

reside on it for three years. The only evidence needed to prove that he had done this was to be a statutory declaration by the selector himself. The terms of payment of the remaining three-quarters of the price were gradually made easier.

This new "free selection" did not, however, supersede the sale of Crown lands by auction; the two systems of alienation were to be used simultaneously. Moreover, any purchaser whatever, either by auction or on condition of residence, might take up as a "pre-lease" three times the area he had purchased. This "pre-lease" gave him a lease of the land for grazing which ranked ahead of any other lease. Yet it was only a lease, and as such was subject to the new right of or liability to selection by any "conditional purchaser" as well as to the older form of alienation, sale by auction.

The second Robertson Act of 1861, the Crown Lands Occupation Act, substituted for the pastoral leases under the 1847 Orders in Council shorter leases for five years only, and limited the lessee's pre-emptive right to one twenty-fifth of the run and to land on which he had effected improvements.

These Acts, though their provisions considered separately might each seem just and indeed generous, were, as a code, without consistency, principle or sense. Ostensibly the Acts opened the public estate to all in the colony who wished to take it—residence and a deposit of ten pounds being the only qualifications for entry into the scramble. An attempt by James Martin in 1867 to be mindful of the colony's imperial trust and to reserve half a million acres for immigrants was denounced by Robertson as "setting apart land for the use of Turks and others" and failed amid "shrieks, yells and view-halloos". Already the pastoralists and "free selectors" had forgotten every other claim and all sense of decency in a bitter contest to assert their jarring legal rights.

Wherever the land was most suitable for sheep the

squatters' wealth weighed down the scales.[1] Half-a-century later a friendly American critic of Australian policies thought "the land laws of the colonies had consistently disregarded the interests of the labourer and the man without capital".[2] The results may suggest this, but the censure on the intentions of the colonial lawgivers is undeserved. But for that regrettable prejudice against "Turks and others" John Robertson might have been counted an Australian King Goodheart who

> In his heart had found a place
> For all the erring human race
> And every wretched fellow.

But economic fact warped his well-meant effort to follow the precedents of the American prairies.

The Crown lands of New South Wales were no longer the empty range of hunting tribes. For a generation or more the pastoralists, whatever their legal status, had made use of the grass those lands grew, and to such good effect that their wool was world-famous and in annually greater demand. Had Robertson and his followers been less obsessed with the idea of spreading agricultural homes as they had been spread in the American West, or, nearer home, in South Australia, they might have realized that grass was the mainstay of the whole rural population in New South Wales, and that tillage was a risky and subordinate matter. "In seventy out of seventy-four of the counties in the intermediate division a patch of arable soil is useless without pasture attached." Perhaps it was a repressed sense of this fact that moved the author of the Act to attach to the right of free selection "the delusion of the pre-lease"—the right to lease for grazing three times the area purchased. But the weapon of free selection on all Crown land turned in his hand and annulled even this touch of realism.

---

[1] For a survey of the contest, district by district, well furnished with general and detailed maps, see Morris and Ranken's *Report on the Public Lands and Land Laws, N.S.W., V. and P.*, 1883, vol. II, pp. 71 *et seq.*
[2] V. S. Clark, *The Labour Movement in Australasia* (1906), p. 27.

As the leases under the Order in Council expired, the Crown lands were thrown open to the free selectors. But the pastoralists were still in effective possession, still entitled to lease their runs afresh and to use their preemptive right to secure picked spots. No attempt was made to partition the colony according to its local suitability to agriculture or pasture. "Two separate forms of tenure were instituted by law, both authorizing the occupation of the same ground."[1] Such a course might have been intelligible had it been a question of supplanting a nomadic barbarism by civilized industry and social security; but the pastoralists were no barbarians, their runs no primitive wastes. Their tenure, though legally inferior, was economically stronger. The spread of their stock had changed the very character of the pastures. As the sheep ate out the saltbush, which in early days stretched from the Lachlan to the Murrumbidgee, grasses both native and new took its place in a soil lightly tilled and compacted by their busy feet. Dams, which when first put down emptied in a few weeks, gained carrying capacity through the puddling of thousands of cattle and sheep.[2] The Riverina of the 'forties was more of a desert than were the lands beyond the Darling a generation later. The men who had initiated these changes and watched their favourable and unfavourable reactions on carrying capacity were led by a law-made war to regard the free-selector who was invited to "jump their claim" much as they had regarded the blacks or as the diggers had viewed the Chinamen. But they were well able to resist the intruders.[3]

Long afterwards, under wiser auspices, it came to be seen that the agriculturalist could render great service to pastoral neighbours, for in dry seasons his haystacks replaced the vanished "top feed," and the grasses and annuals

[1] Morris and Ranken, *loc. cit.* Cf. R. J. Black, *Our Land Laws*, 1905, p. 5.
[2] See Morris and Ranken, *loc. cit.* p. 111 and cf. R. G. Stapledon, *A Tour in Australia and New Zealand* (1928), ch. IX *et passim*.
[3] For an instance of a feud in which blood was shed by both selector and squatter, see C. Amero, *Les Squatters et l'Australie Nouvelle*.

grown on his stubbles raised the whole district's carrying capacity. But these conditions were long delayed. During the 'sixties the seasons conspired with the squatters to defeat agriculture in New South Wales and illustrated the liability of the inland steppes, within the reach but on the margin of both summer and winter rainfalls, to wide fluctuations between drought and flood. 1862 was a year of drought and bushfires. In February 1863 there were floods on the coast, but drought recurred inland until early in 1865. On the coast flood followed flood until July 1864. A favourable season in 1866 was followed by floods with loss of life and much property in 1867, then came drought, followed by more floods in January 1868. In 1869 the Government proclaimed a day of humiliation and prayer for rain. In November 1870 several hundred settlers were homeless after a fresh deluge. "The farmers came to consider it a mere chance whether they would be able to gather in a crop or would lose the fruit of their labours by flood or drought." The area under crop in New South Wales grew only from 254,283 acres in 1861–2 to 378,592 acres a decade later (1871–2), that under wheat from 123,468 acres to 154,030 acres. Meanwhile the sheep depastured increased from 5,615,054 in 1861 to 16,278,697 in 1871. The agricultural revolution had failed to materialise.

The free selectors turned to grazing and the combat deepened. It was bad enough when "cockatoo farmers" tried to "jump" picked spots on the squatters' runs; it grew worse when every "sundowner" might set up as a rival pastoralist. The Act of 1861 made no requirement that a selection should be fenced, and sometimes the selector was a mere blackmailer. "One George C—— selected 320 acres of land on a run in the G—— district. Shortly afterwards he impounded over 700 head of the station cattle, amongst them four bulls upon which he put £5 each, the cost to the station-owners being £78. 1s. 5d." George had evidently chosen a "cattle camp". "After this, one man was constantly kept on watch for a period of five months, at the expiration of which time C—— deserted the selection and it became forfeited. He had neither stock nor improvements on his selection but lived in a calico tent only."[1] It was futile for Sir John Robertson to retort that his Acts had been "framed for honest men and not for rogues". It is the purport of an Act that the courts enforce, and the provisions of Robertson's Act armed even honest men for conflict.

As the law stood until 1875, anyone, adult or infant, might select his or her 320 acres.[2] Many a family settler, by clubbing his own and his children's selections, made up a run of perhaps 3000 acres or even more. If, as often in the Riverina, the whole family came from south of the Murray, the result was the more galling. Inevitably such a grazing selector overstocked his narrow run, perhaps relying on his wheaten hay. In the first dry season encroachments on the station pasture or dams would result. To stop them the Act gave the squatter a complete arsenal of weapons, offensive and defensive. The preemptive right had enabled him long since to buy up water frontages and such points of vantage. By taking a leaf from the family-selector's book, he could defeat the prelease provision, setting employees or "dummies" to purchase, as selections, the selectors' grazing lease. Thus the squatter would "hem in" the would-be grazing selector, making his holding too small to be profitable. But pastoralists disliked "dummying"; "dummies" had a way of turning nasty.[3] Auction-sales of Crown lands were preferable; they were not difficult to arrange, for it was through them the main revenue of the colony was obtained

[1] Morris and Ranken, *loc. cit.* p. 155.

[2] S. H. Roberts, *History of Australian Land Settlement*, p. 227, cites an authenticated story of selection in the name of an unborn child. Put down as Francis, the name had unluckily to be changed to Frances. *N.S.W. Parliamentary Debates*, 1887-8, vol. xxix, p. 3044.

[3] See *Dummies and Mediums, Plain Directions and Hints to*, by "Doodledum Dummy", Kyneton, 24 July 1865, a pamphlet in the Melbourne Public Library, setting forth the various ways in which a Dummy might exact money from his principal.

and unpopular taxation avoided. If land were offered on a sufficient scale, none but the station-owner would be likely to bid. At the worst, rivals could be bought off[1] or left with areas unsaleable save to the station. The banks and financial houses advanced the wool-men the money needed to buy enough of their runs to secure the continuance of the main export industry.

To complete the serried array of the selector's difficulties, the Act empowered the Minister not only to allow land to go to auction at the lessee's request, but also to sanction at discretion purchases by the lessee of land on which he had effected improvements. Otherwise the roving eye of the next selector might light upon the site of a new dam. This was a frequent source of trouble out West. No lessee was safe in improving Crown land. By abstaining from taking possession until the last moment allowed by law, a selector could permit the unsuspecting pastoralist to finish a new dam at great cost: the pastoralist might then find himself a trespasser on a selection it had cost the blackmailer ten pounds to secure after the dam had been begun. As much as £700 was demanded for the fee simple in one such affair. Similar trouble arose later over artesian bores. The parties in this civil war became skilled in using every weapon the law provided. Purchases by virtue of bogus improvements might at times be a necessary preliminary to real ones, but as a rule the improvements were as fictitious as the selectors' statutory declarations of residence. Perjury and corruption vied with cunning and fraud.[2]

Over the broad inland plains the pastoralists held and consolidated their runs by means of the very charter of free selection. Wool and stock-raising, as they practised it, gave a greater net income than the selector's wheat or mixed grazing. But their ultimate economic strength and success

---

[1] *The Warrnambool Examiner*, 29 June 1860, in an article reprinted in *The Argus*, 3 July 1860, accused the member for Portland of accepting a bribe of £350 on condition that he refrained from bidding.

[2] See for some curious examples W. Christie, *Our Land Laws* (1882). The author was a licensed surveyor.

obscure the fact that the pastoralists were on the defensive. Paying more than could then be obtained by cultivation, they bought out many a genuine agriculturalist as well as buying the selections by river or woolshed which had only negative economic value. All such purchases were made to evade an insecurity created by law. All needlessly burdened the industry and lessened its capital resources.

In some areas, notably, but not solely, those unsuited to sheep, much genuine settlement resulted from free selection. Thus in the Bega district, on the extreme south of the coastal strip, a compact settlement of dairy farmers took up holdings and grew maize and root-crops on the river-flats. Easy communication with Sydney by water made the sale of their produce very profitable. Yet even here a preliminary survey would have saved much annoyance through over-lapping selections. At the other extreme of the coastline, the Northern Rivers district, free selectors cultivated maize and sugar by the Richmond and the Clarence. Clashes occurred when they encroached on the cattle stations in the hills, but the station owners learnt to defend their runs by buying 40-acre lots at auction. "No general", it was said, "ever posted his troops in more impregnable positions."

Throughout the old-settled coastal districts from the Macleay River to Moruya Bay, little direct harm resulted from free selection. Selectors took up land alongside the old grants, but brought neither class-warfare nor debt nor monopoly. The old estates were freehold and secure. Patches of good land—isolated in the mountain valleys or hidden amid scrub, where, under another system, no surveyor would have looked—were settled by free selectors, sometimes with legitimate success.

On the New England and Monaro Tablelands, too, positive results were won by selectors combining sheep-farming with tillage. The squatters, unable to buy at auction the freehold of their well-watered runs, most of which were worth bidding for above the upset price of a pound an acre, had perforce to admit the grazing farmer. Selectors quarrelled more among themselves than with the squatters. Dummying was freely employed to fill out selectors' holdings and to cancel pre-leases. In New England 4405 selections had been consolidated into 1560 by 1883. On Monaro, under the snow-clad Australian Alps, the natural combinations of summer and winter grazing with tillage were established on holdings of from two to twenty thousand acres.

It was on the Western Slopes, by the Darling tributaries and in the Riverina, that feuds between squatter and free selector wrought most havoc. However genuine the selector's first desire to make a home by wheat-farming, in these areas of long drought his day was not yet. The squatter could afford to wait patiently—

> It is the land of lots of time
> Along the Castlereagh,

—and he seldom waited in vain. Round Deniliquin in the Riverina the selectors who remained in 1882, out of 1426 who had applied for land since 1865, numbered 244; of these only 48 made any show of living by cultivation. "Most of them make little by it", wrote the Commissioners, "but their earnings are not disproportionate to their exertions." When at long last genuine and dummies' selections and squatters' purchases had alike become station property, in outward appearance there was little to show for John Robertson's great idea but a few broken fences and some skeletons of huts.

Across the Darling on the far western plains

> Where fierce hot winds have set the pine and
> myall boughs asweep

the free selector, making a genuine bid to cultivate, was unknown. Yet even here the Robertson Acts wrought mischief. To prevent selection and, incidentally, to check higher Crown rentals on the back country, the lessees bought the water-frontages at auction, paying a pound an acre. Where nothing less than nine square miles would

make a homestead even at favoured spots, family selection
was not to be expected. Yet by 1882 some 1229 selectors
had taken up 407,000 acres. Two-thirds were "dummies",
and not one in five pretended to make a home. "Shanties"
were commoner than farms. Debiting free selection together with the loss of revenue from the leaseholds for
which this improperly condoned "peacocking" was responsible, it may be reckoned that the three hundred
shanty-keepers,[1] dummies and selectors in the Western
Division had by 1882 cost the colony £10,000 each. In
so level a country that lost revenue might have built a
thousand miles of railway.

The concessions in Robertson's Acts to the claims of
both land-seekers and land-holders not only armed them
for a social strife inimical to orderly settlement but
created confusion and complexity in a department of law
which above all should be simple and intelligible. For
the land laws "affect the interests of a class who, though
enterprising, are generally unlearned, and affect them to
a degree beyond all comparison in the ordinary affairs of
life".[2] Answering complaints of delay in the issue of
selectors' titles, the Surveyor-General (1880) reviewed the
administrative outcome. "There are nine stages in each
conditional purchase, ten in each improvement purchase,
at which all plans and papers touching the case must be
brought together, whereas in simple auction measurements, or measurements in advance of demand, where no
conflicting interests are to be considered, the few plans and
papers required need only be together twice—on receipt
of the measurement and at presentation of the deed."

Even if a conditional purchase went through without a

---

[1] The menace of the shanty may be gauged from two references in Morris
and Ranken's *Report N.S.W., V. and P.* 1883, vol. II, pp. 122, 143: "The
erection of a shanty, and consequent demoralization of the shearers and
station-employees soon bring the lessee to almost any terms, and the troublesome selector merely abandons the land to seek some other place where
he can carry out the same scheme".

[2] G. H. Reid, *N.S.W. Parl. Deb.* 1881, vol. II, pp. 1495 *et seq.*

hitch, the 27 stages of its course at "the Lands" took a minimum of eleven and a half months. "Draftsmen employed in charting have to observe 74 rules, 65 of which may apply to a conditional purchase, and 36 of them are fundamental, the infringement or neglect of any of which might compromise the office."

Sir John Robertson had rejected the tidier plan of settlement after survey in order that independent freeholders might not be baulked of the little properties on which their hearts were set. This was the ideal—a race of yeomen—which had made him the popular hero and evoked enthusiasm throughout Australia. Had the turmoil and waste been offset by this great social gain? Had family settlement been won, even at an economic loss? In 1883 the official returns showed that since 1862 some 129,571 conditional purchases had involved the alienation of 15,421,877 acres of Crown lands, being more than twice the area (6,365,000 acres) alienated in all ways before 1862. But agricultural activity had not kept pace with this free selection. The area under crop had increased by only 329,545 acres in twenty years.

Were there any social gains? What had become of the 129,571 selectors and their chosen spots? Under scrutiny by the 1882 Commissioners it appeared that only 62,000 purported to be "residential selections", the rest being "additional" purchases. Selectors who were actually resident numbered less than 20,000, perhaps not 18,000. They fell into seven types. (1) Dummies who selected in the pastoral lessees' interests, to prevent others and secure the runs, numbered, at an estimate, six-twentieths. (2) Those selecting with the aid of dummies and, before 1875, of children, to obtain areas large enough for grazing, numbered four-twentieths. (3) The few selectors with capital enough to practise agriculture on sound lines, a type more valuable than all the rest together, numbered only a twentieth. (4) Those who by dogged energy succeeded fairly as farmers and paid their instalments, were about threetwentieths. (5) Those "poor in money, education and intelligence, unable to compete in the ordinary occupations of life" who took up small selections, eked out miserable lives for a time, and finally sank into dummying, formed five-twentieths. People of this type, having votes, would not fail to agitate for fresh advantages, remission of interest and so on.[1] (6) Blackmailers, selecting merely to be bought off, totalled perhaps a fortieth; and (7) Those who would take up selections, at 5s. an acre deposit, rather than pay timber licences, and would cut out the timber and forfeit the selection, numbered another fortieth.

One acre in every fourteen of freehold had been cultivated when the Robertson Act was passed, one in thirty-nine in 1880, one in fifty-four in 1891.[2] The bulk of the land alienated by conditional purchase as well as by auction had gone to the pastoralists and had given them "the perfect security of freehold". By 1881 ninety-six land-holders had freehold estates covering eight million acres, averaging 84,000 acres each. Such was the agricultural revolution effected by unlocking the land to free selection before survey.

Indirectly, the Robertson Acts wrought havoc in the moral standards of all classes. "The social effect of the system", thought the Commissioners of 1883, "has been to bring into the country too many of the poor and unthrifty who have been bolstered up temporarily by the laws, but must eventually be a burden to the community." The whole atmosphere of life in the country was tainted by the many temptations to evil-doing which the Robertson Acts left open. Perjury became a commonplace in the lives of all settlers, young and old. The countryside was studded with dens in which horse-thieves found

---

[1] Over ten ·millions of selectors' purchase-money were outstanding in 1882.

[2] By 1891 New South Wales had alienated or agreed to alienate 45,732,000 acres, including 21,325,476 under the conditional purchase (Robertson) system. See *Report of Lands Department*, 1892, *N.S.W.*, *V. and P.* 1892–3, vol. IV, p. 321.

harbour and sympathy. Every effort to educate a population of rough origins was hampered by bitter family
feuds. Measures for the repression of a fresh outbreak of
bushranging during the 'sixties were impeded by the ease
with which a "gang" might use some secluded free selection, chosen perhaps to fit their purposes. Country juries,
mindful of the adage about glass houses, were almost as
willing to condone robbery under arms as stock-thieving.
The trial of the former offence was entrusted in New
South Wales to a special commission, juries being dispensed
with. When three notorious culprits, caught red-handed
after robbing a gold-escort at Eugowra of £28,000, were
condemned at a second trial, a petition for reprieve,
bearing 15,000 signatures, was presented to the Governor.
Bushranging by large gangs was prevalent throughout
the decade. Perhaps highway robbery was inevitable in
those days before railways, when even telegraph lines
were scarce and portable wealth might be had by resolute
ruffians for the taking. But free selection before survey
made the tasks of the police and the schoolmasters uphill
and dangerous work.

How came it that, in the face of its legal and social
perversion, Robertson's Act remained virtually unamended
until 1884? Chiefly because it won the support of two
classes that were beneficiaries by the Act's provisions, and
ignored the scattering of the colony's great endowment.
To the genuine land-seeker, coveting with narrow intensity
a concrete spot that was all Australia to him, what was it
that posterity would suffer? He would provide for his own
by free selection. A more subtle but equally unworthy
resistance to an economical reform of the law came from
the pastoralists and the financiers. "The squatters were
content to let matters remain as they were, relying upon
their superior command of money, and ability to meet
fraud by fraud, to defeat the free selector, who menaced
their runs." More cynical still was the acquiescence of
political leaders in a scheme that had admittedly failed

H

and was manifestly sowing seeds of social and financial trouble. In the administration of the Act the decision of many a critical question—whether land should be put up for auction, and in what parcels, whether a selector should have his chosen spot—put great power into the hands of Ministers of the Crown and their associates. The legislators had good reason to cling to this patronage. "It is notorious that the most effective mode of getting business done at 'the Lands' whether in terms of the law or with the view of thwarting its operation, is to select a land agent who is a member of the popular branch of the Legislature."[1] Finally, the ease with which the proceeds of land sales financed the public expenditure had its effect. It bought the acquiescence of the general taxpayer.

The system, as worked out under ministerial interpretation, gave the pastoralists the freehold of their runs, but at a heavy cost. They were not philanthropists in paying enormous sums into the Treasury. They would much have preferred definite leases at reasonably appraised rentals, for who would pay a pound an acre for land and load himself with an annual interest charge of 1*s*. to 1*s*. 6*d*., if he might have the use of the grass for ½*d*. an acre? The pastoralists borrowed heavily from the banks in buying the freehold, and thus fell into debt to escape a law-made insecurity. As a result they were tempted to overstock in order to lift the mortgages on their land, and in the 'nineties, when the wool-market was glutted and there were droughts of unheard-of duration, many a big sheep-owner was ruined.

Possibly of deeper significance in the end will be the damage done to the Australian communities by the injury the long feud inflicted on the political standing of the pastoralists. Till well into the 'sixties they dominated most of the legislative chambers in Australia and continued

---

[1] *N.S.W., V. and P.* 1883, vol. II, p. 109. Cf. p. 124 for an instance in which the official machinery virtually invited perjury on the part of applicants and stultified integrity on the part of the official surveyors.

to dominate those of the outer colonies until the 'nineties. In 1883 the Commission on the Land Laws in New South Wales gravely noted: "It is argued that practices cannot be condemned as illegal and immoral in which persons of fortune, position and influence in the community have been largely concerned".[1] It is not so argued now. The position and influence of the pastoralists have suffered owing to the shifts by which, albeit in self-defence, their foremost men in the mother colony used the law to defeat the cause of agricultural and family settlement. As persons of fortune they have succeeded. But parliamentary candidates from their ranks, however high their personal qualifications, have been handicapped ever since by the general knowledge that, in the leading pastoral colony, their class used the forms of law to overreach public policy. There are few representatives in Australian politics to-day of the most characteristic and economically important Australians, the big sheep men; and their absence goes far to explain the persistence with which the politics of "development" ignore the economic facts of environment and overseas marketing. Perhaps this is Australia's "tragic flaw".

[1] *N.S.W., V. and P.* 1883, vol. II, p. 91.

CHAPTER XIII

Agricultural Settlement in the Southern Colonies

THE attractions of gold-digging and gold-mining had raised the population of Victoria from 75,000 in 1850 to 538,000 in 1860, and a provincial journal in the latter year rejoiced that the dwellers in the interior far outnumbered "the once predominant citizens of the metropolis". As gold-digging failed them, it was natural that the new-comers, despising the pre-gold "colony of slaves and task-masters", should seek to supply the lack of "a prosperous and well-principled middle class" by unlocking the land. Virgin and fertile plains stretched north and south on either side of the auriferous highlands they had peopled. City merchants, the press, and the more public-spirited of the squatters alike advocated this obvious policy of settling the diggers in an industry which would win annual and increasing wealth. Yet, being in possession of such pastures as the new volcanic soils of the western districts and the alluvial valleys of the Wimmera, the Lodden, the Goulburn and the Campaspe, the squatters were but human in striving to postpone the change.

Forty million acres of the best sheep-walks in Australia were a rich endowment for defensive action, and the law's tradition of maintaining subjects' rights even against the Crown led the courts to construe the Orders in Council of 1847 in a sense favourable to those in possession. There was no back country in Victoria, like the mulga lands beyond the Darling or in Central Queensland, to which the pastoralist alone might retreat. The eleven million acres of mallee lands in the north-west were to them what they had seemed to Major Mitchell—"one of the most barren regions in the world". The squatters held their ground and the symptoms of a violent explosion appeared.

In 1857 a self-constituted Land Convention assembled almost opposite Melbourne Parliament House. The leader was an Irish-American lawyer, Wilson Gray; and the Convention made no secret of its intention to force free-selection upon the legislature. Their slogan was "a vote, a rifle and a farm", and when the first of these had been conceded they broke into the popularly elected Assembly when it was debating a new Land Bill. *The Age* assured the public that broken windows, bloodshed and charges by mounted police were more than the Eastern Markets demagogues had intended. The "popular oracles", it explained, had, in their desire to show the earnestness of the people, "overdone the demonstration".[1] But the revulsion of feeling occasioned by this violence favoured a compromise, and after a conference between the Houses Nicholson's Land Act of 1860 conceded selection after survey and credit payments.

The terms of the concession to land-seekers, being under equal democratic laws necessarily open to all, proved most favourable to those in command of money and local knowledge. When the Act was passed nearly four million acres of the best Victorian land had already been sold by auction. Well posted in these strongholds, the pastoralists were able to pay for the areas now offered, up to 640 acres in a block, prices which they were not worth as separate holdings. And if more than one selector applied for the same allotment it was put up for a sale by auction at which only the applicants could bid. The scales were weighted still further against the "small man" by the rule that half the minimum purchase price of a pound an acre must be paid at once. Most of the 800,000 acres alienated in the space of eighteen months under Nicholson's Act

---

[1] *The Age*, 29 August 1860.

were in the western district and around the central gold-fields. Cultivation increased, but not by equal steps. Selling out to a wealthy neighbour offered the selector a better profit.[1]

In 1862, Charles Gavan-Duffy tried to prevent competition between squatters and farmers by setting aside "agricultural areas" for selection. When there were several applicants for any of the 640-acre holdings into which these were divided, priority was to be determined by lot. But Duffy's safeguards to secure the agricultural use of the land proved ineffective. The Act gave the selector his title, subject to the condition that he erected a boundary fence or a habitable dwelling or cultivated one acre out of every ten. The price, still a pound an acre, might be paid by instalments of half-a-crown. But it was found that, in the event of the selector selling his holding, the Crown had no power to punish his assigns for failure to fulfil the condition. Anyone might take up a fresh selection each year. By deputy and dummy the squatters bought up the lands resumed. Within one week 800,000 more of the richest acres in the colony had been sold. Before the operation of the Act was suspended by a new Ministry it was computed that a hundred men had obtained 930,000 acres out of 1,423,000 acres that had been alienated in accordance with its provisions. "The very class for whom he legislated", its author complained, "sold its inheritance for some paltry bribe".[2]

Duffy's Act, in effect, completed the transfer of Australia Felix in fee simple to the pastoralists. Save for a compact settlement raising pigs and potatoes around Tower Hill (Port Fairy) and Warrnambool, on basalt soils deriving

[1] Brooke, the Commissioner of Lands, attempted the issue of occupation licences to small agriculturalists, on the analogy of pastoral licences, but these were declared illegal by the Supreme Court.

[2] Cf. John Quick, LL.D., *History of Land Tenure in the Colony of Victoria*, 1883: "The prodigality of the State in parting so extravagantly and incautiously with the common inheritance has been only surpassed by the profligacy and the ingratitude of those who were the objects of the paternal care and anxiety of Parliament".

from the last but long extinct Australian volcano, the Western District remained for another generation a famous sheep country and no more. The farmers, like the railways, went beyond its fertile stretches to the seemingly less favoured grey and red Wimmera soils, or crossed the Divide into the oft-flooded Goulburn Valley, or carved out clearings from the giant forests of Gippsland.

The resistance of the pastoralists did not dispel the land hunger. Where Duffy failed a versatile Scot succeeded. James Macpherson Grant, a Sydney barrister who had turned digger and had successfully defended the Eureka stockade leaders without fee, was Commissioner of Crown lands in the first McCulloch Ministry. He continued the policy of selection after survey, but added by an Act of 1865 the simple rule that *bona fide* settlement must precede alienation. His Act gave the selector only a lease at first, though this was convertible into freehold on easy terms of payment after three years of residence and the making of substantial improvements. Three million acres had been taken up under the new Act, and the area under cultivation had increased from 416,000 acres to 680,000 when parliament felt encouraged to enact free selection before survey under a similar safeguard. Under Casey's Act, as the 1869 measure was called, another 11,000,000 acres were selected in the Wimmera, the Goulburn Valley and Gippsland. In the Echuca district dummying came to light, but it was checked by a special land board. The Commissioner for Crown lands held in reserve a discretionary power to disallow applications, but this was seldom needed. The three years' probationary lease was effective.

Genuine agricultural settlement of the Crown lands was thus made easy; yet it was impracticable to change by such legislation the relative attractions of stock-raising and arable farming. The area under crop in Victoria grew from 410,406 acres in 1861 to 1,548,809 acres in 1880, but the expansion was considerably greater on new selections than in the colony as a whole. The ease with which virgin land might be obtained tempted men to crop their land until it was exhausted, and then to sell out and take up another selection. This was not mere greed. Those who attempted to husband their land's fertility by a rotation of crops and fallow could not escape a soil-exhaustion which made wheat-growing on old land unprofitable. Either the farmer turned pastoralist after buying out his neighbours to provide room for stock, or sold out himself to an older pastoralist, and moved on in semi-nomadic fashion to fresh wheat fields. By the middle 'eighties Victoria's agricultural progress had lost momentum. The area under crop grew slowly from 1,500,000 acres in 1880 to just over 2,000,000 in 1890, while that under wheat was stagnant at 1,100,000 from 1883 to 1890.

Nor did Victoria escape the bushranging revival. The wild tumble of mountains and river-valleys in the north-east of Victoria, opened to selection under the later Acts, had retained since the digging days a name for lawlessness. In 1878 a gang of bushrangers, famous in Australia as the last of the outlaws, and the heroes of a dramatic "last stand", issued from this region. Sons of John Kelly, a convict who was sent out to Van Diemen's Land in 1841 for attempting to shoot his landlord in County Tipperary, Ned, Jim and Dan Kelly had gone with their mother in 1865 from Wallan to Eleven Mile Creek, near Glenrowan. There they were soon plying the family trade as stock-thieves. Ned was arrested as an accomplice of Power, a New South Wales bushranger, but identification failed. Some say he betrayed Power, but a Victorian police Superintendent, named Hare, stoutly denies this charge.[1] Jim, his younger brother, was "doing time" in New South Wales—a ten years' sentence, and his second—when both Dan and Ned got into trouble again with the Victorian police. There had been "bad blood" between them and the troopers, one of whom had made love to their sister Kate, and in April 1878, Dan, a boy of only seventeen,

[1] In his *Last of the Bushrangers* (1892).

fit and historically apt that a schoolmaster, though he limped to do it, rid the colony of a pest which was a reminder of a dark age. No amount of sentiment can disguise its sordid and criminal features.

South Australia started with better human material and her economic development was least warped by transportation and gold-rushes. After half-heartedly attempting to open the puzzling Murray mouth and to play a commercial role in serving the Murray-Darling basin by river transport,[1] the province found prosperity by means of the agricultural resources of her central rift-valley and of the folded hills of rich alluvium beside it.

Isolation and the different quality of her colonists might have made her an Australian and nonconformist South Island. Yet even in South Australia, a land without precious metals of her own, the backwash of the mining rushes forced on the conflict between pastoral and agricultural use of the soil and brought industrial ambitions and standards out of intercolonial rivalry. In the 'fifties the exodus of her adventurous sons to "the fields" caused the thorough use of Ridley's "stripper" in harvesting the wheat crop. The 'sixties saw a rapid extension of stock-raising and agriculture to meet the goldfields' demands, and an exodus of disappointed or would-be farmers to select land under the radical laws of New South Wales and Victoria. Thereupon the province overhauled her land system and for a time her legislators copied, with a certain caution, experiments in the art of colonization which once they had been proud to teach.

Even after the discovery in 1860–61 of the rich Wallaroo and Moonta copper deposits, agriculture produced crops that in normal years rivalled in value the products of the mining and pastoral industries combined. Little farms continued to multiply and spread. From 1862 to 1880 the

---

[1] These attempts are admirably reviewed in A. Grenfell Price's "South Australian Efforts to Control the Murray", *A.A.A.S.*, *Perth Transactions*, 1926, pp. 444 *et seq.*

area under wheat in South Australia and the wheat-harvest were about equal to those of all the other colonies put together. After 1866 wheat was exported in fluctuating but considerable quantities to Britain. By 1881 the cultivation per head in South Australia was 7·5 acres as compared with 1·7 per head in Victoria and four-fifths of an acre per head in New South Wales. The Mediterranean climate of South Australia is far better suited for wheat-growing than the coastal lands then favoured by farmers in Victoria and New South Wales.[1] But in turning that advantage to good use the intelligence of South Australian farmers evolved a labour-saving technique. Until the late 'sixties the ripe crops were gathered with reaping hooks in the slow-ripening fields of the S.E. coasts, and the hay was mown with scythes. The sheaves carted in at "harvest home" were stacked and laboriously threshed with the flail and the grain was winnowed with sieves on windy days. Ridley's "stripper", a header pushed at first by two horses, did its work best in a dry crisp air, such as lasted in South Australia's harvest-time from dewless dawn to dark. This was but the first, though it was the most decisive, of the inventions by which the farmers of that province left vacant the places deserted by those who rushed to the gold-diggings, yet increased production and lowered their costs. Victorians adopted the stripper after a bumper harvest in 1866–7. An average wheat yield of 22·25 bushels tempted the reapers to demand forty shillings an acre to cut the crop. After that the strippers were in great demand. Not only did they cut the crops on the old wheat-growing areas more cheaply than such hard-bargaining fellows, but, what was more important for Victoria's future, they encouraged selectors under Grant's Act to venture inland to districts like the Wimmera where the summers were like those of South Australia. With the strippers the grain could be taken off quickly before the north wind's mighty flail had threshed it for the birds.

[1] See map facing p.252 in S.H.Roberts' *History of Australian Land Settlement.*

One invention suggested another in a community whose best minds were as yet undistracted from the main issue of producing more wheat and wool. After strippers came into use in South Australia, a new method was devised of clearing the scrublands thrown open to selectors in 1869. Prior to this only those who had other land for cropping could afford the five years needed to break in scrub or mallee land. The method adopted had been to cut the scrub at about a foot above ground, to pile the debris around the stumps and burn soon after the new shoots appeared. "Sucker-bashing"—a very arduous business with the mattock—was still needed after this and raised the cost of killing the scrub to fifteen shillings an acre. But the cleared land grew good grass. Those who had sheep could get some return for their expenditure even during the five years before the roots were ready to be drawn from the ground. These, if a market offered, were sold as firewood for the towns.

A settler named Mullens at Wasleys (S.A.) made farms of nothing but scrubland both practicable and profitable. He cut the scrub level with the ground, burnt it off and then scratched the soil with a heavy triangular log through which he had driven strong spikes. From soil enriched by the ashes of a "good burn" this "scratching in"[1] would produce a few crops that showed a good margin of profit above the light costs involved. But such farms in the South Australian mallee needed constant attention with the "fire-rake" to keep down the regrowth of suckers. Other scrubland selectors, of whom R. B. Smith of Ardrossan (Yorke's Peninsula) was probably first, went one better and contrived a plough that thoroughly turned up this "Mullenized" land and incidentally loosened many of the roots. Its two, three or more shares worked independently, and each, as it struck an ungrubbed stump, tripped, passed above it "at the trail", and was sent back into the soil

[1] It is customary to explain the term "cockey farmer" by the analogy between this scratching in and the cockatoo's habits. More probably the phrase is a corruption of "cockney farmer". See reference to *Hobler Papers*, p. 93, note 2, *supra*.

by a strong spring so soon as the stump was jumped. After such multiple-furrow "stump-jump" ploughs came lighter cultivators, seed-drills and complete harvesters, the most successful form of which was the work of a young Victorian farmer, H. V. McKay in 1884. More than one South Australian claimed to have anticipated McKay in making a complete harvester, capable of stripping and winnowing in one operation. Whoever was the inventor, there is no question of the important part in maintaining net profits that "harvesters" have played. With such a machine the farmer may, single-handed, drive his team into the ripe crop and, while daylight and endurance last, pour the wheat into the jute corn-sacks ready for sewing up and delivery at the mill or the railway siding.[1]

After 1876 such aids were badly needed by South Australian farmers. From that year to 1904 not one crop reached a ten-bushel average, eighteen fell below a six-bushel average, and prices ruled low. Nine of the poor harvests were reaped in succession, from 1894 to 1902 inclusive. That was a spell of prolonged drought, but not all the years from 1876 to 1904 were drought years. Soil-exhaustion far and wide was mocking the farmers long before the Big Drought set in.

From the first, South Australia had conceded them effective rights to displace squatters from their leases of Crown land. As a consequence the farmers enjoyed a reasonable freedom to test their relative ability in turning the province's sun-baked soil to good use. No suggestion of security of tenure was granted to Crown lessees until after 1847. Then under the Orders in Council they obtained "permissive leases" up to 14 years in duration, outside the "hundreds" surveyed for agriculture and sale. These did not prevent resumptions. A favourite means of raising revenue continued to be "killing a squatter", i.e. giving a Crown lessee six months' notice and then surveying his run into

---

[1] For a description of the mechanism of H. V. McKay's Sunshine Harvester, see the *Australian Encyclopaedia*, vol. II, p. 664.

hundreds. Despite this slight security, the goldfields market and the northern explorations of Stuart and McKinlay had led during the 'fifties to a fourfold increase of stations shipping from Port Augusta at the head of Spencer Gulf. Goyder, the Surveyor-General, reappraised these northern runs after a series of good seasons, but immediately after his doing so most of them were abandoned. A pitiless drought left them bare from 1864 to 1869. After the drought, Crown rentals, based on stock actually carried, replaced the double impost of fixed charge plus assessment on official estimates of "capacity". But what made restocking practicable after the drought was not the easier rentals so much as the fences, wells and dams which took the place of the sod-huts and movable hurdles of shepherding days.

By 1872 the expensive yet economical ways of capitalism had universally replaced the nomadic patriarchal style. Capitalism, being expensive, called for some security of tenure. This came through the operation of radical land-laws.

In the south of the province sale by auction of Crown lands withdrawn from pastoral occupation did not satisfy the farmers' land-hunger after the 'sixties. Land-agents— some called them "land-sharks"—divided the spoil at or near the upset figure of a pound an acre. They deterred genuine land-seekers by threatening to bid against them for the particular block they sought. For this reason, to quote Stephen Roberts, "the trek of the covered waggons of the German settlers was a common sight in the late 'sixties, and a continual stream slowly wound across the plains towards Albury and the easily acquired land". Such sights were a scandal in the chosen home of systematic colonization and many were the proposals and investigations for a remedy. In November 1865 the Surveyor-General went north to mark where the rainfall had extended, even during drought. He found the "line of demarcation extending considerably further south" than he had anticipated and traced it from Swan Reach through Burra Hill, Oak Rises, Mount Sly, Mount Remarkable and Broughton across the gulf to Franklin Harbour and N.W. to the west end of Gawler Ranges. As a result of Goyder's investigations the stock runs were re-graded into four classes,[1] and his work was naturally given prominence as an historical generalization upon the incidence of drought. Botanists think Goyder based his judgment on the prevalence of perennial and other salt-bush and of mallee. But such was his prestige at the time, as a permanent official well endowed with both knowledge and pluck, that "Goyder's Line" was almost immediately accepted as marking the "safe country" for wheat farming.[2]

In 1869, Goyder reported on the working of Grant's Act in Victoria, and in that year Henry Strangways, an English barrister who had quickly taken the lead in South Australian politics, carried a measure similarly designed. It maintained auction sales of land for the sake of "revenue", but permitted deferred payments while restricting the transfer of blocks sold on credit. Selection was allowed only after survey and within defined agricultural areas. As usual, selection tempted men into dummying, especially in the competition for rich pockets of land round Mount Gambier in the south-east. Conditional purchase after survey was extended by a Waste Lands Act of 1872 to the whole area inside "Goyder's Line". Some farms beyond this line had been under cultivation, however, as early as 1867, and after 1874 there was increased activity in taking up areas offered for selection in the far north, i.e. north

[1] S.A., V. and P. nos. 62 and 78 of 1865–6, no. 133 of 1865–6, 16 February 1866.

[2] T. G. Taylor, *Australian Environment*, 1918, p. 98, praises Goyder's work as a model in estimating the possibilities of new country. It was essentially a brilliant surmize but its definite nature has been overstated. His maps and journeys show evidence of indecision and he made minor alterations subsequently. It does not coincide with the 14 inch, the 12 inch or any line of rainfall, and follows the salt-bush closely only near the Burra. Wheat-farming with modern methods has gone far beyond it and the modern geographer hesitates to mark "The Line" on his maps for fear of reviving the deterrent power it once had.

of Port Augusta. Good seasons flattered the venturesome and many were ready to argue that rain followed the plough.

The outward surge of agriculture was met by a shift of wool-growers to the south. When the policy of resumption was active, banks were chary of advancing money to Crown lessees for expensive improvements; and all the pastoral leases were to be put up for auction in 1888, not a distant date in risky country where repayments are often delayed by "act of God".

To make insecurity worse, rabbits came in waves down the Murray valley and over the interior, and in the 'eighties drought returned. Soon it was seen that "good stations had been ruined to make bad farms". The plough had out-paced the rain-clouds and there was nothing for the northern farmers but to abandon their bare, wind-swept fields and "toe the Line" once more. For some of them benevolent governments found southern holdings in exchange. Payment of interest on purchase money was remitted and payment of principal postponed. In areas thought doubtful for farming some were induced to stay by renewable leases in lieu of purchase. Representative boards were created to adjust rentals and renew the pastoral leases, to keep watch against dummying and to classify land so that selectors' obligations might vary with the productive power of their land.

Under flexible administration by these standing boards, the Acts of 1869 and 1872 grafted conditional purchase after survey on to the Wakefield system, as a corrective to the vice of speculation that had beset it. The primary aim was still agriculture, in a moving equilibrium with pasture. Kindly, intelligent amendment maintained the province's name for progressive idealism in her land laws. Yet neither parliament nor representative boards had it within their power to amend the soil. Its exhaustion continued to make the cultivators restless. From 1880 until well into the new century, about 1907, the total area under the plough was stagnant at 2,200,000 acres, while that under wheat fell back from the 1,942,453 acres recorded in 1884–5. The cause was evident. From an average of 11·2 bushels an acre from 1861 to 1865 the yield had fallen to 5·43 bushels an acre for the years 1881 to 1885. Worse was to come during the great drought. For the years 1896 to 1900 inclusive, South Australian farmers harvested an average of 4·1 bushels to the acre. Well might Sir William Crookes, in surveying the world's wheat resources, wonder why they persisted. By that time, however, hope had dawned. At Roseworthy Agricultural College, founded in 1879, Professor Custance, the first principal, put his finger on the weakness that was depressing the yield—an exhaustion of the phosphates always in short supply in Australian soils. He advocated as remedy the dressing of the land with soluble superphosphate. For more than a decade the practical men smiled at Custance and his successor, Professor Lowrie. Then they gave "the handful of magic dust" a trial, and a new era in the Australian economy began.

To face the double insecurity of drought and legislative changes the pastoralists of South Australia relied on another but equally rare type of insight, and succeeded so well that they bought up many a baffled farmer's freehold in the central area of the province. The sheep brought by the first colonists were largely of Leicester and Southdown breed. Angas's South Australian Company added Merinos from Saxony, Mecklenberg, Tasmania and New South Wales. These and the overlanders' flocks of the same breed throve at once, and South Australian sheepbreeders evolved a special type of Merino which won the province high fame for her weighty fleeces. Darwin held that not one man in a thousand had the accuracy of eye and judgment adequate to the breeder's task. The flockmasters of South Australia numbered several such breeders amongst them, notably John Murray of Mount Crawford, and early learned to follow their lead. Without bringing in fresh blood, but simply by inbreeding and culling the unwanted variants, generation after generation, they fixed a robust and vigorous type with a heavy fleece of long-stapled fine wool, an animal, because of its lack of wrinkling, least likely to suffer from the dreaded blow-fly. As a rule, South Australian flockmasters eschewed "artificial feeding", looking to the survival of the fittest chosen to maintain the vigour of their stock and to adapt it even to the chronic drought of the northern salt-bush country.

Tasmanian and Western Australian colonists strove during the second half of the nineteenth century to rid their communities of the economic stigmata of transportation. The Tasmanians had the more obvious need to do so. In 1840 there were 27,246 convicts in the island as against 40,432 free, of whom only 13,000 were adults. Between 1841 and 1852 some 35,378 more convicts were sent thither. Making all allowance for the eagerness of expirees to quit the scene, the population of 68,870 in 1850 was saturated with "lag" blood.[1] The road construction and other pioneering tasks done by the prisoners were stultified for decades by the handicap, largely but not wholly psychological, with which "the system" and its products weighed down a little country by no means poor in natural resources.

In 1858 the new legislature thought to try the fashionable policy of unlocking the land as a corrective of the inertia that had resulted from the exodus to Victoria. But there was little good land left to be unlocked. East of a line from South Cape to Surrey Hills three million acres had already been sold, two million were under grazing licences, and a million in guaranteed "quiet enjoyment" for ten years. These were the "settled lands". The wet Western third of the island remained smothered under almost impenetrable scrub. The new law retained auction sales of Crown land and, as in New South Wales, there was more alienation than agricultural settlement. In 1863

---

[1] According to J. B. Brigden, *Tasmania, an Economic Sketch* (1927), p. 14, in the ten years 1851–1860 some 88,660 emigrants were replaced by 77,080 immigrants, yet the population "had fallen in productive quality".

"agricultural areas" in the north-east were offered for selection but succeeded little better. The offer bore witness to a consciousness of one of Tasmania's natural handicaps, the scattered deposition of her assets. But the root cause of the colony's trouble was that, in wheat growing as in wool, her resources were inferior to those of the mainland, though her climate was attractive to colonists fresh from England. Van Diemen's Land had been exporting wheat to the Sydney market before her settlers took up wool under Governor Sorell's guidance, and in 1850 she had produced more than the mainland. But the transition from gold-mining to agriculture in Victoria and the superior advantages and energy of the South Australians brought the price of wheat below the marginal costs of production in Tasmania. The area under wheat began to shrink in the 'sixties. Farmers in the island were victims of soil-exhaustion even earlier than those in South Australia, and their government provided no such technical instruction as the Roseworthy College men gave their competitors. So Tasmanian wheat was driven out of its natural market in Victoria by South Australian and Californian competition. Emigration continued. A quarter of the land revenue was ear-marked after 1864 for roads and wharves, but as land sold very slowly both revenue and public works fell away. Even sheep-pasturing barely held its own. An attempt was made to extend it into the rainy "unsettled lands" towards the West Coast. Areas of from 60 to 640 acres were offered as free rewards to any settlers who might possess capital equal to a pound per acre acquired and would use it to effect improvements.

To bait the hook, grazing leases of as much as 10,000 acres in adjacent mountainous country were added. On these the grantees might expect at least to reimburse clearing costs by felling timber and exporting it to the builders of Victoria. But Tasmania's luck held. In the 'sixties even that market slumped, for, once more, superior resources were found north of the Straits.

When Victoria set up her tariff wall, Tasmanian depression grew even deeper. Projects of reciprocity were "gravelled for lack of matter". What had the island to offer that David Syme should relent from his ideal of self-sufficiency? A retaliatory tariff failed to put any pressure on the wealthier and younger community. It extended "the dull indigence of Hobart" to the northern half of the island, which had hitherto extracted some prosperity from trade with Melbourne. The expenses of government, when severely pruned, were almost met in good years by the sale of as much Crown land as buyers could be induced to take, but the banks had little liking for advances to enable their clients to buy land on which fluke and scab were prevalent.

In 1871 came the first signs of change. As usual a man named Smith turned the colonists' attention to mining, though in this instance he was reversing the process of economic change on the mainland. The Tasmanian Smith—James by name—returned from the diggings but refused to settle down at farming. He earned the nickname of "the Philosopher", apparently by his eccentric persistence in searching for gold-bearing quartz. He found tin in 1871 at Mount Bischoff in the north-west. Tin-mining, though it seemed a tame thing after Victoria's gold, did something to revive enterprize, and in 1875 further deposits were found in the north-east. In the year following, Hobart and Launceston were joined by rail, and in 1877 gold was found at Beaconsfield near the Tamar mouth. Finds of silver-lead and copper followed in 1885–6 at Mount Zeehan and Mount Lyell on the west coast where Tasman had first seen the land long before. For the first time for many decades immigrants came to swell the island population. Tillage increased in the scattered valleys. Potatoes from the north-west and apples in the Derwent and Huon Valleys were added to the island's tally of exports. Governments took courage and launched into active loan expenditure on transport facilities, railways, roads and bridges. The spell over the island seemed to be broken at last.

In Western Australia, transportation, deliberately accepted, and triply safeguarded by the reform of the penal code in Britain, by the exclusion of female prisoners and by the employment of the men solely on public works, did less harm, on balance, than anywhere else. The "chronic despondency" of the stagnant decades passed after 1870 when a representative council was called to a wider vision and solid achievements by Governor F. A. Weld[1] and the native-born explorer-statesman John Forrest. The pastoral horizon widened when in that year grass-land was found on the Hampton Tableland, and when in 1874 splendid salt-bush and mulga were found on the Murchison and Sandford water-courses inland from Champion Bay. Governor Weld had had experience in New Zealand both as settler and administrator, and dealt with the patchy character of the land available for tillage, as South Australia was doing, by classifying each area and varying the terms of selection with the quality of the land. To squatters he offered the security of fourteen-year leases with rights of pre-emption. In 1880 pastoral occupation followed Alexander Forrest's exploration of Fitzroy Plains in the far north. In 1885 a railway reached York in the sweeter lands of the Avon Valley beyond the Darling escarpment, and wheat farming prospered there in a quiet way. It may have been only by comparison with days of narrower things that the colonists felt satisfied. To John Forrest, acting "comptroller of expenditure" after 1880 and surveyor-general after 1883, free selection of small blocks for agriculture meant nothing very grand. He bowed to the strong desire for its retention, but thought "free selection had in many places resulted in spoiling the country, having dotted over it quite unimproved small locations securing water-holes,

[1] For an able review of the state of the colony emphasizing the urgent need of representative institutions as an expedient of political education for a younger generation which had not felt responsibility, see F. A. Weld to Earl Granville, 1 March 1870.

springs and small pieces of good land which it would have been better for the colony never to have sold".[1]

To check such peacocking and to protect the pastoral tenants from blackmail, Forrest adopted the usual devices of liberal land-laws such as "agricultural areas", long terms of sale on credit, the issue of titles only after a probationary lease and due improvement. Pasture alone made headway as yet, but he had laid on sound lines his long campaign in favour of agriculture. The sheep in the colony passed the first million in 1879 and two millions in 1888.

By then the whole atmosphere had changed. Gold was found in 1883 in the torrid East Kimberley, and, though most who rushed thither in 1884–5 rushed back to Cambridge Gulf in a thirst-stricken retreat, gold was won in fair quantities. The sententious report in which E. Hargraves, the New South Wales gold discoverer, had discoursed on "the non-auriferous character of the rocks of Western Australia" lost its authority and men found traces of gold at widely scattered points from Albany to the de Grey. All was excitement[2]; the Swan River awoke from somnolence to an eager expectancy.

The general result of the period of land reform surveyed in the preceding two chapters was disillusionment. Unlocking the land had opened no door to unlimited gains by farming. Neither the go-as-you-please policy of New South Wales, nor the survey of agricultural areas in advance of settlement favoured in the other colonies, had enabled the farmers to make much headway in displacing the squatters. Save in South Australia, wool remained the staple by virtue of the greater net returns it brought. Even in South Australia, the norm of an unforced colonial

---

[1] Surveyor-General's *Report for* 1883, *W.A. Leg. Council V. and P.* 1884, no. 15.

[2] The story goes that Colonel Angelo, the Government Resident at Pilbara, when gold was found there, wired to the Colonial Secretary (Malcolm Fraser): "Young Withnell picked up stone to throw at crow" and omitted to report what Withnell found in it. Mr Fraser replied: "Did he really? What happened to crow?"

economy, neither liberal land-laws, nor rich soil, nor both together had been enough to assure settled prosperity to the farmers. Only rare qualities of invention, tenacity and insight had kept them from faltering and were to restore their strength at the end of the century. In the 'seventies and 'eighties, throughout the south-eastern colonies the banks spread their branches into the squatting districts, the station men bought their runs, fenced them, watered them and bred up their flocks. Certainly wheat was not yet the master word. The Australian farmer had much beyond politics to learn before his strength came upon him.

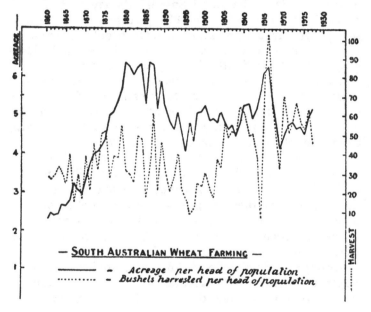

Graph of South Australian Wheat Farming, comparing the effort of the province to develop this industry, as shown in the acreage cropped per head, with the success achieved, as measured in bushels harvested per head. The slump from 1875 to 1903 is very apparent.

The ineffectiveness of radical laws to promote the farming interest at the expense of pasture might well

have impressed on thoughtful observers the social meaning
of the price of land. Wakefield had had a glimmering of
that meaning when he advocated a "sufficient" price,
one that would impede all and sundry from becoming
"land poor" by taking up land they could not profitably
work. But he did not appreciate that in land values,
which are to keep the varying parcels of town and
country land in hands capable of putting them to the
best use, variation with changing circumstances is essential.
It may even be doubted if he saw that, apart from
changes in the market value of land-products, the
sufficiency of a price varied with the fertility and situation of the land. A price sufficient to put an end to
settlement at Australind and in Western Australia
generally was so low in South Australia as to invite the
speculative purchase and re-sale of metalliferous land at
the Burra and even of good wheat land on the Plains
and broad highland valleys. For political reasons the
price at which the government sold public land had to be
given a false uniformity. The government could not, without an appearance of hard-bargaining, charge what the
traffic would bear. Yet democracy's benevolent intention
to temper the wind to the farmer's shorn lamb could
not endow the tender creature with the vigour that enabled the pastoral ram to survive and fatten. And it
came to pass that demagogues dispersed the public estate
and pastoralists gathered up the freehold thereof.

CHAPTER XIV

Plantation Slavery and Secession for North Queensland

I N spite of some variation in their minor economic
activities, the Australian communities, festooned along
a coast-line of ten thousand miles, are nowadays
strangely uniform in social structure. In each port—there
are less than a score that count for much—you will find a
group of importers' warehouses, some big wool-stores, a
railway terminus, a wharf-lumpers union and a number
of public houses tied to breweries. If there is a capital
city in the near background, it is inhabited largely
by a civil service concerned with Crown lands, public
works and education. Its environs will boast some industries engaged on the simpler manufactures or on the
repair and maintenance of the mechanism of land transport. Ships, if they can, seek cheaper repairs elsewhere.
Dairying, grape-growing and its derivatives, sugar and
other tropical plantations may seem to flourish on the
coastal areas, but do so largely through Government aid.
Over the range is the scene of the peculiarly Australian
work, done by a scattered population of miners, farmers
and station-hands, who turn out staple raw-products on
a rough, grand scale with labour-saving machinery that
is the worthiest output of the town factories.

Brooding over the coastal capital, and browbeating with
their vociferous claims the mercantile and professional
classes who, but for fear of the "wowser" vote, would
mould the economic policies of the country on more
orthodox lines, stand the federated trade unions. Their

Trades Hall is the scene of a fluctuating contest between the capable leaders of three groups: (i) the shearers, miners and timber workers of the bush, (ii) the town artisans, and (iii) the transport workers and public works employees. These contend for mastery, somewhat noisily at times, through the primaries or "selection-ballots" that name the labour candidates for the local or national parliament. More continuously they learn the arts of parliamentary debate and constitution-making in holding or capturing the state party machine. The farmers, with some aid from pastoralists and the middle class, are learning political organization from the workers, but are still clumsy and inarticulate. This social structure varies little with the minor staples that differences in local climate may add to the dominant wool and wheat. The Australian communities have set in these forms with a surprising uniformity. In the politics of each the drive comes mainly from a hard-eyed, hard-headed, hard-mouthed working democracy.

Queensland once promised to evolve quite a different social tissue comparable to the planter-aristocracy of the Old Dominion and the Carolinas in the days of Calhoun and Henry Clay. Miss Flora Shaw (the late Lady Lugard), stressing the contrast between temperate and tropical Australia, at the Colonial Institute in 1894, predicted that "if North Queensland obtains the political separation for which it is agitating the nucleus of the development of tropical Australia will have been formed. The creation of other tropical colonies, in which the habits of thought, the aims and traditions will differ widely from those of the existing Australian communities, will be only a question of time". But Southern Queensland, with effective aid from Whitehall at more than one juncture, offered so determined a resistance to secession and social differentiation that economic forces had time to assimilate the north and to cut away the bases of the planters' will to rule.

After the wild scramble for alluvial gold, the wool-growing industry resumed its sway as premier industry throughout Australia and tightened its grip on the south-eastern colonies under cover of the radical land laws. In so doing it pressed into its service the bigger and better resources of money and men that the golden age had furnished. But its geographical centre had moved definitely northward. Before the gold discoveries, the flocks of Port Phillip District vied on almost even terms with those of a New South Wales that still included Queensland. Twenty years later the wheat-growers were restlessly disputing for the land south of a line from Port Augusta in South Australia to Mount Kosciusko. North of that line the superior power of the pastoralist to make profitable use of the land grew more marked as the winter rains gave place to the summer rains. Queensland seemed to the pastoralists "their promised land". Leslies, Campbells and Archers showed the way, and in the 'sixties scores of southern squatters sought safety there from the free selector. Black spearsmen ambushed their stock in the brigalow scrub. They besieged even numerous station households in a strength and determination forgotten farther south, and murdered isolated shepherds and carters with tragic cunning. In Queensland men went about their daily task with shot gun in hand, and nightly folded their sheep because pastoral occupation was still an invasion of territory held in force by resolute enemies. But native resistance could not stop the invaders. "The natural progress of the aboriginal race towards extinction"[1] soon made fences, boundary riders and the "kelpie" feasible there too.

But climatically the north was less suitable for sheep than were the western plains of New South Wales. The excessive evaporation in summer more quickly turned a season of light rainfall into complete drought. Good "top-feed" might remain on saltbush, gidgea, leopard-wood and mulga and in the dried Mitchell grass, but the drying of the rivers and water-holes meant sweeping losses of sheep. Cattle

[1] Sir W. Denison to Sir E. B. Lytton, 6 April 1859.

could travel farther to water, and therefore, as the 'eighties opened, the northern colony became the chief cattle area of Australia. Deep bores tapped artesian supplies in that decade and made sheep safe long after the evaporation of surface-water. The increased carrying capacity of paddocks thus watered was marked by the growing numbers of both sheep and cattle.[1]

Even with assured supplies of drinking water for man and beast, Western Queensland remained a pastoral domain, but on the Darling Downs round Toowoomba there was one debatable land over the range where tillage and cereal crops were also practicable. Just before and after the grant of self-government in 1859, pastoralists and speculators had rushed to lease the favoured areas, and had taken up twenty-five million acres. To sort out operative from speculative squatters, the new legislature allowed a fourteen years' lease only to those who proved their runs stocked during the first year of occupation. But the same herd of cattle might "prove" many runs to the satisfaction of the Government inspector. Though he might know the herd by heart, how could he "give away" such charming hosts? In any event, cancellations of lease brought no new population, while squatting remained "the only productive interest in the colony". Governor Bowen and Premier R. G. W. Herbert, the two ex-secretaries to William Ewart Gladstone who launched Queensland into responsible government, set out to promote agriculture wherever it should prove possible.

In addition to selection on easy terms after the survey of chosen areas they made lavish use of land orders to immigrants. These would buy eighteen pounds' worth of country Crown land on the immigrant's arrival, and another £12 worth two years later. The legislators still

---

[1] Production Statistics Bulletin, no. 20, p. 210:

1876	Cattle	2,079,979	Sheep	7,315,074
1882	,,	4,324,807	,,	12,042,893
1892	,,	6,591,416	,,	21,708,310

planned farms on an English scale. These orders might be issued to anyone who paid an immigrant's passage. H. Jordan, an active agent sent to England in 1861, found a firm of shipowners who were willing to bring out immigrants by the thousand and to take payment in land orders. Darling Downs pastoralists saw their chance and stood ready to buy such orders in any quantity. The plan suited everybody. It relieved the Government of direct cost in financing immigration. It gave the new colonist, if he had paid his fare, most of his money back on arrival. But few tried cultivating their blocks immediately they landed. Even earlier than in New South Wales the financial strength of the wool-growers exploited the legislators' wish to see little farms on the inland downs. Land orders helped them to build up freehold stations with surveyors' agricultural blocks.

For a few years this went unnoticed. Parliament and ministers were engaged in buying and "trying on" the outfit of separate existence—the task Governor Macquarie and Governor Gawler had found so absorbing—a task, indeed, which, since the Tower of Babel, has again and again drawn rulers on into exhilaration and folly and their subjects into discord and remorse. They were building, in haste and on credit, the nineteenth century equivalent of city walls. Self-government brought freedom to start a "national debt", and the energetic Herbert set himself to replace the primitive bullock tracks of the squatters by the macadamized roads, railways and public buildings of a civilized community. He easily obtained from London investors loans of £123,000 in 1862, of £707,000 in 1863, and of £1,019,000 in 1864. He spent them almost as rapidly. Immigrants came in shoals, adding 52,855 newcomers to the population between 1861 and the end of 1865. High wages were waiting for all able-bodied men as navvies on the railways, roads and bridges.

About the middle of 1865, however, the Union Bank, as the Government's financial agents, received word that the colony's debentures had become a drug on the London market. It was only a temporary phase, men said. The bank continued to advance money on the security of the unsold debentures, at the usual ten per cent. discount. But the cold fit in London persisted. For some decades British investors had been losing capital in States of the American Union now prostrate in defeat, in South American republics and in Spain, Egypt and Turkey. They recognized the fever of over-borrowing.[1]

The inexperienced ministers at Brisbane plunged on. Herbert, intending to return to Oxford, had handed the reins to Arthur Macalister, his Minister for Lands and Works, but in May 1866 he drew his successor's attention to the need of a new loan to replenish the Treasury. Within a week an Act authorizing an issue of £1,170,000 debentures had passed both houses and received the vice-regal assent. The Union Bank demurred at further advances, but the Sydney agents for the Agra and Masterman's Bank accepted the business of discounting and placing the new debentures. Early in July, however, word came that the Agra and Masterman's Bank had failed, and that Peto, Brassey and Betts, who were engaged on large railway contracts in the colony, were in difficulties. It was the Overend Gurney smash in London. Chaos and unemployment fell upon the colony in a day. Without a word of warning the Union Bank refused to cash the Government cheques. Macalister proposed an issue of inconvertible legal-tender notes and short-dated Treasury bills. Sir George Bowen made public announcement that he must refuse his vice-regal assent to any such expedient. Macalister resigned. Herbert, resuming charge as minister without portfolio, rushed a bill through Parliament for an issue of £300,000 in ten per cent. Treasury bonds for two years. He was assaulted in the streets by a mob resentful of the Governor's high hand, and resigned after eighteen days, undefeated himself but discredited by the

[1] See Leland Jenks, *The Migration of British Capital to 1875* (1927), *passim*.

defeat at a ministerial by-election of his intended successor, Attorney-General Pring. The Bank of Queensland failed. Bankruptcy spread wide among companies and pastoralists. A coalition under Macalister, despite Governor Bowen's resistance, introduced an issue of Treasury notes, though on a small scale. August brought an ugly situation when hundreds of immigrants swelled the workless mobs. Railway navvies thrown out of work at Helidon and Ipswich marched on Brisbane to exact relief. Their first attempt was stopped, but another in September threw Brisbane into panic. Police and unemployed clashed in the streets. Relief works absorbed some; but hundreds left the colony and depression was universal.

Then in September 1867 James Nash found gold at Gympie in Wide Bay District. Diggers threw up selections and wages jobs in the south and poured thither. A liberal Land Act was framed (1868) to meet the difficulties shown up by Herbert's Acts and to retain the diggers as settlers. It offered large areas, up to 7680 acres of second class land, to grazing farmers who were to cultivate as well as to stock their holdings. This *via media*, though long quoted in the southern colonies as a statesmanlike reconciliation of interests, brought the usual dummying. The land was found by giving pastoralists ten years' extension of lease and substantial pre-emptive rights in return for the surrender of half their holdings. By 1874 some 9000 selections had been made and 3,000,000 acres alienated, but half of these had been obtained by 267 persons of whom all but 90 were squatters' agents. They had surrendered leaseholds to buy them back as freehold. There was considerable selection of grazing farms, especially in the Lower Burnett and Wide Bay Districts. Up on the Darling Downs, a liberal Douglas Ministry tried free selection when the pastoral leases expired in 1878. The new Act (1876) distinguished between (i) conditional purchasers or grazing farmers who could buy from 640 to 2560 acres at auction at an upset price of 10s. an acre, and (ii) agricultural homesteaders who could get their 80 to 160 acres at half-a-crown an acre. But bad seasons intervened. Stations were resumed for selection but while the drought lasted no one would buy. Railways and better seasons brought some settlers along the lines. Brisbane and Toowoomba were joined by rail in 1875, and this made the sale of farm produce more profitable. By 1884, however, it was clear that on the inland downs alienation had far outrun the spread of cultivation.

The coastal strip, a thousand miles long, is another country. The S.E. trade winds bring rain to it off the Pacific in any month of the year, usually in abundance. At its extreme southern end is the seat of government, and on the frequent patches of rich alluvial soil thereabouts men soon found that sugar-cane grew well. Thomas Scott had "tried it out" on a commercial scale at Port Macquarie in New South Wales as long ago as 1823, but damage by frost sent its later advocates to the Northern Rivers and Moreton Bay. In 1843, James Backhouse, a missionary, found it growing as hedges between the beds in the "Commandant's Garden" near Government House, Brisbane. In 1856, John Dunmore Lang, always an eager advocate of the production of cotton and sugar by European labour, rode out from Grafton to a creek on the Clarence River where he saw 350 acres under cane, grown by a settler from Mauritius, M. Adam. He thought it very superior, yielding four tons of sugar to the acre. In July 1862 a correspondent of Lang's at Moreton Bay waxed enthusiastic over plots in the Botanic Gardens and told of "sets" of cane distributed to cultivators in all parts of the colony John Buhot had already made sugar on a commercial scale at Brisbane. Among the pioneer planters was the Hon. Louis Hope, a cadet of the Hopetoun family. In 1862 he left a sheep station at Kilcoy on the Upper Brisbane to grow sugar near Cleveland. With infinite labour he cleared, enclosed, broke up and cultivated twenty acres of forest and scrub. Having planted, trimmed, cut and carried the cane, he watched its crushing in a mill of his own erection. Next he set up boiling vats, and finally he had to turn merchant and sell his own wares. To keep down labour costs when wages were at boom levels owing to railway construction, he employed in 1864 some Kanakas brought by Captain Towns to cultivate and pick cotton in the same district. The Queensland Parliament marked the significance of his success by voting him its thanks in 1867, and making him a grant of land. Within two years over 5000 acres were under cane. In 1872–3 some 65 mills turned out 6266 tons of sugar and 161,473 gallons of rum. The colony's own needs were already met and an export trade to the value of £36,803 provided the moist brown sugar that remained familiar in station rations until the 'nineties. Here was the main chance for settlers on the steamy coastal rivers—an export industry with an almost unlimited market.

Clearing was expensive, but soil and climate were so favourable that crops could be won from only half-cleared land. The heavy work was done in May, June and July— the winter months—"when we usually have very fair working weather as regards heat". After the biggest trees were felled and burnt up at a cost of £10 an acre, forest land was ready for a heavy plough and a bullock-team. To clear scrub land and remove the stumps would have cost £40 an acre. So a variant of "Mullenizing"[1] was practised. The scrub was cut and burned at a cost of about £4 an acre, and cane sets were planted among the charred stumps in holes made by hand with a hoe. After five ratoon crops from this planting and after the stumps had rotted, the land was ploughed for the first time. Putting white labour to work the mills and vats, and Polynesians to do the hoeing, cutting and other drudgery, the sugar-planters counted on averaging out wages at four shillings a day. They planned to compete with other sugar colonies owing to "our having millions of acres of background whereon can

1 See chapter XIII, *supra.*

be raised horses, cattle, corn, beef, mutton and all plantation necessaries at the cheapest rate, without importing, as is generally necessary in other places at a very exorbitant price".

Had it been left to the pastoralists and planters, the two Queenslands would have made black labour the instrument in this mutual service. As sugar boomed, more and more Kanakas were drawn in for the plantation gangs. Moreover, the fount and origin of the squatters' demand for separation from New South Wales had been their intention to obtain convict labour again; and, when Southern opposition barred the way, the leaders in the new colony had looked about as a matter of course for other supplies of cheap service on the stations. Quests for Chinese and Indian coolies broke down under the pressure of Imperial and Indian officials for proper regulation. In the 'forties, Benjamin Boyd, a cool scamp, who sought to found a rival to Sydney on Twofold Bay in Southern New South Wales, had brought in Polynesians to act as shepherds on the Riverina stations. But the British authorities had objected to forced recruiting, and Boyd's shepherds died of the climate and homesickness. In 1863 Captain Robert Towns brought over 67 more of these islanders in the 'Don Juan' to work his Moreton Bay cotton fields. When cotton-planting came to nothing as the American War of Secession died down, Hope used them in his sugar-plantations and thereby added an expansive demand for rough cultivators and cane-cutters to the standing pastoral demand for station hands. The colonies were now self-governing and British opinion was wary of fresh responsibilities in the Pacific. "Black-birding" rapidly rose to considerable proportions. 1237 islanders were brought over in 1867, and 900 more during the first four months of 1868. By this time there were 700 Kanakas in station employment.

A cry for regulation of what looked very like a revival of both slave-trading and slavery arose both within and without the colony's boundaries. The self-respect that the young nation had been taught by British humanitarians in the movement to abolish transportation of criminals revolted afresh against forced recruiting of men of other and alien stocks. Democrats feared the presence of a race which they held incapable of an equal franchise. The wage-earners to a man drew together to resist the menace of cheap and unfree labour.[1] As early as 1868 the Queensland Parliament made a law to regulate recruiting in the islands and the treatment of Kanakas on board ship, but its ability to enforce the law was negligible. The Admiralty had predicted as much. "Whatever regulations may be made for the liberty and well-being of these people, or their being brought nominally within the laws and tribunals of Queensland, no proper and efficient control can ever be exercised over the manner in which these people are obtained and placed on board ship." Recruiting was going on for island plantations and South America as well as for Queensland. It was likely "from the nature of the work to fall into the hands of an unscrupulous and mercenary set who, under pretence of persuading natives to make engagements as labourers for a term of years, would not hesitate to commit acts of piracy, kidnapping and murder".[2] A Polynesian Protection Act was passed by the British Parliament in 1872 and a High Commissioner of the Western Pacific was appointed in 1875. These measures strengthened the Navy's hands, but, so long as Britain refused to annex the islands, foreigners defied both Navy and High Commissioner. Kidnapping, massacre and reprisals continued. When various powers had annexed the Pacific Islands east of Australia, the labour vessels, hailing

---

[1] See Myra Willard, *History of the White Australia Policy*, p. 161: "The labouring classes hated the Kanaka brother whom they saw with as much zeal and heartiness as the philanthropists in England loved the dusky Islander whom they had not seen".

[2] M. Willard, *op. cit.* p. 144: "Whoever else has reason to be ashamed of the part they played in the Pacific Island traffic at least the naval authorities have nothing to regret".

not from Queensland ports only, betook them to New Britain and New Ireland in 1882, and in 1884 to New Guinea. The German Foreign Office bluntly called British attention to their misdeeds and asked British aid "to prevent any transgression at the limit which divides the lawful traffic of Polynesians from slave-trading". A Liberal government in Queensland, under Samuel Griffith, thereupon amended the Polynesian Labour Act with the aim of ending the traffic altogether in 1890.

In the conflict of opinion within the colony, liberal and selfish motives, political and economic ambitions, crossed and criss-crossed. Between 46,000 and 47,000 Kanakas were brought into the country. So long as they were employed on stations, about the towns and on casual work—mostly contrary to their "agreements"—they died like flies, at nearly five times the rate for Europeans of similar ages. Under the liberal laws and regulations in force after 1888 they were legally employable only on tropical agriculture and there was an appreciable decline in the mortality. It was not that the sugar-planters were more humane than squatters and others, but that the Kanakas on the plantations could be more readily watched, and their masters more easily charged with hospital expenses. At best, however, the mortality among Kanakas remained four times as heavy as that among the white colonists. In 1893 it was 52·57 per thousand when that of European men, women and children was only 13·3. Forced to rough pioneering work to which they were unused and in which they felt no joy or personal interest, despised and cursed by the average colonist, they were in fact, if not at law, chattel-slaves.

With such "hands" the sugar-planters worked northward from one fertile pocket of land to another. In the early 'seventies they were booming the Mary River. Farther north at Mackay, John Spiller, after studying the industry in Java, tested twenty acres in 1865. He succeeded so well that many others followed him thither.

Planting sugar-cane was to all appearance a form of agriculture exempt from such irksome tasks as the annual ploughing and sowing. Shoved into holes in the untilled surface of half-cleared land, the favourite "Bourbon" variety grew large and succulent canes that seemed immune from disease. Small owners planted it up to their cottage walls, and neglected weeding and "trashing" when new areas could be turned to profit so easily. Large mill-owning planters plunged into debt to extend their machinery. Any one who had ever lived on a sugar plantation elsewhere was *ipso facto* an expert, to be put in charge of such construction.

The dream was too rosy to last. On the Brisbane and the Mary in 1873 and around Mackay with greater virulence in 1874, there appeared, in a night, a "fire-blight" or rust at first attributed to frost. The Bourbon cane looked as if it had been burnt. All were heavy losers save a few who had tried "Black Java", a quick-maturing smaller cane, which proved immune. This grew in one season, as against two for Bourbon, and the warmer north matured it better than the southern river-valleys. So the disaster pushed the industry farther north, and, as it was then believed that whites could not work in the tropical sun,[1] its dependence on the Kanakas was increased.

Mackay boomed once more. Those who had won through the crisis had learned their business under Queensland conditions. By 1877–8 there were 15,220 acres under sugar-cane, the yield had recovered to more than its pre-blight level (12,000 tons of sugar), and 196,662 gallons of rum were made from the residues. The sugar exported reached a value of £286,222 in 1880, partly through a temporary rise in price. So eager became the rush of selectors for "homesteads" in the sugar areas, under the Douglas Land Act of 1876, that the McIlwraith govern-

---

[1] Miss Flora Shaw wrote in 1893 of the difference between a Javanese or black man and a European working in the tropical sun as "the difference between a humming bird and a sick sparrow".

ment suspended homestead selection at half-a-crown an acre, and re-classified the land. Even at trebled prices and more, 240,000 acres of sugar land were sold between October 1881 and March 1882, and sales continued. Many bought to sell at future prices rather than to grow sugar, for the area under cane only rose from 20,000 acres in 1880–1 to 48,000 in 1883–4. Once more, established wealth seized upon openings meant by the lawgivers for new men. As the lands filled from which cane might be carried by water to the crushing mill, tramways came into vogue and empty land held by speculators meant longer tramways and dearer hauls.

The high price of sugar in 1880 did not hold. The period from 1860 to 1900 was marked, as a whole, by a persistent fall that was due to the competition of beet-sugar, stimulated by bounties in Continental Europe.[1] Yet, through three phases in which differing expedients were found to answer, the Queensland industry steadily grew, with but little tariff advantage in its southern market. In bringing under cultivation extremely fertile though limited areas the planters used—and used up—a supply of cheap and servile labour. In meeting European competition the industry, with government aid, learned economy in crushing its cane by central mills. In replacing brown and "mill-white" sugar by the best refined grade it was most competently served by the Colonial Sugar Refining Company.

So long as Queensland was a separate colony the planters fought with success to retain their coloured labour. Their fight compels the admiration few can withhold from a minority resolute to the end, but Australian opinion was heavily and increasingly adverse. They forged, in the North Queensland Separation Movement, a weapon which (like the Confederate States of Jefferson Davis) gave their purpose the guise of a crusade for self-determination. When the popular hatred of Kanaka labour sent to Bris-

---

[1] W. H. Traill, *A Queenly Colony* (1900), p. 71, quotes prices of £27 to £28 in 1872, £11. 15s. in 1893 and £8. 10s. to £8. 14s. per ton in 1899.

bane parliamentary majorities pledged to put down slavery and slave-trading, the North cried aloud for local autonomy, exposed every electoral and public works scandal, and reasoned at Westminster that the Crown should set up a new colony or colonies north of Dawes Range or the tropic. But when friends trod the stage at Brisbane and islanders might be had more easily, the hot fit passed and constitution-making was forgotten like a tropical fever.

On geographical and financial grounds they had as good a case for local autonomy as ever colonists had; indeed, after the 'seventies they had a better case than the Darling Downs and Moreton Bay had made good in the 'fifties.[1] When separated from New South Wales the infant Queensland had boasted only 28,000 white colonists. By 1871 those north of Dawes Range already numbered 27,000, and the gold and silver found inland as well as the sugar-planting that spread steadily up the coast gave every promise of further rapid growth. The very prosperity of the North debarred its active participants from making their voices effective in Brisbane. How could the planter busy with his crop and with the development of his estate, the miner battling for gold over the rough coastal range and the inland pastoralist on guard against natives and drought neglect their work to attend long sessions in a capital far away in the south-east?[2] Brisbane is nearer to Sydney than to Bowen, nearer to Melbourne than to Cooktown. Kennedy, a northern constituency, elected John Bright in a conventional gesture of despair. But whether they attended or no, the Northern representatives were powerless to pre-

---

[1] See *Queensland V. and P. passim*, Correspondence *re* Separation of North Queensland, and *Q.P. Debates*, 20 August to 3 September 1886.

[2] A brilliant Australian journalist, A. G. Stephens, who had lived in the North, asked in 1893: "What would you think of a man who told you the circulation of the blood would be more perfect if the heart were placed in the big toe?...The result would probably be to make us crippled, blind, deaf, dumb and idiotic. Long before that, however, we would be exterminated by some race of men whose hearts were normally situated". *Why North Queensland Wants Separation* (Melbourne Public Library, *Pol. Econ. Pamphlets*).

vent a Southern majority from pledging the revenues to pay for loans and public works that developed the South alone. The Colonial Office had beyond doubt contemplated further divisions of the Northern mass when Queensland was severed from her mother colony. Dr J. D. Lang, its protagonist in Sydney, had more than once mapped out and named the future northern colonies. The Imperial Parliament had by statute made explicit the Crown's power to proclaim them. In the name of self-government, justice and clean administration, the planters, when the occasion called for their eloquence, claimed for their chosen domain the logical, legal and honourable gift of freedom.

Both at Brisbane and Westminster ministers found that all they could attempt against such tempestuous bowling was to play out time. In 1872 the Earl of Kimberley asked for a full discussion in the colonial parliament and an expression of policy from ministers possessing its confidence. Without these Her Majesty's Government could not "entertain a question of such paramount importance". This was a rebuff. A worse setback was the acceptance in that year of a policy of Imperial supervision of the recruiting of islanders. For a decade separation had to wait. The planters were on the defensive. In 1883 Samuel Griffith, having fought and won an election on the issue of Indian and Kanaka labour, enacted stricter regulations limiting the employment of Kanakas to tropical and semitropical agriculture. The aliens should at least be confined to the tasks for which they were ostensibly indentured and, as was alleged, were uniquely suited. What was more, Griffith enforced his regulations and made the importation of more Kanakas illegal after 1890. Immediately the separation movement revived both in the North and in Britain.

The petitioners contended that the Earl of Kimberley's stipulations had been fulfilled. Expressions of policy had certainly been forthcoming from the Premier of the colony, though they were emphatically against separation, and a discussion in the Brisbane Parliament had ended in the defeat of a motion favouring separation by 36 votes to 9, the Southern members voting with one voice against it. But such opposition, contended the Northern leaders, made good their case for liberation from such rulers. A new Secretary of State (H. T. Holland) sought fresh ground on which to set aside the new petitions. With much effect the Northern colonists quoted an Imperial statute passed two years after the separation of Queensland from New South Wales, giving the Crown authority to change the boundaries of colonies "established or to be established". They cited, too, an explanation of that Act by the Duke of Newcastle to the first Governor of Queensland. "I am not prepared to abandon definitely, on the part of Her Majesty's Government, the power to deal with districts not yet settled as the wishes and convenience of future settlers may require." But the Colonial Office unearthed another condition precedent. The Secretary of State announced to the House of Commons (1887) that the Law officers advised that no step could be taken by the Crown without fresh legislation. Such legislation would be proposed only after some resolution in favour of the change had been carried in the colonial legislature.

This was a hard ruling. If the concurrence of a majority in the New South Wales legislature had been required in 1859, it would certainly have meant the strangling of Queensland at birth. Such a rule meant the cessation in Australia of that internal colonization, under the name of territorial organization, which had created self-governing frontier-communities across the North American continent. There were, no doubt, powerful forces in alliance in 1887 to frame and applaud such a ruling. The petitioners had been tactful enough to scout the bare idea that their Separation League was a Home Rule movement. Nobody could be more fervently loyal than they. Yet if local autonomy had been granted in Queensland, what torrents of awkward questions about Ireland would have poured upon the Unionist ministers of 1887! Moreover, separation would cut in two not only the map of Queensland but also the taxing-power on the future growth of which London investors had counted when they had taken up Queensland bonds to the amount of sixteen millions between 1859 and 1885.[1]

Thought for bondholders' interest in the undiminished taxing-power of the government responsible for the service of the debt may already be traced in 1887. In the replies made to the separationists thereafter it was put more and more plainly. Yet the planters would not admit defeat, though they knew that their arch-enemy[2] had stated the case against them in terms that carried full weight with the Colonial Office. Westminster might be unfriendly for the nonce. They were not dismayed. The party that normally countenanced coloured labour as a means of extending the industry might acquiesce in Griffith's amending act giving notice of the cessation of all "black-birding" and importation of Kanakas after 1890. Such turns and twists of the political weathercocks did not shake the planters' faith in a course they thought to be dictated by the facts of soil and climate. The flag of secession still flew high in the North. Griffith's dream of "preserving Queensland as a future field for European settlement" would fade as light dawned even on that restless mind. Governor Musgrave, though he commended to his official superiors at Westminster Griffith's "clear, temperate and able exposition of the views of the ministry", could not share his opinion that sugar-cane would eventually be cultivated successfully in the tropics by white labour.[3]

[1] The analogy between the North Queensland movement and the formation of new states in the American Union would not reassure the City. Cf. W. E. Adcock on "The Separation Movement in the North", *Victorian Review*, February 1885.

[2] At their social gatherings in North Queensland it was customary to drink to the toast of D. S. G., i.e. "D——n Sam Griffith". "Sugar", as *The Times* remarked 12 October 1885, "does not sweeten the temper of its growers."

[3] Sir A. Musgrave to the Secretary of State for the Colonies, 13 April 1885, covering a statement by the Premier to the Governor, 1 April 1885—an admirable state paper.

Griffith waved aside all doubts. "The same thing used to be said of Moreton Bay.... It was not to be thought that Europeans would work on the plantations on the same conditions as coloured races." They would, he contended, cultivate it under different conditions, as a large population of resident owners working their own properties, unless that result were prevented by the introduction of inferior races in large numbers. Rather than the colony of the planters' dreams, with a government, representing employers for the most part absentees, exploiting an inferior race or races, he would prefer "a separate territory governed as a Crown Colony" by an impartial civil service. But the coastal strips where tropical agriculture was possible were few and not continuous. The mineral lands in the ranges and the pastoral lands on the plateaux by reason of their high elevation differed in no important particular from the rest of the pastoral lands of Australia. The present ascendancy of the planters at Mackay was not valid ground for entrusting them with the future of such wide territories.

Popular opinion in Queensland and in the Southern colonies applauded, even though they did not fully comprehend, the vision of this lean, impatient idealist.[1] He saw in the North the field for an experiment in European settlement unimpeded by any attempt to unite races of wholly different culture in a constitutional colony. Like every great-hearted Australian, he rated high the opportunity of constructive progress unembittered by racial feuds. And from an unexpected quarter there came means to further the experiment he desired that carried it to within sight of full success.

Planters like Hope of Cleveland who crushed and made sugar from their own cane were puzzled, impoverished and held back by agricultural, chemical and engineering

---

[1] C. A. Bernays, *Queensland Politics during Sixty Years*, p. 73, draws a pen portrait of Griffith, justly emphasizing "a strange trait in his character that he never entirely pleased himself".

difficulties beyond their training. To accept the advice of *soi-disant* experts was to incur capital costs which the output did not justify on the falling market in which their sugar had to be sold. Only the finest calculation, the best engineering and chemical skill, extracting the last pound of sugar and turning out the most attractive quality, could make headway against the technical energy and state aid behind the best sugar of Continental Europe. The necessary capacities could be trained, however, by separating the tasks of growing, crushing and refining.

Angus Mackay, a Sydney engineer sent by Queensland in the early 'eighties to investigate cane-sugar production in the French, British and Spanish West Indies, reported immense advances in the French islands and decline elsewhere. This he ascribed to the Central Factory system, which had separated cane-farming from sugar-manufacture, making them even more distinct than wheat-growing and flour-milling. Powerful machinery and boiling *in vacuo*, economically feasible only on a large scale, enabled the genuine central mill to give the grower more for his cane than he could win from it himself with obsolete plant.[1] The system had already been put into operation by the Colonial Sugar Refining Company on the Clarence and Richmond Rivers of Northern New South Wales. There the company bought from the growers the standing cane at from ten to fourteen shillings a ton, cut it by gangs of its own employing, brought it in large shallow-draught droghers to its mills and there crushed and boiled it. Final manufacture took place at the company's refinery at Pyrmont, Sydney.

Mackay predicted the rapid extension in Australia of this plan—"one of the most certain solutions of the labour difficulties which beset sugar production all over the world". The main desideratum would be skill capable of supervising in the mills and the refinery powerful machinery

[1] Angus Mackay, *Sugar Cane in Australia*, 1883, pp. 136 *et passim*.

and subtle processes. Good machines and good management in the field and the boiling houses would extract sugar at falling cost as experience increased. The colour of the labour tending the cane would become a matter of taste.

So, in the ripeness of time, it may happen. But Griffith, true to the idealists' trade of being disappointed, wished to speed up the slow crawl of events. He clutched at the central mill as an expedient to force the transition to white labour in sugar production. In 1885 unemployment in Queensland had been aggravated by assisted immigration. He induced Parliament to vote £50,000 to build or subsidize cane-growers' companies in building central mills. The cane brought to them, he stipulated, must be grown by white labour alone. Plantations were already being cut up into small farms and Griffith meant the new mills to make sugar for these small-holders. But they proved unready as yet to grow cane by white labour only as some of the farmers on the northern rivers of New South Wales were doing. At the mills erected in the Mackay and Port Douglas districts the rule against "black" cane could not be maintained. While Kanakas remained, the whites would not work with them in the cane brakes, though they willingly took work in the mills from which Kanakas were habitually shut out.

Yet the change-over made progress. Though they had shown the way on the northern rivers, the directors of the "C.S.R." were still arguing as late as 1890 that sugar planting in the tropics could not do without coloured labour; but in the very next year the company was selling its North Queensland plantations on easy terms to farmers, as "a partial solution of the labour difficulty". The gentleman-planter who had owned broad estates and worked them through an overseer by Kanaka gangs, who had crushed and, as far as he knew how, had refined his own sugar in a plantation mill, was losing his economic ascendancy. The small farmers into whose hands such estates were divided employed perhaps a Kanaka or two each, but no Kanaka might own land. Now that the rough pioneering of the industry—the clearing and planting—had been done, coloured labour had become an anachronism and a clog. The hardest-headed Australian trust had reorganized the work among small farmers growing the cane, seasonal white labour cutting it and machine-fitters, tenders and chemists manufacturing the sugar.[1]

Political separation for North Queensland in the 'seventies or 'eighties would have set up the type of colony which had an unhappy record in the West Indies—an aristocracy of white planters deriving wealth and ascendancy from the exploitation of semi-servile labour. Though the planters refused to admit political defeat in 1887, the small farmers and the skilled employees in the mills and refineries were cutting away the economic basis of their leadership, and in the 'nineties the Northern Separation Movement collapsed in its hour of seeming triumph.

About 1890 it had been reinforced and supplemented by a demand from the Rockhampton district for a third

---

[1] The Colonial Sugar Refining Company took over in 1855 the refining business of a predecessor, the Australasian Sugar Company, which was established in Sydney in 1842 with an initial capacity of a thousand tons a year. The original shareholders of the C.S.R. Co. were J. H. Challis, James Robey, Edward Knox, Walter Lamb, Alfred Spry, Daniel Cooper, William Fanning, T. J. Nankivell, William Walker, Archibald Walker and Edwin Tooth, and its capital was £75,000. From 1855 to 1887 the liability of the shareholders was unlimited—at law—and accounts were not published. The ordinary shares of the limited liability company registered in 1887 were "paid up" to the value of £600,000. Amalgamation with the New Zealand Sugar Company was sanctioned at the first ordinary meeting of the new company. The volume of *Reports and Speeches, C.S.R. Co.* 1855–1912 in the Mitchell Library is a most impressive record of the company's success and power to mould political action. See especially the Chairman's speeches for the half years ending 30 September 1889, 31st March 1890, 31st March 1892, 30th September 1894 (the acquisition of the Australasian Sugar Refining Co. of Melbourne—Poolmans'), 31 March 1895 (reflections on the effects of the company's production out-growing the needs of the Australasian markets), 31 March 1899 (Parliament has agreed to continuance of duty of £3 per ton on sugar imported into New South Wales).

colony of Central Queensland, and in this demand the pastoralists of the West, notably those about Winton and Boulia, played a part. They petitioned in 1887 and again three years later, when the hour for the exclusion of black labour was striking, that in the event of separation they should be placed in the severed area. Sir Samuel Griffith, now in coalition with his old antagonist Sir Thomas McIlwraith,[1] sought to turn the flank of this massed attack by a plan for a federal Queensland. United Provinces, either two or three in number, should enjoy local autonomy under a central legislature. On the formation of an Australian Commonwealth this central legislature would merge into that of the nation. First framed in 1890 as a means of side-tracking separatist motions in the Brisbane Parliament, Griffith's new plan was dropped because no one but its author was interested enough to comprehend such complexities. In 1891 it came up again as a counter to the draft bill in which at Lord Knutsford's invitation the Central Separation Committee set out to demonstrate the consistency of its ambitions with the security of the public creditors of Queensland.[2] The Griffith plan was defeated, however, in committee of the Brisbane Assembly.

Still the Colonial Office held the ardent separationists at arm's length. Sugar was tumbling in value, and cheap labour, the separationists urged, was their one way to prosperity in their competition with the bounty-fed product of Europe. Sir Samuel Griffith's proposals for local autonomy while preserving the union, said Westminster, had not yet been fully considered. If the bill were defeated a

[1] "A big portly frame with a bulldog head and neck, McIlwraith in his day filled a niche in Queensland politics which no one else could fill, but perhaps it was as well that a brake was put upon him just as he was getting into his stride. He should have lived in the United States of America." C. A. Bernays, *op. cit.* p. 56.

[2] Griffith's Constitution of the United Provinces of Queensland would have done this by leaving a reserve taxing power, untrammelled by any limitation, in the General Assembly. Here again its influence on Australian political development has been great.

second time, the occasion would then have arrived for Her Majesty's Government to consider whether Imperial legislation was necessary to cut the knot. Griffith fought on, fertile of expedient after expedient to avoid complete separation and the irretrievable breach between tropical and temperate colonies which he knew it would involve. He was not helped by the strikes and guerilla warfare on the stations in which his former working-class allies were engaged. He admitted that good government of the North was not practicable from Brisbane and conceded the case for local control of expenditure. Three united provinces would be best, he advised, but he drafted alternative bills for three or two.

The Assembly preferred two, and in that form sent up the bill to the Legislative Council. There it was rejected on the ground that it had not been passed by the two-thirds majority in the Assembly which constitutional amendments required. Griffith's last guard seemed beaten down when, on the top of that defeat, he had to admit in March 1892 that Kanakas were still needed to bridge the gap of time until estates had been sub-divided and the North peopled with white farmers. The coalition government, to relieve the paralysis of the sugar industry by falling prices and the refusal of white labour to cut cane at low wages, conceded a temporary renewal (no set term being stated) of the Polynesian Labour Regulation Act. Griffith's warmest admirers shook their heads. What malign influence, they asked, had made so great a man recant his ideal after spending the best years of his life in cleansing an Augean stable?

The planters made haste. The rough force of facts and prices had tripped up their enemy. In February 1893, full of high hope, they put their overwhelming case to a new Liberal Secretary of State, the Marquis of Ripon. Griffith's last expedient, the Decentralization Bill, had been rejected after full discussion. As they had predicted, the South still refused to listen to reason. They had fulfilled every condition precedent. But still Westminster would not move. A general election was impending in Queensland. It would be improper not to await the result.

That election brought forth a puzzling situation. The new political labour party, representing the miners, station hands and wages men of the coastal towns hitherto opposed to northern separation, polled so strongly in the North that they grew confident of winning power in a separated parliament. Such sinister support of the old cause, financial chaos, coastal floods, and inland drought confused and divided the planters' counsels. Desperately anxious to avoid any obligation to these new allies, they approached still another Secretary of State for the Colonies late in 1895. The reply they received from Joseph Chamberlain proved cold comfort to men all too well aware how southern Australians viewed their peculiar institution. "The people of Central Queensland will no doubt find the Federal Government, when constituted, ready to listen to any reasonable scheme which may be submitted to it with the object of giving them that independent control of their own affairs which they now seek."[1]

Abandoning hope of aid or action from Whitehall, the planters gathered all possible allies for a last sally in the Brisbane parliament; and by the casting vote of one of their leaders in the Speaker's Chair they carried the day. The Assembly resolved that the time had arrived when the Central and Northern divisions of the colony should be constituted separate colonies in compliance with the petitions of the inhabitants thereof (4 November 1897). Yet the separation was not made. The time had not arrived. Sir Samuel Griffith, though now as Chief Justice "above the thunder", was still too much for them. He pointed out to Dickson, the Queensland Premier of 1898, that federation offered a way of escape. With federation the White Australia policy was sure of overwhelming and nation-wide support. That November resolution made

[1] J. Chamberlain to the Governor of Queensland, 15 January 1896.

certain not Separation, but Queensland's tardy entry into the work of founding the Commonwealth.

Such was the last contest in Australia between a landed aristocracy and the industrial democracy, the leaders of the past and the clamour of the future. It compares strangely with the war of secession in the American Union. The warning roar of that conflagration awakened Australians in good time to the menace of a servile under-race. By legislation they barred its growth. But unluckily, their timely determination to check the establishment of planter communities in the Australian tropics became entangled in a resistance to any devolution of effective governing powers by the colonies of 1863. The North Queensland planters and their allies associated the cause of internal colonization with coloured labour for long enough to damn both together. The Colonial Office refused to use the Crown's power to proclaim fresh colonies save at the request of the colony to be sub-divided. This was an insuperable veto. Embodied in the Commonwealth Constitution it still prevents in the self-governing states of Australia any alteration of the haphazard boundaries drawn before 1863. In one instance the discrepancy between the political and the economic boundaries of the regions served by the existing ports is so great that the railways of one state penetrate deeply into the hinterland of another. The makeshift is better than the customs barriers of pre-federal days, but it is eloquent of an inability in Australian leaders, despite the vaunted homogeneity and the re-markable social similarity of the communities they govern, to adapt the map of the Continent to the needs of the nation.

CHAPTER XV

An Apostle of Restriction

AT the opening of the period of colonial particularism (1860–1900), Victoria, thanks to her endowment of alluvial gold, stood far above her neighbours in population and prestige. For a generation she retained her lead and set the tone of intercolonial relations. But her ways were ungenerous, like those of an inept man defending a fortune won by luck.

In 1860 the Australian population had grown to 1,145,585, of whom 538,234 were in Victoria, 348,546 in New South Wales, 125,582 in South Australia, 89,821 in Tasmania, 28,056 in Queensland and a handful of 15,346 marooned at the far-off Swan River. With 6·1 persons to the square mile as against Tasmania's 3·4 and New South Wales' 1·1, the Victorian hive was still attracting most of the newcomers, and its governors, uplifted with pride, were loth to abandon the faith that this would continue and that callings would be found for the ex-diggers, for the rising generation and all new arrivals.[1] What did it matter that the squatters bought out the selectors and elbowed wheat-growing into the plains beyond the Divide? Unprecedented progress had given the people an exhilarating sense of power. They had done great things together and had the will to do them again. Here, ready to a leader's hand, were the core and fibre of nationalism, "that simplest of all ideals which has in its nature no political affinities either with

---

[1] By 1870 the estimated population of Australia was 1,647,756 of whom 723,925 were in Victoria, 497,992 in N.S.W., 184,546 in S.A., 115,272 in Queensland, 100,886 in Tasmania and 25,135 in W.A. See *Australian Demography*, Bulletin no. 43, p. 239. The density of population per square mile in 1870 was: Victoria 8·2 persons, Tasmania 3·8, N.S.W. 1·6.

liberty on the one hand or with tyranny on the other; it can be turned by some chance current of events or by the cunning or clumsiness of statesmen to run in any channel and to work any wheel".[1]

The leader, or rather the driver, came in the shape of a newspaper dictator. David Syme, a tall, square-shouldered, thin-lipped, grey-eyed Scot of Scots had been brought up by an austere father, a North Berwick dominie and a solitary Tory among Whigs. Seemingly the old man had no "melting" left in him towards the youngest of a family of seven, five of whom were boys. "I have no recollection", said David Syme long afterwards, "of ever having addressed him directly in my life, even to the extent of asking him a question. If the idea of doing so ever entered my brain I never had the courage to carry it out. It had been firmly impressed upon me that I had to do as I was told and ask no questions."[2] He impressed the same lesson on the public and the Premiers of Victoria for over forty years. "Time after time", records his pupil and biographer, "the people saw *The Age* use political leaders and parties with the indifference of a carpenter who flings his hammer carelessly aside after it has driven in the nail. Syme only supported men as long as they were whole-souled ministers of the principles he advocated."[3] He practised persuasion by a simple, effective method. "His first step was to announce clearly and lucidly his ideas, and to couch his announcement in a form that assumed, however startlingly original his views, that he was merely expressing a settled public opinion. There was no hurry, no flurry, no forcing, no impatience. He was often greeted with an outburst of popular derision. He ignored it, and when it was over

---

[1] G. M. Trevelyan, *England Under the Stuarts*, p. 117.

[2] Quoted by Ambrose Pratt, in his *David Syme: the Father of Protection in Australia*, p. 4.

[3] For examples of "King David's" disciplining of ministers of his own creation who hesitated to do his bidding, see Pratt, *op. cit.* pp. 167, 175, how his editor, Windsor, attended Cabinet meetings to dictate his ultimata, and p. 249, how James Munro followed Syme to a distant country estate, to beg reprieve from a sentence of dismissal, in vain.

he returned placidly to the charge. The process often extended over years. But gradually his ideas fertilized. Each reiteration made them a little more definite, a little more familiar, a little more acceptable...until at last his ideas with all their consequences were publicly embraced."[1]

Those ideas reflected the history and character of the man who propagated them. Life had reiterated his father's lesson of self-reliance. He had studied theology of an unorthodox hue under Morison of Kilmarnock, had tasted at Heidelberg the Hegelian dialectic of progress through contradiction, had learned proof-reading and privation in Glasgow, gold-mining in California and hostility to the squatter-rulers of Victoria when they evaded his appeal to be reinstated on a "jumped" claim (which proved a most successful one) at Mount Egerton. Socially he was a "thrawn body", retiring to the point of being a recluse, but in thought he was as adventurous and as contemptuous of convention as the diggers were in action. With the zeal of an anchorite he summoned them to make Victoria a "self-contained, self-supporting, independent nation—a nice-balanced industrial community, composite, stable and progressive".

In 1860, on the death of his brother Ebenezer, who had left the staff of the *Westminster Gazette* to seek relief from phthisis by emigration to Victoria, David Syme became both proprietor and editor of the *Melbourne Age*, a struggling newspaper which he had purchased for a small sum four years earlier to ensure its continuance. He made it the mouthpiece of views of which he thought himself the sole prophet[2] and in his advocacy of which he no doubt

---

[1] Ambrose Pratt, *op. cit.* preface, p. xxvii. Even the pious Pratt confesses to doubts of the effects of "ruling the state by a process of plausible suggestion". "It breeds public apathy" (p. 251).

[2] Cf. Pratt, *op. cit.* p. 59: "I know of no one in Australia who believed in Protection except myself". But in this he was mistaken. T. A. Coghlan, *Labour and Industry in Australia*, p. 1140, draws attention to the American and artisan influences "latent in the minds of a large section of the population" and to the formation of a Tariff League in 1859. A pamphlet by G. W. Cole, M.L.C., *Protection as a National System suited to Victoria*, published

pictured himself as a young David going forth to do battle with a sling against the heavy-armed squatting and mercantile interests.

From the first Australian tariff imposed by Governor King to the days of colonial self-government British goods had enjoyed preferential treatment in the Australian market. That was fundamental in the old view and treatment of colonies as means to the mother country's enrichment. From 1808 it took the form of a general levy of 5 per cent. *ad valorem* on all goods not of British manufacture. With small changes according to the needs of revenue this tariff remained until the finding of gold and the era of self-government. When New South Wales and Victoria were separated there were specific duties on spirits and tobacco and *ad valorem* duties on imports generally, 2 per cent. being levied on goods from the United Kingdom and 10 per cent. on those of all other countries. In the tariffs of pre-gold days, despite some traces of protection to local industries such as distillation and sugar refining, and an element of preference to British traders, the dominant idea was undoubtedly to raise revenue by an all-round impost easily collected at the ports.

The preference to goods from the United Kingdom was swept away by the colonial legislatures in 1851. They needed revenue badly and felt themselves to be no longer means to the ends of British trade. Apart from this, the tariffs in New South Wales and Victoria remained much as they had been before the gold discoveries and the grant of self-government, though New South Wales kept a higher duty on sugar in defence of the refinery on Parramatta Road. The Deas-Thompson Tariff of 1852, the new starting-point of New South Wales fiscal history, imposed duties on spirits, wine, beer, tobacco, tea, coffee and sugar. That of 1855 in Victoria also set import duties on seven classes of goods and an export duty of 2s. 6d. an ounce on gold.

in Melbourne in 1860 and consisting mainly of extracts from List, shows that German thought was not without influence.

By 1860 the eager and somewhat raffish men who were finding less and less gold each year were clamouring for other openings, and Victorian legislators, even those who had at first regretted the diggers' coming, could hardly acquiesce with folded hands in the passing of the young colony's attractiveness. Manhood suffrage left them no choice. Carried in 1857 by Haines, a squatter Premier, it gave power to make the laws, or at least to choose the law-makers, to strata of the population that were impatient for their turn of the good things government could give and in their inexperience disinclined to count the cost.

A purely revenue tariff is a late product of fiscal experience, born of disillusionment with the complex results of government manipulation of trade. It implies an abandonment in the general interest of log-rolling by sections. Among the newly-enfranchised strata, however, were British artisans accustomed to action through trade societies in defence of particular markets for their skill, and Americans and Europeans to whom protective duties against British manufactures were familiar boons. The golden age was fading to the light of common day. Late in 1861 nine thousand able-bodied diggers went off to track the rainbows in New South Wales and Otago. To fill their places the colonial parliament continued to subsidize immigration, voting in that year £79,000 to pay passages. During 1862 five thousand immigrants arrived, and a land act, setting aside a quarter of the land revenue, provided an additional £120,000 for the purpose of immigration in 1863.

At this juncture the man in the street worked out an easy corollary from Wakefield's theorem. As the government had used public revenues to bring labouring folk to the colony, it was under an obligation to find work for them. The Protection and Anti-Immigration League was a natural working-class retort to middle-class prejudices against Gawlerism. Let the government stop glutting the labour market with "new chums" and, if it will not itself employ men on public works, let it impose a tariff that will enable local manufacturers to do so and compete with imported goods. Such reasonings found an incisive champion in David Syme in his new rôle of leader-writer. "By the system of naked competition our manufacturers or mechanics are prevented from even making a beginning in the work of opening up new sources of industry among us", he wrote in what his biographer claims to have been the first unequivocal Protectionist article in any Australian newspaper. To found new industries seemed simple enough, but "a ban is put upon the attempt at the very outset; and in a few short years hence, if this prearranged practice of national industrial abortion is continued amongst us, the people of Australia will be as utter strangers to all scientific skill and practical dexterity in the arts and manufactures of highly civilized nations as are the Bedouins of Barbary, or the Tartars of Central Asia. Is this a desirable result? Is it desirable that, instead of carrying with us the arts of advanced civilization from the parent State in Europe to this remote land, we should purposely, and as it were with 'malice afore-thought', upon quitting the shores of that parent State, cast behind us and abandon the knowledge and the practice of those great industrial arts, which have constituted and still constitute the sole groundwork of her characteristic pre-eminence in trade, commerce and wealth? Is it not on the contrary rather desirable that we should endeavour to perpetuate amongst us, in our new home, that civilizing and enriching skill and trained industry which is a part of our national inheritance?"

The importing interests attempted to silence Syme by withdrawing their advertisements from his paper. He reduced its price from 6d. to 3d., to 2d., and finally in 1868 to 1d. The Government of the day, under John O'Shanassy, joined his enemies in 1863 and withdrew the Government announcements. But Syme's unflinching stand and powerful attacks on the self-interested motives of his opponents caught the popular imagination. His paper's circulation doubled and trebled. Advertisers could not afford to ignore such a medium of publicity. By the general election of 1864 he had won his fight and was in command of the enthusiastic popular following which remained faithful to him till his death in 1908, "marching to the ballot box and voting in a placid phalanx for reform".[1]

James McCulloch, who had displaced O'Shanassy before the election, though continuing to declare himself a free-trader, carried, after a severe constitutional struggle with the Legislative Council, a tariff of moderate duties on apparel, textiles, boots, saddlery and earthenware, while reducing the duties on tea and sugar. He argued that local industries must be helped through their days of infancy and high costs.[2] Logically such a justification should have suggested subsidies rather than import duties. For a subsidy to the infant industry would have enabled it to sell its wares at the same price as the imported goods, thereby sparing the consumer the rise in price consequent on import duties and confining the cost of protection to the taxes required to provide the subsidy. Even the choice of import duties should logically have been tempered by a plan for their steady reduction as the industries became "naturalized" and efficient.

Syme, driving his fellow-colonists on the way of "reform" that he had chosen, sought no temporary protection. Any suggestion of infantile inefficiency in colonial manufactures he met by a characteristic counter-offensive. "The articles with which the Victorian market has been deluged would have been dear at any price. They were, and they continue to be of a kind almost worthless,

---

[1] Ambrose Pratt, op. cit. p. 251.
[2] John Stuart Mill (Principles of Political Economy, Book v, ch. 1, sec. 1) regarded temporary duties on imports as defensible on economic grounds where industries perfectly suitable to a young country had still to be "naturalized" there. But C. H. Chomley (Protection in Canada and Australasia, pp. 81–2) quotes a letter by Mill to a Victorian student of his work emphasizing the limitations which he placed on their safe use.

becoming unfit for use with a month's wear-and-tear; and however low in original price, they are a source of constant and excessive expenditure and their purchase-money in the end turns out to have been but a profitless and wasteful outlay. This is no exaggeration; it is the simple fact which is obvious and patent to all." It certainly became the *credo* of every *Age* reader. He denied, too, that import duties raised local prices. They were meant to shut out the "foreign-trader" with his trashy wares, but internal competition would infallibly keep local manufacturers and dealers from raising the prices of their honest products.

Why, in such a small and sheltered market, they should compete to spoil the proffered chance of charging prices near the foreign trader's landed cost plus duty was not made plain. Presumably the local manufacturers would always and in all instances be patriots as disinterested as David Syme undoubtedly was.

For him the tariff of 1866 was no temporary expedient but merely a beginning. He overthrew its author McCulloch in 1871 and Charles Gavan-Duffy, another free-trader, in 1872. They had dared to reason with him and had refused to impose higher duties. Syme was by this time impatient to make high import duties the stimulus to an all-round progress in the industrial arts.[1] One might have expected such a student, and a Scot too, to have known that necessity, not affluence, is the mother of invention and that the industrial arts have grown with painful slowness here and there, seldom transplanting easily or in assorted collections. But the need for protection was self-evident to expectant employers and artisans. Nor did the danger of interruption of the colony's supplies from overseas fail to receive emphasis, every war-cloud being greeted in Syme's columns by thunder-claps of headlines.

[1] G. W. Cole, *Protection as a National System suited to Victoria* (1860), had urged "a comprehensive scheme that would foster every branch of manufacturing industry and give security to those who would embark their capital in manufacturing enterprise".

It was "good journalism", and the phalanx of his followers swelled to numbers as formidable as they were faithful. All the old allies who had fought to unlock the land were enlisted in its ranks. Duties on imported flour and grain won the allegiance of farmers with whom South Australian foreigners were still competing for the Victorian market. Miners dreamed of industrial jobs at regular wages when the anxiety and exposure of rush and gully-camps would be no more. Prosperous manufactures would make Victoria a great nation. "A country given up purely to pastoral and agricultural pursuits would afford no scope for men of artistic and constructive talents." The scepticism of the squatters—the old "stinking fish" party—only roused the fighting ardour of the protectionist forces. Was it not to the interest of such men that the colony should depend for revenue on selling its Crown lands to the longest purses?

After a series of unstable ministries, Syme triumphed in 1877. McCulloch, still recalcitrant, was overwhelmed at the polling booths, and Graham Berry, Syme's ex-Chartist protégé, pushed through Parliament after a momentary reluctance "a Protective tariff in every sense of the expression", dictated by the great silent chief himself.[1] The *ad valorem* duties it imposed ranged to 30, 40 and in a few instances 45 per cent., and were backed, where these were thought more effective, by high specific duties. "King David" ruled supreme. By 1883, James Service, the stiffest free-trader left in public life, bowed to his majesty and was installed as colleague with Graham Berry in a coalition required and forced by Syme to straighten out the finances of the colony. Service accepted Syme's condition that he should not interfere with "the declared economic policy of the country", that is, a tariff of duties on imports averaging 25 per cent.

In its ostensible and immediate purpose of increasing employment in Victorian manufactures, protection was

---

[1] See Ambrose Pratt, *op. cit.* pp. 170–2.

successful. Between 1864 and 1874 the number of factory hands in Victoria increased fourfold. Twenty-eight thousand were "in work" where there had been only seven thousand. Yet this was hardly a decisive advance in artistic and constructive talent. At an intercolonial conference on tariffs in 1870 the protectionist Treasurer admitted that Victorian manufactures "consisted mainly of goods which are made up wholly or in part from imported materials".[1] The sewing machine was largely responsible for a big increase in the industrial employment of women during the 'seventies and 'eighties. As the policy of borrowing tens of millions in London to build railways and ports accentuated the need for exports to pay interest on this capital equipment, industrial employment was not found capable of swelling the list of staple products exported. Industry came to the aid of agriculture in that the best agricultural implements were of local invention and make. But the necessity that produced them had arisen before the days of Syme, and the most rapid agricultural development of this generation took place in the 'nineties under free trade in New South Wales. Prior to federation, Victorian factories sold the bulk of their output in the Victorian market and, if a contemporary pamphleteer is to be trusted, "dumped" at cut prices such of their goods as they sent to other colonies to compete with the foreigner.[2] That would assist New South Wales farmers rather than their fellow-Victorians.

Yet in young communities like Victoria, so long as growth is rapid and virgin resources remain to be developed, hope takes every plan conceived for an accomplished fact. In 1887 *The Age*, attributing to protection the turn of immigration back into Victoria that accompanied the railway mania and land boom of the mid-

---

[1] J. G. Francis, *Report of Intercolonial Conference on Tariffs*, Melbourne, June–July 1870.
[2] Max Hirsch, *Protection in Australia* (1900), Table XXIV, p. 31, showing the prices charged in Sydney and Melbourne for certain Victorian manufactures.

'eighties, announced "the startling fact that protectionist Victoria...in a few years will have left New South Wales far behind in the race for commercial supremacy".[1] But while the scribe was yet writing, the hours of Victoria's greatness were fast running out. Ten years later, New South Wales, in spite of her adherence to "Cobdenism", had drawn ahead of Victoria in population, had gained upon her even in manufactures and exceeded her in the industrial arts that call for brain and sinew. If, indeed, Victoria's policy of protection had been judged by its efficacy towards the grand object for which it was shaped—the absorption of the population left without callings by the exhaustion of the alluvial diggings—by 1881 it had already been found wanting. Sixty thousand men had departed during the intercensal period 1871–81 and had left the colony with fewer adult males than it had possessed when that decade opened.[2] Protection had not, in popular estimation, made it easier to find employment in Victoria. The demand that state aid to immigration should cease was enforced by the prevalence of unemployment as early as 1873.[3]

The colonies other than Victoria rested content, for the most part, with tariffs designed primarily to raise revenue. Queensland duties on refined sugar and "golden syrup" impelled the Colonial Sugar Refining Company of Sydney

[1] "Protection in Victoria and Free Trade in New South Wales", a series of articles published by *The Age* in March and April of 1887. As evidence that "our exports are largely and increasingly exports of our own manufacture" the writer relied on (i) the trade in agricultural implements to the Riverina, a part of N.S.W. nearer Melbourne than Sydney to which the Victorian Railways quoted special railway freights, and (ii) exports of flour.

[2] T. A. Coghlan, *Labour and Industry in Australia*, p. 1481.

[3] State-aided immigration continued in South Australia until 1886, in N.S.W. until 1888, in Queensland until 1891. It had been intermittent only in Tasmania between 1835 and 1887. See *Commonwealth Demography, Bulletin* no. 44, p. 276. For phases of public opinion regarding it the following pamphlets should be read: (a) *How Victoria may be more Prosperous and Wages Higher*, by an old M.L.A. (1867); (b) *British Work for British Capital and Patriotism*, by Anglo-Australian (1869); (c) *State Aided Immigration*, by D. Bennet, 2nd Inter-Colonial T.U.C. (1884).

to establish a branch refinery there in 1892.[1] In South
Australia "fiscal indecision" was the normal state both of
leaders and tariff. The main interest of a community very
active in primary production was free inter-colonial trade,
but protective duties aided the establishment of clothing
factories and a woollen mill.[2] In New South Wales Sir
Henry Parkes was as earnest an advocate of free trade
as David Syme was of protection in Victoria. In his
political youth he dallied with the idea of protecting local
industries[3] but on his return from a lecturing tour in search
of British immigrants he proclaimed himself an ardent
free-trader (1862). Pastoral and financial opinion inclined
to a policy which kept down the cost of living and of
production for export, while the abundant revenue from
the sale of Crown lands left its rulers relatively untempted
by the ease with which big sums might be raised at the
Customs House. Under Parkes's dominance of her politics
during the 'seventies and 'eighties the mother colony adhered to his fiscal faith. Nor did that policy indefinitely
retard, as David Syme thought it must, the establishment
of manufactures. Not in population only but in the
opportunities of employment New South Wales steadily
overhauled Victoria.[4] The industries of the former colony,
moreover, not only afforded more employment to men,

[1] See the speech of the Chairman of Directors (T. Buckland) at the
general meeting for the half-year ending 30 September 1892, *C.S.R. Co.
Reports*, Mitchell Library.
[2] See T. A. Coghlan, *op. cit.* pp. 1155–59.
[3] See resolutions proposed in N.S.W. Assembly of 22 May 1860.
[4] The following table showing excess or deficiency of arrivals over de-
partures is from the *Commonwealth Year Book*, 1901–1907, No. 1, p. 154:

Period	Victoria	New South Wales
1871–1875	− 5,595	+ 29,741
1876–1880	− 5,865	+ 73,459
1881–1885	+27,786	+109,863
1886–1890	+86,231	+ 52,565
1891–1895	−46,848	+ 21,464
1896–1900	−63,582	− 997
1901–1905	−51,803	+ 21,073
1871–1905	−59,676	+307,168

but exploited the natural advantages of coal and raw materials and were therefore better able to weather the crises of the 'nineties. Victoria's "national policy" did not maintain her primacy in population and wealth. Perhaps that ambition was too high. But the attempt set up stresses in inter-colonial relations which made the period one of disin-tegration and drove the leaders in all the colonies into a jealous provincialism. Six intercolonial conferences, in the years 1863, 1865, 1867, 1870, 1871 and 1873, sought relief from the irksome restraints of customs barriers at the borders. At each the disagreement grew more bitter. The first conference drafted a light revenue tariff of duties on wines, spirits, beer, tobacco, sugar, coffee, cocoa, opium, dried fruits, candles, oil sand salt—with one excep-tion "conventional necessities" in ordinary consumption and therefore admirable objects for indirect taxation. The delegates, being the Premiers of their respective colonies, agreed to urge their parliaments to accept this common tariff as the means of intercolonial free trade and joint prosperity. It was to be maintained unaltered until changes proposed by any one colony had been considered by all in conference. Out of such an agreement would quickly have grown a Customs Union collecting revenue at coastal ports only and distributing it among the colonial treasurers according to population. The Premiers went home proud of having found a happy solution of border problems, only to find themselves a generation ahead of their followers.

At the moment New South Wales needed additional revenue. The sale of Crown lands under the Robertson Act had hardly begun to bear fruit. Nor was there wanting a feeling that Victorian protectionism would add to the attractiveness of Sydney's harbour and make Sydney's warehouses the distributing centres for the Eastern colonies and the islands.[1] Victoria, in the first fever of Syme's

[1] Throughout the 'sixties and early 'seventies Victoria tried hard to induce

inoculation with the protectionist serum, felt strong distaste for even intercolonial freedom of trade. Both the major colonies rejected the simple unalterable tariff and without them the others were scattered members.

As the Premiers had foreseen, awkward problems arose on the inland borders as a result of the enactment of different tariffs at the far-distant capitals. The boundaries of New South Wales, Victoria and South Australia cut up the Murray-Darling river-basin, scene of the main pastoral activity, without the least regard for the unity which the area should have derived from the navigation of the rivers. In September 1853 Francis Cadell had proved that navigation was feasible by piloting a little river steamer built in Sydney, the "Lady Augusta", from the Murray Mouth to Swan Hill and bringing back 441 bales of Riverina wool. Before 1860 he had traded with Albury, Gundagai and Menindee on the three main streams.[1] The value of stations on the Darling doubled, it was said, on the day he reached them. To be rid of such irrational things as customs houses in the back blocks, Victoria and South Australia arranged that duties on goods passing up the Murray into Victoria should be collected at Adelaide, while New South Wales and Victoria assimilated their tariffs. That was in 1854. Two years later the discovery of a goldfield in New South Wales but near enough to the Victorian border to be better served from Melbourne than from Sydney tempted the elder colony, at the instance of its merchants, to handicap the Melbourne trade thither by charging duty a second time at Albury and other Murray River crossings. Smuggling proved easy and the manœuvre was futile. In 1864, however, as settlement became active in the Riverina, New South Wales talked of strict administration all along the Murray, especially at Moama opposite Echuca, the Victorian river port,

the P. & O. Company to make Melbourne the final port of call for its mail steamers. See *The Argus*, 25 July and 25 August 1860, and *The Postal Question*, 1873 (Mitchell Library Pamphlets).

[1] A. G. Price, *Founders and Pioneers of S. Australia* (1929), pp. 221-53.

K

unless Victoria would pay over as subsidy a fair share of the duties collected at Melbourne on goods that passed through Victoria into the Riverina.[1]

Melbourne had but lately made herself a more effective centre for the Riverina trade by the construction at very great expense of a railway to Echuca. This would afford a regular and rapid service far superior to the tedious and seasonal navigation of the Murray. Unwilling to lose the traffic, Victoria managed to exact a *quid pro quo* for the subsidy asked by New South Wales. She expressed a willingness to pay the subsidy if, while refraining from setting customs officers on the Victorian border, the mother colony would post them where the Murray entered South Australia to tax goods coming up the river. Melbourne merchants would then have free access by rail to the Riverina, but South Australia's ambition to increase the river-borne trade would be effectively scotched. Along the Murray the country settlers talked of shooting any customs officers that appeared and their threats did not go unreported even by *The Age*, usually given to admiring such officials. After an acrimonious negotiation New South Wales and Victoria entered into a "treaty" in 1867 at South Australia's expense.[1]

Such a bargain suggested to Victoria's smaller neighbours, Tasmania and South Australia, that they should bargain too in defence of their export to Victoria of agricultural products. Mutual concessions, they were astonished to find, were barred by the terms of their constitutions which forbade the grant to anyone of tariff advantages which might be inconsistent with British policy, including British treaties of trade and commerce with European countries.[2] The Colonial Office, regarding this provision as a spur to complete freedom of trade, made the most of the diplomatic difficulties which intercolonial

---

[1] Sir John Young to the Earl of Carnarvon, 24 January 1867. The agreement, as the Colonial Office preferred to call it, was duly ratified by the N.S.W. Parliament in August 1867.

[2] Duke of Buckingham to Governor of New South Wales, 7 January 1868.

reciprocity would involve. Tasmania, impatient of adversity, sought to retaliate against Victoria with a raised tariff if she might not negotiate with a lowered one. She proposed to levy on imported goods duties varying with the treatment accorded to those of Tasmania in the country of the imports' origin. This, too, was "reserved" for the Colonial Office's consideration. Another intercolonial conference was called at the suggestion of Tasmania. It met at Melbourne in June 1870 to consider again the project of a Customs Union. This the Colonial Office would allow, for it would constitute a new diplomatic unit. Freedom of trade between its constituent parts would not be open to "the objection of principle which attaches to differential duties".[1]

Again a common tariff and a unified customs administration dividing the revenue from indirect taxes according to population slipped through the colonial leaders' grasp. New South Wales stood firm for a revenue tariff only, and withdrew as soon as Victoria, intent upon playing the part of Prussia in this Southern Zollverein, demanded that all should adopt her national policy of protection. Nay more. She refused to contemplate a tariff alterable by general consent alone. For a specific term she demanded full and sole power to make changes in the tariff.

The only point upon which the conference could reach unanimity was in proclaiming to the Colonial Office the right of free colonies to make their own terms for reciprocity in trade. Bills designed to raise this constitutional issue passed the Tasmanian and South Australian houses and were duly reserved for the Royal assent. In reply, the Secretary of State for the Colonies (13 July 1871) thought it would be inexpedient to invite the Imperial Parliament "to legislate in a direction contrary to the established commercial policy of this country" and to admit intercolonial reciprocity. Charles Gavan-Duffy as

[1] Circular Despatch from the Earl of Kimberley to the Australian Governors, 15 July 1870.

Premier of Victoria certainly spoke for all when he expressed the colonists' impatience at "being treated as persons who cannot be trusted to regulate their own affairs at their own discretion". Julius Vogel, the able Attorney-General of New Zealand, sought to persuade the Colonial Office that its refusal to countenance reciprocity was actually fostering retaliation and aggravating the tendency towards protection.[1] More conferences, one in September 1871 and another in February 1873, at long last persuaded Downing Street. The Australian Colonies Duties Act of April 1873 allowed them to make whatever trade agreements and laws between themselves they might desire.

The light had dawned too late. Divided sovereignty had done its work, and faith in common action had wilted while the power to move towards it was withheld. Growing discrepancy between the tariffs of the two main colonies inevitably broke down even their sinister agreement about trade across the Murray. When Victoria adopted a heavier tariff and New South Wales in 1873 cut hers down to 45 specific duties, it became worth while to send goods in bond from Melbourne to the Riverina, to release them free of duty on New South Wales territory and send them back at low freights into Victoria. Victorian Ministers promptly denounced the "treaty" of 1867 and established customs houses on their side of the border. But South Australia did not gain by this dispute between her rivals for the Murray trade. The Victorian railways still quoted special freight rates on goods and produce to and from the Riverina. To obtain what she held to be her share of the trade within her own territory, New South Wales extended her railways and cut the rates again. At Albury in 1876 Sir Hercules Robinson, her Governor and a staunch advocate of railways to serve primary produc-

---

[1] The most incisive comments on the effects in Australia of the Colonial Office's attitude towards tariff-making may be found in the Tasmanian Governor du Cane's despatch to the Earl of Kimberley, 29 September 1871.

tion in the interior, deplored the disintegrating effect of intercolonial tariffs, railway feuds and breaks of gauge. "The policy of railway extensions has been almost solely one of isolation, directed mainly to the object of securing by one device or another, for the rival capitals, as much of the traffic of the country as possible.... It is the interest of the country at large that the traffic should flow through its natural and most economical channels, and any attempt to divert its course by restrictions or artificial regulations is simply a waste of wealth and power and a common loss."

In that generation, however, the interest of the country at large had no means of expression. Continued bickering between New South Wales and Victoria over the inland customs barrier came to a climax in 1877 when Victoria imposed heavy duties on the transfer of live stock over the Murray. It was the night of provincialism. Difficulties and habits of mind that have since proved fruitful of ill-feeling and absurdities were being aggravated by local leaders, each intent on serving the part he loved and unconscious of a common weal.[1]

On one issue—perhaps the most fundamental of all—the colonial leaders in Eastern Australia reached unanimity of thought and action, that is, on the exclusion of Chinese

[1] John Robertson, the "King Goodheart" of Free Selection before Survey, rose at a banquet held in Sydney during November 1872 to celebrate the establishment of telegraphic communication with England, to congratulate South Australia on filling the last gap. "Mr Robertson", reports the *Sydney Mail*, 23 November 1872, "put in a claim on behalf of New South Wales for its mead of praise on the ground that it had the largest extent of telegraph lines, and to himself for having been the Minister under whom the first construction contract in N.S.W. was carried out,... South Australia, with more eagerness than wisdom or courtesy, has seized a coveted opportunity of forestalling its neighbours and had completed a bargain which, having been made in haste, would have to be repented of at leisure. The line through Central Australia would some day prove a failure." Possibly a reference at the end of the report to failure on the part of the caterer for the banquet may explain, though it may not excuse, Mr Robertson's "courtesy". The party was "shrewdly out of beef!" Yet, tragically enough, there was much truth in his libel on South Australia and her line. See chapter xx, *infra*.

labour. The restrictive laws by which the coming of Chinese miners had been impeded in the 'fifties were quietly repealed in the 'sixties, having served their purpose. In the early 'seventies a Queensland Government even opened negotiations for the introduction of Chinese coolies to work under indenture in the sugar industry. Then alluvial gold and silver were found on the Palmer River (1873) and on the Hodgkinson (1875). Both are in torrid country, and when a fresh influx of Chinese came to dig for gold the feeling once generated at Buckland River and Lambing Flat was accentuated by the virtual monopoly the Chinese obtained. In 1877 on the Palmer field behind Cooktown there were 17,000 licensed Chinese miners and only 1400 whites.[1]

The Thorn ministry passed through the Brisbane Parliament a measure imposing heavy licence fees, which Governor Cairns reserved for the Royal assent on the old ground that such laws were inconsistent with British treaties with China. The Earl of Carnarvon confirmed his action but let it be known that the Royal assent would not be refused to a Bill which refrained from singling out the subjects of China for onerous treatment.

Governor Cairns' reservation of the measure called forth a loud outcry from the Queensland liberals, which was echoed farther south by ministries to which Thorn appealed for common action on this constitutional issue. But the Earl of Carnarvon's hint was taken and in 1877 and 1878 restrictions on the coming of Chinese were framed in forms consonant with the British treaties. Those who returned to China within a limited period, moreover, were offered the refund of their entrance fees. As in the earlier episode, the decline of alluvial digging ere long made any such taxes prohibitive. By 1881 the Chinese in Queensland were only 11,200 in number and newcomers were barely a hundred a year.

---

[1] P. C. Campbell, *Chinese Coolie Emigration* (1922), pp. 61 *et seq.* and Myra Willard, *White Australia Policy* (1923), chapter III.

Before that natural solution was reached on the tropical diggings, however, Chinese labour had become a formidable problem on Australian coastal ships. On this issue it fell to New South Wales to lead in proposing exclusion. In 1877 the Australasian Steam Navigation Company, under pressure of competition, replaced British seamen by Chinese on three of its vessels. The arrival of a hundred more Chinese seafarers at Sydney in November 1878 gave token of an intention to extend their employment. Almost throughout the Company's fleet the white seamen struck, and the wage-earners of the ports and capitals supported them with enthusiasm by public demonstration and union levies. The Queensland Government, closely sympathetic with the popular feeling, notified the Company that it would withdraw the mail subsidy from vessels so manned. Thereupon, early in 1879, the Company agreed to reduce gradually the Chinese element in the crews. Sir Henry Parkes having fought and won an election on the issue of Chinese exclusion, the New South Wales Assembly at his instance adopted a Bill to revive the old restrictions and to add a prohibition of the employment of Chinese on vessels registered in the colony. As the excitement died away after the success of the strike, the Legislative Council postponed the Bill. But the working men in all the eastern colonies were in grim earnest. They had learned the extent of their influence on political leaders and they kept up their pressure until, about 1881, practically uniform laws against Chinese immigration had been enacted in all those colonies. Public opinion on the question was kept alive by California's troubles with a much bigger inroad of Celestials, by fears not altogether groundless that the Chinese would bring to Australia diseases like smallpox and leprosy that were endemic in Asia, and by an untimely project for indentured Chinese labour on the north-west coast of Australia.

This proposal, though of small moment, precipitated united action at an intercolonial conference called by Sir

Henry Parkes in 1880. It involved the importation of some fifty Chinese only and was termed a "temporary expedient". It served, however, to evoke from the Conference a warm protest which was sent in its name to the Earl of Kimberley.[1] The Governor of the Crown Colony of Western Australia sought through the Colonial Office to reassure the governments concerned. It was a matter of sentiment without practical moment. In that sentiment, however, the self-governing colonists were more nearly unanimous than in any other. Only Tasmania neglected to levy a heavy capitation tax on immigrant Chinese and to define strictly the number which any vessel might introduce. At the instance of the Adelaide Legislative Council the South Australian measure was not to apply to the Northern Territory then under that colony's jurisdiction. But in 1886 even Western Australia, now that gold-digging had spread to her tropics, fell into line.

Recklessly lighting the fires of class conflict, the colonists were all too ready to bicker among themselves on internal problems such as free or safeguarded selection. They might build railways to divert and divide, and tariffs to impede, their central trade. Their notion of progress in industry was to "protect" faint copies of industrial triumphs in their old home. But the general will was agreed that the wage-earner's standard of living must not be spoiled by alien intruders whose docile assiduity, however charming to employers, was unwelcome in British Australia.

[1] *N.S.W.V. and P.* Session 1880-1, vol. III, p. 325.

CHAPTER XVI

Inland Transport

THE early pastoralists had to live the whole year round on the wide tablelands and plains that the explorers had glimpsed and scrambled through. Once he was sure of water, the squatter's main problem was transport. In days when the industry had to find its own convoys, stores and wool carried by packhorse and bullock-waggon moved painfully, straining endurance near to breaking point. Tropical rains would make the black soil plains of Queensland virtually impassable for weeks on end, and it was no unusual thing in the 'sixties for a bullock-dray to take three months on the way from Mitchell's "Fort Bourke" to Bathurst.

In 1847–8 Alan Macpherson formed a new station at Mount Abundance, west of the Darling Downs near the junction of the Cogoon River and Bunjeywargorai Creek. In January 1848 he found himself, after a flood, under the necessity of pushing out to it with rations from Keera on the Gwydir in northern New South Wales. He started on February 1st with a dray lightly loaded, ten bullocks, two drivers and a Keera black to track any bullocks that strayed. In three weeks they covered a hundred miles, about a third of the way. Then they entered boggy country. They spent February 28th getting stores over the Boomai River in a tub. Finally they wrapped the flour in a tarpaulin and set the bullocks to drag the dray through "the shoalest part of the river". On the far bank the team were bogged up to their middles, so the men carried the flour from the dray, still in mid-stream. It was well they did. After further attempts to scramble up the west bank, the bullocks turned in mid-stream and, despite a well-plied whip and much bush rhetoric, pulled out again on to the east bank. Twenty-two times that day Macpherson had swum what in writing he termed "this unpleasant river". Towards dark, another tremendous thunder-shower caught them with the sugar uncovered. They spent ten days more in crossing a dozen miles of bad country. Then conditions mended. The "boss" was able to push forward to Mount Abundance with word of the relief, and to reach it on March 25th.[1]

George Hobler met similar trials as he journeyed slowly down the Murrumbidgee after March 1845 in search of relief from the catarrh which had decimated his Merinos on Mummele, south of Goulburn. In August he was forced to put his stores across the flooded river on a raft made from six casks. Then they swam the bullocks over. Hauling the waggon through, under water, was a heavy business. "It soon sank so deep as not to leave a ripple on the surface, and it was rather an anxious time as we gained steadily on the rope. At last the point of the pole" —which had been lashed upright to prevent its getting foul of any timber—"broke the water again and the whole machine gradually emerged. As we could not pull it up the bank, we put a team of oxen to it, when lo! the rope broke and the waggon began to walk back again into deep water. But it stopped before it got too deep for us. We made fast with chains and dragged it out safely. The same by the drays."

Such strainings alternated with endless slow trudging over flats,

When the wool teams in season came down from Coonamble
And journeyed for weeks on their way to the sea.

Until the digging days, "made roads" were unknown beyond the coastal settlements. Major Mitchell surveyed the main northern road as far as the Hunter River in 1829.

---

[1] *Mount Abundance: Experiences of a Pioneer Squatter*, by Alan Macpherson, Blairgowrie (1875), Mitchell Library.

Newcastle had till then been accessible only by sea. A year later, Mitchell was at work on the southern road and on a new road to Bathurst to replace what remained of "Captain Cox's wonderful but somewhat primitive highway". Over the gullies and water-courses wooden bridges, too often destroyed by bush-fires, were one by one replaced by stone after 1832. In this Mitchell was aided by David Lennox from Ayrshire, a pupil of Thomas Telford. Lennox, a working mason, had been foreman on a bridge that Telford built near Gloucester. He brought to the colony clear memories of its 150 foot span, a thing of beauty borrowed by Telford from a bridge over the Seine at Neuilly. "Thus originated", wrote Mitchell in 1855, "all the bridges this colony possesses worthy of the name." Lansdowne Bridge over Prospect Creek on the Southern Road, though not Lennox's first stone bridge in New South Wales, was the first in which he re-copied the Neuilly arch.[1]

But Mitchell was not happy in his control of the "government men" on the roads. In 1836 actual construction was handed over to the Royal Engineers. They could certainly discipline the convicts, but unluckily they could not work the survey instruments. When the supply of convicts petered out in the 'forties, the roads, according to the Constitution Act of 1842, became the care of district councils empowered to levy local rates for their upkeep. But the districts into which, in 1843, "a few scratches of the Governor's pen" had divided the settled areas around Port Jackson and Port Phillip failed to excite the local patriotism of either councillors or ratepayers.[2] The colonists

[1] In 1844 Governor Gipps sent Lennox to bridge the Yarra at Melbourne, which he did by Old Prince's Bridge, a single span of 150 feet opened on 15 November 1850. It was demolished in 1884 when the river was widened. Under the new Victorian Government Lennox built over 50 bridges, and had charge, at a salary of £300 a year, of all construction of roads, wharves and jetties. See his biography by Henry Selkirk, *Journal of the Royal Australian Historical Society*, vol. VI, part V.

[2] Cf. Sir G. Gipps' homily on finance to the N.S.W. Legislative Council, 29 July 1839, quoted in "Notes on History of Local Government in Victoria", by A. W. Greig, *Proceedings of Victorian Historical Society*, 1925.

thought the building of roads a proper charge on the "land fund". This flowed into the central treasury and seemed a desirable alternative to the imposition of local rates and taxes.

After an interval in which the excellent "convict roads" fell into disrepair, Mitchell resumed charge of the turnpike roads. But the tolls did not go far. Labour was scarce, and, as the settlers jolted over roads that had once been the colony's pride, they no doubt sighed heavily for the days of the government gangs.[1] For use on the unmade inland tracks to and about the diggings, newcomers from America brought with them the idea of vehicles that dispensed with the need of roads. These were the bush-coach, always associated in Australia with the name of Cobb & Co., and the American buggy. The main feature of their construction was a light body suspended by straps above four wheels of large diameter. This simplicity made repair possible anywhere. A wheel or swingle-tree might come to grief in collision with a stump that a sleepy driver had failed to notice in the dark or the dust; but he was a poor hand indeed if he could not cut a sapling to replace the broken spoke or fix up the broken traces with the aid of the local fencing wire. As a means of rapid conveyance the bush-coach was hardly comfortable. "When drawn at a smart trot—its usual pace—on a jolting road, sometimes running in a rut from which it jumps now and then with a shudder, or upsetting in a hole hidden by a puddle of water", a French observer was ready to term it "an instrument of torture."[2] Nor was its rough charm enhanced by the usual concomitants of dust, heat, and incessant attacks on ears, eyes and nostrils by a cloud of flies which rode on each traveller's back, and reserved their best efforts for the sandy uphill pinches where to ease the horses everyone got out and walked. Yet for all

[1] See Major Mitchell's *Report upon the Progress made in Roads and Public Works in New South Wales 1827–1855* (Sydney 1856), Mitchell Library MSS.
[2] F. Journet, *L'Australie* (1885), p. 215.

their discomforts and inelegance the American coach and buggy admirably suited the countryside. Light and supple, they rattled over the inequalities of thousands of miles where the formation and upkeep of roads were beyond the means of a thin skirmishing line of settlers. You might drive them up a hillside or through a forest, or over a "road" which had set into a thousand deep ruts of baked mud. To arrive anywhere, if you did not ride a horse, there was no other choice.

The leathern "springs" of Cobb & Co.'s coaches date back to 1853 and the Bendigo diggings.[1] Four Americans founded the firm—Freeman Cobb, John Murray Peck, James Swanton and John Lamber—but its best brain was another American, James Rutherford, who with five partners bought out Cobb & Co. and reorganized the lines about the Victorian diggings. Having gained a monopoly of the Victorian mail-contracts, Cobb & Co. drove a cavalcade of 103 horses, 10 coaches and 2 feed waggons over the border to Bathurst in 1861. There Rutherford and Walter Russell Hall fixed their headquarters. Thence they spread their services throughout the back country. After 1865 they conquered Queensland. "By 1870 Cobb & Co. in the three eastern colonies were harnessing 6000 horses per day, their coaches were travelling 28,000 miles per week, their annual pay-sheet exceeded £100,000 and they received £95,000 per annum in mail subsidies.

> Swift scramble up the siding
>   where teams climb inch by inch,
> Pause, bird-like, on the summit—
>   then breakneck down the pinch
> Past haunted half-way houses—
>   where convicts made the bricks—
> Scrub-yards and new bark-shanties,
>   we dash with five and six—

[1] William Deakin, father of Alfred Deakin, was an accountant in the firm of Cobb & Co. when the future Prime Minister was born in 1856. See Walter Murdoch's *Alfred Deakin* (1923).

By clear ridge-country rivers,
    and gaps where tracks run high,
Where waits the lonely horseman,
    cut clear against the sky;
Through stringy-bark and blue gum,
    and box and pine we go:
New camps are stretching 'cross the
    plains the routes of Cobb & Co.[1]

Their routes showed the way to the railways, the motor-lorries and airways of to-day. As the locomotive appeared on the main lines, Cobb & Co. went farther out. In the 'eighties they plied on 4000 miles of Queensland "roads", and the last coach was taken off the Yeulba-Surat run only in 1924, passing thence to the Queensland Museum.

Bullock-waggons and the red coaches of Cobb & Co. were crude makeshifts at best, very wasteful of the time and endurance of their users. Yet with them men proved the land and showed what it could produce. In the 'seventies and 'eighties, British capital, seeing the big markets for Australian wool, metals and meat, helped to fence and water the station properties and to link them with the ports by railways and telegraphs. Served by these, the flocks increased from 20,980,123 in 1861 to 106,419,751 in 1891, cattle multiplied from 3,846,554 to 11,112,112 in 1891, and the better care and breeding of the sheep showed in a seven-fold increase of the wool-clip from 78,485,900 pounds to 543,495,800.

Such progress within a single generation could never have been made with road-transport alone. Neither the art nor the administrative machinery of road-building made effective advance. Attempts at construction on tender virgin soil by half-trained engineers, though they cost from five to six thousand pounds a mile, ended in deep mud or flying dust clouds. "It is absurd", wrote Governor Hotham, "to go on spending £500,000 a year

[1] Henry Lawson, *The Lights of Cobb & Co.*

in making roads which disappear after a winter's wear. This colony, for political as well as for financial reasons, should borrow money for railways on the security of the land fund."[1] After Melbourne folk had been tormented for decades by the dust which the north wind drove in thick clouds along their broad straight streets, a civil engineer told them how unsuitable to a dry climate with boisterous land winds were the water-bound macadamized roads of Britain. Concrete roads, he explained, though expensive at first would call for little upkeep and would minimize the dust nuisance.[2] But local governing bodies equal to the technical and financial tasks of building such roads were but slowly created. In Victoria, where local government was most active, the "shires" received wide rating powers in 1863, but borrowing powers for boroughs and shires were not added until 1874. In New South Wales municipal institutions did not become general until after 1905. It was the railway age, and the need of good roads or local road authorities was not felt.

When in the 'fifties the carriage of goods to the gold-fields normally cost more than the goods themselves when landed on Sandridge or Williamstown wharves; when consumers were paying between two and three million pounds per annum to carriers, as well as heavy charges for police protection, Victoria had looked a fresh and promising scene for "associated enterprise" in railway construction. But it was not enough to prove macadamized roads expensive, and wages and fodder-prices exorbitant: it did not follow that, because railway companies had won through their infant ailments to success in Britain, they would do so in a new colony. There were far better openings in Australia

---

[1] In a letter to Captain Cole quoted by *The Age*, 18 October 1862.

[2] I. Tipping, *Suppressing the Dust Nuisance* (Melbourne 1884). "The interstices of the metal should be filled with a material not liable to softening in wet nor to blowing out in dry weather. The only known available material supplying these conditions is Cement Mortar which, after the interstices have been closed to the utmost by rolling, should be grouted to a depth of three or four inches."

for speculators than railways could hope to offer.[1] "The colonists have so little disposition to embark their capital in such undertakings that even with a dividend secured by a Government guarantee, it has been found wholly impossible to finance any extensive scheme of railways by means of local shareholders." "Railways enterprize does not offer sufficient temptation for investment to those who desire to become rapidly rich." The Melbourne, Mount Alexander and Murray River Railway Company, projected in 1852, had received "an extent of encouragement to which", thought Captain Andrew Clarke, "the history of associated enterprize in railways affords no parallel". Five thousand pounds was advanced for preliminary expenses. Government guaranteed a dividend of five per cent. for twenty years on all paid up capital, and granted free land for the line and stations, including fifty acres for a Melbourne terminus. But by April 1855 only 5127 shares of twenty-five pounds had been sold out of 40,000, and, instead of a line to the goldfields and the Murray, the great Company had decided to confine its attention to the line to Williamstown, ten miles long. Commissioners on Internal Communication reported in 1854 that "the opening up of great lines of railway will be a work of time, it will cost millions of money and will require a combination of talent and perseverance, a command of large resources and an amount of confidence on the part of the public which are not likely for some time to come to be the attendants on private colonial undertakings of this magnitude".[2] In May 1856, the Melbourne, Mount Alexander and Murray River Railway Company sold out to the Government for a nominal sum. The Hobson's Bay Railway Company and two smaller concerns prospered on suburban passenger traffic, but only by charging high fares.

[1] Captain Andrew Clarke, R.E. *Report on Railways*, *Vic. P.P.* 1856–7, vol. IV, p. 551.
[2] Report of 1854, *Commissioners on Internal Communication*, *Vic. P.P.* 1856–7, vol. IV, p. 801.

The record of private or associated enterprise around Sydney was even more discreditable. The Sydney Railway Company, after struggling for eight years to raise enough capital to build a line from Sydney to Parramatta, collapsed and left the uncompleted task to the State. Its engineers earned eternal infamy for it by involving the two leading colonies in their disastrous choice of different gauges.[1] Though, in the generation after the convict system had ceased, political opinion was very hostile to government action, it was plainly beyond local resources to link the capitals with the goldfields, or to build lines that would handle the all-important wool traffic at lower freight-charges. "The intervention of the authorities of the country is no longer a matter of expediency but of necessity."

Men were not wanting to plan a transport system for the distant future, with a spacious disregard of cost. One pamphleteer urged the necessity of a North-South line from the Gulf country to Melbourne, with an extension through Queensland to the Northern Territory.[2] Another urged the substitution for rails of great trunk roads on which rubber-tyred locomotives should run.[3] The Lieutenant-Governor of South Australia, Sir Henry Young, sought to harmonize the use of river and railway transport. The enlightened nature of his proposals for connecting

[1] See Sir G. Grey to Sir C. Fitzroy 8 November 1854 and enclosures. Also T. A. Coghlan, *Labour and Industry in Australia*, pp. 841–3. The company begged more capital from the Government than it raised for itself. In a pamphlet published in 1854, T. S. Mort advocated the issue for its benefit of government-guaranteed bearer shares. Circulating like bank-notes, these, he argued, would be a sure means of attracting small savings and thus of avoiding the need of borrowing abroad and "the danger of government taking part in industrial operations".

[2] Edwin Trenerry, *Plan for a Grand Central Transcontinental Railway* (1879). It was to be built on the land-grant plan, from Deniliqum to the Gulf, and linked by branch-lines to Roma, Wagga Wagga and Euston, to join the Queensland, New South Wales and South Australian railways. "Booligal would be the Chicago, merchants there having the option of sending to either one of the ports of Sydney, Victoria or Adelaide."

[3] G. E. Dalrymple, *India Rubber Tire and Tram Steam Traction* (Brisbane 1869), advocating (a) wooden railways or macadamized roads on which should be run rubber-tired locomotives, and (b) a central means of land communication through Echuca, Bourke and the Warrego Valley.

Sydney, Melbourne and Adelaide was recognized. But each of the new colonial governments was intent on the transport needs of its own constituents and inclined to see these as opposed to those of others rather than as reconcilable in a common system.[1] A French visitor in 1885, thinking of the carefully planned railway web of France or Belgium, was shocked to find no general plan for the railways of any one colony, still less for those of Australia.[2]

A central authority, had it existed, might have planned a railway system for the pastoral and agricultural areas with due regard to easy gradients to coastal ports and to the spacing of the lines in proportion to traffic. The latter was perhaps the more fundamental task. Though a valuable commodity per bale, and thus able to bear the cost of long land transport, wool is a sparse crop. An acre will produce at best only some ten pounds in a year. Therefore the railways that collect it into big trainloads for haulage to the sea may be spaced a hundred miles apart. The wool could well bear the cost of haulage to the railway, even by the bullock dray, from stations fifty miles from the line. The economical network of railways for wool traffic was a wide-meshed one. The savings possible by rail transport as compared with road transport were still adequate, after being shared between the pastoralists and the railways, to extend greatly the two margins of profitable sheep-running, its limit in the interior and its degree of capital equipment and care everywhere. When the fancy prices of the gold-digging days had gone, two shillings per ton-mile had remained the ruling charge on the waggons. The freight for miscellaneous goods over the private railways of the 'fifties was a quarter of this, viz. 6d. per ton-mile.

[1] Cf. Lionel Curtis, *Letters to the People of India on Responsible Government*, p. 69. "The moment you begin to establish electoral governments, the boundaries of their jurisdictions, lightly sketched by the pencils of officials and diplomats, begin to bite into the political map like acids." The economic map, too, if you leave development to elected rulers!

[2] F. Journet, *L'Australie* (1885). T. A. Coghlan, *Seven Colonies of Australasia*, 1901–2, pp. 843–4, gives a valuable table showing the length of line opened in each year, 1854–1902.

Ideal plans for the railways of Eastern Australia as a whole were beyond the ken of colonial engineers fighting to build a railway of any sort into the productive interior. In New South Wales, after Penrith and Picton had been reached on the Western and Southern railways, there was so little traffic that the politicians of the hour thought of extending them by horse-tramways. It was all that the engineer-in-chief could do, with the vigorous seconding of Governor Sir John Young, to obtain authority to build for the locomotive, albeit with sharp curves and gradients. But Sydney, for all her deep, safe harbour and abundant natural wharfage, is separated from the wool lands by a rough and sterile area where railway construction was costly, haulage heavy, and traffic light. Zig-zags and gradients of one in thirty were needed to climb the ranges. The cost of such stupendous work—for such it was in proportion to a traffic of forty tons a day on the main Western line—forced the Government to meet interest payments out of fresh loans. This lapse into bad finance, however inevitable, was difficult to recover from when once made.

Benevolent governments were urged to ignore cost of service, and to set rates of freight that would develop the traffic. And freights that were reasonable, even cheap, to the wool men in comparison with the costs of transport by bullock teams, were still high to farmers. Free selectors grumbled that the railway was too dear for them when in the 'seventies it cost 8½d. per bushel to send wheat from Echuca to Melbourne, a haul of only 156 miles. When agricultural implements were charged £4. 11s. per ton for the same journey, the farmer jibbed and sent his team to Melbourne to bring plough or stripper up by road.[1] Agricultural settlements made a demand not only for light freights but also for closer lines. Wheat is by no means comparable with wool in value, weight for weight. An acre under cultivation, however, will produce from ten to twenty

[1] J. L. Dow, *Our Land Acts* (Melbourne 1877).

bushels, weighing over five to ten hundredweight, and as much as three tons of hay. Such a bulk of produce will load many more trains but, as the cost of hauling it to the siding by horse or bullock team mounted rapidly with the distance from the line, fifteen miles out became the limit of profitable settlement. This meant that, if settlement by farmers was to fill in the blank spaces on the railway map, the mesh of the network had to be reduced to thirty miles.[1]

No doubt it would have been wise, had it been feasible, to wait for the agricultural settlement of the land within access of the main wool lines before making ready for the wheat-farmers elsewhere. But in this matter railway construction, even within each colony, was embarrassed by the guerilla warfare on the Western front between squatter and free selector. The wool-growers outbid the selectors for the freehold of land well served by the railways, and soil-exhaustion made farmers restless even where they did get land. Colonial treasurers, too, were only too glad to see them given access to virgin land by the building of more railways. These opened up the prospect of more land "revenue". New South Wales could rely on a light revenue tariff and do without an income tax until the middle 'nineties because of the abundant money received from sales of Crown land. Twelve millions, mainly from sales, figured as land revenue between 1876 and 1880.

Yet financial considerations cramped any grand style in railway-building because low freights in proportion to cost of service made the railways unproductive of net revenue. Construction work had to wait upon supplies of capital borrowed abroad. While the line over the Blue Mountains was being built, the contractors were warned not to go too fast, lest the Treasury should run out of funds with which to meet their claims. The credit of the colonies

---

[1] H. Deane, *Presidential Address to the Royal Society of New South Wales*, 1908: "Railways Required for Carriage of Wood and Wheat".

in the London market was a plant of uneven growth. It flourished well in the 'sixties, and Queensland and Victoria built railways fast. Then came a check, not unconnected with continued repudiation of debts in the states of the American Union and with foolhardy railway contracts in the Near East.[1] "It was a favourite maxim of the sixties", notes Coghlan, "that what America had done Australia would do." The parallel did not hold good, however, as regards the forms of security pledged. Taught by bitter experience, the British investor who lent his capital in America learned to prefer railway bonds charged on the assets of a railway company rather than the bonds or debentures of a state government. In his dealings with Australia he relied upon government securities. The earliest loans to the colonial governments had been raised by the sale of debentures redeemable out of the land fund. Though in process of dissipation, the public estates of the various colonies were very large and tangible assets. Other specific revenues came under pledge for a time, but an episode in Tasmania in the 'seventies suggested to colonial railway-users that all loans for railway construction should be made a charge on the whole of the borrowing colony's assets. The lenders in London were nothing loth to accept the wider security.

A private company had undertaken in 1868 to construct and operate a western railway from Launceston to Deloraine, the Government guaranteeing interest on the cost. This was done at the petition of the landowners along the line who agreed that, in the event of the receipts failing to cover interest as well as running expenses, the Government should find the guaranteed interest by levying a special local rate upon them. The railway receipts proved too small even to meet running expenses, but when the Government took over the line and sought to collect from the landowners a part of the sum they had contracted to pay, these beneficiaries repudiated their contract. Circumstances alter cases, they said. The main railway from

[1] Leland Jenks, *Migration of British Capital to 1875* (1927), *passim*.

Hobart to Launceston had in the meantime been made a charge on the general revenue. Why, then, should the western line be an additional local burden? Attempts to enforce payment of the rate by distraint of their goods called out a violent resistance. "Griffin's horse", an animal seized for non-payment of the rate, became a symbol of defiance until in 1872 the Government abandoned the plan of local assessment to meet local railway deficits.

Though Griffin's horse is now dead and forgotten, its influence is still potent. For good or ill every project in Australia involving substantial expense became thereafter "a public work of national importance". The high horse which the otherwise silent member rides when he demands of ministers a proper recognition of his constituents' importance is really Griffin's.

In the same decade, all the colonies followed New Zealand's lead in the issue of inscribed stock, instead of debentures chargeable on this or that source of revenue, and the British Parliament in 1877 provided by a Colonial Stock Act for inscription and transfer in the United Kingdom. Though not yet listed as trustee securities[1]—a boon Colonial government agents were already seeking—colonial stocks were thus made familiar and easily handled "lines" on the London stock market, the central source of loanable capital.[2]

The honest broker who brought together the willing buyer and the willing seller of colonial securities appeared in 1872 in the person of Sir Hercules Robinson. As governor of New South Wales from 1872 to 1879, he advocated at every opportunity a spirited public works

[1] They were not trustee securities until 1900, when Joseph Chamberlain passed another Colonial Stock Act in their favour. Thereafter, trustees might legally buy them as, in effect, gilt-edged investments, and the savings of the British middle-classes were at the disposal of Australian treasurers.

[2] Regarding brokerage and other expenses of negotiation, see a despatch of the Duke of Buckingham to the Officer Administering New South Wales, 23 January 1868, and T. A. Coghlan, *Seven Colonies of Australasia*, 1901-2, pp. 1024 *et seq.*

policy. When he arrived, Australia had less than 1200 miles of railway, and nowhere did a line penetrate more than 180 miles from the coast. But the engineers had scaled the mountain barrier behind Sydney. The true home of the pastoral industry lay before the railheads; and, both in Victoria and New South Wales, railway men and private brokers concerted plans for the capture of the main wool traffic. Sir Hercules was ready to urge a larger courage on lenders and borrowers alike. Full-bearded audiences at the opening of railway extensions roared applause when he told them "this country possesses almost boundless natural resources which only require population to develop them", and went into ecstasies over the moral he drew, that ministers ought not to be satisfied with the construction of less than fifty miles of railway in each year.[1] Each colony in turn enthusiastically drew up ambitious plans of railway and other development works, to be financed by loan monies. From 1871 to 1875, eleven borrowed millions and a half were found for public works.

Those who decided what railways were to be built and what rivers to be bridged tried hard to limit the schedules to works urgently needed. But what should be taken as the criterion of urgency? Should it be the ability to meet the interest on costs of construction? If this criterion had been abandoned on the roads when the toll-bars were removed, why should it be applied to the railways? As money grew cheaper, importunate members mounted Griffin's horse in turn. Opening up the land ahead of settlement was held to be the saving grace of Government ownership of the railways. By the end of fifteen years of easy money and political pressure, treasurers' ideas of urgent necessity had been pushed so far ahead of population and production that the recurring deficits on the railways troubled even the

[1] T. A. Coghlan, *Labour and Industry in Australia*, devotes an admirable chapter to the origins of "vigorous public works policies". See pp. 1405 *et seq.*

optimists.[1] Always, however, came the reply that increasing traffic was in sight, and that settlers were about to fill the vast empty spaces.

Public expenditure of loan funds far exceeded in the 'seventies direct private investment into Australia. Between 1871 and 1875 only a million and a half of private capital came to augment the 33 millions already so invested. Between 1876 and 1880, however, depression ruled in Europe, and with it low rates of interest. Investors at home were increasingly ready to put their money into land companies and other private Australian ventures. During that quinquennium £11,600,000 came privately to Australia in addition to the £22,000,000 borrowed by governments. New South Wales, Victoria, Queensland and South Australia each took five millions on government account. So far, so good. In the decade 1871 to 1880 inclusive, 2681 miles of railway were built, and the length of line open to traffic was almost quadrupled. By 1881, telegraph lines, erected mainly during the 'seventies, crossed 25,604 miles of country. The stimulus to wool production was proved by the expansion of the wool-clip from 211,413,000 pounds in the grease (1871) to 324,286,000 pounds (1881). The totals of shipping entered and cleared at Australian ports, 3,690,000 tons in 1871 and 8,110,000 tons ten years later, were equally significant of expanding trade.

Sir Hercules Robinson had urged that the "true policy" of a young country was "to loosen every band that hampers industry, so as to lessen the cost of production, to extend your markets, and by making the country year by year a cheaper and cheaper place for working men to live in, to attract them in numbers to your shore". The leaders in each colony heard with prophetic ear the tramp of millions who would soon people Australia. Population was growing at a phenomenal speed. From 1,647,756 in

[1] Correspondence between the Minister of Railways and the Railways Commissioners, *Victorian P.P.* 1891, ch. xvi.

1870 it had risen to nearly two and a quarter millions in 1880, an increase of 35·4 per cent. in a decade, and even this was exceeded in the 'eighties.[1] If any among the leaders had paused in providing railways, wharves, and water supplies for the oncoming hosts, the days of his leadership would at once have ended.

As is usual when a new expedient of economic progress is first tested commercially, practical men saw only its merits, and speculative financiers egged them on. Pastoralists, putting back into the purchase of freehold land almost the whole of their profits and a big share of the new capital that banks and land companies were bringing in, over-capitalized their runs, and then over-stocked them in the effort to reduce their indebtedness. A lucky run of seasons lured them out of their depth. Colonial governments built railways for wheat-farmers who had not yet solved the problem of permanent agriculture. The investing public, both in Britain and Australia, little suspecting these defects and growing foolhardy in land and mining speculation, lost all regard for the practicable. Then an economic winter came to check the general exuberance and to initiate a more varied and more competent use of the land and its railways.

---

[1] The increase from 1880 to 1890 was 41·2 per cent.

CHAPTER XVII

The Land Boom

NO community lacks would-be leaders who confuse city-streets, railway mileage and tall chimneys with civilization, who mistake speculation for prosperity and money-grabbing for the good life. Perhaps it was inevitable that such men should dominate Victoria a generation after the gold-rushes. They had dreamed of and achieved the transformation of so many "canvas towns" into cities that it had become a part of their character to look at finance and government with contractors' eyes. "The whole real business of Australia is to construct and strengthen the material frame upon which its future greatness will depend." So Melbourne was telling the world[1] on the very eve of its fall from the financial leadership of Australia. But a material frame, however strongly constructed, does not ensure the progress of an economic system. Government is finance, and the major part of sound finance consists, not in amassing money, so much as in directing a country's commerce so that its industries incessantly reshape themselves to consumers' needs, as consumers express them in market prices at home and abroad.

The banks which had discounted the bills of merchants and squatters at the capital-ports in pastoral days had a sharp lesson in the danger of short cuts to fortune by land-speculation, when the Bank of Australia and the Port Phillip Bank failed during the "Bad Times". During the 'fifties, however, ten millions' worth of gold flowed each

[1] Through Miss Flora Shaw, *The Times* special correspondent, March 1893.

year out of the up-country gullies. Banks old and new pushed branches into the mining areas to buy gold outright or to act as agents in transferring it overseas. The new banks had not bought the experience of the "Bad Times". The London Chartered Bank of Australia, the Bank of Victoria, the English, Scottish and Australian Chartered Bank, the Colonial Bank of Australasia and the National Bank of Australasia were all founded in the 'fifties, and the Commercial Bank of Australia in 1866. Large profits, easily made in the digging days, multiplied branches in pursuit of a fluctuating business. Easy money bred an incautious zeal to lend.

In pre-gold days, the Colonial Office had coached colonial legislators in banking principles as understood in London. A despatch by W. E. Gladstone to Sir Charles Fitzroy had stated the limits which should be set on the dealings of banks by any laws submitted for the royal assent.[1] These would have precluded banks from advancing money on lands or houses or ships, or on pledge of merchandise, from holding lands or houses save for the transaction of their own business, and from engaging in trade, save as dealers in bullion and in bills of exchange. Banking, as London understood it, was an advance of rights to draw ready money from the "bank" or consolidated purse of the shareholders and depositors, given on the security of a right to a little more money at a future date. The commercial bill of exchange, signed by at least two solvent traders, was the ideal form of security because it represented staple raw materials on their way to market. In the worst times, such bills turn themselves into cash by the sale of the goods. For men must eat and be clothed even when merchant-bankers fail, stock-exchanges close their doors and land is "cheap as stinking mackerel". The rule favouring such bills is ideal, too, in keeping to the fore the banks' best service to society. To the extent that they enforce repay-

---

[1] W. E. Gladstone to Sir Charles Fitzroy, 30 May 1846, *H.R. of A.* series 1, vol. xxv, pp. 74–5.

ment of such advances, banks remind traders of their duty to meet the market's "bread-and-butter" demands.

When, however, the volume of Australian production changed back from the bullion in which, as raw cash, they might deal, to the "sheep and wool, cattle, hides and horns" in which they might not deal, colonial bankers felt this orthodoxy of bill-discounting to be a field too narrow for the employment of their abundant gold-reserves. Colonial legislators, mainly consisting of merchants and squatters, had already exacted from their Mentors at home permission for banks to make advances on wool and stock while still in the pastoralists' hands. Towards the end of the 'sixties, the banks took a further step. They dispensed with the bill of exchange drawn on a London merchant-broker when financing pastoralists whose wool was on the way to the sales. "The legislature", argued a prominent banker, "has encouraged bankers by special enactment to advance money to squatters on their current clips of wool. Surely the advance is as safe when represented by a bill of lading and policy of insurance as when on the backs of the sheep?"[1]

If, however, advances on wool and sheep were sound, why not advances on land? Every squatter was eager to borrow enough capital to buy his freehold and thus save his run from free selectors. The way was made easy for the banks when in 1870 the courts and the Privy Council decided that a bank might acquire, hold and pass a good title to land or other property which fell into its possession as the collateral security of an advance, even though that acquisition were in violation of the bank charter.[2] Bankers might persuade themselves that they had little choice but to make such advances against land. How else could they

---

[1] Adam Burnes, General Manager of the Colonial Bank, in a controversy with James McBain, a director who had resigned rather than countenance the innovation. See *Innovations in Colonial Banking Practice*, by C. M. S. (Sydney 1869) (Mitchell Library Pamphlets).

[2] See Ayers *v.* S. A. Banking Co., 3 *P.C.* and National Bank *v.* Cherry, 3 *P.C.* (1870), p. 548.

prevent the ruin of the industry that grew the golden fleece? Yet such advances were bound to be based on speculative values. Repayment depended on expectations of production coming true, and values holding in years to come, not on goods already produced and made the basis of short-term commercial bills. Inevitably, advances on land were long-term credits that locked up the banks' resources and thus lessened the power of the community to adjust itself to changed circumstances. Nor did the banks long confine the practice to pastoral lands. As the greater pastoralists paid off mortgages, or transferred them to the finance and mortgage companies which were ready to share in this business, competition for openings in which to lay out loanable funds led banks to make advances against the title-deeds of farmers, small graziers and others. "This class of advances", wrote an active Victorian banker in 1880, "has acquired an importance to which what the conservative banker still calls legitimate banking business bears a very diminutive relation."[1]

Two-thirds of the total advances were "outside the current discounts", he estimated; yet the results to bank-shareholders fully condoned, in his opinion, this departure from English practice—"unless it could be shown to be fraught with some latent danger requiring only a hitherto

[1] H. Gyles Turner, of the Commercial Bank of Australia, "Victorian Banking considered in relation to National Development", *Australian Insurance and Banking Record*, 8 December 1880.

According to its prospectus, *The Commercial Bank of Australia Limited*, Melbourne 1866, was "projected especially for the purpose of affording banking accommodation to large and important classes whose claims for assistance entitle them to a much larger share of credit than has hitherto been afforded by the existing banking institutions, viz. the manufacturers, small traders, farmers, vignerons and other producers". This drew from Syme a typical diatribe in *The Age* against the "foreign banks". "We send away to be expended amongst strangers an annual aggregate amount of profit which would suffice for the capital of one new bank per annum.... The Commercial Bank of Australia aims at being the first of the series....It will possess all the privileges of the incorporated Banks without the restrictions which harass them." *The Argus* also welcomed, in its more urbane style, advances to small producers on the security of title-deeds.

undiscovered combination of circumstances to develop".
Nemesis had whispered as he wrote.

Bankers and colonial publicists generally were agreed
in scouting any real possibility of danger. Banking, like
wool-growing and everything else, had to be adapted to
Australian circumstances. Land values in a young country
rose so inevitably, it was said, that a wide margin was
assured and the banks' money was abundantly safe.
Transfer under the Torrens system was so easy that a
clean certificate of title was as negotiable a security as
government stock or a first-class trade bill. "At the worst
the land remained." Gyles Turner smugly ascribed
Australia's freedom from the bank disasters so frequent
in Britain to "the soundness of judgment and moderation
of aim" of the colonial bankers.

Cautious men wondered. London bankers knew well
that the yield of gold from California and Australia
was falling, and that monetary demands for the metal,
especially for the new German Empire, were looming
large.[1] The value of gold was sure to rise and therefore
the general level of prices would fall, more goods being
needed to obtain a unit of gold. Australian exports, they
noted, had escaped the first impact of this fall in prices,
being necessaries of life. Perhaps more thorough occupation of the back country would enable the pastoralists to
maintain their incomes on a falling wool market, but
such increase of supplies "might become a prospective
danger if too largely relied on by the producers". Even
the most optimistic saw a risk of over-capitalization through
the pushing in of more British capital by finance companies,
and conceded that competing bank branches in the
country towns made for excessive lending.[2]

[1] W. Purdy, *The City Life* (1876), p. 11. This little book is the more
significant because its author had an intimate experience of Australian
banking and finance.

[2] In 1880, England and Wales, according to Gyles Turner, *loc. cit.*, had
a banking office for every 11,810 persons, Scotland had one for every 4031,
and Victoria had one for every 2760.

For a time all continued well with Australian finance. Artesian water assured the occupation of wide areas of mulga country inland, and a long run of favourable seasons flattered the hopes of continuous progress that are in the hearts of every generation, but never come true. Men smiled at the thought of financial crisis in a land which exported gold in bulk, and where bank-reserves were normally equal to half the total of notes circulating and deposits at call. In 1866, it was said, a New South Wales Treasurer, Geoffrey Eager, had proposed a national bank of issue, but had planned no more than a branch of the Treasury printing paper money for government. In the remote contingency of a panic such an issue might have afforded the aid of legal tender notes wherewith to satisfy the scared, but it carried the danger of political money, local depreciation and dislocated exchanges. Such risks, and the threatened loss of their own convenient note-issues, led the banks to oppose Eager's plan and all later plans for an emergency issue. Colonial banks went on competing for public favour, and David Syme approved.

Australia in the early 'eighties certainly presented a strong contrast with Britain, in prospects as well as in banking methods. The price of wool was steady. The area under crop had increased in the previous decade from 2,143,709 acres to 4,560,991. The problem of sending surplus meat to Europe had been solved by the refrigerating engine. Good seasons had followed one another as though droughts were no more. It seemed, too, a world where the speculator might still "strike it rich". At Mount Morgan in Queensland a veritable hill of gold was found in 1882. It was known to contain millions of ounces of the metal.[1] A year later, another of silver, lead and zinc was found near the South Australian border of New South

[1] Up to its closing in September 1925, the Mount Morgan Mine treated 9,196,605 tons of ore, containing 5,305,979 oz. of gold and 139,427 tons of copper. It had paid £9,379,166 in dividends. See its *Annual Reports*, 1886–1925, and Rees Jones' *Gold-Mining in Central Queensland* (1913).

Wales.[1] Australia was still the speculator's El Dorado. The gold yield, it was true, had fallen to half what it had been in 1861, but the world wanted gold so much that each ounce bought more imports, and, as costs fell, mining prospects bettered.[2]

So, too, with the other staple industries. Manufactures overseas fell more rapidly in value after 1873 than did raw materials. Competing industrialists in Britain and Germany cut their prices, and for a time sold at finer margins rather than lose their footing in the world's market. For the time being, colonial populations bartered their goods for those of Europe at an increasing advantage.

British investors seeking this attractive distant field paid attention first to New South Wales and the main pastoral industry. Private investment in Australia between 1876 and 1880 amounted to £11,600,000, and of these some eight millions went into the mother colony as deposits or share-capital for banks or land and finance companies. There all financial channels led to the stations. With the new money, squatters bought, fenced, watered and improved their runs. Their purchases swelled the government revenues from land. Improvements and added production kept the railways busy. New South Wales treated £12,000,000 from land sales and rentals as revenue during that quinquennium. Victoria drew an abundant customs revenue from an equally temporary source. To transfer to its Melbourne Treasury the money it borrowed in London over and above interest due there, the Victorian Government or its bankers sold drafts on London to Melbourne merchants wishing to pay in Britain for imports thence. Such liberal offers of money-in-London, and the certainty

---

[1] Up to 1924 the value of Broken Hill's mineral output was 121 millions sterling, the dividends paid by the various companies having totalled nearly £28,000,000. Thirty-four million tons of ore had been extracted. See the *Annual Reports of the Broken Hill Proprietary Co.* from 1885 (Adelaide Public Library).

[2] See T. A. Coghlan, *Seven Colonies of Australasia* (1902), p. 944 for the gold yields per annum from 1851 to 1901.

that the local money they gave for it would quickly be set spinning again in Victoria as loan expenditure, greatly heartened importers. On their big imports the Government collected the usual duties. Active borrowing thus lent an appearance of abundant strength to the colony's public budget. This in turn was the justification of more borrowing to meet growing public needs. "Development" was the blessed word, and between 1881 and 1885 British investors lent at low rates of interest thirty-seven and a half millions to the four larger colonies. Privately, it is estimated, they put thirty millions more into Australia.

Colonial Premiers and Treasurers felt much concern over the responsibility of spending wisely their share of this money. In a young country with centralized habits of development, log-rolling for the favour of a line in the loan estimates was inevitable. The first Victorian Parliament brought it on itself when it approved of railway construction by Government on the ground that Government was best qualified to decide in what directions settlement should be promoted. But after thirty years Parliament was not so sure of that. To a legislature sick of the scandals associated with railways and public works during the O'Loghlen-Bent regime, the Service-Berry ministry proposed that decisions about new construction should be delegated to experts. Parliament heartily agreed. Richard Speight, from the staff of the English Midland Railway Company, was given a high salary to preside over a Railway Commission of three. They were appointed for seven years and were instructed to work the Victorian railways at a profit, but at the lowest fares and freights consistent with a profit, and with development.

The measure establishing the Railway Commission did not give the new experts a free hand in making the rates at which goods and passengers would be carried. The Commissioners could only alter the by-laws and regulations fixing fares and general rates of traffic if the Ministry of the day concurred. Public opinion in a democratic colony

L

would not tolerate on publicly owned railways the apparent favouritism of "charging what the traffic will bear" when this took the form of specially low freights to particular stations. On the other hand, in the name of Development, public opinion did demand low freights that would build up the traffic on all lines. In the long run little is gained by the benevolence which government railways have been required to show in charging freights and fares lower than those needed to balance the railway budget. Duncan Gillies claimed that the state had always in view a higher object than profit, viz., to enable country settlers to market their produce at reasonable cost. "Reasonable" rates, however, mean that in years of lean traffic the Treasurer must meet the railway deficit out of consolidated revenue or fund it, and years of deficit proved far more frequent in Victoria than years of prosperous development. By the end of the century, the Victorian railways had accumulated losses of nine millions. And as a government cannot write off its losses of capital which it owes mainly to external investors, benevolence to country settlers resulted in dead-weight burdens on the general budget. The full cost of railway transport must be paid, either by the class served, by the taxpayers at the time, or at compound interest by posterity. To spread the cost over a long period in the name of constructive benevolence is to dull the instrument of financial criticism by which a well-ordered community locates and analyses its weak services. Worse still, it may tempt posterity to the all-shattering risk of repudiation.

Speight and his colleagues, though they were prevented from rate-making along constructive lines, and were not altogether free in matters of personnel, did manage to break the long series of railway deficits, mainly by limiting political interference in the engagement of employees. Yet their success was not a clear gain. Log-rolling about new construction only shifted from the lobbies of Parliament House to the corridors of the Commissioners' Office at the opposite end of the city. And the railway surplus was too well boomed as evidence of the colony's ability to absorb more British loans for railway-building.

Sir Henry Parkes in 1887 adopted a better plan to place the New South Wales railways above the pettifogging "local members". Not content with the form of independent management by a Commission, he made it a reality by becoming the parliamentary spokesman of the Commissioners and defending their independence even against his colleagues in the ministry. This won for them power to shape the book of rates on lines nearer to sound railway practice. Contrary to the Victorian plan, he refused to load his Commissioners with decisions about new lines. He foresaw the disrepute into which their helplessness to withstand the politicians was to lead Speight and his colleagues, and set up a standing committee of both Houses to deliberate on all works involving a cost of more than £20,000. By this means, reminiscent of private bill procedure at Westminster, he used publicity and delay to check the insidious log-roller, but left on cabinet and Parliament the ultimate responsibility for the spending of public money.[1]

Possibly such well-meant policies encouraged home investors in their taste for Australian securities. In the period 1886–1890 their lending certainly placed another hundred millions at the colonists' disposal, through public and private channels.[2]

But by this time drought had returned. Only Victoria escaped its ravages, and the population there, which numbered a million souls for the first time in 1887, was given the disposal of half the plethora of loaned money. In South Australia, where the drought was most prolonged, it brought to light dishonest speculation in pastoral

---

[1] Regarding log-rollers and their ways, see *N.S.W. Parl. Deb.* 1887-8, p. 805, an account by William Lyne, a recognized authority on the matter.

[2] Cf. H. Gyles Turner, *History of the Colony of Victoria*, vol. II, p. 296, and T. A. Coghlan, *Labour and Industry in Australia*, p. 1633.

land by managing officials of the Commercial Bank of South Australia. The Bank suspended payment in February 1886. Almost simultaneously wool dropped in price to 9¼d. a pound from the 12¼d. which had ruled for a full decade. Apprehension damped down incipient land-booms in the cities and suburbs of Sydney and Adelaide, but not in Melbourne, then the financial centre of Australia. The countryside was flourishing; the city was agog with excitement over Mount Morgan and Broken Hill mining shares. What was this talk of a scarcity of the precious metals and falling prices? Who could doubt the ability of debtors to meet their future obligations in a country of unlimited potentialities?

Bank advances of all kinds had reached a total of 58½ millions in 1880. By 1891 the banks had on balance lent another 73½ millions and the total of advances was 132 millions. Australian deposits, however, had only grown from 62½ millions to 93 millions. The extra loanable funds had been obtained by accepting, or rather, canvassing for British money on fixed deposit for one, two or three years. Before 1880 such deposits had been rare. By 1891 Australian banks held just under 40 millions of them. Insidiously, too, the drought had stopped the repayment of pastoralists' overdrafts, and low wool-values threatened to cause their growth. Banks and finance companies looked to quick profits in the city of Melbourne to provide them with dividends. Gyles Turner's criterion of sound banking would perhaps justify this business too. For a time advances on city land and on stocks and shares showed amazing profits. Wool prices, too, rallied in 1887, and Melbourne financiers ignored the changing equation of trade and the mortgage over their gold reserves which their acceptance of overseas deposits had given to British investors. Millions of borrowed money were profit-hunting in their city, and an inexperienced generation of land-banks played without scruple the exciting game of unlimited gambling on land-values.

Several factors helped on the land boom. During the 'seventies, a rise of wages had started in the pastoral industry of New South Wales under the stimuli of lessened transport costs, heavy expenditure on fencing and dam sinking, and good prices for wool and stock. Then in the 'eighties, Melbourne had to be rebuilt on lines in keeping with her wealth. As the phase of prosperity and capital improvement passed in New South Wales, workers poured into Melbourne. The net immigration to Victoria for 1886 was 18,007, for 1887 some 14,721 and for 1888 no less than 35,385. The spending of loan money on railways and other public works maintained and increased the level of wages. A strong demand arose for suburban houses on time-payment. Building societies purchased and subdivided suburban estates. The building trades could not get enough labour, and wages went on rising. To the end of 1887 banks financed building by advances against title deeds. At last they saw that speculation had pushed land values too high. "What goes up must come down." They refused further advances on real estate. Thereupon, building societies bid against them for local deposits and followed them to England in canvassing for more. Nor did the societies care about such elementary precautions as dovetailing their obligations to repay depositors into their clients' contracts and probable abilities to repay them.[1] "At the worst the land remained."

The bubble reached its iridescence in 1888, the centenary of Australia's colonization. Its most sensational phases were the speculative dealings of the big men in city land and in mining and "investment" shares. During a phase of depression in 1879, patriotic citizens of "marvellous Melbourne" had been encouraged to plot the curve of its future progress by an article in the *Melbourne Review* from the pen of David Syme himself.[2] His authentic figures of

[1] Cf. T. A. Coghlan, *Labour and Industry in Australia*, pp. 1680 *et seq.*
[2] "The Increment in the Value of Land in Melbourne", *Melbourne Review*, vol. IV, pp. 221 *et seq.*

the increase in city land-values, though intended as arguments for more taxation, were interpreted as a prophecy of continued expansion. Syme predicted explicitly that "country land, which is at a low price now (1879) owing to the extraordinary facilities which exist for acquiring it, will go up with a bound as soon as there is the slightest check to the supply, which will be long before the last acre has passed into private hands". As the country prospered, men argued, the city to and from which all its business radiated must grow in equal measure. The City of Melbourne had an area of 410 acres, and when, during the 'eighties, millions of money were seeking investment in Victoria, and millions more were being spent close to Melbourne on railway construction, new wharves and a cable-tramway system, David Syme's prophetic vision was held to have been abundantly justified. After 1884 prices paid for city land became prophetic too. They had lost any link with the rentals that could be paid for the present use of the land. Early in the boom, James Mirams caused general astonishment by giving £700 a foot for a block at the corner of Elizabeth and Collins Streets. During its height the same land was sold to the Equitable Insurance Company for £2300 a foot. "In 1887 you could not have bought a property in Collins Street at any price without being hunted next day by someone offering you a profit on your bargain."[1]

The activity on the Stock Exchange, started by the scramble for Broken Hill and Mount Morgan shares and by more dubious operations in land companies' scrip, may be gauged by the volume of cheques and bills passing through the clearing house. This rose from £3,600,000 a week in 1887 to almost £6,000,000 a week in 1888. In the early months of the year, brokers' offices were working all night to cope with the business in silver-mining shares. Broken Hill Proprietary shares, which were at £176 when

---

[1] H. Gyles Turner, *The Australian Insurance and Banking Record*, October 1896, pp. 731 *et seq.*

the year opened, reached £397 in March. They fell back to £240 after Easter, but the mine was a wonderful producer, and though the "bears" might check excessive optimism, its output justified high prices. It is impossible, however, to "bear" a land boom by selling f.a.q. land for future delivery. Land is too individual a commodity for sale by grade or description. Buyers would contract to pay any price for city land because nobody intended to pay for his purchase in full until he had re-sold at a higher figure.

As the town population grew dubious of the prices they were asked to pay and wary of risking their past gains, "boomsters" sought in the provincial cities and country towns for fresh counters in the game.[1]

The banks had started this wonderful game when, about 1881, they allowed city land as security for considerable advances. Their old business of lending on pastoral land had become cramped by new land and mortgage companies. But before a decade was out, they were puzzled by the problem of stopping the inflation of city values. When at the close of 1887 they refused further advances on land, the ball was in play and they merely left the field. Others played on and the crowd still cheered. British money was eagerly seeking investment in Australia, and the decline in pastoral prospects piled up deposits unused. A disagreement among the Associated Banks[2] postponed a raising of the rates of interest for fixed deposits which was intended to retain the surplus in their keeping and to prevent its misuse by others. An amendment of the Victorian Banking Act (1864), passed in 1887 and assented to a year later, removed any legal doubts that "any incorporated banking company" might "advance money

---

[1] The writer was interrupted at this point (in August 1929) by an emissary of a Melbourne land firm, seeking to sell him a block of land in a riverside suburb of Perth, Western Australia, within sight of his study windows.

[2] The larger banks which were associated in handling the Government account.

on land, houses, ships and merchandise".[1] The land companies thereupon stepped into the place vacated by the Associated Banks, assumed the style and title of banks, and by a competitive canvass for deposits prolonged the land boom for two years after its insanity had become common knowledge in Australia.[2] While the London rate of interest was low—this was the period of Goschen's conversion of Consols to 2¾ per cent.—the land-banks decked themselves with London Boards, on which ex-Governors, ex-Premiers and Agents-General contrived to look reassuring to British depositors, while substantial commissions for their collections enlisted the good offices of English and Scots lawyers.

The money market hardened in 1889. The land-banks went gaily on, giving five per cent. for money at call in Australia. No scruples troubled or cramped their use of money. They lent to speculative builders up to the full "estimated value" of their buildings and land. They advanced money to purchasers on the security of land they had themselves "sold". They declared dividends out of profits calculated by assuming all the land subdivided to have become worth the prices paid or promised for a few blocks. "Free conveyances carried people to the sales, champagne lunches gave them courage to bid, and extraordinary terms of credit reconciled them to their purchases."[3] For any whose eyes still saw, the bubbles had all burst when on December 20, 1889 the Premier Permanent Building Association of Melbourne suspended payment. Liquidation showed up the most irresponsible management. Yet for nearly three years more the borrowing from Britain continued, on both private and public account. The Associated Banks trembled to assist

---

[1] T. A. Coghlan, *Labour and Industry in Australia*, p. 1694, states that this relaxation did not become law although recommended by a Commission on Banking. It was enacted as section 6 in Vic. Statute No. 1002.

[2] Cf. *The Age* and *The Insurance and Banking Record* on the failure of the Premier Building Association in December 1889.

[3] T. A. Coghlan, *Labour and Industry in Australia*, p. 1693.

the land-banks and building societies. Land was fast becoming unsaleable. Thousands of houses built at boom costs were being left without tenants. Emigration from Victoria started in 1891-2. "These cancerous growths", as the London *Economist*[1] called the land-banks, had no realizable assets whatever to set against huge liabilities. Barings failed in London. Wool prices slumped lower and lower, to 9*d.* a pound in 1890, 8*d.* in 1891 and 7¾*d.* in 1892. Strikes stopped trade and industry on an unprecedented scale. The game was up; the whole fabric of Australian credit shook.

The optimists still ruled, however. Parliament was their last refuge. The outstanding fact that Australia had received between 1880 and 1890 more British capital than she could use in producing wealth did not deter the colonial governments. They tried busily to paper over the cracks by raising more loans. The Gillies-Deakin Government in Victoria spent £4,400,000 in 1889 on public works and another £5,000,000 in 1890. In 1891 the Munro Government was only stopped by London's reluctance to find more money, even at higher rates of interest. In April, Munro wanted another £3,000,000, but the public only subscribed £1,800,000. When Barings trembled in November 1890, William Westgarth & Company, a small house which held large amounts of recent Victorian issues, fell headlong, and the sale of its holdings lowered the price of all Australian stocks. Queensland, whose public debt had been swollen by £16,212,000 during the decade 1881 to 1890, mainly by London flotations, sought in May of 1891 a further £2,500,000 at £94. The public offered only £300,000, and the remainder could only be sold to banks and financial houses at £88. New South Wales, though provided with abundant money by the sale of public lands, had added £36,000,000 to her debt by borrowing in Sydney and London between 1881 and 1890. The vicious circle of government deposits of land revenues,

[1] *The Economist*, 12 September 1891.

and bank advances out of these to private clients for the purchase of more land had, as in 1841-3, produced a furious boom, but drought in 1884-5 and again in 1888 saved Sydney from the worst excesses of Melbourne. She had not become a magnet for her neighbours' workpeople. Failure of land companies and building societies did, however, spread unemployment there, and in September of 1891 her Treasurer sought a fresh loan of £4,500,000 in London. He could obtain only £2,500,000, and at the close of the year his successor was seeking with poor success to sell there Treasury bills which he was unable to place in Sydney. South Australia, whence population and capital had for a time flowed to Melbourne, decided in February of 1891 to meet increasing unemployment by public works, and sought a loan of a million and a quarter in London. Only a third was subscribed, and though the balance was obtained, the loan was the last of South Australia's external borrowings for the century.

The revelations of fraud which came with the crash of each land-bank, and London's discovery of similar doings in the similar country of Argentina, created a critical atmosphere. More decisive in sapping Australian credit was the falling value of staple colonial products. The increase of their flocks and herds in the early 'nineties brought little power to station-owners to pay their interest and repay bank advances. Wool fell in 1893 to 7d. a pound and bullocks which had been worth £5 a head in 1884 to £2. 10s. Land, after all, was not such a good basis to bank upon. Mining shares were not much better. Copper from Yorke's Peninsula (S.A.), worth £94 a ton in 1873 and £59 in 1884, was down to £44 in 1886. A ring of European speculators had lifted it to £99 in September 1888, but they burned their fingers and the price was down to £35 a ton in March 1889, from which it recovered with painful slowness. Silver had been at 4s. 3½d. an ounce when Charles Rasp, a station-hand, found Broken Hill in 1883. In 1889 it was down to 3s. 5½d. Then the American and Indian mints closed to its free coinage and its value fell to 2s. 11¼d. in 1893. The new prices afforded scanty prospects of meeting old commitments. When the net profit to be made in the primary industries threatened to disappear, losses had to be cut, costs reduced and capital values calculated afresh. In his struggle to pay interest and reduce his overdraft, many a pastoralist, with the rabbits' aid, ruined his tender out-back country by over-stocking, and further depressed an already weak market by bringing to it a bigger clip. After 1889, stations came in large numbers into the possession of the banks. New men had to be found, or old owners employed in new capacities, to manage re-valued properties on costs consistent with lower prices.

The bankers and public financiers of Australia had failed in their main duty. They had forgotten, if indeed they had ever realized, that an economy, to be sound, must maintain in equipoise its material equipment and the production this exists to aid, that capital values have no meaning apart from actual net income. Income is by no means a hardy annual "aye growing" while financiers sit tight. The borrowed funds for which too many banks strove to find room had inflated the capital values against which, very dangerously, Australian bankers thought it good business to lend. Much had been consumed in extravagant living. Receipts from sales of land, easy customs revenue on luxury imports, still easier bor-rowings abroad had made governments as reckless em-ployers as the land-booming builders. Then prices and employment on high wages sagged together. Public em-ployment vanished. On the rank and file of private employers in the export industries fell the thankless task of reshaping their expenses in harmony with the world's markets. Their calling was to maintain production. They could not do so at wages which gave labour a share calculated on the vanished values of the joint product. But at this point, a new intercolonial federation of trade unions sharply challenged the right of employers, even of federated employers, to dictate labour's share.

CHAPTER XVIII

Labour Shows Fight

AS there were wicket-keepers before Blackham, so there were labour unions before the gold discoveries. Convict artisans and labourers had, without unions and through sheer scarcity of man-power, even enjoyed an active government's pay and conditions when Macquarie was building to Greenway's plans,[1] though not for long. "The loose and easy times of Macquarie gave way to theories of adamant." The convicts, scattered and weak in bargaining against the squatters, were downtrodden as shepherds and hut-keepers. Expiree mechanics about Sydney, though burning with resentment for past wrongs in Britain and Ireland and in the colony itself, had not the quality of mutual loyalty. The system had broken them. Its centralization and brutality had killed initiative in its human tools. Hence the first essays in labour organization "centre round the more arresting figures of the newly arrived immigrant. What the emancipist lacked in direction and management the emigrant who had braved so great dangers was able to supply. Movement, direction and decision were his contributions, but the peculiar form and colour had long ago been set in convict moulds".[2]

[1] See L. M. Thomas, "The Development of the Labour Movement 1788–1848", an unpublished work in the Fisher Library, Sydney University, p. 10: "The convict labourer combined the functions of serf and freeman within a curious economic frame...Government regulation (of wages etc.) proved ineffective because of the scarcity of labour. A natural monopoly exacted its own price of regular hours, government tasks and a wage system".

[2] L. M. Thomas, *op. cit.* p. 15. Cf. p. 13: "For the germ of the labour movement we do not look to the freeman but to the government convict, particularly to the mechanic with his regular hours, his definite wages and his economic worth".

Of the unions and benefit-societies formed in the 'thirties and 'forties, whose records Miss Thomas has faithfully conned, some may have had a continuous life into the golden age. They, and the post-gold societies of typographers, cabinet-makers, shipwrights and engineers, were all copies, and some were offshoots, of British craft-unions.[1] The first Australian branch of the Amalgamated Society of Engineers was formed in 1852 on the good ship 'Frances Walker', outward bound. But as long as dreams came true and men escaped to independence through luck at the diggings or success with a free selection, wages necessarily ruled high. Unions might swell into prominence in resisting the importation of Chinese labour, in concerting a demand for an eight hours day or in resisting some daring oppression by employers.[2] When the aim of the moment was achieved they would dwindle again into "aristocracies of labour" concerned mainly with sickness and accident benefits to their members in the capital towns. In relatively few trades was there a sufficiently stable body of fellow-crafts to maintain continuity.

When capital reorganized mining on a wage-earning basis, a unionism native to the country began to stir. The transition form appeared successively on the Newcastle coalfield in New South Wales and in the consolidated gold mines around Bendigo and Ballarat. The Hunter River District[3] Miners Mutual Protective Association was formed in 1861. A sliding scale of wages varying with the price of coal was exacted by a stoppage of work in August 1872 and occasioned an early "vend" among the Newcastle

[1] See J. T. Sutcliffe, *History of Trade Unionism in Australia* (1921), passim.
[2] Concerning the Eight Hours Day see H. Murphy, *History of the Eight Hours Movement* (1896); W. G. Spence, *Australia's Awakening* (1909); T. A. Coghlan, *Labour and Industry in Australia*, p. 1473 *et passim*; and the *Australian Encyclopaedia*, vol. I, pp. 403-4. *The Argus*, 23 July 1860, contains an account of a strike of railway navvies against monthly instead of fortnightly "pays", which that paper strongly supported.
[3] Concerning this richly endowed district which has contributed greatly to the economic achievement of Australia, yet far beneath its power, which produces wealth by pasture, agriculture, dairying, fruit-growing, wine, coal, iron and steel, see F. R. E. Mauldon, *The Hunter River Valley* (1927).

colliery proprietors. In 1874 the Amalgamated Miners'
Association was formed at an intercolonial conference of
gold, silver, copper and coal miners held at Bendigo. Its
founder, W. G. Spence, sought to bring all miners into
a federal union which could arrange financial aid to any
in need, but would leave each colonial district self-governing in its own area. For a time he succeeded, and the
A.M.A. numbered 23,500 members, but its intercolonial
council broke to pieces when in the late 'eighties Spence
turned his remarkable talent for organization to a greater
task. Till the century's close the loosely associated craft-
unions among the miners paid most attention to accident-
benefits, essential to maintain their membership before the
days of workers' compensation. Latterly they have joined
with the other unions in common political action, though
still proudly given to direct industrial action.[1]

Many of the younger miners and miners' sons went
shearing in New South Wales and Queensland from August
to December. Some followed the shearing almost all the
year round from the Gulf to Warrnambool. One of these
poured out their grievances to Spence and besought him
to form a shearers' union to fight the unfair tactics of the
squatters and win decent conditions for these migratory
piece-workers. Spence accepted the call. When he opened
the books of the Amalgamated Shearers Union at 30
Armstrong Street, North Ballarat, on 3 June 1886, the
foundation was laid of what was to become the central
pillar of the Australian Labour temple.

The pastoralists had announced a cut of half-a-crown
a hundred in the rate for shearing sheep. The union
answered by enrolling 9000 members in six months
throughout Victoria, New South Wales, South Australia
and New Zealand. Until 1904 Queensland had its own
Shearers' Union. Then its shearers joined the A.W.U. or

---

[1] In the mid-colonial period they exerted strong pressure on the legislatures
for effective laws governing the inspection of mines and machinery, beginning
from a Victorian Act in 1877.

Australian Workers' Union, the name which the original body adopted in 1894 with a proper discernment of its native quality and a fine disregard of demarcations between crafts and colonies. Under Spence's leading, the union, while providing "benefits", relied rather on the power of ideas than of money, and spent freely on the education of its members in "union principles". Its main aim was to shape an agreement or contract excluding unfair practices, and to make this contract the universal rule between squatter and shearers. It objected to (i) "the second price", a right which squatters had hitherto reserved of paying at a reduced rate for all the sheep a shearer had shorn if any were badly shorn, cut or otherwise injured; (ii) the rule that shearers must buy food and other requirements at the station-store where often the tradition of the officer-traders of early Sydney still lingered; (iii) the common "men's hut" in which bunks, cook's oven and meal-table made an unsavoury jumble.[1]

In the campaign for better days the union enlisted men in press-gang style. On the eve of the date set for shearing to begin, a union "organizer" would gather the shearers, most of whom had come to fill a "stand" bespoken a year before, would fan their indignation over the rumoured cut in the rate and propose a resolution that they should stand together for "union terms". If the pastoralist, forced by the falling price of wool to cut his costs, insisted on the wages-cut, and ordered the organizer off the run, the unionists went with him, but not far. Probably the organizer had picked out a waterhole nearby which had been proclaimed a reserve for travelling stock by a friendly government, in the days when the squatter's

---

[1] The men's hut was usually a long, draughty, slab building without windows. Two and sometimes three tiers of bunks would occupy the sides, and from them came a nauseating stench of clothing saturated with "yolk" from the wool and perspiration. The table for meals ran down the centre. Cooking was conducted partly in the open, partly at an oven in the fire-place across one end of the hut. The men were often expected to make their own sanitary arrangements. Typhoid was an ever-present risk in the shearer's life.

father was fighting free selectors. There the unionists' camp was the scene of frequent "revival-meetings" in which a new religion of mateship was feelingly unfolded to the bushmen. The prelude to conversion was often conviction of sin—the deadliest sin of "scabbing". "The man who fell once may be forgiven", Spence ruled, "but he is not fully trusted. The lowest term of reproach is to call a man a 'scab'." To avoid that black pit the only way was to join the union at once and to stand firm always. Force was unhesitatingly used, however, to persuade the mulish. The men's hut would be rushed under cover of darkness, and if the squatter sought the release of "his men" from the union camp he learnt from their own lips that they had gone there voluntarily. Many thus enlisted remained true to union principles. According to the founder, the union practised a form of "dipping", being "great believers in immersion as a cure for 'scab'".

Such guerilla warfare brought the agreement for union rules into operation far and wide during 1887 and 1888. The Masters and Servants Acts[1] were often invoked, and prosecutions for assault were not infrequent. But the speed of Spence's success had caught the squatters in disarray. Often the drying of the grass enforced acceptance of the new contract or the old rate. For grass seeds in the wool may mean "carbonizing" wool only and low prices. They may work into and kill the sheep. In a time of booming employment in the towns, imprisonment of the most skilled shearers was an economic blunder. The "ringer" was often as good a unionist as he was shearer.

Over the Queensland border the fires of union enthusiasm were blown to greater heat by an immigrant journalist breathing "socialism in our time". William Lane called for new and revolutionary unions which should federate to win this goal. He was a Bristol man who, after a grammar school education, had found his

[1] See L. M. Thomas, "The Development of the Labour Movement, 1788-1848", ch. v.

vocation in Canada and the United States. At twenty-
two he reached Brisbane (1883) and had soon attracted
a following by articles on labour problems in *The Brisbane
Courier* and in a paper of his own, *The Boomerang*. In
March 1890, he established *The Queensland Worker* to pro-
pound the doctrines of Karl Marx, Bellamy and Henry
George, and to be the mouthpiece of the Australian Labour
Federation. This was his masterpiece. The ferments of
socialist criticism of private enterprise and of union action
to mend wages and working conditions were just as active
and sporadic in Australia during the 'eighties as in England.
Lane added to youthful visions the task of linking the two
movements so that they should pursue a socialist objective
with union discipline and power. He had formed out of
the Queensland unions in 1885 a Trades and Labour
Council of the type that arose easily out of craft-unionism
in each capital city; but it lacked power to control piecemeal striking. These spurts only alarmed employers and
spent union resources on bread and butter.

Lane wanted a more compact federation which would
gather into a disciplined movement the semi-skilled and
labourers as well as craftsmen. During 1889 a busy consolidation movement knit together the shearers, the maritime workers and the building trades of Queensland into
minor federations, and on 11 June of that year the Australian Labour Federation, which Lane had advocated, began
its existence at the Maritime Labour Hall, Brisbane. Its
first adherents were the city craft and waterside unions,
but the shearers soon joined. Their aid was vital, for the
migratory station labour made contacts with other wage-
earners throughout Eastern Australia and spread Lane's
enthusiasm for united action wherever they went.

Queensland shearers were even more drastic in their
proselytizing methods than their comrades in the South,
and after two seasons of divided counsels and detailed
coercion the pastoralists of all the colonies realized that
only common action could meet the religion of which

Lane had become the prophet. The heaven it offered to the faithful at no distant date, control of the means of production and exchange by the organized proletariat, had in it no place for them. In August 1889 the London "dockers" won their "tanner" after a world famous fight in which the Australian unions' contribution of £30,000 played a material part. That gift accentuated the tension which Lane's hot-gospelling had caused in relations between employers and workers throughout Australia. Henry George himself came to Sydney late in 1889 preaching the Single Tax against all land monopolists. An ardent worshipper[1] introduced him to the Australian people with the cry "Ecce Homo!" His presence aggravated the itch of rival devotees to tear apart and re-shape according to their creeds an economy plainly working amiss.

Eighteen-ninety opened with the economic barometer low and falling fast. Wool was down. Money was dear in London. The Australian banks were pressing for repayment of over-drafts. Unemployment was increasing and there was talk of public works shutting down for lack of loan money. Lane, through the *Worker*, to which Queensland wages-men became conscript subscribers on paying their union dues, was advocating a "slate", or labour charter of concessions, in return for which employers would be promised industrial peace for two years. But was it likely that his followers, once they had tasted such success, would rest content? Could the prophet of "socialism in our time" hold them back? Employers, and especially the pastoralists, on whom falling wool prices weighed heavily, did not care to wait on united Labour's pleasure. The Queensland shearers decided to shut every "scab" out of the wool-sheds. At Jondaryan Station the sheep were shorn by non-unionists, as all the countryside knew, and the wool, declared "black" by the unions, was forwarded to Brisbane. The waterside workers or "wharf-lumpers"

[1] Charles Garland, M.L.A., President of the New South Wales Single Tax League.

refused to load it into the ship. W. G. Spence went north and stopped an upheaval for which the employers were evidently ready. An indemnity for the delay of their vessel was paid to the British India Company. In the southern colonies the diplomatic Spence and his Amalgamated Shearers were content to do their own recruiting and sought from the pastoralists a collective bargain of "no shearing save under union conditions". Negotiations were proceeding on a basis promising continuous and peaceful adjustment of the price and conditions of shearing when suddenly a fresh storm broke into fury at the southern ports.

On the intercolonial steamers a Marine Officers Association had applied for higher pay and better conditions aboard ship. Receiving scant attention, their Melbourne branch announced that it had joined the other maritime unions in affiliating with the Trades Hall. The shipowners raised objection to such a bond between officers and seamen. It was likely to undermine discipline, to the peril of ships at sea. At Port Adelaide on 15 August 1890 the ships' officers gave the shipowners the choice between recognizing the affiliation with the Maritime Labour Council or their own abandonment of the ships after a day's notice. It was a challenge. The employers took it up. Both sides made public preparation for a general battle between their organized forces. A union conference in session at Sydney adopted the name of "Labour Defence Committee". Early in September a "Pan-Australian Conference of Employers" also met in Sydney. It announced a "right to freedom of contract between employers and men", a "determination to oppose the use of force and boycotting" and the employers' "intention to retain labour engaged during the strike".

The dispute raised the very first issue of unionism, the right of men to form a union and to join one union with another in mutual support. It had at once involved every maritime calling but one, and paralysed every port. The exception was an important body—the marine engineers. Picketing and riots in both Sydney and Melbourne could not prevent the manning, loading and discharging of ships so long as the engineers stuck to their posts. And there was an abundance of non-union labour to be had among the hosts of unemployed. The colonial governments provided fully adequate police protection. When the Newcastle coal-miners tried to stop the ships by refusing to coal those manned by non-unionists, they were themselves locked out. On 19 September, a clash on Circular Quay, Sydney, between strike-pickets and wool-carters recruited from station-owners and others of the directing class, ended in the reading of the Riot Act and a charge by mounted troopers. Desperate at the increasing activity along the wharves, the Labour Defence Committee tried to bring trade to a stop by calling out the shearers. The telegrams went out to every wool-shed at work on 24 September, and sixteen thousand shearers, ignoring the squatters' threats to forfeit their wages and sue them for breach of contract, answered the union call to down tools.

At once it was seen by both sides that by that call the union leaders had over-taxed their resources. The main source of funds that had maintained the waterside and maritime strikers vanished. The shearers were involved in fines for offences against the Masters and Servants Act. They had lost the wages due to them. When the Mayor of Sydney made a fresh offer of mediation, the employers stipulated that the shearers must be sent back to the sheds. The Labour leaders, in complying on 2 October, were palpably weakening. On the following day the employers again refused the proposed conference unless the "freedom of contract" for which they were fighting were first accepted. The union leaders were scattering. Funds were almost exhausted. Return had not saved the shearers from the legal consequences of the "call out". Non-unionists were working even in the coal mines. At Bulli they were under artillery protection. The stalwarts stood their ground, but on 17 October the marine officers, in whose very cause the unions had taken action, agreed to abandon affiliation with the other unions and to return to their ships. That was the end of the Maritime Strike. In one calling after another, the men, bitterly disillusioned, returned on whatever terms and to whatever jobs they could get. Instead of looking forward to "socialism in our time", as pictured in the glowing phrases of Lane, the unions found their strength gone, their very existence threatened, and themselves put on the defensive for a full decade. "The unions", Lane confessed after that rude awakening, "are threatened with possible destruction by very reason of their instinctive but at present unregulated desire to stand by each other."

Before the year was out, the Queensland pastoralists were dictating terms of shearing which made no mention either of union or eight-hours day, which gave the station-owner a right to limit the number of sheep to be shorn and to say when the wool was wet,[1] and required shearers to tar all cuts and to find their own combs and cutters. Public opinion whispered approval when Chief Justice Darley in New South Wales spoke of the union shearers as "a closely knit band of criminals with commissariat arrangements, firearms and ammunition, devastating sparsely inhabited country, holding the few inhabitants in terror and compelling honest labourers to desist from work". Disheartened, the men at many inside stations accepted the terms offered. Out back in the Central Division the fight began again and the strikers organized a camp at Clermont. "Make your choice within a fortnight", said the squatters, "or others will fill your places." Though this was represented then and since as a threat to bring in Chinese labour, the squatters undoubtedly had in mind the "free labour" they had recruited and could bring north by shiploads from Melbourne and Sydney. A thousand

---

[1] The shearers object to wet wool as it causes rheumatism and sores on the hands which are hard to heal in the fly-infested back country.

shearers at Barcaldine talked openly of their resolve to exclude the southern strike-breakers by force. The Queensland Government proclaimed such doings an insurrection (23 February 1891) and despatched mounted police under a resolute officer to maintain the peace. After a month of tension and incendiarism at isolated points, the Government ordered the arrest of the strike leaders. They were charged under an unrepealed but almost forgotten statute of 6 George IV, c. 129 with conspiring "to induce others to depart from their hiring". Most were convicted and some sentenced to gaol with hard labour for three years. Fines and imprisonment for rioting were meted out to many, and the strikers scattered, powerless to prevent the drafting-in of as many non-unionists as the pastoralists needed. At a high cost in money and embittered feelings, the Queensland pastoralists had brought it home to labour that times had changed.

When in August 1891 the shearing was due to commence in the southern colonies, squatters' and shearers' leaders alike showed cooler judgment. The former agreed to maintain the union conditions, while the latter raised no demur at the employment of non-union men. Unemployment was still rife and prices were still falling. The mines felt the pressure no less than the wool trade. The contract system, a form of piece-work, was enforced in the Moonta copper mines (S.A.) in October 1891, after a futile resistance by strikers. In June 1892 it came back to Broken Hill, from whose stopes the unionists had banished it by a dramatic strike when the boom was at its height.

The effect of these turmoils on the financial situation, though by no means helpful, operated through vague opinion and fears rather than by changing economic realities. In the darker days that so soon followed many saw in the strikes the cause of every misfortune. They would have made the labour unions the scapegoats of unhappy communities. Such views ignored, however, the unsound practices in private and public finance which had destroyed the equilibrium of town and country and over-capitalized almost every industry. The maritime and pastoral strikes perhaps drew the attention of overseas investors to the rotten superstructure and thoughtless direction of Australian finance.

As the strikes involved the pastoralists in heavy additional expense during two exceptionally good seasons and made them hasty sellers of their wool, they may have hampered the repayment of pastoral advances and so the mitigation of the financial crisis. But that crisis arose out of financial malpractice. Wage-cutting and conscription for the class-war, the aims of the contending leaders, were short-sighted measures when the cool diplomacy and resource of constructive minds could alone have reorganized business and production and redeemed the colonies' credit after the monstrous abuse of it by "boomsters". Possibly the labour troubles aroused in the British investing classes a fear of labour-socialism. They were in a position to call the Australian directing class to an account of its stewardship, and did so in 1893 by seeking to withdraw investments. Yet the labour unions had been crushingly defeated in 1890–91. Was it that British investors knew with John Bright that coercion cures no evil and suspected that much remained to be mended in Australia?

CHAPTER XIX

The Bank Smash and Economic Reconstruction

NEMESIS tarried even after the labour turmoils, choosing her time. The strikes delayed but did not prevent the shipment of a non-perishable staple—wool; and the seasons, especially in New South Wales, continued very favourable. But prices were still falling, and the searching criticism of all expenses that is natural on falling markets put a stop to land-booming. Speculative and all other building ceased suddenly and absolutely. Forty-one land and finance companies failed in Melbourne and Sydney between July 1891 and August 1892. There were four millions of British deposits among the eighteen millions of their liabilities, and as some called themselves "banks", British investors began to wonder about Australian banking in general. The Mercantile Bank had suspended payment in March 1892. The Bank of South Australia was absorbed by the Union Bank. All was not well, but the Associated Banks of issue stood in firm array until January 1893. Then the Federal Bank appealed to its associates for aid, and on being refused it, went into liquidation.

The older banks, it was known, must be finding many worthless finance bills in their portfolios. Advances on city land at inflated values could not all be repaid. Overdrafts to the depressed primary industries were "frozen hard". To obtain liquid resources some banks continued to solicit deposits in Britain even during 1892. Though bought by high and rising rates of interest, such deposits with Australian banks increased in that year by £1,180,000, and the bank that sought them most urgently was Henry Gyles Turner's Commercial Bank of Australia. Its Australian deposits were falling after 1890 at the rate of £400,000 a year, but its British deposits climbed to £5,638,000 early in 1893. Wool and wheat still slumped in value, and land banks and finance companies which were known to have banked with the Commercial stumbled and fell.

All classes in Australia, particularly in Melbourne, were spending on necessaries alone. Trade was so dull that balances in London could not be used to advantage. The rates paid on the later deposits could not be earned in Australia by advances on sound security. Above all, this British money exerted a disintegrating force among the banks themselves when solidarity alone could have saved the weaker ones. If withdrawn, a British deposit would deplete London balances renewable only by shipments of gold or additional exports, a different matter from the withdrawal of an Australian deposit which was almost sure to be paid into another local bank. The older and more wary banks which had kept down the mortgage on their gold and London funds—most important funds in financing a community whose foreign trade bulks so largely—could hardly be blamed if they fought shy of others' burdens. But their caution became known and spread fear among a sorely tried public. The resolutions by which the Associated Banks thought to reassure the world at large after the collapse of the Federal Bank were so guarded that they were read as "Sauve qui peut!"

A run on the Commercial Bank was soon draining away its reserves. In three months, deposits totalling a million were withdrawn, £115,000 being paid over the counter in one day. The Board knew that most of the British deposits which fell due on May the first would be withdrawn. Gyles Turner appealed to the Victorian Treasury and the other associated banks. The Government had no funds to spare in London and would not risk a Government note issue in Victoria. The banks would find £1,750,000, but this was not enough. The great "Commercial" suspended payment on 5 April.

Before the month ended it had "reconstructed". The process meant that nine millions of deposits were impounded as ordinary or cumulative preference capital. Five and a half millions of these were British, but the depositors, after their long-drawn suspense, accepted the compromise with eagerness. It saved something from the wreck. Warnings of withdrawals at due date led to a general epidemic of reconstruction among the other Melbourne banks early in May. When word reached J. B. Patterson on Sunday, 30 April, that the National Bank of Australasia would close next day, he gathered his fellow-ministers, hastened by special train to the Administrator's country house where, as Executive Council, they drew up a proclamation of five days' bank holiday. Next morning, the news precipitated all Melbourne white with panic, into Collins Street. Had all the banks failed? Those whose headquarters were in Sydney or London opened, ignoring the moratorium. All the Victorian banks but a small one went into reconstruction. "We are all floundering", confessed the Premier.

In Sydney, Sir George Dibbs played the man. By the third of May he knew that the banks could not act in unison and at once pushed two emergency measures through parliament.[1] One of them made bank notes a first charge on their issuers' assets, the other gave the Governor-in-Council power, at any bank's request, to declare its notes legal tender. A little later a third emergency law empowered the Treasury to issue its own notes and to lend these to the banks up to half the total of the current accounts locked up by any bank suspension. This was the traditional policy of choking a panic with cash. For some

---

[1] See T. A. Coghlan, *Labour and Industry in Australia*, part VI, chapter IX, and part VI, chapter VII. The author, as Government Statistician, shaped the measures described. They are said to have been suggested by the Hon. R. J. Black, a director of the Bank of New South Wales.

reason, perhaps an old antagonism to government intervention, perhaps the palsy of despair, the big Sydney banks hesitated to ask in set form for the aid offered. The Commercial Banking Company of Sydney, of which Dibbs' own brother was the brain, suspended payment on 15 May, though it possessed a million in hard cash and owed only £600,000 to British depositors. Thereupon the Premier wrung applications from the other leading banks and, willy-nilly, made their notes lawful cash. This cleared the air. Sydney's gold reserves, no longer needed there, could be used to meet demands elsewhere. Little need for them arose, for confidence, or rather courage, had by this time returned everywhere. Cecil Rhodes as Premier of Cape Colony cabled on 25 May that he would invest his Government's balances in Victorian or New South Wales securities or in a new loan to either government, if desired. His offer was declined, but "as an indication of the pathway of future events" a British Treasury official, writing later in the year, thought it "more to be studied than all the schemes of all the imperialists".[1]

The very ease with which wealth had come to the directing class in Melbourne had been its undoing. The bank smash cancelled out the gold rushes and the land boom. The whole cycle of events made up an economic episode that left the population in Victoria with little constructive experience. Some 232 millions in gold, out of about 320 millions found in Australia prior to 1893, had passed through Victoria's hands. Her fortunate sons had investments in every colony, more especially in Queensland. They had had first use of £54,690,000 out of the hundred millions lent and invested in Australia by British capitalists between 1886 and 1890. The habit of assuming that wealth would always fall into the lap of "marvellous Melbourne" had been too easily acquired. But 1893 broke the spell.

[1] A. G. V. Peel, "The Australian Crisis of 1893", reprinted with a reply by Sir George Dibbs in *N.S.W., V. and P.* 1894, vol. I, p. 1021.

The prestige and momentum of financial power were gone. One source of expenditure which in the past had increasingly stimulated trade in Australia went with them. During the boom years the export of securities had raised funds equalling a quarter of the colonies' recorded production. During the five years from 1891 to 1895, although investment in Western Australia was fast growing, withdrawals from Australia as a whole almost equalled receipts. On balance, only £821,000 of outside money came into the country. Victorians were forced to call up the funds they had invested in other colonies, ten millions being withdrawn from Queensland alone, Coghlan estimates, during a run of exceptional seasons there.

In these straitened circumstances some of the banks found need of legal permission to pay on the locked-up deposits lower rates of interest than they had contracted to pay in their plans of reconstruction. Colonial courts and legislatures gave them the easier terms they asked, but such action at the expense of British shareholders did not mend the repute of Australian investments. Of the British deposits in the keeping of Australian banks in March 1893 there were only thirteen and a half millions left in 1900. Much had become preference capital; but three millions had been lost outright, and much had been repaid and withdrawn. Local deposits in Victorian banks stood at £39,279,000 in March 1893; at £29,698,000 when the century ended. Advances went down from £50,000,000 to £29,400,000. Melbourne had shrunk as marvellously as it had grown.

Victoria was not helped out of her debility by wise political leading. The policies of her governments during the 'nineties were starveling and uninspired. Through the long crisis from 1889 to 1893 she looked in vain for a statesman. Her most brilliant politician, Alfred Deakin, had withdrawn in disgust after holding office in the Gillies administration throughout the boom, and had vowed not to serve again save in a federated Australia.

David Syme, with a mind set by age and by the atrophy of unresisted power, could find only a scapegoat and a row of puppets. Speight, the Chief Commissioner of Railways, had succumbed to the boom and joined hands with the politicians in building a spider's web of parliamentary railways. Inevitably, construction costs at boom wages rose higher, and the marginal railways, serving undeveloped and less important areas, earned less. The interest bill swelled more rapidly than the railway revenue and the old dreary succession of deficits ominously recommenced. After March 1891, *The Age* attacked him as chiefly responsible, owing to his extravagant over-building and lax administration, for the alarming state of the colony's finances. Political patronage, Syme proclaimed, had not even been scotched, but was still rampant. One man, sheltered by the privileges of a permanent public servant, was being used by ministers and members for their own political ends.[1]

By December 1891 Syme had convicted Speight before the supreme tribunal of Victoria—his own editorial desk— of incompetence, extravagance and dereliction of duty, of contempt of Parliament and public. He and his fellow-Commissioners must go. James Munro, whom Syme had put up in place of the Gillies-Deakin coalition in November 1890, hesitated to do his master's bidding and was allowed to retire to London as Agent-General. William Shiels, installed in his place in February 1892, obeyed orders and suspended Speight, Ford and Greene, the three Railway Commissioners. Being given compensation in lieu of salary, Speight spent it in litigation against Syme on the score of libel. After two trials, which dragged an expensive course through three years, he was awarded a farthing damages.[2] Having thus vindicated and confirmed his

---

[1] *The Age*, leading article, 22 June 1891.

[2] The charges made by *The Age* and the addresses of counsel are reprinted in full in *The Great Libel Case: Speight v. "The Age"*, a report of the proceedings in the second trial, 18 April to 26 September 1894 (Melbourne 1894).

power, Syme magnanimously contributed a cheque for a hundred pounds to help the scapegoat to start life again in Western Australia.

Graham Berry, the veteran protectionist leader, was called to office again as Treasurer in the Shiels Ministry and proceeded to set the finances right by increasing the customs duties. This was not quite the old protectionist policy, for it depended for success on a continuance of imports, but it seemed to conform with recent experience. Berry made the duties 35 to 50 per cent. *ad valorem* where in Syme's earlier tariff they had been 20 to 35 per cent. But for some reason the remedy failed. Instead of the increase of £625,000 the duties had been expected to yield, the customs revenue went down by £600,000. The cessation of loans had dried up the London money and the local spending upon imports which it financed. Higher customs duties only cramped still more a shrunken trade. J. B. Patterson, succeeding Shiels and Berry in January 1893, had to face an accumulated deficit of £2,650,000. He suggested lower duties and an income tax of sixpence in the pound. These might have been accepted, but when he proposed a retrenchment of all civil servants' salaries as well he provoked too many opponents at once. A general election swept away the rash fellow. In his stead came, as the best substitute Syme could put up, George Turner—a suburban solicitor, myopic, cautious and tactful.[1] From September 1894 he continued as Premier and Treasurer of Victoria—save for a temporary displacement in 1900— until in February 1901 he became first Treasurer of the Commonwealth. During those years of gloom he served his country faithfully. The newspaper dictator behind him and his own native caution alike forbade any bold experi-

---

[1] Walter Murdoch, *Alfred Deakin*, p. 185, describes Turner's appearance at the Adelaide session of the Federal Convention in 1897: "Early in the proceedings he stood up and recited a catalogue of radical proposals"— possibly from a newspaper cutting—"he looked and spoke like a busy little shopkeeper rattling off a list of cheap lines". But his appearance did scant justice to a spirit of rare tenacity.

ment in re-casting indirect taxation, but he carried an income tax in 1894 and did not shirk the task and duty of retrenchment. In addition, he set every government servant a personal example and, in his shirt sleeves, worked for unheard-of hours at his desk, watching over pennies and points of which no predecessor had known. He cut expenditure to the bone, and scouted every suggestion of more borrowing abroad. By a system of rigid economy he made certain that Victoria reduced her public spending and lived within her income. After 1897 he was proud to show an annual surplus in her greatly shrunken budget. Yet it was a family solicitor's success, not a statesman's. Between 1895 and 1900 Victoria lost 75,000 of her folk by emigration, chiefly to people the goldfields of Western Australia. The increase in the Victorian population numbered during those years less than one-fourth of the excess of births over deaths. Economic relief came from private energy little helped by the state's policy, and from the success in primary production elsewhere of the colony's emigrant sons.

New South Wales followed other leaders and other policies. E. M. G. Eddy, Sir Henry Parkes' Chief Commissioner of Railways, had a reasonable chance as well as the courage to control the railway service he reorganized. Parkes' Public Works Committee checked for a time the baleful art of log-rolling in which the local members of that over-centralized colony had been too skilled. There was still waste to stop, however, and reform was hampered by the colony's lack of a clean-cut annual budget. Ministers might initiate without the consent of the Treasurer expenditure up to £20,000 on any item—an opening for commitments which made a firm control of the finances hopeless. Under a system which also carried over, from one year into another, votes which had not been spent in full, it was hardly possible to know how the public finances stood. Deficits could not but appear, and there was no definite reckoning-time to spur public and Parliament into the task of meeting them. Public revenue per head had remained stationary at £8. 15s. 6d. between 1881 and 1891, but ordinary expenditure had grown during that decade from £7. 11s. 2d. per head to £9. 3s. 3d. In addition, forty millions of loan money had been spent, not all of it on "reproductive" works.

Sir George Dibbs had shown the quality of decision during the bank crisis, but he incurred the discredit of a state of chaos in the public accounts for which he was not responsible. His advocacy of protective duties as a cure for the colony's ills made no appeal to a community that saw what Victoria had achieved, that had an old distrust of monopoly and that had been aroused to enthusiasm for free trade and direct taxation by Henry George. At the general election of 1894, Dibbs' followers were routed by a double attack from radical freetraders under George Houston Reid and from the Labour Party.

In five busy years in office, Reid enacted a series of financial, agrarian and fiscal reforms which set free to considerable purpose the resources of the land and the energies of its people. First, he made provision for an annual budget in which, as in the other colonies, the public accounts would be balanced on a cash basis on 30 June of each year. Appropriations from the consolidated revenue which had not been spent during the year when they were voted would lapse at its close. He sought to clarify the main budget of the colony by relieving it of local expenditure and setting up local governments and municipalities throughout the colony. Incidentally this measure would have lessened the intrigues and bargains for local favours that poisoned the atmosphere of Parliament and corrupted both electors and elected. It provoked, however, a combination of the regular Opposition, Labour and "local members" from Reid's own party who felt they could acquire merit in their clients' eyes by no other means than petty services. The allies inserted an abolition of plural voting by property owners which Reid would not accept. His zeal for simplification was tempered by Scottish caution.

Joseph Carruthers, his Minister for Lands, carried, however, a revision of the laws governing the selection of Crown lands which time was to prove a little too bold for democratic sentiment. In conjunction with the land taxation on a basis of unimproved values which Reid started then and which Carruthers later developed, the new land laws reasserted the public interest in sound settlement. They separated the combatants in the old agrarian feud; they afforded farmers fair access to land which they could put to uses more profitable than pasture, and they relieved out-back pastoral lessees from the worse forms of bogus selection.

Earlier amendments of the Robertson system[1] had in large measure eliminated the conflict between leasehold and free selection by dividing the pastoral leases into "resumed" and leasehold areas. The former, though legally resumed, remained in occupation by the pastoralist until someone saw fit to select. The incentive to dummying on such areas therefore remained. On the leasehold areas, however, selection was barred and the pastoral lessee was secure for five, ten, or fifteen years in the Eastern, Central and Western Divisions respectively. But all such expedients short of the full security of freehold call for watchful administration if the interest of posterity in a plastic land system is to be upheld. The amending acts limited the patronage of Ministers of Lands and wire-pulling members by setting up sixteen local land boards. These would judge the good faith of applicants for land and scrutinize their fulfilment of the conditions of purchase. The most important condition, that of residence, had in 1884 been raised from three to five years. This was intended to make more expensive the practice of storekeepers in country towns of subsidizing dummies with rations and taking payment at the end of three years in

---

[1] Notably the Crown Lands Acts of 1884 and 1889.

M

the land they had selected from the pastoralists' runs. The Act of 1889 set above the local boards a Land Appeal Board. This took the place the Minister had held. The Lands Department, it was argued, was an interested party in many cases that were made the subject of appeals. The new court of three members exercised its judicial functions wherever the business before it required its presence. Land causes led to itinerant justice as when the first and second Henries built up the royal courts of England.

Such steps did something to separate the combatants who had warred for the public estate. But more was needed to encourage a financially crippled population to lay out slender resources in the risky business of growing a crop under the sun and the rain. The town population, as Carruthers reminded Parliament, had increased between 1861 and 1891 from 159,834 to 730,000; the country folk only from 189,116 to 338,321. The failure of free selection, with its record of blackmail, dummying, litigation and financial disaster was, he claimed, as plain as Holy Writ. But there have been disputes on the interpretation even of Holy Writ. Carruthers carried the men of New South Wales with him in his reading of remedies for the failure when, for the mad scramble of free selection before survey, he substituted two principles well tested in the southern colonies—selection after survey and the classification of Crown lands. The former substituted orderly surveying for desperate unreason. The latter proceeded along tentative but sound economic lines, (a) setting apart areas suited to specific forms of selection and (b) putting varying values per acre on the blocks surveyed for settlers. He was on well-tried ground, too, when he made extensive use of a five years probationary lease as a test of the good faith of applicants for agricultural land.

Reid and Carruthers broke new ground in an ambitious plan to stay the alienation of the public estate by substituting agricultural leaseholds for freeholds. Robertson's conditional purchase had scattered freeholds throughout the countryside. The 1895 amending act offered long leases and security of tenure on an improvement basis. For grazing farms "settlement leases" of 28 to 40 years were given at rentals of 1¼ to 2½ per cent. on the capital value of the blocks, subject to re-appraisement at the end of each fifteen years of the lease. Within the first eighteen years after 1895 some 8,793,000 acres were taken up on this tenure. But the country residents of New South Wales had seen and done many things in defeat of leasehold. They had small reason to expect security at the hands of government. Early in the next century, before many settlement leases had come up for their first re-appraisement, this tenure was made convertible into freehold for certain areas per lessee.[1]

In increasing from five to ten years the term of residence required on ordinary conditional purchase (Robertson) selections, the Carruthers Act stiffened the tests of agricultural intentions applied to those seeking freehold farms. But it offered leasehold farms as well. These were called homestead selections, and were surveyed before settlement on areas set apart for agricultural occupation "on a face", i.e. unmingled with pastoral runs. The object was to divide resumed areas into blocks which in the ordinary run of seasons would maintain an active farmer's home. Each settler might obtain one block only. After residing on it for five years and effecting specified improvements, he would be given a homestead grant. Both forms of leasehold selection were originally made subject to the condition of perpetual residence by the lessee or his transferees. The lessees of homesteads paid 1¼ per cent. on the appraised value for five years and thereafter 2½ per cent. Nowadays the rate is 3½ per cent. "if residence is performed by deputy".[2] At first, extensive areas were occupied

[1] *New South Wales Official Year Book*, 1927–8, p. 724, shows that of the 8,793,663 acres granted as settlement leases up to 1913 over 5,000,000 acres were converted to freehold between 1909 and 1927.

[2] *N.S.W. Official Year Book*, 1927–8, p. 726. In 1912 a new form of leasehold, the "homestead farm", was evolved.

on such leasehold terms, but with agricultural success the hankering for freehold and security from re-appraisement proved too strong. In 1908 facilities were conceded for the conversion of homestead selections into conditional purchases, i.e. freehold.[1] Though backsliding was to follow later, the method of lending public land at a nominal rental to genuine settlers opened the way in the poverty-stricken 'nineties to a big agricultural advance. Money for the purchase of the freehold was sadly to seek. The little capital that could be found was used as working capital at a time when advances against land were regarded askance. Carruthers' Act opened a way to much active farming in the great central scrub from Booligal to the Bogan, and elsewhere on the Western Slopes and in the Riverina.

Farther west the confusion was not easily mended. On the resumed halves of pastoral leases, free selection of grazing farms under the Act of 1884 had unhappily coincided with the era of falling prices, with drought and with the spread of rabbits through the Darling basin.[2] Even when he meant well, the grazing selector could make no headway, and many a "resumed half" became a mere breeding ground for the rabbit pest. Carruthers granted revision of rents to the pastoral lessees whose land had been devastated, and, whenever any area was withdrawn for settlement, an extension of lease over the remainder of the run proportioned arithmetically to the fractional area taken. But in the west, the great King Drought remained master all through Reid's rule.

Reid's fiscal reforms were, like his financial practice and his colleague's land law, a return to simplicity. He encouraged his fellow-colonists to persist with the colony's natural industries by taking every removable burden off their costs, enabling the miner, the dairyman and the

[1] See V. S. Childe, *How Labour Governs*, pp. 14, 33, as to the political reactions of the "Conversion Act".

[2] See D. G. Stead's article "The Rabbit", in the *Australian Encyclopaedia*, vol. II, pp. 355–8.

cultivator to aid the pastoralist in finding from the land the exports needed to restore confidence and prosperity. Though it cost him half his majority and a sharp parliamentary struggle, Reid removed Dibbs' light protective duties, reduced some of the older duties on conventional necessaries such as sugar, and derived new revenue from added duties on narcotics and stimulants and from light direct taxes on incomes and the unimproved value of land. He was forced to retain certain specific duties on necessaries as concessions to conservatism when pushing the direct taxes through the Legislative Council, but his revenue tariff was simpler than that of Great Britain herself.

Under it, New South Wales made a recovery in bold contrast with the long stagnation that followed 1893 in Victoria and South Australia. Only in Western Australia, indeed, was the mother colony's expansion under free trade surpassed. It embraced both primary and secondary production, commerce as well as industry. The area under wheat expanded from 647,483 acres when Reid took office to 1,426,166 acres when he left it. Sydney recovered her chief place as the distributing centre for Australia, New Zealand and the South Pacific. Her re-exports rose from £4,700,000 in 1894 to £10,000,000 in 1898. After the crisis, 17,000 houses stood empty in Melbourne. Sydney's population hardly ceased growing, and by 1899 the building trades there were as active as in 1891. In every colony men set about increasing production from the soil. The decade 1891-1901 saw an increase in the number of Australian breadwinners engaged in primary production from 419,499 to 535,766, from 30·7 of the total breadwinners to 32·5.[1] Nowhere, however, was such all-round success achieved as in New South Wales. In effect, Reid's tariff stipulated that no manufacturer should make

[1] See Tables on p. 891 in *Commonwealth Year Book*, no. 20. The return to gold-mining in W.A. accounts for much of the increase, but this is the only decade since 1871 in which Primary Production has gained upon Transport and Industry in numbers occupied.

his fellow-Australians' tasks more expensive, that no industry was wanted which did not maintain its footing by fair service at a fair price in the main task of lifting the net income and real standard of living in the colony of New South Wales.

This was uphill work. An unprecedented drought reduced the flocks of New South Wales from nearly 57 millions in 1894 to 36,213,000 in 1899 and 26,650,000 in 1902. Save for a temporary spurt in 1899, wool remained low in value too; yet the wool-clip was maintained at almost its old total by the increased weight of the average fleece. The production of wool in New South Wales fell off by less than twenty million pounds in the decade, from 321,416,000 pounds in 1891 to 301,942,000 pounds in 1901. Moreover the installation of refrigerating engines on steamers plying to Europe added a new source of income from Australian pastures. New South Wales did well with frozen mutton. Even if the lighter carcase of the Merino compared unfavourably with New Zealand's crossbreds, it was worth more in that form than as tallow from boiling down or as meat on the local market. Queensland pastoralists led the way in exports of frozen and chilled beef.[1] But refrigeration helped the small farmers even more than the pastoralists. Their crossbreds produced better lambs for freezing and their butter became for the first time a profitable export.

The Victorian market had been glutted with "dairy butter" in the 'seventies when it was retailed at sevenpence a pound or sold at $1\frac{3}{4}d.$ a pound in casks to the soap-makers. An unrefrigerated shipment of $2\frac{1}{2}$ tons was sent to Leith as an experiment. Why Leith was chosen as its

---

[1] Three men deserve honourable mention for their efforts along different lines to solve the riddle of sending refrigerated cargoes of Australian perishable commodities to Britain. They were (i) James Harrison, a Victorian inventor and journalist (*Australian Encyclopaedia*, vol. I, p. 601), (ii) Thomas Sutcliffe Mort, a Sydney wool-broker and man of enterprize (*id.* vol. II, p. 144), and (iii) Robert Christison, a Queensland pastoralist (M. M. Bennett, *op. cit.* chapters XV and XVI).

destination is hardly apparent. It sold as grease at a penny a pound. There was no future for Gippsland dairy farms in those prices. Then came the refrigerator (1882) and the Danish cream separator (about 1885). The first consignment of refrigerated butter sent to London brought sixteen pence a pound. In this new export Victoria led the way. Her shipments to England rose from 1,286,583 pounds in 1890 to 13,141,423 in 1893 and 22,139,521 pounds in 1894. Co-operative central butter factories turned out a more uniform and dependable product, and raised the value of a dairy cow from £3. 10s. on an independent farm making its own butter by hand-churn to £8. 10s. when the farm supplied cream to the factory or milk to the creamery. Tasmania was pioneer in the export of fruit in cold storage, mainly apples.

At the end of the nineteenth century it was easier to put Australian food on English tables in perfect preservation than it had been to put French or Irish produce there when Queen Victoria came to the throne. Commodities once of little value became the basis of intensive settlement. In this the years following the bank crisis were those of most activity. The new economic strength of dairy farming was shown in the voluntary sub-division of pastoral freeholds, which were sold or leased as small farms to dairymen and fruit-growers. These men could now pay for their land at enhanced prices, and make good incomes too, where the free selectors had failed. Yet since they faced the competition of Denmark and Ireland in butter, and of New Zealand and the Argentine in mutton and beef, their success was conditional on high efficiency and low costs of production. The big share which New South Wales took in each of the new export trades showed an adaptability in agriculture that she had once notably lacked, and in this turning of the tables on her southern neighbours the advantage of her revenue tariff was not slight.

In the 'nineties, also, the riddle of permanent wheat-farming in Australia was solved. Necessity proved again the mother of invention. Edward Lascelles, applying South Australian methods on a large scale, developed a new wheat area which soon spread over a million acres of the Victorian Mallee lands. These had been thought hopeless for agriculture because the eucalyptus scrub stooled out with fresh vigour when the main stems were cut. After 1876 the spread of rabbits led to the abandonment even of pastoral leases there. South Australians first hit upon the idea of "mallee-rolling", i.e. of "Mullenizing" the land by dragging over it with a team of oxen a heavy roller made from an old engine-boiler or a tree-trunk. The snapped stems and foliage were then burned off and the stump-jump plough set to work among the mallee-roots that had not burned in the dry soil. Lascelles planned the conquest on a large scale of a new virgin area for agriculture. He provided water by irrigation and transport by a light railway. Having demonstrated that cultivation on extensive lines would cover the light costs, he sub-let to share-farmers his "pastoral lease" at Lake Corrong (now re-named Hopetoun), and his example set flowing a vigorous current of settlement.

Irrigation works initiated by the Gillies-Deakin government in the Goulburn and Wimmera valleys under an Act of 1886 had been stultified by the doubt whether the market could absorb much fruit and small produce. Nor had governments after the boom the resources of money or courage needed to educate the settlers on the irrigated lands into paying the cost of their reticulation. Lascelles, however, had found another use for the irrigation channels northward from the Wimmera, as means of supplying stock and domestic water over wheat-growing areas. The winter rains watered the crop, but there were as yet few sound catchments, and summer rains were too capricious to refill the dams. Government railways were constructed with light or second-hand rails, and gravitation channels were extended from the Grampians watershed to enable new farmers to test Lascelles' ideas. Their conquest of the

Mallee for agriculture enlarged the Victorian area under wheat from 1,145,163 acres in 1890 to 2,017,321 acres in 1900.

In South Australia the wheat area fluctuated from 1,673,573 acres in 1890 to 1,913,247 acres in 1900, though still remaining smaller than it had been in the 'eighties. But South Australian farmers were at last listening to the professors of Roseworthy College and dressing their wheat fields with superphosphate. In 1896 they used 600 tons of "artificial manures", mainly superphosphate of lime. By 1900 they used 24,000 tons, and the average yield in a season of by no means favourable rainfall rose to 5·88 bushels. Since then, South Australian yields have abundantly borne out Professor Lowrie's prediction that they might well be doubled when normal seasons returned. The Victorian Wimmera and Mallee districts, largely settled by South Australians, were quick to follow this lead. Superphosphate was first used around Nhill in 1897—"the year of the cyclone".[1] In spreading it, a selector named Salter took a hint from an old practice of steeping seed-wheat in liquid manure and nitre. After he had pickled his seed with bluestone, he mixed superphosphate or Thomas phosphate with it so that each grain received a coating of manure, rushed the seed to the field and sowed it broadcast by hand before it had time to dry. This obviated the difficulty of sowing with the old seeding-machine that had a centrifugal action; it had sent seed and "super" flying in different directions. But Salter's method was little better. Though 9·75 inches of rain fell during the growing period that year, only three bushels an acre were harvested. During the next two years, the Department of Agriculture showed the farmers how to "drill in" both seed and manure. The imported superphosphate "ran" badly, being lumpy with moisture absorbed when crossing the tropics,

---

[1] W. E. Dahlenberg, "Thirty Years of Wheat-growing at Nhill", in the *Ganmain Express*, 7 May 1926—an excellent summary of the methods which have made the Wimmera pre-eminent as a wheat district.

but the value of the new method was at once apparent. Supplementing the stump-jump plough and harvester, the drill and its later derivative the combine (cultivator and drill) have made the Australian farmer master of his little world and almost independent of hired labour.

More than the general use of superphosphate, however, contributed to the rapid advance of wheat-growing that marked the decade after the drought. Fallow, repeatedly worked to give a firm level seed-bed covered with a mulch of dry tilth, conserves for the crop plenty of nitrates and much of the previous year's rainfall. That is the essence of "dry-farming", taught by stern necessity in South Australia and Victoria during the persistent drought of the 'nineties. But the greatest lesson then learned came from an amateur botanist in New South Wales—the lesson of pedigree and graded seed.

The western slopes of New South Wales are within the zones of both the summer and winter rains. Sometimes they receive both, sometimes neither. The wheat crop is thus exposed to dangers of drought and rust. An English surveyor with a love of botany decided that the heavy-flagged, soft-grained wheats, favoured for their big yields in lucky seasons by his neighbours near the present site of Canberra, were ill-adapted to face such climatic vicissitudes. In 1889 heavy losses through rust had spoilt a favourable prospect even in South Australia. William Farrer knew that the nature of the rusts precluded any curative treatment of the growing crop, and set himself to breed varieties of wheat that could resist or escape their onslaught.

He chose to breed, by careful cross-fertilization, varieties that would have the characters he wanted, rather than await and select nature's chance crosses. With a constructive method such as this, he thought he might achieve as well two further objects—to produce types suited by their economy of flag and early maturity to the short growing-season of western New South Wales, and to improve the gluten-content and milling strength of Australian wheats. He wanted, in other words, a rust-and-drought-resistant wheat-plant, the flour from which would absorb much water and produce more well-risen loaves. He began his researches in 1886 at Tharwa near Queanbeyan, and in 1890 attracted the attention of the more intelligent officers of the Department of Agriculture. They invited him to Sydney in 1891 and sent him to Adelaide in 1892 to conferences on the rust problem. Even with the old wheats, New South Wales was advancing fast as an agricultural colony. In 1897 she exported bread-stuffs for the first time; her subsequent success, however, was largely Farrer's achievement. By 1898 he had bred wheats resistant to the rusts of his own district, and his new wheats, "Bobs" and "John Brown", were being eagerly sought for their ability to stand up to drought and their yield of stronger milling grain. In 1902–3 he was able to distribute in bulk a seed-wheat called "Federation" which has literally changed the whole aspect of the Australian wheat fields. It makes a short-strawed crop, unattractive in the paddocks because of a bronze appearance quite unlike the golden harvest of tradition; but it won favour by sheer yield. Produced to be cut by the stripper-harvester, the plant wastes little of its time and strength on straw, but throws a moisture-content that the sun drinks greedily from soil or leaf into heads well-packed with translucent grain. Farrer's work and that of his pupils neither started nor stopped with "Federation", but it was that variety which, as dramatically as McArthur's Merinos, laid the firm basis of a great exporting industry, in this case the high quality of the dry white wheats of Australia. His "abstruse experiments in cross-fertilization" put the staple crop of Australian farmers into something like competitive equality with wool inside the ten-inch winter rainfall line.[1] They

[1] In a paper on "The Making and Improvement of Wheats for Australian Conditions", read before the Australasian Association for the Advancement of Science at Sydney in 1898, Farrer explained in detail his aims and technique and the economic possibilities, as he saw them, of Australian

did more. At last settlers had the means—in labour-saving implements, dry-farming, superphosphate and pedigree wheats—of accepting the land so long offered them and of making permanent homes in it.

But the generations of semi-nomadic agriculture had wrought a havoc with the settlers' standards of domestic comfort which it will take much time to repair. Still to the Australian farmer "home" recalls

A track winding back
To an old wooden shack
Along the road to Gundagai.

wheat-growing. The paper was printed in full in the *Agricultural Gazette of New South Wales*, vol. IX, parts II and III.

CHAPTER XX

Back to Colonizing

WHEN in the 'nineties British investors looked askance at Australian public and private securities, other exports were needed to meet Australian commitments abroad. Mining, and especially the old simple gold-digging, played a big part in producing the goods. Some of the city unemployed in Victoria and New South Wales went fossicking on old alluvial fields, with considerable success. Companies treated the tailings of old crushings by the new cyanide process. As a result, the New South Wales gold output rose from £460,285 in 1890 to £1,315,929 in 1895, that of Victoria from £2,354,244 to £2,960,344 in the same period, and the Australian output from £5,231,466 to £7,708,029. The last figure included a new contribution—£879,748 from Western Australia.

Here alone the days of the diggings had come again, with their sudden rushes, their flamboyant style, with fabulous gains for a few, excitement and toil for all. But there was a big difference in the West. To make life bearable or even possible on the diggings there, the aid of the state was from the first essential to a degree that had never been known at Bathurst or Ballarat. The widely scattered discoveries of alluvial gold made in 1887 at Golden Valley and Southern Cross in the Yilgarn Hills, in 1888 on the de Grey and Oakover Rivers in the Pilbarra district, and in 1889 at Lake Austin in the Murchison, were all in regions of intense heat and prolonged drought. Supplies of water for considerable populations in such places would cost time and money. In spite of official warnings, however, inexperienced miners and camp-followers crowded thither and by their very sufferings forced the officials of the Crown Colony to take urgent measures to avoid wholesale disaster.

Luckily the grant of responsible government freed the courage of John Forrest from the curb of Westminster. This was no race to be won with tight reins. As an explorer he had known what thirst meant in that inland country, and though attacked and reviled by the noisier element on the "fields" whose growth and needs outran even the boldest measures, he laboured faithfully with the aid of subordinates as great-hearted as himself to make habitable the harsh, ill-watered areas where the "t'othersiders" swarmed. Self-government had brought release from the veto of the Colonial Office on colonial borrowing. A few years earlier, when the public debt of the colony was a million and a quarter, Governor Broome had been refused leave to borrow £500,000 for public works. The first Parliament elected under responsible government (1891) authorized the flotation in London of a loan of £1,336,000 to build an Eastern Goldfields Railway from Northam to Southern Cross, to make a harbour at Fremantle and to provide water out back. The contractors pushed the line out quickly and made good profit by private operation of it for some months before it was handed over to the government.

Before the railhead had reached Southern Cross, John Ford and Arthur Bayley, a lucky prospector from the Murchison field, had pushed eastward from "the Cross" with two months' provisions on their pack-horses. In July 1892, finding good grass on a flat which the natives called Coolgardie, they rested their horses. In an hour or two they had picked up twenty ounces of gold in small nuggets. Supplies ran short and they were compelled to return to Southern Cross. The raw gold in which they paid for more provisions brought others on their tracks, but not until they had taken from the cap of a reef five hundred ounces of free gold.

On 17 September 1892, Warden Finnerty at Southern Cross granted Bayley's reward claim. On camels, horses, bicycles or afoot, almost every man there rushed helter-skelter to Coolgardie. "In Perth and Fremantle everyone seems to be either carrying tents, picks, shovels and dishes or otherwise preparing for the road."[1] Four hundred men had won three thousand ounces at Coolgardie before the end of October. Then the lack of water drove almost all of them back until the long hot summer was over. From Melbourne, Adelaide and overseas, unheard-of numbers came to Albany and Fremantle to be ready for the rush when the winter rains returned. Officials made ready to dig big dams and to bore for artesian supplies. In 1893 the colony spent £15,000 on water supplies at Coolgardie and along the Goldfields road, a big sum for a community inured to economy. It proved, however, ludicrously low for the needs of those now arriving. Four thousand five hundred had come in 1892, five thousand came in 1893. By ships that risked foundering in the great winter rollers of the Bight, heedless of any discomfort, they made the passage from the depressed towns of Victoria and South Australia to share in the glittering prizes of Fly Flat. A few hardbitten "overlanders" made their way with camels or horses across the Nullarbor Plain that till then had separated East and West as completely as a sea. From Britain too came adventurers of all classes and qualities; they made a new and vigorous community with all the variety and fecklessness of the old Victorian days.[2]

Sensational finds by prospectors continued and the new government's difficulties in providing water and transport were extreme. The gold occurred here and there in rich pockets. The richness of the finds brought great numbers to the scene, but the limited extent of the rich patches in every early discovery made Perth officials reluctant to

[1] *West Australian*, 21 September 1892.
[2] Pierre Leroy-Beaulieu gives an excellent picture of the Western Australian "Gold Fever" in *Les Nouvelles Sociétés Anglo-Saxonnes*, chapter VII (1896).

incur heavy expense on permanent water-works. Yet, without water in plenty, permanent mines were impossible. High working costs would prohibit any attempt to extract gold from the lower grade ores. Boring for artesian supplies had revealed only salt water. Public and private "condensers", stoked up with the salmon gum timber that grew as a sparse but almost universal forest on the Coolgardie goldfields, distilled fresh water from this, but only in expensive driblets. By the end of 1895 the government had built at a cost of £37,700 tanks and dams to hold 13,500,000 gallons, but by then the population was increasing by tens of thousands each year. Moreover, surface water was not safe. Typhoid fever, already endemic on the fields, showed a significant spurt of virulence after each rain. Sanitation was of the crudest. Soil and dust around the camps were charged with germs that too easily infected dams and the tanks supplied from roofs.[1]

Another reason for caution was the atmosphere of bluff and knavery that gathered around "new finds". Authentic and really wonderful samples of ore from these might even be sent to London, but they seldom continued at depth. Before operations could continue, local managers had sometimes, so the story goes, to request London to "send back the mine". Such fields had already attracted company promoters whose market rigging threatened to accentuate their speculative repute. Clear vision and bold action were needed if a stable community were to establish itself in the wilderness. Yet courage and chance did achieve that end.

In June of 1893 a rush of about 150 men had set off from Coolgardie towards a locality termed "Mount Youle", said to be fifty miles out, to the north-east. Perhaps a trader started the rumour as a ruse to sell stores. Most of

---

[1] See J. H. L. Cumpston and F. Macallum, *History of Intestinal Infections* (Comm. Dept. of Health, 1927), p. 402, for a letter from C. H. Hill, Health Officer at Coolgardie, May 1895.

the party camped for two days in some rocky country by Mount Charlotte, held up by lack of water. Rain fell, and all but two pushed on. Hannan and Flannigan stayed, the latter having "spotted" some surface gold; in a day or two they had found a hundred ounces. Hannan pegged out a reward claim; it was granted, and in two days more half Coolgardie was encamped at "Hannan's", now Kalgoorlie. Almost as a matter of course London companies were formed to exploit the gold-bearing lodes at depth. To the general surprise it was found that here the rich patches did have considerable depth, and length too, over a full Golden Mile. When Sir John Forrest visited the fields in November 1895 he found several mines assured of ranking for years to come among the world's biggest producers.

The evidence of their permanence, backed by vehement clamour from the diggers, convinced the Premier that ample water must somehow be supplied both to the mines and the city growing up around them. Early in 1896, C. Y. O'Connor, the colony's Engineer-in-Chief, decided that the best plan was to build a weir on the Helena River, in the Darling Ranges near Perth, at a spot called Mundaring. The rainfall there averaged well over forty inches a year, and from the Mundaring Reservoir five million gallons daily could be pumped, along a pipe line thirty inches in diameter, 330 miles to the eastern goldfields. Men gasped, but Forrest stood by his adviser, and at his wish Parliament authorized the borrowing of a million and a half to build the weir, install the pumps and lay the pipe-line.

While the work was in hand, the gold yield rose from £1,068,807 in 1896 to £3,990,699 in 1898 and passed six millions in 1900. London investors readily found money for public works in the colony, even though they were fighting shy of other colonial securities. In 1896 and 1897 Western Australia was the only Australian colony to raise new loans in London. Masses of rich ore had been discovered in the Murchison and other northerly fields and railways were pushed out from Cue to Meekatharra, from Kalgoorlie to Laverton and Leonora. The boom-time congestion of goods on Fremantle Wharf—"the farm"—was at last cleared, and in appearance, though by no means in truth, the newcomers had taken charge of the busy community of 175,113 in 1900 which contrasted strongly with the sleepy 47,081 to whom, ten years earlier, responsible government had been granted. All but a few were waiting eagerly for the impetus to mining which should come with the operation of C. Y. O'Connor's great water scheme.[1] Early in March 1902 the "Scheme water" reached Kalgoorlie, but when it did so the great engineer who had planned and achieved this triumph had resigned his cares. Worn out by his labours in substituting for the open roadstead of Fremantle a safe harbour at the Swan River's mouth, and in pumping a river up to the arid interior, he died by his own hand on the eve of the popular celebrations. It was enough for him that the pessimists were confounded.

Never has an Australian colony employed a better public servant. It was his brain that enabled Forrest, by public works built with British capital, to remove the great natural impediments to colonization in the south-west corner of the continent. Yet his death is additional evidence of the breaking strain that a centralized economy must impose on its most capable men. He had been in the colony's service less than eleven years when at the age of 58 his spirit of tempered steel was broken.

The Coolgardie, or, as it is now called, Goldfields Water Supply, though for a time a financial burden on the revenue, has been more than an engineering success. Both the critics who loudly proclaimed it needless and extravagant, and the optimists who expected it to make possible the

[1] Among the sceptics one of the most persistent was J. H. Curle, in his *Gold Mines of the World*. See first edition (1899), p. 154, and second edition (1902).

real greatness of the mines, missed its true value. Here, as in the eastern colonies, gold brought people but could not hold them. Indeed, world-wide monetary changes drove them out of gold-mining much more quickly in Western than in Eastern Australia. The trading world was being supplied with so much gold by South Africa, Western Australia and the Klondike after 1896 that its value, as measured in commodities, went steadily down, i.e. prices of goods as stated in gold-units went up. As soon as this rise in gold prices offset such particular economies as the cyanide process of producing it, the Western Australian mines were limited to richer ore by the rise in general costs. Those of Victoria had been helped to survive by falling costs in the 'seventies and 'eighties. Thus the change-over to agriculture had to be made quickly in the West if the state was not to lose its ex-miners more rapidly than Victoria had done.

It was well that Sir John Forrest had made a lifelong study of the land problem. In 1892, before Coolgardie arose, he had introduced a Homesteads Bill to enable the government to assist settlers by loans up to half the value of the improvements needed to turn virgin land into farms. At first, prejudice against state interference was too strong for him, but in November 1894 an Act was passed establishing the Agricultural Bank. Using £100,000 of trust money as its capital, the Manager of the Bank was to make advances of not more than £400 each to enable new settlers to ringbark and clear their homesteads. Within areas of safe rainfall they might well grow some of the farm produce which the colony was then importing to the value of half-a-million a year from the eastern colonies. Under careful and conservative management the Bank felt its way for eight years.[1] Early in the new century, however, when gold-mining showed signs of

---

[1] *The Agricultural Bank and Industries Assistance Board*, by Gordon Taylor (1921), though marred by some immature judgments, gives a valuable résumé of the development of government credit to farmers in W. Australia.

waning, two or three vigorous spirits among the colony's public men realized that superphosphate and the other new wheat-growing methods of Eastern Australia could be applied with unusual chances of steady success over a broad belt of lightly-timbered country, of mottled quality but safe rainfall, stretching from Geraldton towards Albany and eastward as far as Southern Cross and perhaps Esperance. They seized upon the Agricultural Bank as a means of providing government money by which anyone, ex-miner, civil servant or immigrant, might clear and equip a wheat farm. The category of improvements for which advances were to be made was widened, and such advances were allowed up to the full value of such improvements.

Almost equal in importance to the Agricultural Bank's advances, in this transition to agriculture, was the aid given in the new wheat areas by the Goldfields Water Supply. At first it had relied for financial support on its services to the mines and goldfields towns, but nowadays farms and wheat-handling towns draw water from it along two-thirds of the pipe-line.[1] Rapid settlement, as in the Victorian Mallee, was made easily practicable in country where, during summer, water for stock and domestic use had been hard to find. O'Connor had builded better than he knew. Over a far wider range of country, north and south of the belt which the pipe-line crosses, one of C. Y. O'Connor's lieutenants, P. V. O'Brien, has provided water supplies piecemeal by a more economical method, conserving the water around the granite bosses that occur like natural roofs throughout the south-west of Western Australia. By low retaining channels around the base, the rain-water is led into covered dams of considerable size. In other instances wells at favourable spots have revealed unsuspected sub-artesian supplies. By such ways much of the land that seemed utterly inhospitable in the 'nineties

[1] "In 1925–6 the Railways consumed 8 per cent., the mines 22 per cent. and 'other' 70 per cent. of the water supply." *C.Y.B.* no. 20, pp. 136–7.

has been made the scene of agricultural settlement or, farther out, of light pastoral occupation.

Under the brave rule of Forrest, Western Australia thus began a recapitulation in an artificial setting of the main themes of Australian colonization. Superphosphate and the acclimatized wheat-farming of the Eastern States enabled the immigrant "t'othersiders" and a new generation of "gropers" to break the spell of her long pastoral slumber. But that dramatic awakening of the Swan River colony seems to have exhausted the capacity of Australians to colonize in the old makeshift, venturesome fashion.

The planters' dreams of a separate North Queensland had come to nought, and South Australian ambitions to plant a tropical sub-colony in the Northern Territory ended in costly failure. Forts Dundas and Wellington were abandoned in 1824 and 1827. Another defensive post under naval auspices lasted at Port Essington from 1838 to 1849.[1] Crawfurd, the Administrator of Singapore, wrote of the North Australian coast that, owing to the uncertain character of the monsoon, he could not conceive a tropical locality more unfavourable to cultivation. Yet in 1864 the South Australians projected its official development from a "first town" on the coast, around which small farming areas and pastoral estates would be sold and leased on the good old Wakefield plan.

Pastoralists had indeed trekked from the south and east into the high inland country. Some had followed the South Australian explorers, Stuart and McKinlay; and in spite of the resistance of Newcastle, the Secretary of State, the whole territory, save a strip known as the Albert district southward from the Gulf of Carpentaria, was assigned to South Australian government. Quarrels between the officials sent to determine the site of the "first town", delays in the survey of land and the defection of

[1] The following paragraphs owe much to the *Cambridge History of the British Empire*, vol. VII, ch. VI, "Experiments in Colonization", by A. Grenfell Price.

a North Australian Company, made up a record of blundering that was not expunged by Surveyor-General Goyder's choice of the fine harbour at Port Darwin and rapid survey of 600,000 acres on the tableland behind. But it was not only initial errors that "damned the Northern Territory"; as subsequent events showed, the permanent disabilities of soil and climate counted for more. It was absurd, in any circumstances, to attempt its government from the colony farthest from it by sea, the only means of communication then available. Newcastle, who saw this, acted unwisely in sanctioning an absurdity.

The leaders in South Australia sought in 1870 to correct this weakness by a telegraph line joining their northern and southern territories. The projectors of a submarine cable proposed that the colonies should co-operate in the construction of a land-line from Wentworth near the Darling-Murray junction to Burketown on the Gulf of Carpentaria; there it would meet the terminal station of the cable they were to lay from Singapore. On his way to Melbourne, an emissary from the company asked at Adelaide whether South Australia would facilitate its operations if Port Darwin were made an intermediate station.

Premier Strangways was eagerly favourable. His government would either guarantee the cost of constructing or would itself construct an overland telegraph line along McDouall Stuart's track from Adelaide to the north coast. According to Charles Todd, the Superintendent of Telegraphs, such a line would cost £120,000. While the negotiation was proceeding, John Hart displaced Strangways as Premier, and, being a more cautious financier, reverted to the plan of co-operating with the other colonies on the Wentworth-Burketown route. The House of Assembly, however, was not to be baulked of the prize and insisted that South Australia should at least offer to shoulder the full responsibility. As a result the province undertook to finish the line from Port Augusta to Port

Darwin before the end of 1871. It was expected to "promote the success of the new settlement at Port Darwin as well as the occupation of those large tracts in the interior which are suitable for pastoral occupation".[1]

Four days after the reception of the company's acceptance of this offer, the government rushed a Construction Act through both houses, the "house of review" doing its part at a single sitting. Within the next month contracts were duly let for the three sections into which the line was divided. A year later, news reached Adelaide that the contractors for the northern section had failed. The energetic Todd was sent to fill the gap; he did it, but the total cost mounted up to £420,720, more than £300,000 above the first estimate. The line was completed by 22 August 1872. The cable company, as Adelaide no doubt expected, saved itself the expense of a cable between Port Darwin and Burketown, so that the province secured "the monopoly which", so she said, "South Australia had scarcely coveted and certainly has not striven for".

Power to send messages at a shilling a word from Adelaide to Port Darwin did not, however, solve the Territory's problem. More formidable obstacles to tropical agriculture remained in the climate, soil and lack of labour in North Australia. Post holes for the telegraph line revealed gold at Pine Creek in 1871, and in the following year there was an attempt to mine by companies there. But costs were phenomenal, and men would not stay save at such high wages that "ounce stone" showed no margin of profit. The heat was terrific. Chinese coolies were brought from Singapore to work for the companies, but these collapsed and the coolies tried their luck at mining for themselves in a primitive fashion along the Margaret. They were "a poor diseased lot of creatures", pirates and

---

[1] *S.A. Parl. Papers*, no. 24, 1870–1, House of Assembly. See also no. 38, 1870–1, both Houses. Correspondence finally fixing Port Darwin as terminus of cable from Europe.

port riff-raff. Gold had brought no permanent white settlement.

Perhaps a transcontinental railway would bring the settlers. As far back as 1862 a Port Augusta Overland Railway Act had authorized the government to negotiate for an overland railway to be built on the land-grant principle.[1] No effective offer to do so was made during the five years of the Act's currency. Talk of state construction arose in 1877, but parliamentary opinion was almost unanimous that the Territory must first be developed and made prosperous by coloured labour before anything so ambitious as a railway were undertaken. A Northern Territory Immigration Act passed in 1879 failed to obtain the Queen's assent. The Indian Government had made representations that the provision it contained for the welfare of coolies was inadequate. That government stipulated that such a measure should protect Indian coolies through an officer responsible to itself. In 1882 a further Act embodied this principle, and in the year following the Palmerston and Pine Creek Railway Act authorizing state construction passed both Adelaide houses amid enthusiasm.

Little came of all this. Drought and financial stringency tied the Adelaide Government's hands. Opinion in other colonies was very adverse to the introduction of coloured labour. The Indian Government waited for the appointment of the protector responsible to itself before it would permit the recruiting of coolies. In 1887 the Pine Creek Railway was begun with Chinese coolies. It made no difference. The country along the line was as empty when it was finished as before it was begun. The Chinese had been brought under indentures for railway building and "evaporated" when it was built. A southern section from Marree above Port Augusta was built as far north as Oodnadatta, 688 miles from Adelaide, between 1878 and 1891, when once more lack of loan funds called a halt. A gap of 1063 miles remained.

[1] H. A. Parsons, *The Truth about the Northern Territory*, Adelaide, 1907, *passim*.

The advocates of tropical agriculture as the key to the development of the North were not silenced, though plantations failed through neglect at Delissaville in 1882, at Manton Hill on the Adelaide River in 1884 and at Shoal Bay from 1885 to 1890. Sugar-cane, coffee plants and rubber trees throve despite long periods of neglect. This was true, but men will not tend tropical plantations which cost more than they produce. Some still argued that cheap indentured labour would show a margin of profit, but others pointed to the poor soils of the Territory, mainly weathered from sterile sandstones and watered by summer rains alone. Why should men cultivate these in preference to the Queensland coastal strip, whose richer patches enjoyed rains at all seasons?

The dream of tropical agriculture by means of coloured labour faded as federation dawned. Queensland planters, on the defensive against the new political labour movement in North Queensland, offered to transfer their mills to the Territory if guaranteed coloured labour for twenty-one years. The Chief Secretary shook his head. In the coming Federal Parliament both houses were to be elected by the widest suffrage.

Federation meant stagnation to the Northern Territory so long as the state of South Australia continued to administer its scanty affairs. It was an empty land. There was a port in outline at Darwin. A few Chinese fossicked for gold. The population had been 5366 in 1890: in 1909 it was 3538. Cattle exports had expanded from 20,495 to over 100,000 a year during that period. But what was such a trade as a basis of taxation to provide interest on a debt of £2,748,063? In 1909 South Australia washed her hands of the business with relief. "It is obvious", wrote H. A. Parsons, "that it will not pay to grow any tropical products in the Northern Territory with white labour for export in competition with the productions by coloured labour of other countries". But though leaders might be concerned about the empty North, the man in the street was little interested in a place "not on his map". Throughout federated Australia men acquiesced in the restriction of settlement and industry to areas and enterprises which would provide white Australians with a defined and state-guaranteed standard of living. To the realists this was the substance of the White Australia decreed by the Commonwealth.

BOOK THREE

THE COMMONWEALTH

CHAPTER XXI

The Origins and Extension
of Wage-Fixing

"SYDNEY or the bush!" cries the Australian when he gambles against odds, and the slogan betrays a heart turning ever towards the pleasant coastal capitals. But the percentage who found industrial employment—predominantly a city category—diminished after the bank smash from 30·7 in 1891 to 26·1 in 1901. Building and construction work in and around the cities were dead. Factories cut down their staffs. Bush-venturing on farms and alluvial diggings had a fresh innings; but there were still too many in the towns. Trade unions fell to pieces or stood shrunken and powerless. Their defeats in the early 'nineties, attributed by their leaders to class-antagonism in high places, had borne witness to Lane's foresight in trying to unite town and country labour and to bring unskilled as well as skilled men within his Australian Labour Federation. For their deadliest foes during the struggle had been the as yet unorganized labourers. Yet unionists knew full well it was the scabs' poverty, not their will, which had made them consent to fight capital's battle.

The solution, said Spence, was to spread trade unionism throughout the length and breadth of Australia. On the old lines of craft benefit societies this would take time and long endeavour. The "new" way of propaganda by strikes had not prospered. Political action would cost less. The traditions of British unionism were against it, but Graham Berry in 1884 had advised the second Intercolonial Trade Union Conference to "make labour's voice heard in the councils of the nation". The Conference had contented itself with a parliamentary committee, to watch over the passage of measures beneficial to labour. During and after the great maritime and pastoral strikes, however, friend and foe alike bade them regard the ballot as the proper means of righting wrongs, and in the bitter hours of weakness and isolation Labour took up this challenge and resolved to send artisans to speak for artisans, miners to represent miners. These might some day seize the machinery of government which had beaten them down.

In New South Wales, members of the Legislative Assembly were to be paid for the first time after the election of 1891. With energy unimpaired by poverty, the unionists formed Labour Electoral Leagues and enlisted such general support that thirty-six of the forty-five candidates endorsed by the Trade Union Council won seats in Parliament. To the gifted correspondent of *The Times*[1] the new party might seem cursed with "inept chatterers at the head and larrikins at the tail", but her appraising eye valued highly its main ranks of determined men who resented unearned vicissitudes of pay and living. As yet they had no leader, no policy that they could call their own, and their ways in Parliament were clumsy.

Sir Henry Parkes, a man of the people leading his fifth government, accepted their support but found it irksome—"given after a manner of their own, as an ungracious man gives charity". In October 1891 he refused to proceed with a Coal Mines Regulation Bill because his allies had thrust into it a clause making eight hours the legal day's work underground. One of his lieutenants harped upon supply and demand. "That", retorted a mining member, Fegan of Newcastle, "is a principle we do not recognize and in the opinion of all readers and thinkers it will not survive very long." Parkes gave up office for the last time rather than enact restriction. With leonine mien and his

[1] Miss Flora Shaw, afterwards Lady Lugard, in her *Letters from Queensland* (1894).

surprising high voice, the old statesman bade the defiance of his generation to the new power. "Civilization would lose its charm and value if it did not lighten the burden of the masses of humanity. But I distinguish very broadly between eight hours being sufficient for a man to labour and Parliament presuming to say how many hours he shall labour. The working classes of this country are sufficiently strong to make good—indeed they have made good—their right to work eight hours without asking Parliament to exercise a power which in all moral justice it does not possess.... Tyranny is an arbitrary interference with your fellow-men and whether it is in the guise of a trade-union or the edict of an autocrat it is tyranny just the same."

His successor, Sir George Dibbs, broke up the inexperienced Labour group by raising the fiscal issue. Their ranks were further torn by recriminations over the very pledge of solidarity in the division lobby by which they sought to close them. The party's candidates fared badly at the elections of 1894 and 1895. A leading member, Joseph Cook, joined Reid's free-trade ministry as Postmaster-General. Yet the main body regained the balance of power in 1895, and when, after five years fruitful of liberal reforms, Reid demurred at further concessions in return for support, it nipped in the bud his ambition to be first Federal Prime Minister. Then it proceeded to squeeze a protectionist ministry under William Lyne.

The Labour Party had in these years learned much. From being "an impotent group of hysterical, blocking, unpopular intransigents", it had become "a compact body of artful parliamentarians who knew how to drain the last drop of reluctant honey from the Reidite hive".[1] But it was still fumbling in search of a distinctive programme. In January 1895 the "Solidarities", as the core of the party called themselves, adopted six new planks at the Political Labour League Conference. The first urged

[1] T. A. Coghlan, *Labour and Industry in Australia*, p. 218.

extension of government ownership and operation of "such works as railways, tramways, water-supply, public lighting or other works for the good of the community". After such extension their parliamentary power might dictate the improvement of wages and working conditions for all state employees. The sixth new plank was "Compulsory Arbitration".

This plank told of a changing balance of power both in the political and in the economic spheres. Unionists foresaw the coming of governments unlike those which had outlawed them in 1890 and 1891, and the prospect has softened the antagonism of miners and shearers to government intervention in industrial disputes. But it was with reluctance that they admitted the claim of the community to be the dominant party in such disputes. Lane's and Spence's federated unions had practised negotiation with the employers, though rather as an art of bluffing enemies than as an adjustment of sound relations between partners in a joint service of the public. They had relied on the strike as the final arbiter in the war of the classes.[1] But the association in point of time of the great strikes with the looming of financial chaos had made the strike weapon profoundly unpopular throughout the land. Everywhere men discussed plans of public action to prevent the appeal to force. Should public intervention take the form of conciliation—the good offices of disinterested men, nominated and paid by the state—or of compulsory arbitration after the fashion of the criminal courts enforcing the king's peace? Till 1894 all such proposals were coolly received by miners and shearers as well as by employers. The latter thought any state action likely to tie their hands lately freed, as they imagined, by the victory of "freedom of contract". The unions still thought themselves equal to renewing the battle.

---

[1] In W. G. Spence's *Australia's Awakening*, ch. xxxii, "Trade Unionism", may be read the old leader's naïve advice to union negotiators. It would be amusing if it were not so sinister in ignoring the need of sound principles.

The trend of prices, however, was strongly against the men. Without consulting the A.W.U., the Pastoralists' Federal Council imposed in 1894 a new agreement, reducing the piece-rate to 17s. per hundred for machine-shorn sheep, and making each pastoralist sole interpreter of his agreement with shearers. The union leaders, powerless to say them nay, tried to save their own faces by a conference. The pastoralists refused it. Into strike camp went the shearers, as in the brave days of Lane. The station-owners promptly fetched non-unionists by the hundred from Victoria, Tasmania and New Zealand and filled the stands. Riots flared here and there. A river-steamer, the 'Rodney', carrying non-unionists up the Darling, was burned to the water's edge at Pooncarie. Wool-sheds, too, were burned at Ayrshire Downs, Cambridge Downs, Cassilis, Manuka and Dagworth in Queensland.[1] The Nelson government therefore proclaimed a state of insurrection and the camps scattered.

In New South Wales, while the commotion still boiled, Williams, the A.W.U. President, appealed to the new Premier, G. H. Reid, to compel the disputants to confer. Reid asked first for a guarantee that disorder would cease. It was not given. An elaborate offer by the A.W.U. to settle on the wages of 1891, and individual bargains at the sheds on other matters, drew the scornful rejoinder from the pastoralists that "as it has already appeared in the newspapers it calls for no further reply". The union's funds ran low, and supplies of non-unionists were inexhaustible. Its own men left the strike camps to find work on the pastoralists' terms at other sheds. The strike died out.

It was after this experience of supply and demand that the A.W.U. joined in adopting "Compulsory Arbitration" as a Labour plank. Its own rough power to impose "restrictive conditions on the trade, business or industry of the members" having waned, it sought the aid of the

[1] M. M. Bennett, *Christison of Lammermoor*, pp. 193–200, 215. The note on p. 197 refers to the strike of 1891.

N

state's power of legal compulsion. Ever since 1891 Charles Cameron Kingston, a South Australian radical intimate with Labour, had pleaded for a compulsory registration of unions of employers and employed and for the enforced reference of their differences to a "Court". In 1894, after three abortive attempts, he succeeded in carrying through the South Australian Houses a Conciliation and Arbitration Act embodying, though ineffectively, this principle of compulsion. The awards of the State Board were only to bind the parties to the dispute submitted to it.

Kingston's compulsory arbitration in the name of industrial peace, adopted in 1895 by the New South Wales Labour Party as a new plank, became at once an important issue in Australian politics, second only to that of the federation which was to prepare a wider scope for its triumphs. Reid fell from the height of his power because he would not grant the new province to law and order.[1] He was willing to compel the parties to a dispute to confer, but would not enact the legal enforcement of an arbitrator's award.

For five years after Labour's conversion opinion among employers remained adverse. Reid's mild Bill in 1895 for compulsory conferences seemed to the *Sydney Morning Herald* "extreme and one-sided legislation calling new and highly unfair powers into existence". The Legislative Council gave its second reading short shrift by thirty votes to one. But in 1896 a renewal of turmoil at the Newcastle coal mines preyed upon the public's nerves. Victoria had set up minimum wages boards in that year. New Zealand also had set up a compulsory arbitration court as the coping stone of a system of state conciliation. That was the year, too, in which the sinking prices which had troubled the economic world since 1873 touched bottom. Unconscious that a heavier gold production was at last causing buoyant markets, men readily attributed

---

[1] T. A. Coghlan, *Labour and Industry in Australia*, pp. 2105–9, and G. H. Reid's *Reminiscences*, p. 188.

success to the experiments in New Zealand and Victoria. A commendation of the New Zealand Court by the Chairman of the Union Steamship Company,[1] the leading employer of that colony, did much to persuade Sydney to acquiesce in an extension of the experiment to New South Wales. When Bernard Ringrose Wise, Lyne's Attorney-General, introduced his Arbitration and Conciliation Bill in 1900, he put it forward as "an experiment designed to overcome evils the gravity of which we are fully acquainted with, and which cannot possibly bring in its train other evils at all equal to those it is intended to do away with". Labour and middle-class opinion applauded his optimism when he asserted: "There cannot be a strike under this bill. There may be disputes but there cannot be any interruption of industry". The Legislative Councillors were not so sure, but in the calm after the campaigns for federation they let it pass.

To attain industrial peace, that heaven of all men's wish, Wise's Act of 1901 went further than Pember Reeves' New Zealand variant on Kingston. The New Zealand measure prohibited strikes and lock-outs only when one party to a dispute had appealed to the Arbitration Court and while the appeal was pending. The element of legal compulsion came in ostensibly as a last resort, a weapon in reserve when the parties would not agree upon a settlement. The whole purport of the New Zealand Act was to lay emphasis on conciliation—the original aim of all this legislation. Collective bargaining, through innumerable brains, would continue to adjust the flux of prices and terms in which the values of men's services to one another were registered from day to day. But events did not work out thus, even in New Zealand. Disputants often brushed aside the boards of conciliation and sought

---

[1] Mr (afterwards Sir James) Mills was reported by the *Sydney Daily Telegraph*, 3 July 1899, to have said: "I think this method of settling disputes is, on the whole, satisfactory. Under the operation of the Act the parties can meet together and after a little discussion the strength of each case can be pretty well judged".

to present an unprejudiced case before the bench armed with compelling power. Let the Court make their collective bargains for them.

This subtle but all-important change in the atmosphere of business was not lost on the sensitive brain of Wise. In a colony where, as he thought, it seemed "a permanent condition of industrial enterprises that there shall be a perpetual liability to industrial strikes", his Act unconditionally prohibited strikes and lock-outs pending consideration of every dispute by the Court. By it a strike or lock-out became a misdemeanour against society. It was immaterial whether the parties applied for an award or no. Existing terms and conditions of employment could not be disturbed at the will of one party alone. With one sweep the New South Wales Arbitration Court threw its sanction over the terms upon which, when the Act came into force, men were employing and serving one another. The assumption, implicit in the New Zealand Act, that a legal tribunal was competent to direct every needed adjustment in the conduct of business and that at its bidding peace would bless the Court's decision, became more positive in New South Wales. The Supreme Court, possibly with raised eyebrows, ruled that the Arbitration Act "deprives the employer of the conduct of his own business and vests the management in the tribunal formed under the Act".

Victoria was not so bold. There "union rates and conditions", though still proclaimed, were hopeless of achievement by industrial action and the Labour group in Parliament was weaker. Its sway of the balance in the Assembly was enough, however, to exact from Turner the establishment of minimum wages boards. Their machinery was simple, their aim immediate. The helpless poor congregated in Melbourne after the collapse of the boom were being exploited as out-workers by clothing and other manufacturers. Factory laws were no new thing in Victoria, though they had not yet regulated wages. As early as 1882, *The Age* had been shocked to find low wages and evil conditions in the protected industries it had fought so hard to rear. An Amending Factory Act of 1885 had prescribed better conditions of space, sanitation and safety, and had set public inspectors to enforce them. Probably a House of Lords investigation into the sub-letting of piecework at "sweated" rates to East London home-workers gave the Victorian Labour leaders their fresh cue in 1895. A sharp agitation by *The Age* against sweating, understood more widely as home-working, was answered by evidence that such work was all too general in the over-populated capital and too essential in eking out family sub-sistence to be declared illegal. The Legislative Council and Assembly conferred and agreed upon (i) the establishment of minimum wages boards representing both sides under official chairmen, to fix legal piece and time-wages in the clothing, furniture, baking and butchering trades, (ii) the making of a register of home-workers, and (iii) "policing" of wages board determinations by the official factory inspectors. Though modelled on conciliation boards, the new machinery was not explicitly directed against strikes; the Act did not declare them illegal. The home-workers were too helpless to fight. No dispute or threat of a dispute was needed to call a board into existence. Nor did the Act require the incorporation of industrial unions of employers and employees as juristic units for a formal litigation, as the Acts inspired by Kingston did. The boards brought representative employers and employed face to face in order to set up limits below which the state might forbid the purchase of service at prices which offended public opinion.

The new method did, however, promote labour organisa-tion in providing for regular negotiation. The election of representatives to sit on the boards brought scattered workers together, and thus eliminated any weakness due only to their dwelling apart. Its piecemeal extension waited upon the ripening of opportunities. A resolution of either House of the Legislature might create a fresh board. For a time the enforcement of determinations was dubious. The task was hardest in the furniture trade where Chinese masters and men were too inscrutable for the inspectors. But the danger that the determinations might restrict employment was offset by rising prices, and by the exodus, mostly to the goldfields, of 63,582 Victorians, of whom 39,805 were males, during the quinquennium 1896–1900. The first fear of wage-fixing quickly faded. Of thirty-eight boards established prior to 1906 eleven had been applied for by employers, the best of whom welcomed restraint upon hard taskmasters. An attempt in 1904 to limit the boards' option in defining minimum wages to the average paid by "reputable employers" proved short-lived; it was abandoned two years later. The average is not always divine. Boards numbered 186 at the end of 1927. The only check upon their determinations was a Court of Industrial Appeals which might review and upset determinations not legally arrived at, and exercise for the nonce all or any of a board's powers.

William Lane had endowed the Queensland Labour Party with an early strength which was to carry it to the ministerial benches even before federation. Before he set out for his New Australia in Paraguay, Labour was represented by fifteen members in the Assembly (1893). Yet the very success of Labour in elbowing aside the radical party and taking from the first the direct opposition benches put out of possibility the fruitful method of "support in return for concessions" pursued in the southern colonies. As a result, legislation to set up industrial courts made a slow start in Queensland. Elsewhere such laws were the work of individual Liberal leaders, such as C. C. Kingston, Pember Reeves, B. R. Wise and Alexander Peacock, rather than of Labour conventions or caucus. For six years the Queensland Labour Party gained nothing but parliamentary experience in a hard school. Then, on 1 December 1899, they had the honour to form the first Labour Government, under Anderson Dawson. It held office for only six days. In 1908 a coalition ministry, led by William Kidston, who had been Dawson's Treasurer, but was no longer a Labour leader, adopted the Victorian Wages Boards (8 Ed. VII, No. 8) and to these in 1912 a Liberal Government added a Court of Industrial Appeals by an Industrial Peace Act (3 G. V, No. 12). On its accession to power in 1915, the Labour Party lost little time in exchanging the wages board method for a Court of Industrial Arbitration (1916). Of the less populous states, Tasmania and Western Australia, the former has followed the Victorian Wages Board methods, while Western Australia has made consistent use of a Court of Arbitration, first successfully established in 1902. Its supervision of apprenticeship has been notably thorough and sound under the care of W. Somerville, the workers' representative since 1905.

After 1907, in a Commonwealth tribunal, a greater man than Kingston had elaborated a principle of wage-fixation which led boards and courts alike to interpret the wage-earners' share in production as a sacrosanct family maintenance. An American observer who reviewed the Australian Labour movement in 1906 found in it "something of the Chinese jealousy of the outside world, of the parochial spirit extended to a continent",[1] and held that this weakened its moral appeal. In 1907, however, a Judge of the High Court of Australia, presiding over a Federal Arbitration Court, took high moral ground in claiming for the workers a wage independent of supply and demand. A glow of idealism warmed what had seemed a class egoism. Aided by many outside the union ranks, Labour rose to power in both states and Commonwealth, expecting and expected to reconstruct the Australian economy on the firm basis of a legal living wage.

The Convention which drafted the Commonwealth Constitution had inserted among the subjects with respect to which the new legislature might make laws for the peace, order and government of Australia "Conciliation and

[1] V. S. Clark, *op. cit.* p. 291.

arbitration for the prevention and settlement of industrial disputes extending beyond the limits of any one State ".[1] The regulation of industry remained a state responsibility, but memories of the great strikes and of the dark days that had followed had bitten deep. Men reasoned that the new Government alone could wield effective powers to stop the paralysis of callings such as the pastoral, which knew no state boundaries, and the maritime, the ships of which plied beyond them. Out of a stormy passage through the Federal Legislature there emerged in 1904 a Commonwealth Conciliation and Arbitration Act. Three Federal ministries had died during the drafting of its provisions, and the decisions and personnel of the Court it called into being soon became the main matter of political argument throughout the Commonwealth. Here Labour found its programme.

Henry Bournes Higgins, as Convention delegate and as legislator, had been chiefly responsible for the creation of the Court, and, by renovating as a novel extension of democratic jurisprudence the mediaeval ideal of the just price, he was now to show the Labour Party the path it had sought by which those on whom had fallen the sharpest pains of adversity might reach a just and reasonable security. The ideal, transmuting the old rations habit and the instinctive solidarity of men facing a trying climate, soon caught the national imagination.

Immediately on his appointment in 1907 as second President of the Court, Mr Justice Higgins had to decide whether the wages and conditions of work in H. V. McKay's harvester factory could be held "fair and reasonable" and could thereby entitle its products to exemption from the excise duties imposed by a new Excise Tariff Act (No. 16 of 1906).[2] The learned judge reasoned

---

[1] Constitution Act, section 51, subsection xxxv. As to the hesitation over the insertion of this subsection, see G. Anderson, *Fixation of Wages in Australia*, pp. 128–9, a very valuable work of reference.

[2] See H. B. Higgins, *A New Province for Law and Order*, passim; 2 *Commonwealth Arbitration Reports*, p. 1; G. Anderson, *op. cit.* pp. 188 *et seq.*

that, as the Act offered exemption from excise duties to those employers who paid "fair and reasonable" wages, it must mean by these words something more than the level set by the "barbarous" higgling of the market. He decided that "the primary test in ascertaining the minimum wage that would be treated as 'fair and reasonable' in the case of unskilled labourers" must be "the normal needs of the average employee, regarded as a human being living in a civilised community". After some inquiries into the costs of a workman's household of about five persons, he named 7s a day, 42s. a week, as the lowest wages that he could certify to be fair and reasonable.

The Excise Act was soon afterwards held to be invalid on constitutional grounds; it was beyond the powers entrusted to the Federal Legislature. But the "Harvester judgment" could not be expunged from men's minds. It was acclaimed at once as the much sought *eirenicon*, the way of industrial peace for which arbitrators and boards had so long been groping. The tide of opinion, which had been running in favour of wages boards as being less provocative of "disputes", turned again towards Courts of Arbitration. New South Wales, after changing in 1908 to a wages boards plan, returned to a mixed one of courts and boards in 1912. Several state legislatures embodied in their industrial codes the inspiring words "the normal needs of a human being living in a civilised community" —with local variants. Yet the nation-wide realization of this standard by state tribunals was hampered by fear of inter-state competition, a fear which could not be laid as long as any important state, such as Victoria, failed to impose the new doctrine on its wage-fixing tribunals.

The power of the Federal Court to enforce as well as proclaim the *eirenicon* was limited. It could hear only the parties to disputes extending beyond any one state. Unions with inter-state affiliations could overcome that limit by extending their disputes. But the capacity of the federal tribunal to hear parties was also finite, and the

High Court, as interpreters of the Constitution, restrained its action. An award bound only the parties to the specific dispute, and could not be made a common rule. Sometimes it was practicable with the aid of the six Australian directories to cite every employer in every state as a respondent; but this was at all times costly. For fourteen years (1906 to 1920) it was held by the High Court that the Commonwealth Arbitration power did not extend to fixing the wages and conditions of employees on the railways and other industrial activities owned by the state (i.e. provincial) governments. These, thought the majority of the High Court Justices, were state instrumentalities. To control them, it was then held, would be inconsistent with the freedom and financial responsibility of the states.[1] Awkward situations arose, too, from the overlapping of state and federal jurisdictions and the zeal of employees to make the rival courts compete to be fair and reasonable.

Four times federal ministries have appealed to the nation to confirm by popular vote constitutional amendments designed to give the Commonwealth more control over industry. The reasons for the repeated rejection of such proposals, though made by governments of all the political colours, are matters for political rather than economic history. The fact of rejection has made the process of re-shaping wage-standards to the ideal of fairness and reason a complex and litigious business. Yet both the process and the ideal have grown in strength.

At the time of its promulgation the Harvester wage of 42s. was a bold step forward. Its general adoption promised relative plenty to those who had come through great tribulation. In 1907 unskilled men in regular employment were getting, on an average, 33s. a week. Some wages boards had fixed 30s. a week as the minimum.

---

[1] An article in the *Round Table*, vol. II, pp. 358 *et seq.*, written in 1911, indicates that the reversal of decisions restraining the federal control of industry was expected almost as soon as those decisions were given.

Carters and drivers were getting 25s. for a week of 56 hours. The advance was consolidated between 1907 and 1914 by two out-works of federal and state regulation. One was the inclusion in the awards of grades higher than the unskilled day labourer. The other was the adjustment of the wages legally awarded so that they should be fixed real wages, not mere nominal wages stated in a money whose value was falling.

The Victorian boards, set up as a means to prevent sweating, were originally confined to the tasks of defining the minimum wage and conditions of apprenticeship. But the power to fix wages implied power to fix overtime rates and so by further implication the length of the working day. Their determinations, nevertheless, were of the baldest simplicity. The Arbitration Courts, interpreting more boldly their mission to settle disputes, felt impelled to lay down not only the "basic wage", as "a wage below which employers ought to be forbidden by the State to employ its citizens who are labourers",[1] but also to safeguard the advantages of the skilled men by awarding "secondary wages" or margins for skill. The fear of discontent was held to justify awards of the same basic wage in different industries, on the ground that unequal wages were "anomalies over which men brood". That extended it laterally to labourers in all industries. In other awards that fear did not prevent the grant of generous margins to machinists of high specialization "however much specialization tends to monotony, to industrial discontent". This set up a competition for margins. The conception of the margin for skill was joined with that of "just minimum time wages" in finding a fair and reasonable piece-rate for shearers. "Having found that the shearer should, as a 'skilled worker', get a net wage of £3 per week for the time of his expedition to the sheep stations to shear, and that a rate of 24s. per hundred sheep would give this net result, the Court fixed 24s. per hundred

[1] Higgins, J., *Meat Industry Employees' Case*, 1916, 10 C.A.R. pp. 482–4.

as the minimum piece-rate. Allowances had to be made for days of travelling and waiting, expenses en route, cost of mess, and combs and cutters ".[1]

The threat of industrial discontent was a trump card in this process of extending the sway of judicial arbitration over all wages, conditions and hours of labour. At times the second President resisted the finer drawn distinctions by which union advocates claimed secondary wages for "skilled labourers" or for the handling of special cargoes by wharf-lumpers.[2] But the dripping of water wears away the hardest stone and, whatever propagandists may cry from the house tops, they know full well that arbitration judges' hearts are not of stone. Concessions once made are with difficulty reviewed, even when anomalies arise. Unpopular awards have been withdrawn more than once "for the sake of industrial peace", under threat or actual pressure of strikes.[3]

The Arbitration Courts have been led on, pushed on, and drawn into an increasingly elaborate rule over industry very widely defined. Men may be expected to discover and brood over anomalies when benevolent justice may thus be moved to essay their correction. But industry and commerce are very complicated, and one may in recent years mark a weariness in the economic Titans of the Court. Surely, they plead, margins for skill are fit matters for settlement by masters and men according to changing

[1] H. B. Higgins, *A New Province for Law and Order*, p. 14, and 5 *C.A.R.* p. 48. The Shearers' awards have greatly raised the standards of accommodation at the wool-sheds and "men's huts" on the stations.

[2] See G. Anderson, *Fixation of Wages*, pp. 322–7, 359. In 1914 Mr Justice Higgins was led to remark in a Waterside Workers' Case: "The grounds on which special rates are claimed seem to be as numerous and varied as the well-known excuses for drinking beer....The union now claims a list of some 30 special cargoes and in this are included case-oil, log-timber, pig-iron and even ballast".

[3] See G. Anderson, *op. cit.* pp. 450–64, and cf. pp. 476–80. On p. 457 the learned author writes: "The position in regard to the adoption of an extended system of payment by results in Australia is worse today than it was before Judge Beeby's award, for there has been a trial of strength between the unions and the Court, and the unions have won". Cf. Higgins, J., on p. 472.

needs, and might not some mechanics be paid for what they do? The unions frown on all this.

Awards not only became more inclusive, but as Mr Justice Higgins warmed to his life-work they took on a scientific method of remaining the same. A wage which was intended to cover a labourer's household needs could not do so if it remained unchanged while prices rose. Until 1912 no exact measurement of the rise in prices was ready to the Court's hand, but in that year the Commonwealth Statistician, Mr (afterwards Sir) G. H. Knibbs, put forth "certain curious and interesting figures, the result of much valuable research and compilation".[1] These were index-numbers designed to measure the purchasing power of money over a composite unit of commodities, derived from the aggregate expenditure of Australians on certain household necessaries. From 1913 the Federal Court has made use of the index-numbers in finding, by rule of three, the "Harvester wage equivalent", i.e. the sum of money capable of purchasing at current prices what 42s. purchased in 1907.[2]

Thus through all the vicissitudes of war and post-war prices, those who drew the basic wage were secure of their real wages, of the normal needs of the average employee regarded as a human being, so far as the Harvester judgment covered those needs. It may be hard to regard that average as divine, but it has certainly been placed, so far as laws can do it, upon a pedestal of privilege. When prices were rising rapidly after the war, the third President added 3s. a week to the "Harvester equivalent" in order, as he said, "to secure at least to the workers the living

[1] The description is Mr Justice Higgins' first reference to them. See *Labour Report of the Bureau of Statistics*, no. 1 (1912), "Prices, Price Indexes and Cost of Living in Australia" as to the "weighting" of the standard articles of consumption included. In G. Anderson, *op. cit.* p. 229, may be found an account of the precautions to ensure their accuracy, by C. H. Wickens.

[2] After April 1923 the Court made a regular practice of inserting in awards a clause providing for quarterly adjustments in accordance with the "cost-of-living index-numbers".

wage adopted by the Court, whatever increase in the cost of living there may be in any quarter". This shock-absorber, known as "Powers' Three Shillings", has been retained in almost all subsequent awards, both when prices were falling and when they were rising.

Yet the wage-earners have been beset by doubts whether the "Harvester equivalent" really did provide for the normal needs of the average employee. When during the war clothing prices were rising more rapidly than those of foodstuffs and rents, the complaint arose that the aggregate expenditure on which the Commonwealth Statistician based his index-numbers did not include clothing. Under war conditions the effect was that Knibbs' index-numbers understated the change in the purchasing power of money. Their use assumed that the prices of items omitted were varying *pari passu* with those of the items included. By the time the ingenious officials in the Bureau of Statistics had provided index-numbers based on total household expenditure, including clothing and miscellaneous items, the relative levels had altered. The inclusion of clothing was then found to result in index-numbers substantially lower than those calculated on the original basis.[1] Prices of clothing in Sydney, according to the Bureau, increased only 24 per cent. between 1914 and 1927. Those of food, groceries and housing had gone up by 53 per cent. Under these circumstances the doubts of union advocates as to the adequacy of Sir George Knibbs' original indices were waived. Their clients had been at some disadvantage while clothing prices ruled higher, but since 1921 they had made greater gains by the Court's continued use of the index-numbers based on food, groceries and housing only. And these, after all, are the *normal* needs of the average employee.

Critics delving for a richer content in the doctrine of the sacrosanct wage next turned their attention to Mr

---

[1] *Commonwealth Year Book*, no. 20 (1927), ch. XIII, especially pp. 520–1. But cf. J. L. K. Gifford, *Economic Statistics for Arbitration Courts*, pp. 24 *et seq.*

Justice Higgins' original finding. Did it in very truth cover the needs of a family of five persons? "Treating marriage as the usual fate of adult men", wrote the learned President in 1915, "a wage which does not allow of the matrimonial condition and the maintenance of about five persons in a home would not be treated as a living wage". It was not hard to show, however, that the Harvester judgment of 1907 had been based on very meagre evidence furnished by nine housewives and a few tradesmen. It had embodied as much the wages policy of the best employers as "the normal needs" of the average working-class family. To allay these new doubts, Mr W. M. Hughes, protesting that it had been settled "long ago" that such a basic wage should be paid as would enable a man to marry and rear a family under decent, wholesome conditions, appointed in December 1919 a Royal Commission on the Basic Wage. It consisted of representatives of employers and employees and was asked to determine the "ordinary expenditure of a household of five", its cost, and how the basic wage should be automatically adjusted to changes in that cost.

The Commission took much evidence. It made out "indicator lists" of food adequate to the most scientific dietetic scale, of clothing good in wearing quality and of sound workmanship. It decided that a five-roomed house, in sound tenantable condition, not cramped as to allotment, in decent surroundings and provided with bath, copper and tubs, set in, was the "fair thing" for a man on the basic wage. Then it totted up the prices and found that for such requirements the basic wage in Sydney, November 1920, ought to be £5. 17s., and in other capitals similar amounts ranging down to £5. 6s. 3d. in Brisbane. The "Harvester equivalent" on which Federal and State minima were directly and indirectly based was then £4. 13s. in Sydney, Melbourne and Hobart, £4. 9s. 6d. in Adelaide and £4. 0s. 6d. in Brisbane and Perth. The Chairman of the Commission himself urged that the adoption of its findings would ruin any industries manufacturing for export, and by raising the costs of Australia's primary industries would set up a formidable drawback to their development, perhaps to their continuance. He regarded the findings as a *reductio ad absurdum* of the family wage, based on the needs of a man, wife and three dependent children. The payment of such wages to all adult male workers would provide for 2,100,000 non-existent children and nearly half a million non-existent wives. He made the announcement of the Commission's findings an opening for propaganda in favour of wages based on the needs of man and wife only, and of a plan of family endowment, financed by a levy on industry.[1]

Out of a *furore* of discussion there became perceptible the doubts of consumers about the whole dogma of sacrosanct minima; and all who buy Australian products at home or abroad are consumers. Was there not need of evidence as to the effects of such fixed wage-standards on demands for goods and therefore on demands for labour? Could increased wages be passed on indefinitely? What of the industries which sold their goods at the prices ruling in competitive markets? Should not evidence be gathered of the ability of industries to pay wages? From Queensland, the hotbed of Australian political ideas, came a suggestion in 1925 that wages should vary with the productivity of industry, and that an index of the general capacity of industry to pay might be compounded in each September from changes in income per head, past production per head and estimated future production per head.[2] Unluckily the President responsible for the suggestion died suddenly before the Commission's report had been con-

---

[1] For Australian developments along these lines see *Report of Royal Commission on Child Endowment or Family Allowances*, 1929, especially pp. 35 *et seq.* No industrial court prescribed the basic wage as defined by the Piddington Commission, but cf. J. L. K. Gifford, *op. cit.* p. 44.

[2] *Report of Economic Commission on the Queensland Basic Wage*, 1925, pp. 66–70. A criticism of the proposed index as a guide to capacity to pay wages is ably set forth by J. L. K. Gifford, *op. cit.* pp. 46 *et seq.*

sidered by the Queensland Court. Changes calculated by
rule of thumb have been made in the wages awarded to
workers in industries below and above average prosperity;
but no statistical index of capacity to pay has yet been
adopted.

Even this rule of thumb recognition, however, was a
breach in the rampart of sacrosanctity. In 1909, Mr Justice
Higgins ruled that the Federal Court could not prescribe
a lower rate in order to keep an unprofitable mine going.
"If shareholders are willing to stake their own money
on a speculation, they should not stake part of the employee's proper wage also." The propriety of a wage the
legal award of which would abolish their jobs was not
plain to the copper-miners at Wallaroo and Moonta in
South Australia in 1921. They entered into an industrial
agreement to work, while the market for copper was low,
for less than the basic wage and the usual margins. This
agreement the Federal Court somewhat reluctantly recognized. *Fiat justitia* is a high doctrine. The danger involved
is that wage-fixing tribunals may raise their conception of
justice more rapidly than the price which can be allotted
from the joint product of the industry to the contributors
of routine service. Prices, even of routine and skilled
manual service, are ultimately encouragements or dis-
couragements to persistence in that service. If sacrosanctity
and increase of wages go hand in hand, more may be
attracted into the callings so blessed than can be found
regular employment in them. Fluctuating wages have a
social function to perform in minimizing unemployment
and sending labour to Sydney or the bush.[1]

[1] Cf. F. C. Benham, *Prosperity of Australia*, pp. 209-10, and A. C. Pigou,
Principles and Methods of Industrial Peace (1905), *passim.*

CHAPTER XXII

Strength and Protection

THE three decades of the Commonwealth have witnessed a remarkable advance by the Australian pastoral and farming industries in the teeth of natural and imposed handicaps. In 1901 primary products from the mines, stations, farms and forests made up 93·8 per cent. of exports worth £49,696,000. In the decade ending June 1927, though the mines' quota had fallen away, pasture and agriculture had grown so strongly that the percentage of primary products among Australian visible exports had risen to 95·51, in a total value averaging £125,622,000 per annum. Manufactures, which in 1901 contributed 6 per cent. of the exports, provided barely 4½ per cent. in the decade 1917–1927. A full third of Australia's recorded production is exported—a proportion exceeded by few countries[1]—and the part of the primary industries in buying Australia's share in the products of the world has continued to increase.

The century dawned on a land seared by the worst and widest drought the white man has seen. In New South Wales, after six years of abundant rainfall from 1889 to 1894, eight successive years of subnormal rainfall culminated in 1902 with a Sahara year. The mean rainfall for the whole state fell below 11·91 inches. That at Balranald for the first eleven months was 3·65 inches, at Booligal 2·73, and at Bourke, from January 1 to October 31, 2·44 inches. The colony's flocks, usually about half

[1] Great Britain exports less than 30 per cent. of her production, the United States of America less than 10 per cent.

the Australian total, shrank from 57,000,000 in 1894 to 26,560,000 in 1902. That was "The Great Drought".

Queensland, the region of summer rains, fared little better. The onset was milder, 1895 and 1896 being years of average rains in most districts though ending badly in the West. Ninety-seven was a bad year and though 1898 was better, there followed four years of despair. When the grasses were eaten and the saltbush was leafless, the best of the sheep and cattle could only be kept alive by cutting "the mulga". At the sound of an axe the poor skeletons would come running from every direction. "By the middle of 1899 trains were running day and night, transferring nearly a million sheep from the great stations beyond Winton to the Eastern Tablelands and the coast, on whose coarse unsatisfying grasses no sheep had been kept since the early sixties".[1] The men out West hung on, watching clouds gather, drop a thin shower and vanish in the night. Months passed; overdrafts mounted. Though the experienced sold early or knocked on the head all but their breeding ewes and stud stock, in such a drought heavy purchases of fodder and costly bores to deep artesian water were imperative to keep even the remnant alive. "What a lot of money these pastoralists must make to be able to afford such things!" said the bush publican to the teamsters. Months dragged out into years. In 1902 the mean rainfall for the state—coast and tablelands thrown in—was 12·63 inches. Hard frosts cut down the sugar cane even in the far north. Out West, sheep and cattle, to save which mortgages had been piled up for years, perished by the hundred thousand. The live stock in Queensland had numbered over twenty-seven million in 1894. In 1902 there were barely ten million.[2]

---

[1] M. M. Bennett, *Christison of Lammermoor*, pp. 222–3.

[2] *Production Statistics, Bulletin*, no. 20, pp. 209–11. In 1894 Queensland depastured 19,587,000 sheep, 7,000,000 cattle and 444,000 horses. In 1902 there were 7,213,000 sheep, 2,540,000 cattle and 399,000 horses. For a graph of the annual rainfalls see *Rainfall Observations in Queensland*, by H. A. Hunt (1914), p. 12.

Not even Victoria, slowly convalescent from her financial fever, was spared. Of the eight years 1895 to 1902 only one, 1900, touched the colony's average rainfall and 1902 was the driest year on record. In "the cabbage garden", as envious old John Robertson called it, the tally of sheep fell from 13,180,000 in 1894 to 10,841,000 in 1900 and 10,167,000 in 1904—the only years in which Victoria felt that she could afford to collect stock statistics. In South Australia, nine years, 1894 to 1902 inclusive, each saw less than ten inches for the province as a whole, though the first was a good year in the agricultural belt east of Spencer's Gulf.[1] Flocks on South Australian farms and stations decreased from 7,152,000 in 1892 to 4,880,000 in 1902, cattle from 411,000 to 213,000 and horses from 186,000 to 164,000.

In Western Australia, old prospectors, who in those "dry 'nineties" made forced marches across what is now the Wheat Belt, find it hard to believe that the changed scene will last. Where many that they knew died of thirst and all walked in fear of it, there are now permanent water supplies, and every winter fields of waving wheat. Long rakes of trucks laden with grain pass, all summer through and most of winter, along railways to the coast. Even settlers who have lived through both the drought and the wheat-boom shake their heads. They saw the native fauna driven away by the drought between 1894 and 1902.[2] Were those dry years a startling abnormality? The native game have mostly returned to their old haunts, but will the dry cycle come again too?

The Great Drought taught the women of "the back blocks" to listen for that sweetest harmony "the orchestra of rain, the crashing roar on the iron roof, the deeper roar from the creek, the music of bull-frogs". The hatchet-

---

[1] For graphs and detailed statistics see H. A. Hunt, *Rainfall Observations in South Australia* (1918), pp. 12 *et seq.*

[2] See an article "Seasons since 1860", by Bruce Leake, *Western Mail*, Perth, W.A. 5 July 1928, p. 42. See also the comments thereon by G. L. Sutton and E. B. Curlewis.

faced menfolk who saw it through are not poetic folk, but they respond surprisingly to Dorothea Mackellar's

> Core of my heart, my country!
> Her pitiless blue sky
> When, sick at heart, around us
> We see the cattle die—
> But then the grey clouds gather
> And we can bless again
> The drumming of an army,
> The steady soaking rain.

The decades that followed seemed by comparison a run of exceptionally good seasons broken only by one bad relapse, 1914. That impression is not, however, supported by the official rainfall records. A comparison of the "sheep map" of Australia[1] with the rain maps from 1908 to 1928 reveals a four years' drought from 1912 to 1915 against which large areas of dense sheep-holding had to provide, and seven years of widespread deficiency of rainfall between 1918 and 1929. Drought after all is only a question of degree in the back country. It is the harsh master who has taught the pastoralists to keep Australia's fame for fine wool by a ceaseless culling of their flocks. "If you want to grow the best merino wool in the world", wrote an old squatter in 1883, "you must stop in this dry land which is carefully cultivated by Nature with rotation of crops and allowed to lie fallow periodically—that means a drought. If you had no droughts you would not have the best wool in the world and our sheep would be continually in the hospital as they are in New Zealand, where the merino sheep does no good. All life is a gamble and I like to gamble with Nature, though I know that she always has an ace up her sleeve and can ruin me when she likes".[2]

Sheep and wool statistics have been eloquent of the better selection and management of flocks. In this mature

[1] *C.Y.B.* no. 20, p. 627. Cf. graph on p. 625.
[2] Barton, *Reminiscences of an Australian Pioneer*, p. 269.

industry there has been little extension to new areas, save in Western Australia. Nor did the number of sheep in Australia again reach the 1891 total of 106 millions until 1928. But sub-division and better watering of paddocks from artesian and sub-artesian wells,[1] top-dressing of pastures with superphosphates, the increase of "crossbreds" in mixed farming areas and, above all, the culling of the merino flocks have built up the yield of wool to figures far above those of 1891. Then 106,421,000 sheep gave a clip of 640,752,656 pounds, or about six pounds per sheep. In 1902–3 the wool from 53,675,000 sheep weighed 408,302,146 pounds or seven pounds nine ounces per sheep, a result of selection for survival during the drought. In 1913–14 the clip from 88,947,000 sheep was 771,308,222 pounds and the yield per sheep eight pounds ten ounces, showing that the lessons of the drought had not been forgotten. The improvement has been maintained. In 1921 a total of 723,058,219 pounds was obtained from 86,119,000 sheep, again eight pounds ten ounces from each, and for 1928–9 it is estimated that 950,000,000 pounds came from 106,100,000, a yield of almost nine pounds per sheep.[2] Drought, too, was the headmaster who disciplined the farmers to listen to that quiet scientist, Lowrie, and his advocacy of superphosphate. The farmers on Yorke's Peninsula (S.A.) were first to give heed, as they had been first with mechanical improvements. Their example gave permanence to wheat farming in its old homes and extended its range inland. Two decades later the improvement of the pasture-value of farmers' stubbles taught the pastoralists also the lesson of top-dressing. The

[1] See *Commonwealth Year Book*, no. 20 (1927), ch. XXIII.

[2] The above figures are based on the numbers of sheep recorded in the *Commonwealth Bureau's Production Bulletin*, no. 20, p. 211, and the estimates of the quantity and value of the Australian production of wool set out in the accompanying table, for which the author is indebted to the Commonwealth Statistician, Mr C. H. Wickens. In fairness to him it must be used as a compilation of doubtful accuracy. The deductions made from the two tables in the text are still more doubtful. All comparisons of wool yield are vitiated by the changes in the practice of creek-washing, exporting in

new methods have built up a wheat export industry which under other auspices may well outgrow the pastoral industry in financial weight and international repute.

The Northern Mallee in Victoria, the Pinnaroo country corresponding to it over the South Australian border, a long strip in New South Wales to the west of "Coghlan's Line"[1] and the whole Western Australian Wheat Belt outside the Avon and Victoria Districts have been occupied for wheat-growing since Farrer bred Federation and Lowrie won credence about superphosphate. But the increase of yield won by improved methods in the older farming districts is at least as significant as these extensions inland. A graph prepared by Dr A. E. V. Richardson shows the relation between the district average yield of wheat and the rain that fell on the growing crops in the Victorian Wimmera from 1892 to 1928.[2] The drought years 1902 and 1914 significantly divide the period into three phases. In the seasons before 1902 each inch of rain which fell in the growing season, April to October, gave the farmer 0·59 of a bushel, on the district average. Between 1902 and 1911 an inch on the seed-bed meant nearly a bushel—0·95 to be precise—and in the decade 1912 to 1921 it brought forth almost a bushel and a half of better grain (1·43 bushels). Omitting the drought year 1914, when the rain on the crop was less than four inches, the return per inch of rain in the Wimmera district was 1·66 bushels for the other nine years in the 1912–1921 decade. The best farmers and the students at Longerenong College win

the grease, scouring, etc. and by the varying periods between shearing, but the general fact of increasing yield per sheep is plain in the period under review.

[1] See the final map in H. A. Hunt, *Rainfall Observations in New South Wales* (1916), and compare this line with the "western line of profitable wheat-growing" on the map as frontispiece of the *N.S.W. Year Book* of 1927–8.

[2] *Victorian Journal of Agriculture*, 1925, p. 161. The whole article is an excellent résumé of the progress in agricultural practice made by a district now noted for its high standards. Dr Richardson was formerly Agricultural Superintendent in Victoria, and thereafter Director of the Waite Agricultural Research Institute of Adelaide, in his native South Australia. The graph shown herewith has been continued down to 1928 by him.

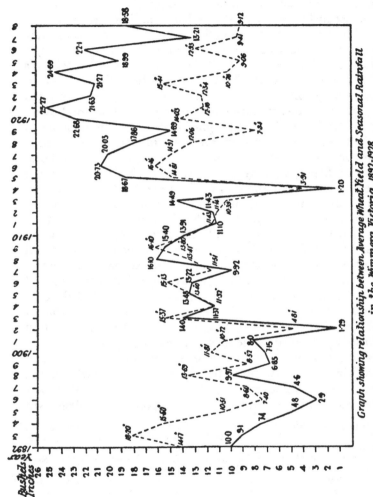

Graph showing relationship between Average Wheat Yield and Seasonal Rainfall
in the Wimmera, Victoria, 1892-1928

Average Yield in bushels per acre thus ——   Seasonal Rainfall (April-October) thus ------

Estimated production of wool—Australia 1879—1928-9

Year	Number of sheep	Quantity in lb.	Value (£)
1879	53,896,345	321,893,655	12,782,264
1880	62,184,252	365,767,269	15,398,171
1	65,092,719	329,200,266	13,405,820
2	67,825,571	355,545,193	14,482,466
3	69,985,297	429,462,805	18,245,403
4	61,570,138	401,040,722	17,177,301
5	67,491,976	387,603,545	13,778,492
6	69,568,993	389,977,852	13,202,050
7	80,510,360	452,322,243	15,681,680
8	80,793,548	464,352,372	15,899,287
9	85,809,405	508,112,532	17,855,353
1890	97,881,221	468,281,600	16,293,789
1	106,421,068	640,752,656	20,648,816
2	103,272,068	644,840,166	19,988,316
3	99,539,889	626,712,559	17,722,234
4	100,411,461	631,908,300	15,926,681
5	90,689,727	623,444,119	16,553,544
6	90,615,847	579,680,037	16,229,889
7	82,653,278	541,017,033	14,409,864
8	79,237,002	538,945,525	15,056,625
9	72,347,509	472,623,278	18,945,013
1900-1	70,602,995	391,401,848	13,348,441
1-2	72,040,211	539,394,377	16,348,000
2-3	53,675,210	408,302,146	13,672,000
3-4	56,932,705	410,388,376	14,959,000
4-5	65,822,918	470,401,503	18,223,000
5-6	74,540,916	516,721,130	21,155,000
6-7	83,687,655	570,733,785	24,111,000
7-8	87,650,263	682,360,564	30,512,000
8-9	88,352,469	647,415,575	24,737,000
9-10	94,453,703	740,249,776	28,830,000
1910-11	98,066,046	787,527,437	30,266,000
11-12	96,886,234	798,390,585	28,846,000
12-13	87,139,184	687,485,825	27,543,000
13-14	88,947,179	771,308,222	30,401,000
14-15	82,491,296	734,826,751	28,766,000
15-16	73,146,460	636,275,674	31,255,000
16-17	80,562,221	636,589,411	41,885,000
17-18	88,863,816	654,443,141	45,076,000
18-19	91,874,362	736,414,694	50,704,000
19-20	79,454,829	762,105,005	52,940,000
1920-21	81,795,727	625,197,486	37,636,000
21-22	86,119,068	723,058,219	39,577,000
22-23	82,700,514	726,683,278	55,608,000
23-24	84,011,048	662,598,085	66,451,000
24-25	93,154,953	776,881,507	81,430,000
25-26	103,563,218	833,738,907	61,633,000
26-27	104,267,101	924,410,553	69,430,000
27-28	99,357,738	888,129,780	75,634,000
28-29	*106,100,000	950,000,000	*69,572,000

* Estimated.

yields far above the district average. The students obtained 3·5 bushels of wheat per inch of seasonal rain during the dry years 1917 to 1921. Private farms have

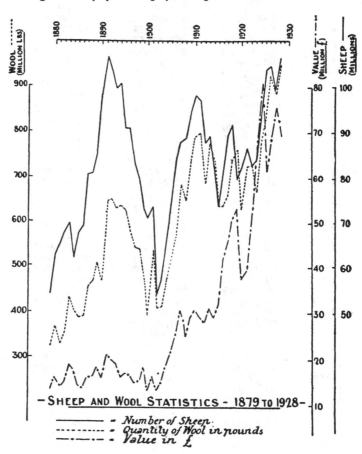

maintained an average of 3·6 bushels per inch. Thus the farmers, like the pastoralists, have accepted the hard facts of drought as a stimulus to skill and courage. Water conservation in the seed-bed supplies the wheat-plant, in the critical months of maximum transpiration, September and October, with abundant sap to turn into grain. Fallowing for fifteen months, late seeding and liberal dressings of water-soluble phosphates give the short-strawed wheats of Farrer and his school their chance to fill heavy ears with plump white wheat, though the north wind rage off the hot interior.

As a direct result the totals of wheat harvested in the Commonwealth and the average yield per acre have strongly advanced. The last year before Federation (1900) saw a record harvest of 48,353,000 bushels from 5,666,000 acres, an average of 8·53 bushels. Before the first decade of the century was over, average yields of more than eleven bushels were usual, and two harvests (1903 and 1909) had yielded over thirteen bushels per acre, a figure unknown since the narrow fields of the mid-'seventies. As prices were on the up-grade, such yields led to bigger acreages under wheat. In 1913 the first nine million acre crop of wheat gave the first hundred million bushel harvest (103,344,000 bushels). After the year of war and drought, 1914, a crop of 179 million bushels was grown (1915) on 12,484,000 acres—an area broadened by the re-seeded failures of 1914. Neither figure was excelled for more than a decade thereafter, but the average yield of 1915 (14·34 bushels) was surpassed in 1920 (16·08 bushels).

The rise of country land values and the eagerness of successful business men to acquire country property may suggest that the net incomes on stations and farms have advanced at least *pari passu* with the expansion of wool and wheat production. This is doubtful. In the land hunger of successful Australians social ambition plays a part, as well as economic calculation; for socially the "hewers of wood and drawers of water" (*vide* any protectionist newspaper) are respected as the most typical Australians and respect themselves in proportion as they remain independent of state subsidies. And by reason of repeated increases in the customs tariff on imports and of other government regulation of trade and prices, costs have risen in the exporting industries to the detriment of net incomes.[1] A recent stocktaking of the effects of protection estimated the burden on Australian prices attributable to such policies at 9 per cent. of the general price-level.[2] But there is no stability or permanently calculable nature in this burden. Its inherent tendency is to grow even when the external price-levels at which exported goods sell are steadily falling. A statistical inquiry at a specific date misses the *vis a tergo* of wage fixation and similar benevolent policies. The continual raising of the tariff and the spread of restrictive schemes designed to secure "sheltered" prices in the Australian market even for exportable goods (see Chapter XXIV) imply a general belief that it does not matter whether the price-level of a country is 9, 10 or 20 per cent. out of line with those of its customers.

Ever since the first federal customs tariff was imposed there has been an unceasing propaganda from the secondary industries for more protection. Latterly the primary industries, one by one, have joined in the chorus. The cause is not mere greed; it is raised costs—raised by policies intended to benefit specific groups through their charges to others. Coal is the most edifying example of a primary industry turned beggar. "Once an export industry, the costs of production rose till it ceased to export and became a sheltered industry—sheltered by the high cost of transport. Finally costs have risen until this shelter became insufficient and it is now (1929) beginning to be exposed to the competition of imports."[3] The in-

[1] In *Production Statistics Bulletin*, no. 20, p. 183, may be found an interesting comparison of the increases in prices of primary and manufactured products. Without commenting on the statistical bases of the index-numbers (p. 173), it may be noted that the greater relative rise for manufactured goods, almost entirely consumed locally, suggests rising levels of cost in exporting industries.

[2] *The Australian Tariff: An Economic Enquiry* (1929), p. 68.

[3] *Loc. Cit.* p. 26.

creased costs laid on Australian industries by such policies are more deadly than those of drought. These have their compensations when the drought ends, but since federation there has been no breaking of the tariff.

A customs and excise tariff capable of raising considerable revenue was made necessary to the young Commonwealth by the Braddon Clause in the Constitution (No. 87), requiring the return to the state governments of three-fourths of the net revenue from the duties. To give the federal authorities the two millions they required, a tariff producing eight millions was indicated. Should it incidentally give Australian manufacturers such advantages as they had enjoyed under the Victorian, Queensland and other tariffs? At the first federal elections a small majority in the House of Representatives, the chamber to which the Cabinet was responsible, was zealous to pursue this aim of protection, but in the Senate the advocates of a purely revenue tariff were about as numerous as the protectionists. The Prime Minister, Edmund Barton, though inclined to restrain the ardour of C. C. Kingston, Minister for Customs, had long been allied with the protectionists in New South Wales. A tariff was proposed which, in defence of established industries, "must necessarily operate protectively as well as for the production of revenue". The tariff which emerged in 1902 was a compromise in whose schedules protection reached a degree most disappointing to the insatiable Syme and his henchmen.

The Labour Party, though holding the balance between Barton's and Reid's followers in the Representatives, came mainly from New South Wales constituencies and had "sunk the fiscal issue", i.e. left its members free to vote on tariff items untrammelled by decisions in caucus. Not unmindful of the sting in George Reid's election cry, "Revenue without concession to private and class interests", many Labour men had helped to limit the duties to a range of from 5 to 25 per cent., and to preserve a long free list.[1] But Victorian protectionists were not slow to size up this political situation. They evolved a "New Protection" policy calculated to make the workers partners on the ground floor in the benefits of protection. They promised to "protect" the consumer too.

A parliamentary Royal Commission, appointed in 1904 to examine the workings of the new tariff, recommended in 1907 substantial increases in many duties, but added "that where protective duties are substantially increased, provision should be made to secure payment of reasonable wages to persons engaged in the industries benefited". Moreover, should the Minister certify that the retail selling prices of protected goods had been unfairly increased, the Governor-General on an address from both Houses might by proclamation suspend the increased duties on imports.[2] These novel proposals were accompanied by a review of the piecemeal and varying care for labour afforded by state wages boards and industrial courts in Victoria, New South Wales, Western and South Australia and a note of the entire absence of such bodies in Queensland and Tasmania. The Commissioners were anxious to apply to all Australia, irrespective of state and constitutional limitations, an idea which Deakin, as Barton's successor in the Prime Ministership, had embodied in the Excise (Harvesters) Act during the preceding year.

This Act imposed on various Australian agricultural implements excise duties amounting to half the customs duties, but the duties were made variable with the behaviour of the Australian manufacturer, which was evidently regarded as a matter of free-will on his part. If he were found to be "taking advantage" of the tariff and charging prices above those declared by the Act to be "the fair thing", the Government took power to reduce the customs duties by executive action. So the farmer would be "protected".

---

[1] For the tariff schedule see *Commonwealth Statutes*, no. 14 of 1902, vol. 1, p. 300.

[2] *Progress Report*, no. 50, pp. 4–5, 2nd session, 1907.

The excise duties in turn might be remitted if Parliament or an approved industrial tribunal certified that a given manufacturer was paying fair and reasonable wages to his employees. The leading manufacturer of these implements was Hugh Victor McKay. A farmer's son, he had as a stripling put together, from old stripper and winnower parts eked out by cut-up "tins", the first "stripper-harvester", and through many a struggle had built up, first at Ballarat and afterwards at Braybrook Junction near Melbourne, a thriving industry making his "Sunshine" harvesters and other labour-saving machines. Mr Justice Higgins, in the famous Harvester judgment, refused him a certificate that the wages and conditions obtaining in the Sunshine works were "fair and reasonable". McKay thereupon refused to pay the excise duty. Had not those wages maintained in employment throughout the long Victorian depression a growing body of workers at standards regarded by their fellows with envy? He was sued by the Commonwealth before the High Court. That Court, however, by a majority judgment of three justices to two, held the Excise Act to be invalid. The Constitution had granted power to the Federal Parliament to levy excises in order to obtain revenue. This was an Act seeking to regulate labour conditions and incidentally discriminating between states and parts of states. The New Protection, with its complicated rewards and penalties by which protected employers were to be led and pushed into treating well both wage-earners and farmers, seemed to have burst like a bubble. Yet the idea had turned the political mill for the nonce and had enlisted the Labour Party to work for high and higher tariffs.

As shown in the preceding chapter, the Harvester judgment at once became the basis of an active regulation of wages and conditions by both state and federal tribunals. Labour, having found where its interests lay, acquiesced in extensions of protection by tariff revisions in 1908–11,

1914, 1921 and 1926. The tariff of 1908–11 imposed rates nearly double those of 1902 and cut down the free list. At Deakin's insistence a 5 per cent. preference to British goods was allowed in items affecting a large proportion of Australian imports from Britain. This gesture of restraint in raising the impediments to British trade with Australian customers was made 10 per cent. when in 1914, 1920, and 1925 the tariff was put higher still.[1]

The New Protection was but the first of a series of outworks of "economic statesmanship". Its importance, at first, lay mainly in the eager drive of self-interest with which it inspired the Labour Party's adherents, a drive which in 1910 placed the party in power over the Commonwealth. The leading brain of the second Fisher Government—first Labour Cabinet to enjoy the support of a safe majority—was William Morris Hughes, formerly a free-trade Labourite. As the new protection policy worked itself out in the wages tribunals, his eager brain saw in the exceptional prosperity of the decade 1910 to 1921 opportunities to put in practice several ambitious policies matured by Labour in the days and school of Deakin. In addition to an important share in passing the tariff schedules of 1914 and 1920, Mr Hughes brought into operation an exclusion from the Australian coastal trade of all vessels, whether British or foreign, not observing Australian conditions and wages-awards for seamen. Simultaneously he purchased and expanded a government line of ocean-going steamers. In these further steps towards a closed economic system the aspect of imperialism, though still proclaimed, was difficult to maintain.

Mr Hughes had first made his political mark as organiser of the waterside workers and seamen in the old Lang division of Sydney. It was but to be expected that he should press on the federal legislature a plan for securing

---

[1] For the later schedules see *Commonwealth Statutes*, no. 25 of 1921, vol. XIX, p. 76, and no. 26 of 1926, vol. XXIV, p. 78.

by law "fair and reasonable" wages and conditions for
workers on the Australian coastal steamers. It was not
his own plan. A Navigation Bill had been drafted in 1902
by a Customs official, Dr H. N. P. Wollaston, following the
lines of a measure designed to control Sir James Mills and
his Union Steamship Company of New Zealand. It had
a stormy legislative history. Kingston having resigned
over the Conciliation and Arbitration Bill, the Navigation
Bill was referred to a Royal Commission and the mantle fell
on W. M. Hughes as its chairman.

The Commission presented a majority report in 1906
adorned with much rhetoric about "a numerous and well-
manned mercantile marine—the only safeguard for our
Empire—sufficient to transport our products in time of
peace and to assist in guarding our shores in time of war....
We shall best serve imperial interests", wrote the majority,
waving the flag of Empire against the critics of restriction,
"by setting an example which the other members of the
Empire may be inspired to follow, in providing for the
defence of the Commonwealth by employing our own
citizens on our own ships". But that policy, tried and
let slip again and again by Britain between 1381 and 1849[1],
signally failed to inspire "the other members of the
Empire" when presented at an Imperial Conference on
Merchant Shipping Laws in 1907. It continued as a
piece on the Australian legislative chess-board during
five sessions 1907, 1908, 1910, 1911 and 1912 and was at
last enacted at the bidding of the Second Fisher Ministry
in 1912.

The debates had discovered no way round the contention
of the Minority Commissioners of 1904, that the proposed
coastal clauses, excluding from the Australian coastal trade
overseas vessels which did not observe Australian wages,
hours, rules of manning and accommodation, would restrict transport facilities and enhance the monopoly powers

---

[1] See G. F. Bastable, *Commerce of Nations* (ninth edition), pp. 34, 53,
165.

o

of the associated inter-state shipping companies.[1] It was
an evasion to say that Australian trade was growing so
fast that whatever was done would still leave a trade
profitable enough to attract "a sufficient fleet of ships to
meet all the reasonable requirements of Australian producers". Tramp steamers, the adjusting factor in the
supply of ocean transport, go where they are most likely
to fill empty space on every "leg" of their voyage.[2] Any
limitation of that likelihood forces the charging, on balance,
of a higher average level of freights.

The Bill, even when passed, was reserved for the Royal
assent as one affecting Imperial interests. War had broken
out before that assent had been received. The proclamation of the "coastal clauses", a step inevitably delayed by
the necessity of giving ship-owners notice of the need of
structural alterations in their vessels, was postponed until
after the war at the request of the British Government.

War-time brought, after a pause in 1914, an increased
sense of secure prosperity. Isolation looked like security,
and a moderate inflation like sound, though easy, monetary
conditions. A prospering countryside after the bumper
seasons of 1915 and 1916, and customers for manufactures
in New Zealand, Java, South Africa and the Islands who
were very ready to pay prices which had risen less than

[1] When a witness who knew the ways of the Associated Steamship
Companies from within (H. McLennan, Melbourne Manager for J. and
A. Brown, Newcastle Colliery Proprietors, and formerly a director in the
shipping firm of Howard Smith, Ltd.) explained to the Navigation Bill
Commission the workings of the deferred rebate system and the monopoly
it had created in the coastal cargo trade (*Comm. P.P.* session 1906, vol. III,
p. 951, and cf. p. 949, questions 24300 and 24322), the Majority Commissioners thought the rebate system "open to grave abuse" and recommended the "introduction of legislation making it illegal". But a system
that built up a "fighting fund" of accrued bonuses amounting to £60,000
in the shipowners' custody, automatically available for use against competitors as their intrusion became serious, was not to be abolished by a wave
of the law-givers' wand, nor indeed otherwise, until its work was done.

[2] "The element of greatest influence in the competition for ocean shipping
between ports is the so-called 'load-factor', i.e. the possibility of a ship
bringing cargo to a port and at the same time getting another cargo out."
Sir George Buchanan, *Transport in Australia*, vol. I, p. 16; *Comm. P.P.*
1926–8, vol. V, p. 106.

those of Europe and America, led men to forget the cost of raising "fair and reasonable" conditions to whatever level the heart of man desired. Increased customs duties went almost unnoticed. Under ever-widening "awards" manufacturers were led to share the good times with the workers in shorter hours and better wages. The times emboldened Mr Hughes, Prime Minister after October 1915, to extend the Australian system to the high seas by means more direct than even the New Protection and the much-postponed Navigation Act. Again he worked upon a plan long conned and argued. As early as 1906 a Federal Royal Commission on Ocean Shipping had reported that "as a matter of principle the sea carriage of goods should be as much in the hands of the state as land carriage now is".[1]

In those days of Socialist enthusiasm, little restrained by the responsibilities of office, it was almost inevitable that a Commission drawn largely from the Labour Party should turn from arguments about the mail subsidy and poundage rates to "the larger question of establishing a line of mail steamers under the direct control of the Commonwealth Government".[2] On such a government line both freights and wages would register the Socialist government's bidding. On four grounds the Commissioners had advocated the building and operation of a National Fleet of mail-steamers. It could be cheaply financed by an internal loan of about three millions on which the Government need pay no more than 3 per cent. An up-to-date fleet of eight vessels would show the way to private enterprize just as the government railways did in Australia. Though it could be just as economically operated, except as regards wages, as any private company's ships, the Government line would not require to show any profit. And as to wages, "the payment of deep sea wages on the

[1] *Comm. P.P.* session 1905, vol. III, p. 1050. *Report of Royal Commission on Ocean Shipping Service.*
[2] *Loc. cit.* pp. 1041–2.

Australian scale would undoubtedly enable the national ships to obtain the pick of all ranks of seamen engaged in the oversea trade".

Early in 1916, though Australian manufacturers were enjoying more spacious markets by reason of Britain's preoccupation with war, it became evident that for want of shipping the bumper wheat harvest of 1915 would rot on Australian wharves and sidings. In that event the farming population, customers essential to the Australian home-market, would be ruined. Mr Hughes, urging in England the pooling for the common cause of all resources of shipping foodstuffs and men, and fearful that the far-distant Australian contribution to the pool would be neglected, suddenly felt impelled to buy a fleet of fifteen tramp steamers. They were not new, nor were they the right size for the long voyage. It would have taken them seven or eight years to shift the accumulated wheat. But they proved useful pawns in the negotiations with Britain for its sale and transport. They could be used where they were suitable, and so set other tonnage free to shift the wheat. This gesture of impatience or independence did its work. The British Government bought and transported the wheat, and Mr Hughes' Strath line, re-christened "Australs", earned big freights carrying petrol from American ports to Australia and on other relatively safe routes. Before the war was over they had more than paid for themselves. They cost originally £2,052,000 and by 1921, on Mr Hughes' computation, they had made a profit of £2,993,245. Perhaps, as a capable critic suggested,[1] the Prime Minister had not allowed for depreciation during those years of hard driving, but in company with nearly a score of interned German vessels the Commonwealth Line had made paper profits of over seven millions.

[1] S. M. Bruce, *Comm. P. Debates*, 29 November 1921, vol. xcviii, pp. 13, 339. But the critic added, "it is impossible either for an accountant or an ordinary intelligent layman to get at the position from the statements as they have appeared in the Budget papers from year to year".

When the war ended, Mr Hughes was no longer at the head of the Australian Labour Party, but he had not forgotten his Kaiser-like enthusiasm for a fleet on the ocean flying the Australian flag and observing the Australian seamen's log of wages and conditions. He was not allowed to forget it. As hostilities ceased the Seamen's Union had become restive. Surely the coastal clauses of the Navigation Act might now at last be proclaimed. In May of 1919 the seamen struck, putting this forward as one of their demands.[1] Though unsuccessful, their action brought the Navigation Act once more to the forefront. Mr Hughes was then absent at the Peace Conference, but before he returned to Australia he had effected a second shipping *coup* by ordering, without the consent of Parliament, a fleet of five large passenger and cargo vessels. Contracts for the construction of these were placed in Britain while the Australian seamen were still defying Arbitration Court, fellow Trade Unions and public opinion alike. These five steamers were to become famous as the "Bay liners". Before their arrival in 1922, the way for their entry into the trade from Brisbane to England *via* all Australian capitals and the Suez Canal had been duly smoothed by the proclamation, in July 1921, of the coastal clauses of the Navigation Act, excluding their competitors from participation in the coastal trade.

Alas! The full tide of war and post-war activity on the seas was now ebbing fast. When in November of that year the House of Representatives debated the position of the Commonwealth steamers, it was plain that the "Austral" and ex-enemy vessels were with difficulty showing any profits. Old age, rough usage and a declining freight-market were telling heavily. Mr S. M. Bruce, from the detachment of the back benches, pointed to a net capital cost of the steel vessels bought, seized, built and building, amounting to £3,648,000. He arrived at it by subtracting

[1] In *The Round Table*, December 1919, p. 166, may be found a useful summary of their other demands.

P

from cost and interest the net profits made. He concluded that "the Commonwealth can either get out of the venture at this moment and look back on a record which shows no loss and probably a slight gain, or hand the vessels over to the Commonwealth Line (under non-political management) on a capitalised basis which would give them a chance to compete with any likely competitor". He advised sale, but the majority of the House still feared the power of the Shipping Conference. The revival of Scandinavian, German and Italian shipping, the expansion of the American and Japanese mercantile marines did not in their opinion offer adequate guarantees against the power of the ring to raise freights.

Selling off the older vessels, cancelling orders for new ones, the Commonwealth Line continued under non-political management for another seven years. But losses mounted up. These did not arise from cutting freights against the Conference vessels to the advantage of Australian shippers. From the first the Commonwealth vessels had charged Conference rates, and the freight index numbers of *The Economist* show no sign of a more rapid fall of Australian freight rates during the period of their ownership by the Commonwealth Government. In mid-1928 the remnant—the five Bay liners and a handful of cargo-carriers—were sold to Lord Kylsant for £1,900,000 and the Commonwealth retained only an accumulated net loss of some six millions.

The unions who had been partners in the splendid adventure did not altogether lose the Australian rates of pay and conditions aboard ship. These had been hammered out in the first instance by negotiation with the Commonwealth Steamship Owners' Association, and thereafter registered with and revised by the Commonwealth Arbitration Court.[1] The generosity of the wages and conditions

---

[1] The first Commonwealth Arbitration Award defining wages, hours and conditions for the Federated Seamen commenced to operate in December 1911 (see 5 *C.A.R.* p. 147). The first Waterside Workers' Award of that Court was given on 1 May 1914 (see 8 *C.A.R.* p. 52).

secured on Australian coastal shipping had not brought about that expansion of the Australian mercantile marine which the authors of the "White Ocean Policy" seemed to expect. In addition to the cramp of legal regulation, economic forces of impersonal origin were checking the call for inter-state vessels around the coast. The Western Australian trade in the 'nineties and the early years of this century had been a busy colonization of an undeveloped area. Men and families had to be carried over the Bight by tens of thousands, with clothing, foodstuff, machinery—all the impedimenta of a big campaign into the interior. The movement and subsequent trade were in many ways reminiscent of the longer-range gold-seekers' migration from Britain in the 'fifties. In the second decade after federation, however, the Western state began a big export of foodstuffs to Europe, and its requirements from the Eastern states ceased to grow. Passenger traffic has expanded very slowly since the East-West Transcontinental Railway between Kalgoorlie and Port Augusta was opened in October 1917. Similarly, passenger traffic on the eastern coast has felt the competition of the new coastal railways in New South Wales and Queensland. Airways already offer a still speedier service between the state capitals. Timber from the West to the East, butter from East to West, iron ore from South Australia in exchange for coal from Newcastle, raw sugar from Queensland mills to the refineries at the capitals' ports, the varied manufactures out of Sydney and Melbourne factories—these things freight inter-state vessels, but they are a fleet of smaller tonnage than before the war. The vessels on the Australian register had in 1928 a tonnage of 284,622, a figure almost coinciding with that of 1908, viz. 284,641 tons. Yet the companies have cargo space in excess of the coastal demand for it at the high Australian freights.[1] "In the

[1] Messrs Anstey, Yates and McHugh, in an elaborate report favourable to the Navigation Act (*Comm. P.P.* 1923, vol. II, pp. 1071 *et seq.*), claimed that there had been no increase in Australian coastal rates after the proclamation of the Navigation Act's coastal clauses, ignoring the fact that

inter-state trade", wrote a recent observer, "Australia is provided with as fine a service of steamers as can be found in the world and one capable of great development in the future".[1] As elsewhere in the Australian economy, the question presses whether the stable has not been improved at the expense of the horses' feed. While war and post-war prosperity lasted, such out-buildings of protectionism as government steamers and a lavish coastal service afforded unique conditions and wages and passed for expressions of our national pride. When drought and falling prices came again, their cost became an appreciable mortgage among many that endangered the national estate's recovery.

on most of the world's routes the period 1921 to 1924 saw heavy decreases. They admitted that coastal freights, under the Navigation Act and Arbitration Award, were 30 per cent. above pre-war rates. Cf. *Comm. P.P.* 1914–17, vol. VI, p. 1606.

[1] Sir G. Buchanan, *Transport in Australia*, vol. I, p. 14.

CHAPTER XXIII

How Tariff Protection Grows

IN the politics of a protectionist country there is no ease. Having given certain industries an advantage in the home market, your protectionist is torn with anxiety that they will take advantage of the consumer. Hence his addiction to boards. Subconsciously aware that he has run a risk of high prices and slack service, he calls on a board of experts to guard against it. But his board, soon or late, advises him that the task is too complex. He gets rid of it, or reconstructs it, and the farce begins again. But the manufacturer or other candidate for advantage ignores these boards and makes straight for Parliament House. From the story of one such board may be learnt the fate of all.

Section 101 of the Commonwealth Constitution reveals the fear of the authors of federation that, in the exercise of its powers over trade and commerce, the Commonwealth would need an organ of adaptation to unforeseen changes, a board whose rulings might be more flexible than the decisions and precedents of the law-courts. "There shall be an Inter-State Commission", they enacted, "with such powers of adjudication and administration as the Parliament deems necessary for the execution and maintenance within the Commonwealth of the provisions of this constitution relating to trade and commerce and of all laws made thereunder". This came true. There was such a commission for seven years, but it was born late and died young. Parliament, like the Federal Conventions, intended it to be both a court of record and a board with wide powers of inquiry and action in defence of inter-state freedom of trade.[1] The High Court ruled, however, that the statutory limitation of the Commissioners' tenure of office to seven years incapacitated them from the exercise of judicial powers under the Constitution. The Commission became an impotent thing, analogous to a Royal Commission or a Parliamentary Committee. It continued in existence until 1920, but the government of the day ignored every suggestion it made for the amendment of its defective legal basis. At the expiry of the first Commissioners' term no fresh appointments were made and the Commission lapsed.

The Federal Conventions may have been wise or unwise in seeking to entrust to a standing tribunal of wide powers the defence of the general interest in free enterprize. But in its absence that general interest has gone unregarded. The voice of the special pleader is never stilled. New Protection, developing through wages fixation, tariff schedules, Navigation Act restrictions and subsidies on export, has wrapped Australian industry in a net of legal rules. The Australian business man is tempted to become a suave concessionaire, exploiting his small corner while yet the system admits it, but explaining that he would gladly treat his clients better if the newest board would but give him a little larger scope and check the unpatriotic greed of others.

During its brief term of existence the Inter-State Commission presented a series of reports on the Tariff, tracing some of the more obvious repercussions of "scientific protection". The natural protection of local manufactures by distance from Europe had been diminished, even offset, by high inter-state shipping freights.[2] While these

---

[1] See *Comm. P.P.* sessions 1914–17, vol. II, pp. 1195 *et seq.*, *Second Annual Report of the Inter-State Commission*, reviewing the effect of the High Court's judgment, in the Wheat Case, upon the functions of the Commission.

[2] See, for instances, their reports on Boots and Shoes, Enamelled Baths, and Iron and Steel, *Comm. P.P.* sessions 1914–17, vol. VI, *passim.* "Freights from Sydney and Newcastle are higher and were so even before the war, than from Middlesbrough, the principal exporting port, to Australian ports direct."

remained the Commission hesitated to recommend protective duties high enough to "compensate" them in
Western Australia and other outlying parts. But were not
the tolls of the inter-state shipping combine, that impeded
local manufacturers in the outlying parts of Australia,
paralleled elsewhere and everywhere by the restriction of
industry through high costs? A tree whose outer twigs
wither has weakened also in trunk and roots. Charges
passed on are borne by someone.

The Commission's terms of reference in these tariff
inquiries drew attention to the need of "lessening the cost
of the ordinary necessaries of life". But the Commissioners
found that none of the 666 applicants for tariff assistance,
whose wares ranged from motor cars to insecticides, from
corsets to canary seed, had any concern with this. "The
cost of living", they reflected,[1] "is everybody's business,
but not the special affair of each citizen in such a sense
that he could give authoritative information on the state
of prices and of manufacturing trades in relation thereto....
Any increase in the cost of living resulting from Tariff
taxation produces its effect only by a total of separate im-
posts on many separate items." Yet all the applicants
stood in separate and urgent need of protection. Some
found it irksome to be precise as to evidence of that need.
The Commission had issued a printed form on which
applicants for assistance were asked the present state of
their business and the progress made during the three
years[2] previous to the date of application. The result was
disappointing, not to say disturbing. They all with one
accord began to make excuse. "The filling in of the forms
involved too much trouble. Details were not available of
the matters specified in the forms. Manufacturers were
averse to disclosing the financial results of their operations." When the Commissioners, armed with formidable

[1] *Comm. P.P.* session 1914–17, vol. VI, p. 3, *First Annual Report of the Inter-
State Commission.*

[2] *Comm. P.P.* session 1914–17, vol. VI, pp. 10 *et seq.* The form itself may
be found in vol. II, pp. 1168–73.

powers and knowledge,[1] persisted by oral examination,
"applications in many instances were considerably modified as the result of the private investigations, and so, too,
was the evidence given in public". One applicant named
Bernstein, who had applied for an increase of 20 per
cent. on duties already at 40 and 30 per cent., was "unable to give any information as to manufacturing costs.
He said 'I am not aware of our profits for the past three
years. I do not know anything about finance'".[2] The
Commission thought it unreasonable "that taxes on the
community should be increased on the plea of unprofitable-
ness of manufacture unless this plea can be made good
by something more than assertion".

Other witnesses, disliking this nice calculation of less
and more, refrained from suggesting the levy of taxes on
the community. They would be content with a simple
prohibition of entry to the Commonwealth of goods likely
to compete with their own. If this boon were granted,
they would enter into bonds not to increase prices save
when wages or raw materials rose in cost; and even then
the increase should be under the Inter-State Commission's
control. With the local market thus secured there would
be, they contended, a *pro rata* reduction of overhead
charges which would "tend to reduce prices!" The Commission politely demurred. "The total exclusion of new
ideas and improvements to which the whole industrial
world is contributing could not possibly act otherwise than
to our substantial detriment".[3]

[1] The Chief Commissioner, Mr A. B. Piddington, K.C., had been offered
a place on the High Court Bench. Mr Nicholas Lockyer had been Controller-
General of Customs and Mr George Swinburne, M.L.A., of Victoria, was
a business man of wide experience in political and industrial administration.

[2] *Comm. P.P.* sessions 1914–17, vol. VI, p. 134.

[3] The authors of the *Australian Tariff: an Economic Inquiry* (1929), p. 116,
have in effect thrown the mantle of their authority over such pleas for
monopoly. Having in mind (see p. 115) the iron and steel and the metal-
lurgical industries, they hold that "the problem of safeguarding efficiency
now requires a different solution in industries capable of great economies
through concentration". Industrial monopoly they regard as "a relatively

Even under the Tariff of 1908–11 the Commission found among manufacturers a widespread neglect of accurate costing, and a lack of attention to what their rivals in other countries were doing. Inspection of factories revealed an "urgent necessity for a greater appreciation of the value of industrial efficiency". Waste of power, unsuitable buildings, double handling of goods, waste of by-products, want of appreciation of applied science had enhanced the cost of manufacture and rendered necessary "higher duties than would be the case if the operations were accomplished by the most efficient modern methods".

The costs of production of Australian manufactures, so far as revealed in official statistics, had increased by £50,235,000 between 1908 and 1913, a time of rising tariffs but also of "exceptional abundance in primary production". The general affluence had permitted the value of manufactured output to rise by £62,031,000. "It thus appears", commented the Commission, "that the great increases in the burden of production have been successfully passed on to the consumer, together with an additional sum of £11,795,000". But some allowance from this total had to be made for increased overhead charges and costs of distribution. Others beside the manufacturers had had their "cut".

The Australian boot and shoe industry, pre-eminent among the secondary industries, afforded a clear view of the process of passing on. The Victorian boot manufacturers, with a perfunctory acquiescence from those in New South Wales, asked the Inter-State Commission for composite duties of 2s., 1s. 6d. and 1s. per pair of men's,

new phenomenon virtually unknown to the classical economists". They think that, with "the automatic and simple safeguard of public knowledge and public criticism...the protection given should be sufficient, not merely to place local production on an equality with imports, but to exclude those which could equally well be made in Australia. The best economic conditions for a protected industry are established when it obtains the maximum market for an organized output, and protection is likely to be most economically applied when it is limited to such industries." One is reminded of Governor Hunter and the trading officers.

women's and children's footwear, plus an *ad valorem* duty of 25 and 30 per cent. These duties, they hoped, would enable an "arrested industry" to win the 13·8 per cent. of the market still served by importers. They hastened to assure the Commissioners that there was no danger to the consumer in increasing the duties. In the main lines of boots already made in Australia "internal competition is sufficiently keen in this trade to keep manufacturers' prices at the lowest rates consistent with safety".[1] The Commission, avid for the facts, confronted the President of the Victorian Boot Manufacturers' Association with a statistical study of increases in costs and values of output. Only one inference, that dignitary admitted, could be drawn from it. Manufacturers were able to pass on to the public their increased expenses, plus an advantage. Nor was indication absent that the wage-earners wittingly shared in gains so accruing. An "Inter-State Conference"—not to be confused with the shipping combine— represented the Boot Manufacturers' Associations of New South Wales and Victoria and the Australian Boot Trade Employees' Federation in all states save Western Australia. It was active in urging the need of more protection.

The Inter-State Commission ventured to remind Parliament that every burden on trade is paid for by someone. "When the finished article of one industry is the necessary raw material of another the Tariff encouragement to both industries may fail to stimulate development in either case." Growing bolder in thought, they predicted that "it may at times be found a distinct economic advantage to withdraw Tariff encouragement from certain subordinate industries when the effect of such encouragement is proved to be a hindrance rather than an aid to the total of industrial development".

What, then, is a subordinate industry? Before industrial tribunals the term "industry" has been given a wide

[1] *Comm. P.P.* sessions 1914–17, vol. VI, pp. 264 *et seq.*

connotation.[1] It cannot now be narrowed to exclude the callings whose success or failure drives fast or slow the wheels of the Australian economy. So long as pasture, mining and agriculture provide almost the whole (95·5 per cent.) of Australian visible exports, there can be no question that the manufacturing industries are subordinate, in the sense that their prices must consort with such costs in the primary industries as enable the latter to make headway against their rivals. The sales of the manufacturers are the costs of the primary producers.

Too long have Australian leaders talked as though no burdens could offset our natural advantages for growing wool and wheat. "Fortunately", sighed the Inter-State Commission, "Australia offers the possibility of unlimited expansion in agricultural, mining and pastoral industries for the products of which the world's demand is practically unlimited."[2] Thirteen years later the Development and Migration Commission, in another First Report, clung with less confidence but more circumlocution to the same hope. "If the industries affected in a complex and disturbing manner are special in their nature and can command a place in the markets of the world, and can retain that place in spite of the adverse conditions—in short, if the world must have their products—they will survive."[3] A nation hoping to progress in numbers and well-being requires a vigorous advance—not the mere survival of its chief industries. The Inter-State Commission foresaw that the market for numerous Australian manufactures would be confined to the Commonwealth and could therefore offer only a limited expansion of employment. Its warning was underlined by the collapse after the war of the sortie which Australian boot manufacturers made between 1916 and 1921 into the markets of New Zealand, South Africa

---

[1] See G. Anderson, *Fixation of Wages in Australia*, pp. 171 *et passim*.
[2] *First Report of the Inter-State Commission* (1914), *loc. cit.* pp. 12–13.
[3] *First Report of D. and M. Commission*, November 1927, p. 8.

and the islands, and by the decline in the export of harvesters to the Argentine, a trade built up by H. V. McKay in days of less protection.[1]

The Commission reasoned, in effect, that when in doubt Australia should lead from her longest and strongest suit, the industry that promised the wider success. Her search for the long suit could hardly pass by wool or wheat. Yet, hard on the heels of reports expressing this general advice the Inter-State Commission put forward a series of recommendations in favour of increased tariff protection on all manner of goods. It commended to Parliament most of the pleas of manufacturers for duties "commensurate with their costs of manufacture and distribution". The implied theory is that the citizens of a "protected" country must be denied the fruits of business capacity in all lands but their own.

Where will the historian find a bridge over the gulf between the Commission's critique of pure protection and its practical advice to Parliament? Not in its recommendation of duties on corsets and stockings. These seemed just and right because it was anomalous that such articles should receive "different treatment from that extended to ordinary apparel". But if no item in a tariff be "anomalous", no protected industry reaps a net advantage from the tariff.

> When everyone is subsidized
> Then no-one's any booty.[2]

A scientific tariff should be like the French criminal who, after being "psycho-analysed", found that his character consisted entirely of defects.

The Commission may have known that Parliament during the war was in a mood to welcome any plea for

---

[1] The Toronto *Globe* announced, 8 October 1929, that the H. V. McKay Proprietary Ltd. had completed arrangements for the manufacture of Sunshine harvesters in Canada and would transfer its export business thither.

[2] E. C. Dyason, after W. S. Gilbert.

home industries. But, to the extent that such knowledge influenced it, the High Court's doubts of its independence were upheld. Parliament showed its mind plainly enough in an ingenious alteration of the duties on agricultural implements. The manufacturers of these refused to deploy for the Commissioners, on the first parade ground of the New Protection, either claim or argument. On behalf of the agricultural implement workers an Adelaide commercial traveller told of their readiness to support any application for prohibitive duties. He confessed that he did not know the manufacturers' costs,[1] but felt sure that duties of £12 per stripper-harvester fixed when such machines were six feet wide ought to be raised now that they were made nine feet wide. In the absence of both application and evidence from the manufacturers, the Commission made no recommendation. Such a resolute stand did not, however, deter the legislature. It enacted alternative duties of £13 or 35 per cent., general tariff, and £10 or 22½ per cent., preferential tariff, that rate to operate which returned the higher duty.[2] These straws showed the way the wind blew in Parliament.

Perhaps the bridge over the gulf of paradox may be found amid the rival and elaborate recommendations of the Chief Commissioner and his two colleagues concerning iron and steel—"compared with which even gold may be looked upon as of secondary importance". The war-time cult of self-sufficiency gripped them.

An economic history of Australian iron and steel has yet to be written. An indication of the stages in the growth of the industry must here suffice. Before the era of gold diggings, men were testing the abundant supplies of iron

[1] *Comm. P.P.* sessions 1914–17, vol. VII, p. 8: "We wrote to the chief manufacturers asking them if they needed further protection, and if they did so we would support them. They wrote to us then. I am unable to give the names and full replies".

[2] The *ad valorem* rates, in a period marked by increasing prices and larger machines, were the effective ones. Concerning reapers and binders, implements not previously made in Australia nor dutiable, see *Comm. P.P.* sessions 1914–17, vol. VII, pp. 13 *et seq.*

ore, limestone and coal scattered about New South Wales.[1]
A small blast furnace and two beam engines were working
at Nattai (now Mittagong) in 1848. Their Fitzroy Iron
Mining Company ran, however, a chequered and unprofitable course. Like all other colonial callings except
wool-growing and sugar-refining, it was laid low by the
superior attractions of alluvial gold. "Australia could
produce gold with comparatively less labour than any
manufactured commodity, and with the gold it could
import its manufactures from countries where they were
produced with comparatively less labour than was gold."[2]
As the exhaustion of the diggings modified this "cardinal
economic fact of the fifties", a larger blast furnace was
set going again at Mittagong and made iron for the girders
used in 1864 for Vickery's Buildings, in Pitt Street. The
Fitzroy works even exported pig-iron to California in
1868, the first 230 tons realizing £6 and £5 per ton. But,
in spite of the coming of the railway to Mittagong in 1867,
the company collapsed in 1870. Its plant and land at
"New Sheffield" were sold by auction for £10,000. In
the blast-furnace's last and most productive run, February
1876 to March 1877, it produced 3273 tons of pig-iron,
52 tons of which were made into "merchant-bars", the
wrought iron that was the raw material of the ubiquitous
village blacksmith. But by that time another scene had
been chosen for Australia's "black country", namely
Lithgow, on the way from Sydney to Bathurst, and James
Rutherford, of Cobb & Co., had turned his organizing
brain to the making of iron.

The Eskbank Iron Works, managed by Enoch Hughes
who had led the venturers to this more favourable

---

[1] See article on "Coal" in the *Australian Encyclopaedia*, vol. 1, p. 274;
Essington Lewis, "Iron and Steel Industry in Australia", pp. 31 *et seq.*
(*Proceedings of Engineering Conference, Newcastle* 1929); and F. R. E. Mauldon,
Economics of Australian Coal. The attention of students may also be drawn
to an interesting study by Louis Hunter of "The Influence of the Market
upon Technique in the Iron Industry of W. Pennsylvania" (*Journal of
Economic and Business History*, February 1929).

[2] G. V. Portus, *Cambridge History of the British Empire*, vol. VII, ch. IX.

scene, set out like its predecessor to smelt pig-iron from the native ore. But as in so many other European callings, including wool-growing and wheat-culture, a simple transfer to Australia of the ways that had served in the old lands did not bring success.

Gradually the emphasis in the works at Lithgow turned to the puddling and rolling of imported pig and scrap iron into "merchant-bars". Production of local pig-iron ceased in 1882, and a little later Rutherford "blew down" the blast furnace and melted up the ironwork in order to put away further temptation to lose money. Government orders for the rolling of rails from scrap offered the best business. Such "parasitic capitalism" did not satisfy Rutherford. His plans for rolling and galvanizing sheet iron having miscarried through the removal of an import duty, he sold out to William Sandford, a Bristol man whom Lysaghts had sent out to run a wire-factory at Parramatta. Paying his men by piece-work and on a sliding scale, Sandford stuck to re-rolling old rails and imported steel blooms. He extended his mills for rolling merchant-bars and boasted, at a political banquet in honour of some new plant, that the Eskbank works could produce 245 sections and sizes from iron or imported steel.

But the days of the general utility smith and his bar-iron were passing. That iron had been malleable, hot or cold, and easy to weld, a commodity of high quality and dear in production but not of exactly defined composition. The day of specialized steels, each with specific characters adapted to a certain use, was coming, and with it the need of the highly trained iron-master.[1] Cheap steel rails from abroad put a stop, by their superior strength and dura-

---

[1] "To produce wrought iron of general merit was comparatively easy but expensive", writes an American historian of a similar time of transition at Pittsburg, Louis Hunter, *Journal of Economic and Business History*, February 1929, p. 279. "To produce iron of specialized quality was very difficult, but, if successfully accomplished, resulted in a material reduction of cost. A first requirement for the control of the quality of the product was an exact knowledge of raw materials."

bility, to the re-rolling of old iron rails at Eskbank. Not lacking courage, Sandford set up a Siemens four-ton open hearth furnace and in April 1900 turned out the first Australian steel. Again a political banquet was held, and, a little later, there was much talk of a London company with £730,000 capital which would greatly extend the industry. But an Iron Bonus Bill proposed by the first Federal Government came to nothing. With it ended the company talk. There were other ways, however, of obtaining a sheltered market, and in September 1905 Sandfords Limited obtained a seven years' contract to supply the New South Wales government's requirements of iron and steel. Two days after the signing of the contract the works manager went to Britain to purchase plant and expert assistance. With their aid a great new blast-furnace at Lithgow began again the smelting of "native" ore from Carcoar in April 1907. Before the year was out, however, the firm was in difficulties. Costs had mounted, and a second Iron Bonus Bill had been vetoed by Mr Deakin's socialist allies; they favoured direct nationaliza-tion. Sandford appealed to the public to subscribe funds to carry on his great work; the public fought shy of it, and his bank foreclosed. G. and C. Hoskins, a Sydney firm of boiler-makers who had made the locking-bar pipes for the Coolgardie Water Scheme, bought the Eskbank property in January 1907. After an experiment with bigger plant, the new firm turned away from the puddling and rolling of wrought iron, to concentrate on steel.

The enterprise of the Hoskins in replacing small furnaces and mills by large ones was stimulated in December 1908 by the passage of a Manufactures Encouragement Act, offering bounties on the production of pig-iron from Australian ore, on bar-iron from such pig-iron, and on steel and galvanized sheet. Their business grew apace. Payments to the New South Wales Railways for freight rose from £28,700 in 1908 to £98,000 in 1914. Veins of mullock in the Carcoar deposit of ore led them to try a fresh supply at Tallawang near Mudgee, and later the big ore beds at Cadia, out towards Orange.[1] A second blast-furnace swelled the out-turn of pig-iron from 30,393 tons in 1908 to 75,150 tons in 1914. The various State govern-ments developed a habit of granting, over and above the prices, duty paid, quoted by British firms, a preference of 10 or 15 per cent. to Australian tenders; this helped. The Lithgow mills rolled the first steel rails made in Australia for the East-West Transcontinental Railway. The number of men on Hoskins' pay-roll trebled between 1908 and 1925, and their plant began to take the shape of a modern integrated iron and steel works.

By 1925, however, another Richmond was in the field. A steel enterprise, planned before its inception on up-to-date lines, was assembling its materials from the most accessible sources in Australia and serving the Australian markets by sea.[2] When, in 1928, Hoskins erected at Port Kembla on the south coast a blast furnace of American design and planned a complete iron and steel plant at tide-water,[3] they were following the earlier lead at New-castle, north of Sydney, of the Broken Hill Proprietary Company.

Between 1900 and 1911 the "B.H.P." had used in its lead-smelting at Port Pirie (S.A.) iron ore from two large deposits called Iron Knob and Iron Monarch, close to the coast on the other side of Spencer Gulf. A trial

[1] The Carcoar ores were limonite and hematite, with occasional patches of magnetite. The manganese content varied from 0·5 to 1·5 per cent. The Tallawang ore is magnetite. Those from Cadia are mostly hematite carrying from 50 to 62 per cent. of iron with a very low manganese content. The missing manganese was supplied from Grenfell.

[2] Be it noted that the new works thus combined American ideas of mass-production with the advantage of sea-carriage that has enabled British steel-masters to hold so long their position in export markets. With a German degree of technical and "rationalizing" skill the B.H.P. works should be formidable competitors in free markets.

[3] This enterprise, under the name of the Australian Iron and Steel Company Limited, involved a combination of Hoskins Ltd. with Dorman Long & Co., Baldwins (England) and Howard Smith Limited, with a nominal capital of five millions.

made at Port Pirie in 1907 showed the ore capable of producing excellent pig-iron, and in 1911 John Darling, the Chairman of the Company, knowing the life of even such a wonderful producer as its Broken Hill mine to be limited, announced that its manager, G. D. Delprat, was to visit Europe and America in search of information and experts "for the development of industries kindred to our resources, as yet barely touched upon".[1] In this search Mr Delprat was embarrassed at times by a readiness in those of whom he asked advice to offer their own services to the great company he represented, but finally he found in Philadelphia the man he was seeking, David Baker, an engineer of New England origin and training, and of wide American and Canadian experience.

Land had long before been acquired (1896) at Newcastle (N.S.W.), close to the main coalfields of Australia. There, on a site enlarged to 1100 acres by purchase and by reclamation from mangrove swamp, the first units of the steel works arose in the year 1914. They comprised a 350-ton blast furnace, 66 by-product coke ovens, three 65-ton basic open hearth steel furnaces, a 35-inch blooming mill and a 28-inch rail and structural mill. Nearly a million sterling had been laid out at Newcastle and Iron Knob when in January 1915 the first shipment of iron ore was unloaded from the Company's steamer, 'Emerald Wings', at its Newcastle wharves. The blast furnace was "blown in" on 9 March 1915, a month later steel ingots and six weeks later steel rails were produced. War-time demands caused a rapid expansion of the plant. In the year ending 1 December 1927 it consumed 692,208 tons of ore, from the quarries and crushers on Spencer Gulf, in turning out 416,532 tons of pig-iron, from which 387,929 tons of steel were made and re-made into a great variety of shapes and sections at subsidiary works that have built themselves around the Newcastle site.

[1] See *The Iron and Steel Industry in Australia*, by Essington Lewis, Managing Director of the B.H.P. Co., *loc. cit.* pp. 15 *et seq.*

But a change has come in the circumstances of the Proprietary. It began operations at Newcastle on estimates which were expected to make it independent of tariff assistance. In quantity, quality and accessibility the iron ore deposits in South Australia, the limestone from the hills by the Don River near Devonport, Tasmania, and the low-sulphur coking coal at Newcastle, when assembled by sea-carriage made cheaper by the back-loading of coal, promised success on economically sound lines in free competition with the world. The first contract for coking coal used in the blast furnace plant was seven shillings per ton delivered at the works. Then over the pall that drifts high above its forest of stacks there descended the deeper fog of war; and its great wheels, for all their might, were caught in the labouring machine of the New Protection.

The tall chimneys did not cease to smoke. Orders came thick and fast to Newcastle as to all the world's steel plants. Australia did not go short; the Transcontinental Railway was built mainly with B.H.P. rails. Rails and munition bars were sent even to France and Britain. But costs mounted. Fresh plant had to be installed at war-time prices and wages rose steadily. The Company purchased coal property and began to sink its own shafts; but this could save it only coal-mining profits. Legal regulation and union enforcement of shorter hours and higher hewing rates were making Newcastle coal dear to win.[1]

In such circumstances it is intelligible enough that the Inter-State Commission recommended in a majority report a step which the authors of colonial tariffs before federation and of the federal tariffs of 1904 and 1908–11 had hesitated to take, viz. the imposition of import duties on pig-iron and on iron and steel products.[2] Only the Hoskins of Lithgow had applied for such duties, but the majority

[1] See F. R. E. Mauldon, *Economics of Australian Coal, passim.*
[2] *Comm. P.P.* sessions 1914–17, vol. v, pp. 1602 *et seq.* Pre-war duties are tabulated on p. 1678.

Commissioners satisfied themselves by an examination of the Broken Hill Proprietary Company's costs up to 30 April 1916 "that without tariff assistance this company cannot compete in other markets than New South Wales, the state in which its works are situated, beyond the stage of pig-iron and even in that particular item it may with free imports be limited in its area of distribution in normal times". The Chief Commissioner was for helping the industry through infantile weakness by continuing the system of bounties and looking into the problem of inter-state shipping. His colleagues conceded that where an article is the raw material for secondary industries, and its manufacture in adequate supply is likely to take time, "encouragement by bounty means the least burden on secondary industries and the community". But the bounty method indicated, they thought, an expectation that the industry would ultimately be able to do without assistance. This, they held, was not the case with iron and steel. "Under the conditions which at present exist in Australia (that industry) cannot continue without help....Any scheme of assistance by bounties would be, in our opinion, an altogether insufficient assurance to capital and enter-prize that a determined and permanent settled policy had been instituted by Parliament. Import Tariff duties, on account of their more permanent nature, are considered the only appropriate means of assistance for an industry which has advanced to a stage when successful development is assured under reasonable protection."[1]

Reasonable protection as a determined and permanent policy, however, has a knack of leading its devotees on and on. The Commissioners regretted that for lack of time their investigation had not "comprehended" "the effect that any alteration in the Tariff would have upon the many branches of engineering and allied trades as well as upon other industries". Yet they did not hesitate to recommend the imposition of duties on pig-iron, of

[1] *Comm. P.P.* sessions 1914–17, vol. VI, pp. 1626 *et seq.*

17s. 6d. per ton in the general, 12s. 6d. per ton in the preferential tariff. This led to a recommendation of duties on scrap iron because it competed with pig-iron; also to iron and steel ingots, blooms and billets. "If steel billets and blooms are left free of duty it may better pay the manufacturers of plates, etc. in some of the principal centres to import billets and blooms rather than use those made from Australian ore. Imports can come direct to any port." Thence to iron and steel bars, rods and angles. "If a duty were put on steel-blooms and scrap without putting a duty on manufactures it would seriously affect the present rolling mills." Such duties, they knew full well, would "have to be taken advantage of to some extent". The duties they suggested on steel rails would be a burden on the public railways. The representatives of the New South Wales Public Works Department were not slow to impress this on the Commission.

> "I weep for you", the Walrus said:
> "I deeply sympathize!"

Perhaps prices would rise only "until increased output, better organization and other factors reduce costs". The Federal Parliament, not unmindful that "other factors" included the legal definition of wages and conditions, went beyond the Commission's lead. Scope was left for future industrial awards by the imposition of much heavier duties than those recommended, on almost every item of the tariff affecting iron and steel.[1]

"The mighty current of a popular movement", Ranke noted, "carries along with it even those who seem to direct it." The surging nationalism of war-time, maintained at high tide by the discussions after the war of international relations in the Pacific, made Australians ready to pay any price their trusted leaders asked "to make this great Continent independent of outside supplies

---

[1] Customs Tariff Acts, especially no. 25 of 1921.

Q

of iron and steel". Moreover, the tactical skill of the Prime Minister (Mr W. M. Hughes) in imposing the new tariff of 1921 at a time when wholesale prices in Britain, Europe, and America were tumbling down, masked from the Australian public the burden of the new duties. For Australian prices actually fell between August 1920 and December 1921—though maintained at a level higher than those in other lands.[1] Facts, for all his skill, have proved persistent critics of popular feelings. In a hundred-and-one ways Australian primary producers have felt the strain of this discrepancy between price-levels in their home and their oversea markets. Like their ancestors in the old land, they are great users of iron and, whereas the price of pig-iron at Lithgow rose by 62·6 per cent. between 1914 and 1927,[2] the average of British iron and steel prices was in 1928 less than 13 per cent. above the pre-war average. In Australia, it seemed, the advantages of improved technique which elsewhere percolated to the consumer, were mortgaged for the employees of town factories and public utilities. Here was fit matter for consideration by a new Board.

[1] See D. B. Copland, "The Economic Situation in Australia 1918–1923", in *The Economic Journal*, vol. xxiv, p. 38.
[2] See Table on p. 15, Essington Lewis, *loc. cit.*

CHAPTER XXIV

"Protection All Round"

SINCE 1913 the place held by the primary producers'
leaders in the State and Commonwealth legislatures
has reflected the growing importance as exports of
wheat and dairy products. Unlike the pasturing of stock
for their wool, hides and meat, these industries keep the
countryside moderately well peopled. The Country Party
came determined to play a lone hand and to sway the
parliamentary balance in the interests of the "man on the
land", much as the Labour men had done twenty years
earlier. Farmers sold their produce, other than sugar-
cane, at values that fluctuated in unsheltered markets.
They objected to both tariff-raising and wage-fixing.
Whether such policies raised town standards of living or
not, they certainly piled up transport and farming costs.
The Country Party sought to free the farmer's costs of
uneconomic burdens. The man on the land resented being
neatly robbed of the reward of his increased efficiency, and
meant to "warn off" both protected manufacturer and
privileged labour.

But the statesman who can compel or induce a democracy to face unpleasant facts is a rare product.
Farmers in annual conference sought to evolve a policy
and a leader from a political machine modelled largely
on that of Labour, but most of the leaders[1] they tried

---

[1] The co-operative activities of Australian farmers which should have
educated such leaders have been curiously patchy. Study of the "Eudunda
Farmers" in South Australia and of the "Westralian Farmers" in Western
Australia are needed. Rather unfortunately the ablest of the co-operative
leaders, having dealings with successive governments of different colour,
think it imperative that they should "keep out of politics".

in Parliament became, like Labour after 1907, pupils in the Victorian school of political conjuring. The first step in their education as new-protectionists was the appointment, in lieu of the defunct Inter-State Commission, of a Tariff Board.

At the election of 1919, the Prime Minister (Mr Hughes) promised a protective tariff so hedged about that the consumer should be secure against "profiteering" prices. The Tariff Board was to do the hedging.[1] This expert body would study the effects of the tariff on Australian industries. Was a manufacturer acting in a manner which resulted in unnecessarily high prices being charged to the consumer? The Board would "deal with" him. The Minister must refer to the Board "the necessity for new, increased or reduced duties, and the deferment of existing or proposed duties" So formidable did the new Board look that an ardent Nationalist who, in subsequent years, earned as Minister for Customs the title of "high priest of protection" voted against the Bill on its second and third readings. But personnel and tenure are important matters; the first Board, appointed for two years only, consisted of a customs official as chairman, a Victorian manufacturer and an importers' representative.

In its youth, reviewed in its annual report of June 1923,[2] the Tariff Board showed a tender solicitude for soldier-settlers' needs. Wire-netting, fencing-wire and galvanized iron it held to be "goods absolutely essential to the primary producer starting out to bring under control and cultivation large tracts of country, much of which was in a virgin state". On its initiative the Government placed these commodities on the free list and talked of a bounty to manufacturers "providing for them a protection equal to the then duty". Before a year had passed, but after

[1] See "The Tariff Board of Australia", by R. C. Mills, in *The Economic Record*, May 1927, pp. 52–81. Proposals for a further re-shaping of the Tariff Board are outlined in *The Australian Tariff: an Economic Inquiry* (1929), parts x and xi.

[2] *Comm. P.P.* session 1923–24, vol. ii, p. 1687.

a political crisis, the Board, finding that the principal Australian manufacturers had accumulated a stock of several thousand miles of wire-netting, reported that British wire-netting was being "dumped" into the Commonwealth to the detriment of an Australian industry. Hastening to the aid of the new suppliant, it recommended the imposition of a dumping duty on cheap wire-netting under Section 4 of the Customs Tariff (Industries Preservation) Act 1921.[1] Free imports of the pioneer settlers' necessities were promptly and effectively stopped.

In its second term, with its personnel reinforced by a representative of the primary producers, the Tariff Board made an elaborate inquiry into the agricultural implements industry.[2] The information as to their costs supplied by the Australian manufacturers, "confidentially but in full detail", satisfied the Board that these gentlemen were not charging excessive prices. On the contrary, not only had they provided implements adapted at all points to local requirements, but their activity and enterprise had also been a valuable check upon the monopoly which American exporters might otherwise have built up, in the supply of mass-produced implements from Canada and the United States. Treatment so good when applied to one secondary industry, they argued, should be extended to all. The Board found it "impossible to imagine that any secondary industry can carry on without protection in a country where it is the policy to protect secondary industries, where the standard of living is high as the result of that protection, and where the volume of output is restricted through the absence of a large home market".

[1] No. 28 of 1921. Section 4 provided that if goods exported to Australia of a kind manufactured in Australia were being sold to an importer at an export price less than the fair market value of the goods and to the detriment of an Australian industry, the Minister, after report by the Tariff Board, might after gazettal impose a special dumping duty representing the difference between the fair market value of the goods at the time of shipment and the export price.

[2] *Comm. P.P.* session 1925, vol. II, p. 1891, *Report of the Tariff Board on Agricultural Implements.*

The Country Party leaders lacked either the skill or the courage to reason with such logical fellows. They faced a nation hypnotized by a myriad press articles into submitting to the protection of all secondary industries as the settled national policy. They did not distinguish between a cost of living made high for all by this policy and standards of living raised for some but depressed for others. They proceeded rather to claim the extension of the national policy to the primary industries as well. The home market might not be large enough for the manufacturers' ambitions of output, but protection had made it a lucrative field for them; and it consumed more than half of the total value of Australian primary products. Why should not the primary producers enjoy a sheltered market there too? The national policy of protection, having taken Labour under one wing, could surely find room under the other for its older allies the farmers. It had already befriended the sugar growers, and war-time expedients had shown how "orderly marketing" might proceed. Out of such beginnings rose the ideal of protection all round.

During the war, truly, wool had been appraised and wheat pooled under the compulsory powers of government. This war-time marketing and distribution of essential commodities was held necessary to prevent their diversion from the resources of the allied powers. It was facilitated by the concentration of shipping under a single Allied Shipping Control. Beyond doubt it had saved the premier industries of Australia from ruin.[1] Five hundred million bushels of wheat were handled by the Australian Wheat Board's agents, including Farmers' Co-operative Companies, during the five seasons of the Board's control. Nearly two-thirds of this were sold to the British Government at an average price of 4s. 8.8d. a bushel delivered in Australia, a figure well above those ruling before 1914.

[1] Vide *The Round Table*, December 1920, pp. 183 *et seq.*, September 1921, p. 931, and F. R. Beasley, *Open-Marketing v. Pooling in Australia, passim.*

Though there were indignant snorts from some when British ministers referred to the price paid for this wheat as evidence of Australian farmers' patriotism, those farmers were mightily impressed by the machinery of mass-marketing made practicable by the simplified commerce of governments at war. After the war, both by the compulsion of friendly state governments in Western Australia and Queensland and on a voluntary basis in all the states growing wheat for export, wheat pooling continued.[1] Despite fluctuating support, the farmers' leaders built up machinery both for sale through a seasonal pool in each state and for cash sales through co-operative companies as wheat merchants. In doing so they entered, in Western and South Australia, into financial co-operation with the British Co-operative Wholesale Society. But some, notably in New South Wales, hankered for a sheltered price in the home market.

Four Australian wool-clips were purchased by the British Government at an average price of $15\frac{1}{2}d$. per pound, *plus* half of any profits it might make from re-sales for civilian use. The total quantity was over seven million bales.[2] At the end of 1920, however, after the British Government had paid the agreed price to the credit of the Australian Central Wool Committee, it found itself with a considerable sum in hand as profits of civilian sales and with a surplus of nearly two million bales of Australian wool, half merino and half cross-bred. As it had also 770,000 bales of New Zealand cross-bred wool, this was indeed an embarrassment of riches. Wool-growers, wool-brokers and wool-buyers had all worked harmoniously and with brilliant technical and administrative success in sub-stituting mass-purchase and appraisement for the older

---

[1] See F. R. Beasley, *op. cit.* pp. 40–45, and *Commonwealth Year Book*, no. 21, p. 1021. Compulsory pooling ceased in Western Australia in 1922.

[2] 7,154,621 bales weighing in all 2,486,721,753 pounds, worth at the flat rate of $15\frac{1}{2}d$. some £160,600,780. See *Comm. P.P.* sessions 1914–17, vol. v, p. 1159, for notes by J. M. Higgins on the Broad Principle of the Wool Scheme.

auction-sales in Australia and London. The British Government had no longer need or wish to control the purchase of the Australian, New Zealand and British wool-clips. Over the market, however, there hung at the resumption of free auction-sales this mighty stock of old wool as well as the 1920–21 clip. In all, the visible supply was over three million bales.[1]

A marketing plan for the transition period was hammered out by Sir Arthur Goldfinch, the Director of Raw Materials for the British Government, in conference with representatives of both wool-growers and brokers. It took shape as a great joint stock company whose name stated its function, the British Australian Wool Realization Association Limited. Nick-named "Bawra", with perhaps the suggestion that it was first cousin to "Dora", the Association was registered on 27 January 1921 as a Victorian company. To it the British Government, through that of the Commonwealth, transferred the cash and the unsold wool remaining from its war-time monopoly. Valuing this wool at 40 per cent. less than its appraised value—for prices had slumped heavily under the pressure of deflation at home and the shadow of such stocks—Bawra distributed wool-certificates and shares in its assets to all growers who had contributed wool to the total appraised in proportion to their contributions.[2] The slump in the wool auction-rooms, bordering on panic, was stayed by a Commonwealth "war-time regulation", 9 May 1921, setting 8d. a pound as the minimum price at which wool might be exported. Bawra then proceeded, not always with the concurrence of wool-selling brokers, to put up its stocks

[1] For an excellent review of the war and post-war marketing problem see the *Economic Record*, February 1928 Supplement, article "Bawra", by E. C. Dyason. Though further research among the papers of the Central Wool Committee and Bawra, in the Library of the School of Commerce at the University of Melbourne, may possibly modify some of the conclusions therein contained, the author of the article was exceptionally well placed and qualified to analyse the events and forces which he appraises.

[2] The British Government also appointed Bawra its agent in the sale of its stock of New Zealand wool.

at monthly auction sales mainly in Britain, carefully rationing the market and setting reserves on its offerings according to its estimate of growers' costs in producing the concurrent new clips.[1] After August 1922 the wool-selling brokers refused to be bound by the Association's allocation of quantities of wool, old and new, to be submitted at the Australian auctions. The plan's success, however, in removing the fear of unlimited offerings, had by then made possible a sharp recovery in prices, especially for merino wool.

At the end of that year, when Bawra's distributions had reached sixteen millions sterling, Sir John Higgins, its Chairman, proposed that the shareholders should use its remaining assets, estimated to be worth to them six millions more,[2] as an insurance fund for the protection of Australia's pastoral and agricultural industries. Sir John, a "self-made" business leader of Cornish origin and Phoenician ability in finance, talked to a meeting of over 500 shareholders, of setting up central re-conditioning works, of grading every lot by type and yield, of abolishing draftage —that old mystery that makes the wool-growers' hundredweight only 111 pounds when he sells his wool—of allocating quantities for auction and of mass-bargaining about freights. By such means he held that a central organization with a capital of six millions might "increase the returns from a normal Australian wool-clip by £2,500,000 to £3,500,000 or eight to ten per cent. of its present value.... The important factor—the material gain—would be in the enhancement of the value of the wool production of the Commonwealth". His proposals were summarily rejected by an adverse vote, without discussion. The powerful wool-selling brokers were active in hostility to

---

[1] Dyason, *loc. cit.* p. 59: "On many occasions the Directors of B.A.W.R.A. refrained from putting their full quota on the market and in some cases suspended sales altogether for a period".

[2] It must be noted that as under the original agreement for the acquisition of the Australian wool, a half share in the assets realized by Bawra belonged to the British Government.

them, for they were not ready lightly to submit their excellently run and lucrative businesses to a central control. But in opposing Sir John Higgins' great "rationalization" they played upon a responsive instrument. The vast majority of pastoralists mistrusted anything that would put their wool nearer to the grasp of governments in whose policies they have seldom had part or trust. Sir John Higgins disclaimed any association between the co-operative company of his dreams and government control. Yet save by fiat of the Commonwealth Government, how could his central organization obtain or retain such control of Australian wool as would be needed for its purpose of mass-marketing? Mr Dyason, as "the student", "is left with the conviction that the Australian wool industry as a whole lost an opportunity, which is unlikely to recur, of creating a powerful instrument for its own advancement".

Bawra certainly served the wool industry well. It distributed over thirty millions as the Australian woolgrowers' quota of the wool salvaged from the war. But the results of other ambitious plans outside Australia for the advancement of values in the world's markets tempt one to regard the veto on its continuance as an equal service. Merino wool is grown in South Africa. How long would Sir John Higgins' disclaimer of any attempt to "uphold unduly the price of wool" have held good in a sense acceptable to the users of wool? Who would have decided what was due?

Other groups of the primary producers showed no liking for free or open marketing. They had before them an impressive example in sugar of the power of an organized industry, based upon an Australian primary product, to secure special prices through a sheltered local market.

Even before federation, the Colonial Sugar Refining Company had shown its political influence in a successful resistance to G. H. Reid's proposal (1896) to remove the long-established duty on sugar. The Company had in the early 'nineties stood up with resource and courage to the attacks of bounty-fed German sugar in its Australasian markets. Fighting funds had been set aside without detriment to the annual rate of dividend, and prices had been cut by £2 to £3 per ton in the colonial markets.[1] But when Reid proposed the abolition of the duty on sugar imported into New South Wales, a duty dating back to 1855, the impending destruction of the industry was loudly proclaimed—"a result which those who wish to place in the hands of German importers a large share in the sugar trade of New South Wales will naturally view with satisfaction". Contracts with farmers on the Northern Rivers for sugar-cane were cancelled. Inquiries were set on foot with a view to "utilizing our N.S.W. plant elsewhere". Reid bowed to this storm of opposition; at his advice Knox was knighted in 1897 and the reduction of the duty below £3 a ton was stayed.[2] The Company's inspecting chemist, Dr Kottmann, went to inquire about new processes in France and in Germany. Knox, a native of Denmark, had himself been educated at Lübeck, though too soon to have imbibed from List his skill in nationalist economics.[3] The usual dividend was declared, free of the new income tax. Sixteen thousand tons of Australasian sugar were exported to British Columbia, Hong-Kong, London and Japan, and shareholders were offered the right to provide £170,000 fresh capital to replace the debentures redeemable in 1899 and 1900. They were not slow to respond.

The old chief died on 7 January 1901 at the sunrise of the Commonwealth, but his creation, the great C.S.R.

[1] *C.S.R. Co. Reports* (Mitchell Library), Chairman's statement for half-year ending 31 March 1895. Apart from their economic significance Knox's statements have a rare charm as a revelation of his vigorous personality.

[2] "The area under sugar-cane in New South Wales reached its maximum in 1895–6 with a total of 32,927 acres." It then fell gradually to 10,490 acres in 1918–9. *Commonwealth Year Book*, no. 6, p. 392, and no. 20, p. 675. The farmers on the Northern Rivers have found dairying more lucrative than sugar-growing, though in recent years high prices for sugar have attracted many back to the old crop.

[3] For a short biography of Sir Edward Knox, see *Australian Encyclopaedia* (second edition), vol. I, p. 704.

Company, entered the new arena armed *cap-à-pie*. Since 1889, £1,100,000 had been added to its paid-up capital and applied mainly to the reduction of interest-bearing liabilities. It had virtually withdrawn from direct cultivation of sugar-cane in Australia, leaving this to white farmers. In times of drought it could draw upon supplies of raw sugar grown on its own plantations in Fiji or upon outside supplies from Java. With inter-state free trade it expected to concentrate the work of refining "to a larger extent than heretofore, at any port where the existing conditions allow of the refining work being conducted at the lowest cost".[1] But federated Australia regarded other aims as superior to the economies of concentration. One of the earliest acts of the national Parliament put a stop to the importation of Kanakas and made provision for the deportation of any in Australia after 31 December 1906.[2] To encourage sugar production by white labour an Excise (Sugar) Act 1902 offered as a bounty on sugar-cane so grown a rebate of two out of the three pounds a ton excise levied on manufactured sugar.[3] The proportion of Queensland sugar grown by coloured labour fell from 85·5 per cent. in 1902 to 12·11 per cent. in 1909. The tariff protected the sugar industry by an import duty of £6 per ton on raw or refined cane-sugar, and £10 per ton on beet-sugar. Thus the white sugar men in New South Wales and Queensland enjoyed a net protection of £5 per ton, paying in effect only £1 a ton as excise. Yet they were far from being happy. The Commonwealth Statistician recorded decorously in 1912 that the system of rebates was producing "effects not anticipated at the

[1] *C.S.R. Reports* (Mitchell Library). Statement by the Chairman, H. E. Kater, for the half-year ending 31 March 1901.

[2] The Pacific Island Labourers Act, no. 16 of 1901, especially 8 (i). Of 9841 Kanakas in Queensland on 31 December 1901, 9269 had been deported by 21 December 1909.

[3] P. A. K. Ewart, in *Melbourne Stock Exchange Record*, February 1929, contends that the bounty was "in no sense paid out of the taxpayers' funds inasmuch as it was paid from a fund collected from the sugar producers themselves" By parity of reasoning customs duties are only taxes on warehousemen!

time the legislation was passed, and that the greater part of the cost of substituting white for coloured labour was thereby being imposed on the States engaged in the industry, instead of being a charge upon the whole Commonwealth". Bluntly the sugar-growers complained that with unions forcing up the men's wages and the refining companies determining the price they would pay for cane—according to sugar-content but by monopoly power—no good came to them from either protection or bounty. In 1912 both excise and bounty were repealed on condition that Queensland prohibited by state legislation the employment of coloured labour in the industry. Simultaneously the state set up machinery to fix the wages of sugar employees. The position of the cane-growers between the upper and the nether millstones of refineries and organized labour remained unattractive. The area under sugar-cane fluctuated but increased little between 1905 and 1914.[1]

At this stage the industry aimed only at the service of the Australian demand at Australian prices.[2] Its uneasy poise was rudely upset in 1915 by the effects of drought and war, but was propped up again on more attractive supports by the state and federal governments. Early in the war, state price-fixing boards fixed the price of sugar, among other commodities. The figure named was considerably less than the market price outside the Commonwealth which had been affected by the blockade of Central European supplies of beet-sugar. But Australia had sugar troubles of her own. Dry seasons in Queensland and New South Wales had sharply threatened supplies. The fixed price at this juncture made it impracticable for the C.S.R. Company to adopt the plan used in former years of shortage, viz. of importing raw sugar from Java or Fiji, refining it and putting it on the Australian market at a

---

[1] See *Australian Production Statistics, Bulletin*, no. 20, p. 204.
[2] Cf. Edward Knox's reflections on expanding production, *C.S.R. Reports*, 31 March 1895 (Mitchell Library).

price reflecting the outside value of sugar. To do so in 1915 would have meant a loss of £7 a ton. The Federal (Labour) Government, obsessed by the dogma that value should bear an invariable relation to cost of production,[1] was anxious to prevent the C.S.R. Company from increasing the value of the Australian sugar in its possession above what ministers held that it had cost. Early in May, however, it became known that the stocks of Australian sugar, freely consumed at the fixed price, would be exhausted in July. The Federal Government then purchased, through the C.S.R. Company, the Java sugar needed to tide the domestic demand over the period of shortage, until the 1916 sugar crop.

Once having entered the sugar business, federal governments found it hard to draw back. In July 1915 Mr Hughes (then Attorney-General) purchased the raw sugar from Australian growers and central mills at £18 per ton, and employed the C.S.R. and Millaquin Sugar Companies to refine and distribute it. A charge of £3. 13s. per ton was allowed for the companies' services in refining and handling the sugar, plus an addition representing the cost of tinning, canning, handling and distributing the syrup. But a provision in the agreement—9 A, a mere afterthought—read: "Should legislation affecting the conditions of the manufacture or refining of the 1915 crop of sugar be passed by any State this agreement shall be subject to such re-adjustment as shall be agreed upon". One Dugald Thomson was named as arbitrator. As war-time wages and costs rose, prices to growers had to be revised. Scanty yields led to imports of oversea sugar, on government account. In 1919–20 and 1920–21 these were both extensive and expensive. The retail price was raised to 6d. a pound.[2] To keep it at that level until the government's costs had been recouped, a complete embargo on

---

[1] See *Comm. P.D.* vol. LXXVI, 6 May 1915, p. 2914, statement by Senator Pearce.

[2] For a table of Australian sugar prices, 1915 to 1925, see *Commonwealth Year Book*, no. 20, p. 678.

imports of black-grown sugar was imposed. Behind this screen of regulation the price of raw sugar to the growers could be and was further increased. Generous prices for cane set up a considerable expansion of the area under cultivation. The long stagnation at between 140 and 170 thousand acres was broken up in 1921 when 197,293 acres grew cane. In 1926–7, 280,000 acres were growing it.

On more than one occasion the Commonwealth Government has announced its intention to terminate the embargo on foreign sugar and to confine the protection of so prosperous an industry to the import duty of £9. 6s. 8d. per ton. But Queensland occupied a pivotal position in federal politics. The swing of its ten electorates in the House of Representatives usually determined the fate of the federal cabinets. Queensland state governments have been nothing loth to support the cause of the sugar-growers. The industry has become an exporting one on a considerable scale. Imports averaging in value £2,693,000 a year in the five years ending June 1921 have given place to exports averaging £1,551,800 per annum in the succeeding five years. The exports were mainly sold in the British market where for several years they enjoyed a preference.[1] The

[1] In 1928 the embargo was renewed until 1931. N. Skene Smith, *Economic Control*, part III, chapter II, traces in detail the scheme by which prices, wages and the right to share in this industry are "controlled". The price of sugar is ostensibly "fixed" by a Sugar Board consisting of "a Government chairman, two growers' delegates and one millers' delegate". But the Board's decision, so far from being a "control", must leave room for the prices allowed to growers and millers by District Boards. These prices in turn are resultants of the wages granted by state wage-fixing tribunals to cane-cutters, cultivators and millhands. The prices allowed for cane have been attractive. Since the present system was elaborated the number of growers has increased from 3930 in 1920 to 6730 in 1925. Since 1925 indeed, the Sugar Board and the Central Cane Prices Board have intervened to stop expansion (i) by refusing applications from present growers to plant new land, and (ii) by putting an embargo on further assignments of land to new growers. There still remains the danger that present growers will raise more cane per acre. The Queensland yield of cane is low per acre in comparison with Java. Similarly with labour. The aim of the wage tribunals has been "to base the wage in the industry upon a minimum as fair to the sugar worker, with his irregular employment, as is the basic wage to an average employee in fairly regular employment". High piece-rates and minima for the 44-hour week have set up a mild rush to work in the industry,

spread of such labour-saving devices as the tractor-drawn cultivator has enabled the cane-grower to draw profit despite a falling average of home and export prices. Further economies are in sight. A motor cane-cutter, invented by one of the Riverina Falkiners, seems to need only the spur of necessity to bring about "alterations and adjustments to enable it to operate successfully in heavy crops of green cane". The anomaly of two prices, however, one for the patient Australian housewife and the other for freer folk oversea, whether they buy sugar neat or in Australian jam and condensed milk,[1] excites the cupidity of other primary producers.

Another industry expanded fast during the war as a result of charging a high price in the home market and dumping its surplus abroad. This was the dried fruits industry, the main homes of which are the irrigation colonies in the Murray and Murrumbidgee valleys.[2] The earliest of these, Mildura (Vic.), established by the Chaffey Brothers from California in the early 'nineties, the almost contemporary Renmark in South Australia and Curlwaa (N.S.W.) obtained water by pumping from the River Murray. Oases of vines and citrus fruits in the dried plains of the interior have always appealed strongly to the Australian imagination. They excited the admiration and hope of *The Times* special correspondent when, after the Bank Smash, she watched the efforts of colonial legislatures to mend matters by promoting any and every form of land settlement. They seemed to offer so much better

even from far-away Italy. Preference to members of the A.W.U., legally established, has seemingly been a brake upon this movement. The Court has had occasion to warn the said Union "to be careful not to refuse tickets to men who are qualified to become members of the Union".

[1] Manufacturers for export obtain a rebate on the sugar-content of their goods equal to the difference between the Australian and foreign wholesale prices, on application to an export sugar committee. In 1925-6, 56 per cent. of the total production of sugar was consumed in Australia, at a wholesale price of £26. 10s. a ton, while the net value of the exported sugar was £11. 5s. 9d. The average price for the whole crop was £19. 10s. 7d. per ton.

[2] *Comm. P.P.* sessions 1914-17, vol. VI, pp. 898-9, *Report of Inter-State Commission on Dried Fruits*, 16 August 1916.

opportunities of maintaining the amenities of life to which settlers from Britain had been accustomed. "On highly productive land, a much smaller portion suffices for the maintenance of a given number of persons: consequently men live nearer together, and are able to employ their leisure in social intercourse, at once natural and mutually stimulating."[1]

Government aid had not been stinted at any stage of their history. Irrigation works on a large scale, spreading water through gravitation channels over the Goulburn and Wimmera valleys, had been undertaken before federation. Alfred Deakin, having visited California and India, was their inspired patron. In New South Wales the Murrumbidgee valley became a scene of busy preparation after 1906. Headworks and irrigation channels were constructed at vast expense. Money was advanced to settlers, on the security of the land taken up by them.[2] Water was supplied at rates far below the maintenance costs and interest on the works which stored and carried it.

Yet it was early apparent that Californian irrigation could no more be transplanted unmodified to Australia than could English farms and factories. The settlers on irrigation "colonies", as Miss Shaw noted, met more easily to "employ their leisure in social intercourse", but their meetings did not discover a McArthur or a Farrer. "Their talk runs always to prices", said Adam Smith of all venturers' meetings for recreation. There was much cause on the irrigation blocks for such talk. Australian markets for fruit and other small produce were soon glutted. High wages and long voyages made those of Europe unremunerative. Bounties of 10 per cent. on the

[1] Flora Shaw (Lady Lugard), "The Australian Outlook", a paper read before the Colonial Institute 1894.
[2] "As a general rule, the rate of interest charged on advances to the settlers by the irrigation authorities is lower than the rate payable by the Government and also less than the rate charged on mortgage transactions with the banks." *Report on Canned Fruit Industry, Development and Migration Commission*, 1929, pp. 12–13.

market value of the dried fruits they exported were paid by the Federal Government after 1907. In 1916 the Inter-State Commission reported that an Australian Dried Fruits Association, behind the shelter of an import duty of 3*d.* a pound—equal to practically 100 per cent.—was maintaining a high local price which, despite the usually lower prices received for exports, gave the grower a profitable average. It doubted, however, whether the Association could have maintained its high local prices save by refusing to supply its local goods to any dealer importing dried fruits without its sanction.[1] The normal economic result of "profitable prices" followed. Considerable additional areas were planted with vines and fruit trees and Australians felt pleased at the conquest of new oases.

During the war the Murrumbidgee Irrigation Area reached the stage of settlement. A huge storage dam at Burrinjuck had impounded 771,640 acre-feet of flood waters, to be spread by gravitation over 200,000 acres in the Riverina some 250 miles below the dam. In large part this land was reserved for returning soldiers. Still more ambitious was a great irrigation scheme with head-works on the Upper Murray, the construction of which was put in hand after the war. When these were well begun, however, men began to wonder what crops would be profitable on the area of 700,000 acres which they would irrigate lower down the Murray. The outlook for dried fruits, in spite of the Australian Dried Fruits Association and its skilful propaganda, was not clear. Both production and exports of dried fruits were favoured by the beneficence of the Baldwin Government in Britain, which by a preferential duty gave the Australian growers a sheltered market oversea, where Australian costs might be covered,

---

[1] The Commission had doubts as to the consistency of this with the Australian Industries Preservation Act, part II, section 4 (i), but the Chairman of the A.D.F.A. reassured it. "Our rules were submitted to the present Attorney-General (the Hon. W. M. Hughes) who said that they were all right."

or, at least, an average maintained between home and export prices that would achieve the end.[1] But could this be counted on permanently?

Governments have certainly occupied an unenviable position as sponsors and guarantors of irrigation colonies. Having bought land for closer settlement and added to its cost heavy capital outlays on headworks and water channels, their action would have been stultified outright had they not tried to induce settlers to cultivate the land they subdivided and watered. Successive governments have hesitated to call a halt in a losing business so long as the block-holders were ready to contribute some part of the interest on the outlay. Assistance in marketing their produce inevitably followed. But inevitably settlers and governments realized the rickety financial position of an industry dependent for much of its market on the good-will of governments half a world away which were responsible to constituents of their own. The number of farms occupied on the Murrumbidgee Irrigation Area, below the great Burrinjuck Reservoir, declined after 1924, owing to forfeitures and surrenders.[2] Work on the mightier Hume Reservoir, on the Upper Murray, which when completed was to impound 2,000,000 acre-feet of water, had to be curtailed.

Country Party leaders had not hesitated, before such portents appeared, to press for the general extension of such plans for the "orderly marketing" of primary products. The Federal Government after heavy losses became unwilling to shoulder by simple guarantees, or by "pools" which were in effect guarantees, the financial burden of marketing surplus produce. It favoured the constitution, at the wish of a specified proportion of those engaged in each industry, of a Board of Control endowed with legal

---

[1] As to the similar subsidization of the later developed Canned Fruit Industry see the *Report by the Development and Migration Commission*, 1929, pp. 11–13.

[2] *New South Wales Year Book*, 1927–8, p. 743.

power to make a levy on all such producers for common expenses of advertising and marketing.[1] These legalized cartels, soviets, boards—call them what you will—were to control the supply put on the Australian market and to send the balance of the production to be sold abroad at what it would fetch. Several acts were passed during the 1924 session to implement this. With them passed an Export Guarantee Act, authorizing the Treasury to guarantee advances by the Commonwealth Bank to marketing boards up to 80 per cent. of the market value of the produce controlled.

Most ambitious was the Paterson Butter Scheme devised, according to its author, "to put the producer in exactly the same position with regard to the Australian-consumed part of his production as would automatically obtain if there were no exportable surplus produced".[2] Butter producers, especially on the Northern Rivers of New South Wales and in Queensland, had long been satisfied that they were as deserving of protection as their neighbours who grew sugar-cane. Why should cane fed into the rollers and vacuum pans of a sugar mill acquire more merit in the eyes, more silver from the pockets, of Australian consumers than the same sugar-cane, or its cousin maize, grown alongside it at the same cost and fed to those paragons of the breeder's art, Strawberry and Melba XV, the milking shorthorns? "The butter workers are entitled to equal advantages in this supposed free country, where justice and equity are said to dominate."[3]

[1] Cf. *The Economic Record*, February 1928: L. R. MacGregor, "The Queensland Marketing Plan", p. 135; and T. Paterson, "The Marketing of Primary Products", p. 129.

[2] T. Paterson, "The Marketing of Primary Products", in *The Economic Record Supplement*, February 1928, p. 132. A note by J. F. Barry in the *Economic Record*, May 1926, pp. 119–21, outlines the scheme as first conceived, and in the February 1928 Supplement, Professor L. F. Giblin dissects "Some Costs of Marketing Control".

[3] John Martin, dairy farmer of Ballina, N.S.W., 24 September 1914, *Comm. P.P.* sessions 1914–17, vol. VI, p. 545. The annual subsidy to sugar-growers was then about one million sterling. According to Professor Giblin it was £4,000,000 in 1928, *Economic Record*, February 1928, p. 152.

In 1925 a Gippsland politician hit upon the means of obtaining for the cow-men this fair deal. A voluntary combination of butter-producers, known at first as the Australian Stabilization Committee, imposed a levy of 1½d. per pound on all factory butter, and out of this fund proceeded to distribute a bounty of 3d. a pound on all butter exported.

Exporters were naturally willing to send more butter abroad, mainly to London. The Australian consumer, to get his share, had to pay 3d. more than export parity, a little bounty on his private account supplementing that on exports financed by the butter-producers "among themselves". Lest greedy New Zealanders should seek to make profit out of the improved Australian market which the associated producers had made for themselves, a duty of sixpence a pound was raised against imports of butter to Australia.

A profitable price, as ever, stimulated the growth of the industry. More butter was exported, for sales abroad, which now bore a subsidy, could be pushed so long as the price paid by the outside buyer was within 3d. per pound of the acceptable export price in pre-subsidy days. But every increase in the proportion exported made a bigger call on the levy fund. The local price, paid on a smaller share of the total production, had to be put higher if the profitable average price of the dairyman's calculation was to be achieved. As Professor Giblin drily remarked: "It is not altogether healthy for any industry to be able to raise the price of its product as it desires without any corresponding effort".

Once the "costs plus" system has been accepted, the producer is lifted into a paradise where economy seems no longer imperative. "Justice" names the price and the other fellow pays it. Yet these "stabilized" costs have a curious quality of restlessness. "There will always be a considerable number of marginal producers who cannot make the industry pay, and will be clamant for a higher bounty".[1]

Such local prices for butter, sugar and dried fruits raised the cost of living in Australia and, through this, the level of wages to a degree by no means negligible. For sugar (460 million pounds), butter (95 million pounds) and dried fruits (28 million pounds) are quite important items in the massed household consumption which guides the Commonwealth Statistician when he "weights" prices and calculates the index numbers industrial tribunals use. The rising costs are passed back to the exporting industries by all and sundry in the sheltered industries. They have no other resort. If wheat-growers, too, should be smitten with the brave notion of evolving a marketing plan by which they too may receive a profitable price—an Australian parity, whatever that may mean—the whole burden would fall back on wool. So would come to pass the strange vision that fell upon the Tasmanian seer, "of Australia as one enormous sheep bestriding a bottomless pit with statesman, lawyer, miner, landlord, farmer and factory hand all hanging on desperately to the locks of its abundant fleece".[2]

These schemes of price manipulation one and all bespeak a hazy appreciation of the function of prices in guiding the economic use of man's resources. Australians have too often legislated as though a price might be made at whatever figure the producer in search of an easier life chose to call "the fair thing". But the prices that direct the goings and comings of sound prosperity are the signs by which men learn from willing buyers their changing needs. High prices encourage production where it affords a margin of profit. Falling prices discourage it by wiping out the margin or hope of profit. A government or board of control

---

[1] L. F. Giblin, "Some Costs of Marketing Control", *Economic Record*, February 1928, p. 150.

[2] L. F. Giblin, *loc. cit.* p. 154.

that seeks to fake the world's prices does so at the peril of the citizens and producers whom the faked prices mislead. It deranges and weakens its whole economy if it forces them to work with costs that the outer world is under no obligation to meet. And if, in doing so, it sees fit to feed other nations with an abundance which its price-faking begrudges to its own citizens, it adds to the strength of others and accentuates the contrast in competitive vigour between bond and free.

Printed in the United States
By Bookmasters